water & heritage

Sidestone Press

water & heritage

material, conceptual and spiritual connections

edited by
Willem J.H. Willems & Henk P.J. van Schaik

Published by Sidestone Press, Leiden
    www.sidestone.com

Imprint: Sidestone Press Academics (peer-reviewed)
For more information and peer-review procedure see:
www.sidestone.com/publishing/

ISBN 978-90-8890-278-9
    PDF e-book: ISBN 978-90-8890-279-6

Lay-out & cover design: Sidestone Press
Photographs cover: © Ruengrit | Dreamstime.com

United Nations
Educational, Scientific and
Cultural Organization

ICOMOS
Netherlands

Contents

Foreword   9
Irina Bokova

Preface   11
Diederik Six and Erik Luijendijk

Culture is the fourth pillar of sustainable development   15
Olivier Blond

Water and Heritage: conventions and connections   19
Henk van Schaik, Michael van der Valk and Willem Willems

Evolution of rainwater harvesting in urban areas through the   37
millennia. A sustainable technology for increasing water availability
Benoît Haut, Xiao Yun Zheng, Larry Mays, Mooyoung Han,
Cees Passchier, and Andreas N. Angelakis

Ancient Water Wisdom. Traditional water systems in India   57
Vasudha Pangare and Ganesh Pangare

Water and heritage in Angkor, Cambodia. The monuments, the ancient   71
hydraulic network and their recent rehabilitation
Peou Hang

Water and World heritage   87
Anne Lemaistre

Beautiful tropical islands in the Caribbean Sea. Human responses to   99
floods and droughts and the indigenous archaeological heritage of the
Caribbean
Corinne L. Hofman and Menno L.P. Hoogland

Pacific Islands on the brink of submergence. Rising seas in an age of   121
climate changes
John A. Peterson

Sand and water – and their effect on the pyramids of Meroe in the   141
Sudan
Alexandra Riedel

Preserving New York City's waterfront industrial and maritime heritage   155
through resilient and sustainable development. New York City's coastal
development
Kate Daly

Heritage values of water and sea defense in Recife. Challenges for a   169
local governmental approach
Evelyne Labanca Corrêa de Araújo

Hazard vulnerability and management of cultural heritage in the   185
context of water-related hazards in the Republic of Korea
Hae Un Rii, Hyo Hyun Sung and Jisoo Kim

Flood Protection for Historic Sites – Integrating Heritage   205
Conservation and Flood Control Concepts. Experiences in Germany
Heiko Lieske, Erika Schmidt and Thomas Will

'Climate is what we expect, weather is what we get'. Managing the   217
potential effects of oceanic climate change on underwater cultural
heritage
Mark Dunkley

Water as an Agent of Creation and Destruction at Petra   231
Douglas C. Comer

Tsunami and heritage after the 2011 Great East Japan Earthquake   245
Katsuyuki Okamura

Reinforcing the link between Water and Heritage in order to build   257
Disaster Resilient Societies
Rohit Jigyasu

Between pragmatism and cultural context. Continuity and change in   273
Ifugao wet-rice agriculture
Stephen Acabado and Marlon Martin

Water Services Heritage and Institutional Diversity   297
T.S. Katko, P.S. Juuti, P.E. Pietilä and R.P. Rajala

The framework of skills and knowledge shared in long-enduring   313
organizations in the improvement of irrigation efficiency in Japan
Mikiko Sugiura, Yohei Sato and Shinsuke Ota

The Deltaworks: heritage and new space for a changing world   331

Marinke Steenhuis

Beyond site protection. Embedding natural heritage into sustainable   351
landscapes

Kenneth Irvine

The Santa Cruz River. Four Millennia of Water Heritage and Security   371
in the U.S.-Mexico Border Region

Rafael de Grenade and Robert G. Varady

Cultural and touristic strategies for preservation and enhancement of   389
Venice and its lagoon

Francesco Calzolaio

The Tennessee Valley Authority. How the Development of the   399
Tennessee River Influenced Archaeology in the Southeastern United
States

Erin Pritchard, Michaelyn Harle and Pat Bernard Ezzell

Development of the WWC world water heritage systems (WHS)   417
program

Avinash Chand Tyagi and Kazumi Yamaoka

Appendix 1: Statement of Amsterdam   431

Foreword

From the beginning of time, humanity has sought out sources of water to sustain life, health and the ecosystems on which they depend. This is especially true today, in this turning point year for the international community, as States shape a new global sustainable development agenda.

Limiting the impacts of floods, landslides, and droughts, water security and cooperation are basic requirements to improving lives and to empowering people to overcome hunger and disease. The stakes are high. Peace and democracy thrive when people and cultures cooperate for water. Literacy, gender equality, economic development, respect for human rights, freedoms, and diversity – all of these depend on water security.

As a basic element of life, our relationship with water is complex, entailing material, and spiritual dimensions, and embodied in heritage that is both tangible and intangible. This relationship has always been a source of inspiration and a wellspring for innovation and creativity, leading us to think not only of the present, but also the future and the security of future generations.

UNESCO is uniquely positioned to explore the relationship between water and heritage. The Organisation helped to launch the theme of 'Water and Cultural Diversity' at the *3rd World Water Forum*, drawing on longstanding work across the natural, social, and human sciences, through the leadership of the International Hydrological Programme and the World Heritage Centre.

Initiated by the International Council on Monuments and Sites (ICOMOS), *Water and Heritage, material, conceptual and spiritual connections* is associated with this collaboration. It tells the story of water heritage in all its diversity. It reveals the technical ingenuity that water heritage has always inspired, and it presents the challenges that this heritage faces, along with possible solutions. Reflecting the depth of cooperation between UNESCO and ICOMOS, this book was launched during the *7th World Water Forum*, as a showcase of cooperation to increase dialogue on water heritage.

In this spirit, I wish to thank the editors and authors for sharing their commitment to highlighting the importance of humanity's water heritage for sustainable development and lasting peace. I am confident this book will help to chart a new course for the benefit of all societies.

Irina Bokova (Director-General of UNESCO)
March 2015

Figure 1. Pont des Arts, Paris, France (48°51' N, 2°21' E). Inspired by the talk of Olivier Blond showing the photographs of Yann Arthus Bertrand during the ICOMOS Netherlands-conference Protecting Deltas, Heritage Helps!, Amsterdam, September 2013. Photograph by Yann Arthus Bertrand.

Preface

Protecting Deltas, Heritage Helps!

Last century the world has changed dramatically. Since the end of the Fifties, the world population has more than doubled in size from 3 to 7 billion people, an increase that covers more people than have ever lived before. The impact of this population explosion is becoming increasingly evident: pollution is choking our cities; food and water shortages are increasingly threatening humankind; and the greenhouse effect is suffocating our planet. Rapid industrialization, technological development and rising prosperity have resulted not only in population growth but also in more short-term thinking and acting, especially among politicians. Long-term solutions for the world's sustainability challenges have become hard to define. Heritage as a crucial long-term source of inspiration is less recognized.

Deltas are the most vulnerable places in the world. More than half of the world's population live in deltas. Fertile land, fishing activities and trade are traditionally the most important reasons for the high density of human settlements in delta areas. Due to the density of early civilizations in delta areas, these places have a high density of cultural heritage sites that makes the relationship between water and heritage clear for the world's urbanizing deltas.

Saving the deltas of the world will be one of the most critical challenges for a sustainable future of humankind. Exposure to water related hazards, especially due to climate change resulting in higher frequency and intensity of disasters, together with an increasing population density and richness in cultural and natural heritage puts communities, particularly in world's deltas, at high risk. Rapid urbanization of delta areas without respecting the historic water structures accumulated over the centuries make these areas, in which economic, social and cultural values are concentrated, even more vulnerable.

Progression and development have caused the loss of cultural heritage. It is now clear that in times of uncertainty and risk, we need heritage as an important contributor to a sustainable future. A better understanding of place and historical continuity is key. Knowledge of living with water and water structures - passed on over generations – is of great importance for a sustainable environment. Ingenious use and reuse of tangible and intangible heritage can offer solutions for the future. Harmony between water and heritage management will not only improve spatial quality but will ultimately contribute to the preservation of civilizations and the wellbeing of humankind.

We believe that heritage can play a role in safeguarding people's lives in the world's delta areas. As the world heritage advisory council for UNESCO, the International Council on Monuments and Sites (ICOMOS) can and must play a key role in promoting and supporting this important role of heritage in protection in deltas. In 2013, we organized the conference Protecting Deltas, Heritage Helps! from 23-28 September in Amsterdam, The Netherlands. The purpose of the meeting was to build bridges between the water and the culture sectors in order to protect world's deltas. This resulted in the Statement of Amsterdam (Appendix 1) as a basis for further action. Furthermore, the city of Amsterdam became the first city in the world to be awarded with the first water and heritage monument shield. Also a movie on water and heritage was produced, which can be found on you tube. A final outcome of the conference is this impressive scientific publication.

During the finalization process of this publication, we were deeply shocked by the death of our beloved and respected friend, colleague and editor of this book, Prof. Dr. Willem J.H. Willems, board member of ICOMOS Netherlands, dean and professor of Archaeological Heritage Management at Leiden University and co-president of the ICOMOS International Committee on Archaeological Heritage Management. Without his inspiration, generous support and dedication, this publication would not have materialized. Together with Ir. Henk P.J. van Schaik,

Prof. dr. Willem Willems †.

Programme Leader ICOMOS conference Protecting Delta's, Heritage Helps, member of the Technical Advisory Committee of the World Water Assessment Programme of UNESCO, former Coordinator Cooperative Programme on Water and Climate, and Lead Water of UPEACE, The Hague, he represented both heritage and water professionals to create a well-balanced and profound publication on the symbiotic relationship between water and heritage. We owe Willem Willems and Henk P.J. van Schaik everlasting gratitude for all they have done to bring the heritage and water worlds together. We would like to dedicate our final words to Willem Willems by quoting Gustavo Araoz, President of ICOMOS worldwide, who said in a moving reaction: "*We are all deeply saddened by his parting, but in our mourning, all (...) should rejoice in the legacy that he left us and that will live on.*"

Jhr. Ir. Diederik Six (president ICOMOS Netherlands) and
Drs. Erik Luijendijk (board member ICOMOS Netherlands)
Amsterdam, December 2014

Figure 1. Sea ice of Ross and Mount Erebus, McMurdo Sound, Antarctica (South Pole) (76°12' S, 163°57' E). Inspired by the talk of Olivier Blond showing the photographs of Yann Arthus Bertrand during the ICOMOS Netherlands-conference Protecting Deltas, Heritage Helps!, Amsterdam, September 2013. Photograph by Yann Arthus Bertrand.

Culture is the fourth pillar of sustainable development

Olivier Blond

Executive Editor of the GoodPlanet Foundation[1]

Suppose the three pillars of the official definition of sustainable development -people, planet and profit- missed out on a fourth that would more firmly establish the concept? More than 20 years after Gro Brundtland presented the sustainability definition to the UN, we propose, along with others, culture to become the fourth pillar.

In housing, the cultural dimension is very strong. With two contradictory aspects: on the one hand an increasing standardization of building forms on the planet. On the other hand, the rehabilitation of local expertise, which allowed people for centuries to live in an appropriate and resilient manner. *"It is not to folklore. But in view of sustainable development, ancestral skills have merit. Thus, when earthquakes hit in China and Pakistan, traditional buildings withstood the shocks while modern concrete buildings collapsed. We must therefore ensure that large construction companies include this dimension, it can be done when there is a demand for it"* explains Jean Musitelli, former Ambassador of France to UNESCO and president of Diversum, the association that encourages consideration of the cultural heritage in sustainable development policies.

At the 2002 Earth Summit in Johannesburg, the cultural dimension has been recognized. Then, in 2010, the third World Congress of United Cities and Local Governments (UCLG) -including numerous cities like Paris, Mexico City, Sao Paulo and Istanbul- national governments adopted a document entitled *"Culture: the Fourth Pillar of Sustainable Development"*. The document states, inter alia, that culture is necessary in all its diversity to meet the challenges humanity faces. *"This vision is based on the notion of cultural diversity brought by Unesco"* said Jean Musitelli.

---

1   The GoodPlanet is a public interest French NGO, based in Paris, chaired by French photographer and movie director Yann Arthus-Bertrand. Its objectives are to raise public awareness of ecology and to inspire a desire to take positive action. The GoodPlanet is optimistic and apolitical – It puts human beings at the center of sustainable development. It proposes realistic solutions by means of programmes aimed at everyone: citizens, local authorities and corporations. The foundation acts in 25 countries.

Figure 2. View of Venice, Veneto, Italy (45°25′ N, 12°45′ E). Inspired by the talk of Olivier Blond showing the photographs of Yann Arthus Bertrand during the ICOMOS Netherlands-conference Protecting Deltas, Heritage Helps!, Amsterdam, September 2013. Photograph by Yann Arthus Bertrand.

The text mentions. *"The world does not only face economic, social or environmental challenges. Creativity, local knowledge, diversity and beauty are all indispensable foundations for the dialogue for peace and progress. These values are, in fact, intrinsically linked to notions of human development and freedom. Cultural challenges of our world are too great to justify that they should be given equal attention to as the other three original dimensions of development (people, planet, profit). The fourth pillar creates solid bridges with the other three dimensions of development, and complements each of them. "*

It is in this context that Diversum introduced in 2011 the purple economy. The purple economy is based on the idea of a new alliance between culture and economy. The idea is that *"it refers to the root causes of the economic downturn: the depletion of the Western society production based model."* The misguided use of natural resources, the world reconfiguration in the twenty-first century and other aspects have not been sufficiently taken into account in conventional economical models. Culture is a value-added growth factor, and therefore a source of employment, a development that should be encouraged.

It is also a cultural responsibility: human activity produces positive or negative externalities that impact on culture as they impact on environment. This aspect was analysed on the environment, but much less on culture. And to continue the parallel with another *"green"* concept, the ecological footprint (the impact on ecosystems), we can imagine one day calculating a cultural footprint.

In short *"We must get back to thinking!"*

Water and Heritage: conventions and connections

Henk van Schaik[a], Michael van der Valk[b] and Willem Willems

a H2Ovan Schaik, henk.vanschaik19447@gmail.com

b CrossVision, info@crossvision.nl, www.hydrology.nl

Water is life. Man cannot survive for more than a few days without water. Water is one of the four basic elements and heritage conveys the fundament of all civilisations on earth. The existential importance of water is testament to humankind's manifold spiritual and material relations with water through time. Innumerable expressions of this relationship are found in all cultures and all countries of our world. As both natural heritage and cultural heritage are related to life, they are inherently linked to water.

Spiritual water-related cultural heritage resources can be defined as expressions of people's thoughts, beliefs and religions that value the inextricable relationship with water rather than humankind's relation to their bodies and physical surroundings, as individuals or communities.

Physical water-related cultural heritage resources are considered to be movable or immovable objects, sites, structures, groups of structures, and natural features and landscapes that have archaeological, paleontological, historical, architectural, religious, aesthetic, or other cultural significance. Physical cultural resources may be located in urban or rural settings, above or below ground, or under water, and their cultural interest may be at the local, national, regional or international level. Over time the focus on the spiritual values of water has expanded to include the physical aspects. Rationalisation and secularisation of water management and water services has developed through objectivised scientific research to provide credibility, investment planning based on capitalised costs and benefits, and the legitimisation of decision processes by stakeholders.

Increased population density, in combination with water-related hazards, enhances threats to the rich and diverse cultural and natural heritage all over the world on the banks of rivers, in lowland deltas and in arid and mountainous regions. Climate change is expected to intensify flood and drought patterns, to affect groundwater and sea levels, to increase pollution and lead to a higher frequency and intensity of disasters. The potential impact of sea-level rise on cultural heritage is of great concern, and communities are faced with challenges to adapt methodologies for the future protection of water-related heritage. It is therefore timely to enrich our understanding about the vital importance of water-related heritage for the diversity of our cultures, the preservation of cultural and natural values for future generations, as well as for spatial planning.

On the other hand, cultural and natural heritage can provide valuable examples of successful strategies to deal with uncertainty and risk; human ingenuity and the capacity to share water management experience across cultures have shaped iconic cultural landscapes enabling societies to cope with water hazards. Today heritage can help us to better understand the dynamic relationship between societies, water management and governance. Protecting natural heritage can provide an effective strategy to address threats. Examples are flood plains and mangroves that provide natural buffers to coastal areas against the perils of the sea. Similarly, modern water management can offer essential technologies to protect heritage sites acutely threatened by natural disasters and prepare for the impacts of environmental change. These examples provide key insights to improving our current approaches as well as for actions towards an equitable and sustainable future for all.

With this book we aim to raise awareness amongst policy-makers, scientists, practitioners and the public in the water community on the contemporary values and uses of water-related heritage. Similarly it contributes to promoting a better understanding amongst the heritage community of the water-related threats to heritage (climate change, floods and tsunamis) and threats to water-related heritage (tourism), as well as the importance to study the impacts of these threats (e.g. climate change impacts studies) and the vulnerabilities of heritage in order to prepare for protection and response measures.

The publication is based on presentations of the international conference 'Delta protection: heritage helps', held in September 2013 in Amsterdam, and is supplemented by invited papers. Whereas the scope of the book cannot cover the vast wealth of relations between heritage and water, it serves to expand and define the multivariate relations between water and heritage, and to articulate and strengthen these relations among the water and heritage communities.

1. Historical evolution of heritage protection: emerging perceptions

The perception of the concept of heritage has evolved over time. One way we can see this is by looking at the many conventions, charters, documents and treaties that have been developed since the first half of the 20th century. In this chapter we present a summary of the evolution in the perceptions, conventions and protective measures for cultural and for natural heritage. There are a few instances where cultural and natural heritage meet.

Cultural heritage

Water and culture have been intrinsically linked for thousands of years, but the concept of heritage is more recent. The understanding of cultural heritage has evolved significantly over the years. Whereas cultural heritage used to be a 'monumental' concept that informed us about the past, there is a growing recognition of the significance of combining the tangible physical values and the intangible aesthetic, spiritual and social values of heritage for the present and even our future.

The roots of heritage policy can be found in Europe. During the 19th century international and regional agreements for the protection of cultural heritage emerged for the first time, codifying the perceptions and appreciation of cultural heritage. For example, the 1885 *Convention on the Protection of Archaeological Heritage of Europe* and the *European Convention on the Protection of Archaeological Heritage* under the Council of Europe created broad legal protection of cultural heritage antiquities and sites valuable to communities worldwide.

The 20th century saw an incremental shift from regional agreements to international consensus in the protection of cultural heritage. The 1931 *Athens Charter for the Restoration of Historic Monuments* outlined a seven-point manifesto to: (a) establish organizations for restoration advice, (b) ensure projects are reviewed with knowledgeable criticism, (c) establish national legislation to preserve historic sites, (d) rebury excavations which were not to be restored, (e) allow the use of modern techniques and materials in restoration work, (f) place historical sites under custodial protection and (g) protect the area surrounding historic sites.

The 1935 *Roerich Pact*, an inter-American treaty on the 'Protection of Artistic and Scientific Institutions and Historic Monuments', represents the first multinational agreement for the protection of cultural property during war and peace. While limited in its provisions for the *protection of immovable* cultural property and cultural and educational institutions, the Roerich Pact allows no provisions for exception by reason of military necessity. Following World War II the *The Hague Convention for the Protection of Cultural Property in the Event of Armed Conflict* (UNESCO, 1954) requires its signatories to *protect cultural property in war*. The Convention attributes a protective sign to facilitate the identification of protected cultural property during an armed conflict, which is also used to mark exceptionally important cultural property under special protection (see Fig. 1). The 1954 The Hague Convention was the first international convention to define property considered 'important' and 'valuable' for humankind, and signalled the protection of cultural property as an international issue.

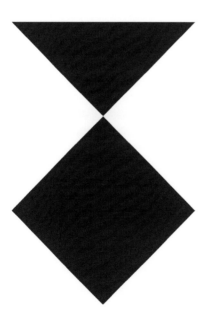

Figure 1. The sign of the 1954 The Hague Convention can be found on many buildings of importance and interest.

In 1964, in Venice, the Second Congress of Architects and Specialists of Historic Buildings adopted resolutions which, among others, created the *International Charter on the Conservation and Restoration of Monuments and Sites*, better known as the Venice Charter. One of the resolutions, put forward by the UNESCO, created the International Council on Monuments and Sites (ICOMOS), to carry out the Charter. The Venice Charter provides an international framework for the preservation and restoration of ancient buildings by means of a code of professional standards. It states that the concept of a historic monument includes not only a single architectural work *but also its urban and rural setting*, which provides the evidence of a specific civilisation, a significant development or a historic event (ICOMOS, 2015).

It was only in the Convention concerning the Protection of the World Cultural and Natural Heritage (UNESCO, 1972) – the World Heritage Convention – that the term cultural heritage was employed to define the cultural objects to be protected at the international level. This Convention founded the well-known World Heritage Programme and is currently the most widely ratified international legal instrument in heritage conservation comprising 191 States Parties. A key concept of the Convention is the recognition and protection of heritage of 'outstanding universal value' for the benefit of all humankind. Currently (spring 2015), there are over 1,000 World Heritage sites: 70% cultural, 20% natural and 3% of both natural and cultural value, in 161 countries.

The 1992 Valletta Treaty (formally known as the European Convention on the Protection of the Archaeological Heritage) is a multilateral treaty of the Council of Europe, also known as the Malta Convention (Council of Europe, 1992). It aims to protect the European archaeological heritage as a source of European collective memory and as an instrument for historical and scientific study.

In 1994 the Nara Document on Authenticity, endorsed by ICOMOS experts assembled in Nara (Japan) (UNESCO, 2015), was conceived in the spirit of the 1964 Venice Charter. It states that heritage today recognises the vernacular values of various countries and cultures in a changing world, and considers the diversity of cultures and heritage in our world as an irreplaceable source of spiritual and intellectual richness of all humankind. The Nara Document adopted *authenticity* as the prime criterion for the assessment of heritage. The responsibility and the management of cultural heritage is in the first place a prerogative of the cultural community that has generated it. Many institutions have endorsed this broad appreciation of cultural heritage.

In 2001 the General Conference of UNESCO adopted the *Convention on the Protection of the Underwater Cultural Heritage* (UNESCO, 2001a). States Parties to the Convention agree to protect 'all traces of human existence having a cultural, historical or archaeological character which have been partially or totally under water for over 100 years,' including shipwrecks, sunken cities, prehistoric art work, treasures that may be looted, sacrificial and burial sites, as well as old ports that cover the ocean's floors.

The 2005 Council of Europe *Framework Convention on the Value of Cultural Heritage for Society* (the Faro Convention) defines cultural heritage as *"a group of resources inherited from the past which people identify, independently of ownership, as a reflection and expression of their constantly evolving values, beliefs, knowledge and traditions. It includes all aspects of the environment resulting from the interaction between people and places through time (Art. 2)."*

The Framework Convention also provides a set of guidelines that includes adopting *cultural heritage impact assessments* and mitigation strategies where necessary to enrich the processes of economic, political, social and cultural development and land-use planning.

A recent development in the heritage debate is the recognition that cities and urban areas make up a large percentage of tangible cultural heritage properties. With increased urbanisation, this heritage is particularly relevant to urban development and the post-2015 development agenda. The UNESCO's *Recommendation on the Historic Urban Landscape* (HUL) (UNESCO, 2011), *presents* a legislative institutional framework with measures, *including a glossary of definitions* as a relatively new approach to urban heritage management. Bandarin and Van Oers (2014) provide by means of examples from all over the world an invaluable resource for architects, planners, surveyors and engineers worldwide working in heritage conservation, as well as for local authority conservation officers and managers of heritage sites, including the link between historic cities and climate change. They describe the Historic Urban Landscape as

"an updated heritage management approach based on the recognition and identification of a layering and interconnection of values – natural and cultural, tangible and intangible, international as well as local – that are present in any city. It is based also on the need to integrate the different disciplines for the analysis and planning of the urban conservation process, in order not to separate it from the planning and development of the contemporary city. [...] All this is part of the day-to-day running of the city in order to respond timely and adequately to the dynamics of the twenty-first century urban condition, which is always in a state of flux and seemingly accelerating."

Bandarin and Van Oers (2014) conclude with a research agenda for planners and designers, facilitating the message that 'the Historic Urban Landscape has different meanings in different places that are shaped by different environmental, economic, social and cultural conditions – these should be recognised and respected in order to fulfil its potential to reconnect the historic city to its urban context and to the dynamics of the urban century'.

The broad recognition of cultural heritage to include both tangible and intangible heritage (e.g., engineering works, music, dance, literature, painting, spiritual heritage) is not new. For example, 60 years ago Ikram and Spear (1955) described the archaeology, architecture, music, painting, calligraphy, literature in various languages and the spiritual heritage of Pakistan. Physical and spiritual water-related heritage is important as a source of valuable scientific and historic information about the prehistoric, historic and contemporary identities of peoples and cultures. As expressed in the Venice Charter, the Nara Document and other documents on cultural heritage it is an asset for an economic and social development and integral parts of a people's cultural identity and traditions.

On a practical level, the 1985 Environmental Impact Assessments Directive of the European Union (*EU Directive on the assessment of the effects of certain public and private projects on the environment*, European Commission, 1985) requires that the potential impacts of proposed developments on cultural heritage are examined. However, in current studies any cultural heritage is mainly restricted to *built* heritage. There is a need for better guidance on how best to consider the implications of proposals on cultural heritage. Cultural heritage needs to be considered earlier in the process and should include greater public participation (Bond *et al.*, 2004).

Natural heritage

Natural heritage can be considered as the aggregate of the elements of biodiversity – flora, fauna and ecosystems – and geological structures and formations (geodiversity). The UNESCO World Heritage Committee recognises important sites of natural heritage as World Heritage, approving of the need to preserve them 'as part of the world heritage of mankind as a whole.' More recent global agreements, such as the 1992 *Convention on Biological Diversity*, provide States sovereign rights over biological resources within their national jurisdictions. The idea of static conservation of biodiversity is slowly being replaced by the idea of dynamic conservation. The agreements commit countries to conserve biodiversity, develop resources for sustainability and share the benefits resulting from their use. It is expected that bioprospecting or the collection of natural products will be allowed by the biodiversity-rich country, in exchange for a share of the benefits.

Natural heritage is defined in the World Heritage Convention. It is further elaborated in the Operational Guidelines for the Implementation of the World Heritage Convention (UNESCO, 2013), which also contains the specific criteria and conditions of integrity for assessing the 'outstanding universal value' of prospective natural heritage properties for recognition as World Heritage.

UNESCO's World Heritage Centre works closely with the IUCN, its advisory body to the World Heritage Convention, in order to ensure the long-term conservation of inscribed natural heritage sites and their World Heritage values. This includes undertaking monitoring missions in cooperation with States Parties and site management in order to evaluate the state of conservation of World Heritage sites, capacity-building activities and providing technical assistance. In addition to the IUCN, major international non-governmental conservation organisations such as the Conservation International (CI), the Fauna and Flora International (FFI), The Nature Conservancy (TNC), the Wildlife Conservation Society (WCS) and the World Wide Fund for Nature (WWF) have figured prominently in the expanding range of activities carried out by the World Heritage Centre.

In 2005, the World Heritage Marine Programme was established in order to protect marine areas of 'outstanding universal value'. The UNESCO World Heritage Centre's Natural Heritage Strategy (UNESCO, 2006), endorsed by the World Heritage Committee, outlines the guiding principles, mission statement, strategic orientations and working methods of all activities relating to natural heritage.

Cultural and natural heritage

There are only a few instances where cultural and natural heritage meet. The UNESCO 1972 World Heritage Convention brought together the recognition and protection of cultural and natural heritage of 'outstanding universal value' for the benefit of humankind. The Convention establishes a system of identification, presentation, and registration in its World Heritage List. The World Heritage Convention has progressively attained almost universal recognition by the international community during its more than 40 years of life. 'Throughout the years the Convention has undergone extensive interpretation and evolution in its scope of application. Operational Guidelines, which are the implementing rules governing the operation of the Convention, have been extensively revised. Links, with the World Bank and the United Nations, have been developed to take into account the economic and political dimension of world heritage conservation and management', state Francioni and Lenzerini (2008). Many legal issues remain to be clarified, however. For example, should World Heritage reflect a reasonable balance between cultural properties and natural sites? What is the meaning of 'outstanding universal value' in the context of cultural and natural heritage?

The World Bank and other development banks recognise the importance of physical cultural and natural resources as (a) sources of valuable scientific and historical information, (b) assets for economic and social development, and (c) integral parts of a people's cultural identity and practises. In its Operational Policy and Bank Procedures, the World Bank aims to avoid, or mitigate, adverse impacts on cultural and natural resources from development projects that the World Bank finances (World Bank, 2009; Freestone, 2013).

Moreover, at the practical level, the legally-binding and globally-accepted guidelines and procedures for the Environmental Impact Assessment and Strategic Environmental Impact Assessments (IAIA, 2015) support the assessments of the impacts and mitigation measures of development projects on both the natural and cultural heritage. The IAIA fosters and strengthens the integration of cultural and natural heritage in impact assessments. However, as to natural heritage, Environmental Impact Assessments are often limited to the assessment of the impacts of development on the adherence to pre-set norms and goals, for example, the impact of a project on a threatened species (Brown, 2008; Akoto and Piésold, 2008; De Jesus, 2008).

Today cultural heritage is firmly established within national policy frameworks across all regions. Particularly in the last 20 years heritage has increasingly become part of the discourse on sustainable development, including its economic valuation.

In Note A/69/216 of July 2014 " Globalization and interdependence: culture and sustainable development" of the Secretary General of the United Nations, submitted to the General Assembly of the United Nations and prepared by the United Nations Educational, Scientific and Cultural Organization the last conclusion states that "building on the lessons learned from the Millennium Development Goals, the international community should be looking for development strategies that foster effective, transformative change and that rely on culture. In this context, and based on the language of the General Assembly in its resolution 68/223, that "Member States, intergovernmental bodies, organizations of the United Nations system, relevant non-governmental organizations and all other relevant stakeholders give due consideration to culture and sustainable development in the elaboration of the post-2015 development agenda", Member States may wish to fully integrate culture, through cultural heritage and the cultural and creative industries, within the framework of the future system of goals, targets and indicators".

In conclusion, cultural and natural heritage are currently firmly established within international conventions, national policy frameworks across all regions, as well as operational guidelines and procedures. Clarification of the role of heritage is required to not only strengthen the role heritage can play in supporting the MDGs and SDGs but also to identify, develop and apply methods of assessing trade-offs and synergies of cultural and natural heritage within sustainable development processes.

2. Water and heritage

Water-related heritage can be considered an icon for the individual and combined paradigms that inform us why our ancestors chose or developed certain solutions (e.g., large dams, water wells, windmills) and why certain governance systems match certain geophysical, economic and cultural conditions. Studying water-related heritage will guide us in assessing the long-term consequences of specific managerial strategies and their applicability in specific conditions. Water-related cultural heritage can indeed provide us with the means and insights by means of which we can better serve the needs of present populations and make informed choices concerning our future.

Numerous iconic examples of water-related natural and built heritage have brought together peoples of diverse origins. For instance, the Iguazu waterfalls on the border between Uruguay and Argentina, Roman aqueducts, qanats in Iran, the flying sand weir at the Dujiangyan Irrigation System in China, the Beemster polder in the Netherlands, the Niger River, and the garden pools in Udaipur, India. Heritage icons are present in all climates: arid and wet, in urban and rural settings, natural and built environments (UNESCO, 2001b).

The development of water infrastructure is closely connected to human development. However, global development targets set in the Millennium Development Goals (MDGs, 2000) and in the Sustainable Development Goals (SDGs, 2015) do not refer to the relevance of water-related cultural achievements. Although Goal 15 of the SDGs calls for the protection, restoration and promotion of the sustainable use of terrestrial ecosystems, sustainable management of forests, combat desertification, halt and reverse land degradation and put an end to biodiversity loss, implicitly supporting the protection of natural heritage, the protection of cultural heritage is not mentioned explicitly or implicitly in the SDGs.

Water and indigenous knowledge, the spiritual connection

In the Essays on Water History, published by the International Hydrological Programme (IHP) of UNESCO, Hassan (2011) wrote: 'For millions of years, hunters and gatherers depended on wild plants and animals sustained by rainfall. Around 10,000 years ago, the structure and dynamics of human societies were radically transformed due to the development of food production.' Not long after food production developed, a reciprocal relation with water management started.

In fact one could say that the attempts of humankind to eke out a living and, whenever possible, satisfy its desires, have defined the history of water management. Water was not only a substance that sustained life, but equally a cornerstone in the way people conceived the world and expressed their thoughts. Water management systems have been embedded in attitudes and practises constituting paradigms that have not only exalted but also operationalised mental, institutional and technical structures.

The spiritual connection to water and water bodies that indigenous societies maintain as an integral element of their culture is often a source of water conflict with external development agents. A more explicit understanding of indigenous value systems by the development community would (a) help relieve the pressure on indigenous societies and (b) serve the cause of sustainable development for humanity as a whole (Groenfeldt, 2013). This way of thinking is reflected in the 4th World Water Development Report of the United Nations (2012b; see also Kelleher, 2010):

> *"Ethical, Social and Cultural drivers are at the heart of the human family's interaction with the natural environment. Collectively they influence human beliefs, values, thoughts, perceptions, knowledge, decisions, behaviours, demands on and use of water."*

In line with this thinking, for example, the Australian Government's Indigenous Caring for Country programme recognises the role that indigenous peoples have in natural resource management and heritage activities. The programme encompasses Indigenous Protected Areas, which are 'area[s] of indigenous-owned land or sea where traditional indigenous owners have entered into an agreement with the Australian Government to promote biodiversity and cultural resource conservation' (Australian Government, 2008). Due to the ownership of water vested with the Crown, in Australia the indigenous peoples' engagement in cultural heritage protection of water places has been a further point of negotiation and compromise. Nevertheless, in most instances, water sites with special meaning to the indigenous peoples are considered secondary to the interests of states, territories and industry stakeholders. The Australian Human Rights Commission (2009) states,

> *"In general, obviously, there is a gap in water policy [...]. The development of water policy has been done in complete isolation to other social and economic areas of policy that relate to indigenous peoples, including native title, land rights, and cultural heritage. This inconsistency and isolation is heightened for indigenous peoples, whose land boundaries do not correlate with state borders. Additionally,*

indigenous peoples are not only forced to try to fit into state water legislative arrangements and make them relevant to their needs, but also to navigate and apply a wide range of other legislation and policy to secure distinct rights to lands, waters, natural resources and cultural heritage."

Climate change: a water-related threat to heritage

Cultural and natural heritage is often threatened by external impacts, be it water-related disasters or human-induced environmental changes and deterioration. Of these external impacts, the impacts of climate change have become a key management concern. In the light of climate change the UNESCO has published a practical guide, entitled 'Climate Change Adaptation for Natural World Heritage Sites' (Perry and Falzon, 2014). It recognises natural heritage as a means to protect against climate impacts and provides a climate change adaptation strategy that can be integrated into an overall management plan. It concludes that for 'any strategy to work, it must be relevant to its users, and above all practical. Too many well-intended strategies fail simply because they are unusable.' This UNESCO guide particularly recommends the UNESCO World Heritage Centre's 'Enhancing our Heritage Toolkit' as it provides the basis of the management approach highlighted by the guide. It stresses, amongst others, that 'climate change is a highly complex process, and we cannot predict in detail what future climate conditions might be. However, we can develop some consensus on likely scenarios based on observation, knowledge and expertise, and professional intuition. What is clear is that change is on the way' (UNESCO, 2008). In Australia, for example, climate change poses the greatest long-term threat to important sea and water elements, including the World Heritage listed Great Barrier Reef (Australian Government, 2008; Australian Human Rights Commission, 2009).

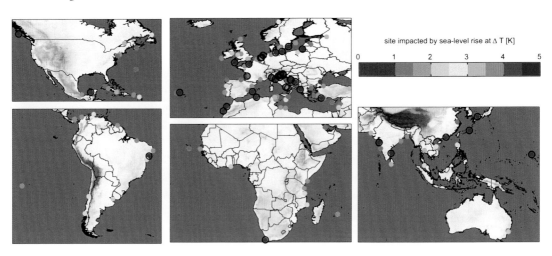

site impacted by sea-level rise at Δ T [K]

0   1   2   3   4   5

Figure 2. The location of UNESCO cultural World Heritage sites impacted by a sea-level rise. Colours: the lowest temperature rise at which the site will be impacted by a sea-level rise. Open black circles: the sites already impacted due to the present-day temperature rise (0.8 K). Source: Marzeion and Levermann (2014).

Marzeion and Levermann (2014) report the results of computations on the impacts on current cultural heritage sites of sustained warming through sea-level rise estimates for the next 2000 years. They estimate that 6% of all the UNESCO World Heritage sites will be affected if the current global mean temperature sustains for the next 2 millennia, while 0.7% of the current global land area will be below mean sea level. These numbers increase to 19% (136 sites) and 1.1% for a warming of 3 K. Given the lifetime of carbon dioxide in the atmosphere – millennia – there are indications that fundamental decisions concerning the cultural heritage and its protection are required. Marzeion and Levermann conclude that in coastal deltas the cultural heritage is especially threatened with inundation due to sea-level rise, in particular in Southeast Asia (Fig. 2).

Including water-related heritage in the global water dialogue

Though many heritage sites are water-related – for example, eight of the eleven World Heritage sites in the Netherlands are related to water – little attention is given to heritage in the global water dialogues or in the sustainable development dialogues. To date heritage has not been mentioned in any of the Ministerial Declarations of the World Water Forums that have been organised triennially since 1997. As mentioned in the foreword by Blond (see above), the definition for sustainable development 'People, Planet Profit' misses Culture (and heritage). Blond coins 'Culture' the forgotten fourth pillar of sustainable development.

Against this background the ICOMOS-Netherlands organised the international conference entitled 'Protecting deltas: heritage helps'. Held in September 2013 in Amsterdam, it brought together more than 100 experts and resulted in the *Statement of Amsterdam* that called for more attention to Water and Heritage. It states that:

- The management of water heritage is dynamic and 'management of change'. Both historic and modern water structures and water works symbolize the need to adapt the function and meaning of sites based flexibility and resilience. Profound understanding of historical continuity is essential to improve planning processes.

- Heritage is a valuable asset as a source of pride and identification, social and economic development, stimulating striving communities. Preparing societies for the effects of climate change will work best where cultural landscapes are improved.

- The societal desire for sustainability has found its expression in spatial planning, but the relation of heritage, development and sustainability is still in its infancy. There is an urgent need to communicate the links to policy makers, professionals and the public. Spatial planning plays a key role in connecting decision makers and experts, including engineers, archaeologists, historians, geographers, ecologists and landscape architects.

The Statement of Amsterdam recommends fostering research, the exchange and dissemination of water and heritage-related knowledge and experience, including any traditional and informal knowledge, between governmental, non-governmental, private and research organisations.

More recently, the *Dresden Declaration on Flood Protection for Historic Sites*, adopted at the international conference (June 2014, Dresden) on 'Flood Protection for Historic Sites' also calls for combining the cultural, ecologic, spatial, structural and social aspects of flood risk management, forming an integrated part of urban land use and development planning.

3.Organisation of the book

The following twenty-four articles from all over the world are centred on cultural heritage, natural heritage and underwater heritage. The articles discuss scientific analysis, advocacy, policy-making and practical protection measures, and have been grouped in three core sections in relation to material, organisational, and spatial, social, cultural, economic and spiritual connections.

Material connections

Heritage in water infrastructure

The four articles in this section describe the aesthetic uniqueness and beauty, technical genius, social appropriateness and the economic values of iconic ancient water infrastructure. The articles elucidate the cultural, economic and social values of these traditional water infrastructures for their contemporary use, as well as their provision of essential services today and tomorrow. These articles could be supplemented by many more examples such as qanats and water wheels in the Middle East, and water mills in the Netherlands. The articles all call for recognition of these values and the protection of traditional water infrastructures – a clear message to policy-makers, water managers and heritage experts.

Haut *et al.* in 'Evolution of rainwater harvesting in urban areas through the millennia: a sustainable technology for increasing water availability' describe the evolution of rainwater harvesting in urban areas in the course of millennia. Rainwater harvesting is a sustainable technology for increasing water availability and reducing flood risk dating back to 5000 BC.

'Ancient Water Wisdom: Traditional water systems in India' by Pangare and Pangare presents an in-depth inventory that also includes water-harvesting techniques serving as valuable lessons for today.

Hang outlines in 'Water and Heritage in Angkor, Cambodia: The monuments, the ancient hydraulic network and their recent rehabilitation' how the rehabilitation of ancient Angkorian hydraulic systems in Cambodia was prepared and carried out, to optimise water and disaster management while safeguarding temples, and how the activities informed advanced hydraulic engineering, thereby meeting multiple needs. The rehabilitation of the cultural landscape and environment has, in turn, recovered their essential functions in safeguarding the monuments.

In 'Water and World Heritage' Lemaistre presents descriptions and illustrations of several examples of water-related world heritage icons.

Disasters and heritage: impacts and responses

The first disaster addressed in this section is climate change: its impact and responses. The articles present specific case studies from around the world, and examine the impacts of climate change on cultural heritage, research findings and response strategies, and present recommendations for their protection.

In 'Beautiful tropical islands in the Caribbean Sea: Human responses to floods and droughts and the indigenous archaeological heritage of the Caribbean' Hofman and Hoogland focus on the evidence of catastrophic events and the water management responses of local communities through a number of archaeological case studies from across the Caribbean.

'Pacific Islands on the brink of submergence: Rising seas in an age of climate changes' by Peterson presents results of archaeological research on the impact of sea-level change on islands in the Pacific and the response mechanisms available to local communities.

In 'Sand and water – and their effect on the pyramids of Meroe in the Sudan' Riedel describes the destructive impacts of changes in precipitation on the pyramids and the need for further study into its root causes, as well as the development and implementation of protection measures.

'Preserving New York City's waterfront industrial and maritime heritage through resilient and sustainable development' by Daly centres on New York City's future waterfront development, and emphasises the importance of respecting its industrial heritage through the development of sustainable, resilient and integrated urban manufacturing of residential, recreational and commercial cityscapes.

In 'The values of sea defence heritage in Recife, Brazil' Labanca Corrêa de Araújo discusses the value of a 400-year old sea defence and its need for protection as it is faced with the impacts of climate change, rising sea levels and intensified storms.

In 'Hazard vulnerability and management of cultural heritage in the context of water-related hazard in the Republic of Korea' by Rii *et al.* the authors present physical and policy responses to improve the conservation of cultural and natural heritage properties threatened by water-related disasters and climate change.

Lieske *et al.* in 'Flood Protection for Historic Sites' introduce a nation-wide study on heritage conservation and urban development confronted with large-scale flood protection, and examine the 2014 Dresden Declaration on Flood Protection for Historic Sites.

Dunkley argues in 'Climate is what we expect, weather is what we get: managing the potential effects of oceanic climate change on underwater cultural heritage' that the effects of natural and anthropogenic climate change on underwater cultural heritage have not been adequately considered or researched. He offers an innovative assessment of the potential effects of oceanic climate change on managing underwater cultural heritage in the UK.

'Water as an Agent of Creation and Destruction at Petra' by Comer describes the degradation of the water harvesting system in the area surrounding the ancient city of Petra. It recommends identifying ways to divert water from the sites in order to address the deterioration of archaeological resources.

In 'Tsunami and heritage after the 2011 Great East Japan Earthquake' Okamura reviews past and current impacts on cultural heritage in a devastated area, the subsequent interventions and the research carried out. It presents a newly-emerging issue: dilemmas concerning heritage and communities during reconstruction processes, and clarifies how these issues and challenges relate at a socio-political level in Japanese contemporary society.

In 'Reinforcing the link between Water and Heritage to build Disaster Resilience Societies' Jigyasu analyses the various impacts of natural disasters on cultural heritage, the contribution of heritage to disaster prevention, and the role of urbanisation in water-related heritage.

Organisational connections

'Between pragmatism and cultural context: Continuity and change in Ifugao wet-rice agriculture' by Acabado describes the centuries old Ifugao water management system on the Philippines that parallels other systems in Southeast Asia (i.e., Indonesia), where communities using the same water channel share irrigation management duties.

In 'Water services heritage and institutional diversity' Katko *et al.* research the role of governance heritage in water services. The authors argue that the development of sustainable and resilient water and wastewater systems requires an understanding of the institutional, administrative and legal frameworks of a country.

Sugiura argues in 'The framework of skills and knowledge shared in long-enduring organisations in improvement of irrigation efficiency in Japan' that unchanged social structures of water user organisations and institutional frameworks of skills and knowledge have supported the sustainability of technological development since the commencement of irrigation.

Spatial, social, cultural, economic and spiritual connections

In 'The Delta works: heritage and new space for a changing world' Steenhuis argues that 55 years after the construction of the first Delta Works, certain changes to the structures are unavoidable, but that these changes should respect the principles of the original design by adhering to the alliance of geomorphology and vegetation and, just as essential, the feeling and experiencing of society about the transitions between sea and land, polder and dam.

'Beyond site protection: embedding natural heritage into sustainable landscapes' by Irvine pleads for the incorporation of natural heritage in development at multiple scales, challenging conventional wisdom and requiring reconciliation of strong views and vested interests, for which Environment Impact Assessments and the Strategic Environmental Assessments are relevant instruments.

'The Santa Cruz River: Four Millennia of Water Heritage and Security in the U.S.-Mexico Border Region' by De Grenade and Varady presents an inquiry into the historical role of water in assuring societal security – via a river's contribution to regional identity and to traditional food production systems – to yield insights into desert cultures of the past. Perhaps, more importantly, it may offer critical clues to the future of water in desert cities.

In 'Cultural and tourism strategies for preservation and enhancement of Venice and its lagoon' Calzolaio proposes redirecting tourist flows towards the lagoon and highlighting the role of its polycentric communities, thereby levering the authentic heritage of Venice and its lagoon, where land and sea, nature and man have become inextricably linked through centuries. The paper describes the complex relationship between the waters of the Venice lagoon and the community of people who share its amphibious space, residents and visitors.

'The Tennessee Valley Authority: How the Development of the Tennessee River Influenced Archaeology in the South-eastern United States' by Pritchard presents how the Tennessee Valley Authority has managed archaeological resources in conjunction with its operation of the Tennessee River from its early days in the 1930s, and is committed to continue its efforts.

'Development of the WWC world water heritage systems (WHS) programme' by Tyagi and Yamaoka proposes to create a 'World Water Heritage Systems Programme'. This programme is meant to encourage the protection of the people-centred practices, institutions, organizations, regimes and rules that serve as soft components of sustainable water management systems across all sectors and geographical areas around the world: intangible water heritage.

References

Akoto, R. and K. Piésold. 2008. Indigenous cosmology of cultural heritage for impact assessment, in: *IAIA08 Conference Proceedings: The Art and Science of Impact Assessment*, 28th Annual Conference of the International Association for Impact Assessment, 4–10 May 2008, Perth Convention Exhibition Centre, Perth, Australia.

Australian Government. 2008. Indigenous Australians Caring for Country. Department of the Environment, Water, Heritage and the Arts. http://www.environment.gov.au/indigenous/index.html (accessed January 2015).

Australian Human Rights Commission. 2009. Climate change, water and Indigenous knowledge: A Community Guide to the Native Title Report 2008, 8 pp.

Bandarin, F. and R. van Oers (eds.). 2014. Reconnecting the City: The Historic Urban Landscape Approach and the Future of Urban Heritage. Wiley-Blackwell, 376 pp.

Bond, A., L. Langstaff, R. Baxter, H.-G. Wallentinus, J. Kofoed, K. Lisitzin and S. Lundström. 2004. Dealing with the cultural heritage aspect of environmental impact assessment in Europe, in: *Impact Assessment and Project Appraisal*, vol. 22, nr. 1, March 2004, pp. 37–45.

Brown, S. 2008. Integrating cultural landscape approaches in cultural heritage impact assessment, in: *IAIA08 Conference Proceedings: The Art and Science of Impact Assessment*, 28th Annual Conference of the International Association for Impact Assessment, 4–10 May 2008, Perth Convention Exhibition Centre, Perth, Australia.

Council of Europe. 1992. European Convention on the Protection of the Archaeological Heritage. Council of Europe, www.coe.int. (accessed January 2015).

European Commission. 1985. Council Directive of 27 June 1985 on the assessment of the effects of certain public and private projects on the environment (85/337/EEC), in: *Official Journal of the European Communities*, 5 July 1985, No. L 175, pp. 40–48.

Evelpidou, N., T. de Figueiredo, F. Mauro, V. Tecim and A. Vassilopoulos (eds.). 2010. Natural Heritage from East to West: Case studies from 6 EU Countries, Springer, Berlin.

Francioni, F. and F. Lenzerini (eds.). 2008. The 1972 World Heritage Convention: A Commentary; Oxford Commentaries on International Law, Oxford University Press, Oxford, 600 pp.

Freestone, F. (ed.). 2013. The World Bank and Sustainable Development: Legal Essays. Legal Aspects of Sustainable Development, Martinus Nijhoff Publishers, Koninklijke Brill, Leiden.

Groenfeldt, D. 2013. Water Ethics: A Values Approach to Solving the Water Crisis, Earthscan/Routledge, Abingdon, 216 pp.

Hassan, F. 2011. Water History for Our Times. IHP Essays on Water History, vol. 2, UNESCO, Paris. Digitally (PDF) available on www.hydrology.nl.

Human Rights and Equal Opportunity Commission. 2009. Native Title Report 2008, Chapter 6, Indigenous Peoples and Water;, Australian Human Rights Commission, Sydney, 422 pp.

ICOMOS. 2015. www.icomos.org (accessed January 2015)

Ikram, S.M. and P. Spear. 1955. The Cultural Heritage of Pakistan, Oxford University Press, Karachi.

International Association of Impact Assessment. 2015. www.iaia.org. (accessed January 2015).

IUCN. 2013. IUCN Standard on Physical Cultural Resources; July 2013 – revised November 2013, IUCN, 7 pp.

Jesus, J. de. 2008. Cultural Heritage, Impact Assessment and the Council of Europe Conventions, in: *IAIA08 Conference Proceedings: The Art and Science of Impact Assessment*, 28th Annual Conference of the International Association for Impact Assessment, 4–10 May 2008, Perth Convention Exhibition Centre, Perth, Australia.

Keheller, A. (2010) Exploring alternative futures of the World Water System: Building a second generation of World Water Scenarios – Driving force: Ethics, Society and Culture. Prepared for the United Nations World Water Assessment Programme (WWAP).

Marzeion, B. and A. Levermann. 2014. Loss of cultural world heritage and currently inhabited places to sea-level rise, in: *Environmental Research Letters*, vol. 9, 034001; doi:10.1088/1748-9326/9/3/034001.

Perry, J. and C. Falzon. 2014. Climate Change Adaptation for Natural World Heritage Sites: A Practical Guide, World Heritage Papers series 37, UNESCO, Paris.

Tilden, F. 1957. Interpreting Our Heritage, The University of North Carolina Press, Chapel Hill.

UNESCO. 1954. Final act of the international conference on the protection of cultural property in the event of armed conflict, The Hague, 1954, UNESCO, Paris, 79 pp.

UNESCO. 1972. Convention concerning the protection of the world cultural and natural heritage, adopted by the General Conference at its seventeenth session, 16 November 1972, UNESCO, Paris, 19 pp.

UNESCO. 2001a. Convention on the Protection of the Underwater Cultural Heritage; UNESCO, Paris, 21 pp.

UNESCO. (2001b. Water – its role in human evolution; special issue of World Heritage, April 2001, nr. 59, 94 pp.

UNESCO. 2008. Enhancing our Heritage Toolkit: Assessing management effectiveness of natural World Heritage sites, World Heritage papers series 23, UNESCO, Paris, 161 pp.

UNESCO. 2011. Recommendation on the Historic Urban Landscape, including a glossary of definitions, 10 November 2011.

UNESCO. 2013. Operational Guidelines for the Implementation of the World Heritage Convention, WHC. 2013, 167 pp.

UNESCO. 2015. www.unesco.org (accessed January 2015).

United Nations. 2012a. The Future We Want, Outcome Document of the United Nations Conference on Sustainable Development, 20 to 22 June, Rio de Janeiro, Brazil, A/CONF.216/L.1.

United Nations. 2012b. 4th World Water Development Report, UNESCO, Paris.

United Nations. 2014. Globalization and interdependence: culture and sustainable development; Note A/69/216 of the Secretary Gewneral to the General Asembly, July, 2014.

United Nations. 2015. www.un.org/en/development/desa/population/publications/urbanization/urban-rural.shtml (accessed January 2015).

Verschuuren, B. 2007. An overview of cultural and spiritual values in ecosystem management and conservation strategies in: Haverkort, B. and S. Rist (2007) *Endogenous Development and Bio-cultural Diversity: The interplay of worldviews, globalization and locality*; ETC/Compas, Leusden, pp. 299–325.

Waterton, E. 2010. Politics, Policy and the Discourses of Heritage in Britain. Palgrave Macmillan, Houndmills, Basingstoke, Hampshire, UK.

World Bank. 2009. Physical Cultural Resources Safeguard Policy Guidebook, World Bank, Washington, 106 pp.

Evolution of rainwater harvesting in urban areas through the millennia

A sustainable technology for increasing water availability

Benoît Haut[a], Xiao Yun Zheng[b], Larry Mays[c], Mooyoung Han[d], Cees Passchier[e], and Andreas N. Angelakis[f]

a TIPs, Université libre de Bruxelles, Av. F.D. Roosevelt 50, C.P. 165/67, 1050 Brussels, Belgium, bhaut@ulb.ac.be

b Yunnan Academy of Social Sciences, 650034 Kunming City, China, zhengxy68@163.com

c School of Sustainable Engineering and the Built Environment, Arizona State University, Tempe, AZ 85287-5306, USA, mays@asu.edu

d Dept. of Civil and Environmental Eng., #35-302 Seoul National University, #1 Daehakro Kwanakgu, Seoul, Korea, myhan@snu.ac.kr

e Department of Earth Sciences (Institut für Geowissenschaften), Johannes Gutenberg Universität, Becherweg 21, 55128 Mainz, Germany, cpasschi@uni-mainz.de

f Institute of Iraklion, National Foundation for Agricultural Research (N.AG.RE.F.), 71307 Iraklion, Hellas, info@a-angelakis.gr

Abstract

In the prehistoric world, the low water availability in several regions of the world, particularly in arid and semi-arid regions, resulted in the construction of various water reservoir types for collection and storage of rainwater (e.g. in Minoan islands, in Indus valley, in China, and pre-Columbian civilizations). Rainwater harvesting was known even in the Mesopotamian plain where fresh water from the Tigris and Euphrates was secured. There, rainwater harvesting was used to secure drinking water supply. Since then, the technology of construction and use of several types of cisterns has been further developed, by different civilizations. Advanced water cistern technologies were invented, with a peak in the Classical and Hellenistic periods that follows Alexander the Great, during which they spread over a geographical area from Greece to the West (central and south Italy) and to the East (Egypt and probably eastern and southern of Egypt). The Romans inherited the Greek cistern technologies and developed them further mainly by changing their application scale from small to large and implementing them to almost every large city. Characteristic paradigms of ancient water cisterns are considered in this chapter. Development of cost-effective decentralized water supply management programs based on the harvesting and the storage of rainwater in cisterns, especially in water-short areas, is a sustainable technology. In addition, during floods, one of the basic ideas is to increase water storage in order to achieve the maximum possible water retention effect together with minimum investment (e.g. construction of local embankments for the towns). This can also be achieved by construction of water cisterns.

Keywords: *Ancient Egypt; Classical and Hellenistic periods; increase water availability; Medieval times; Minoan Crete; Roman period; Ottomans; rainwater; reduction of flood risks; water cistern.*

1. Prolegomena

Water harvesting methods are distinguished by the source of water they harvest (e.g. groundwater, surface water, rainwater and floodwater). Historically, there is a correlation between heightened human efforts for the construction of water harvesting structures across regions and abrupt climate fluctuations, like aridity, drought, and floods (Pandey *et al.*, 2003). The objective is the safe beneficial use of this water and the reduction of the impact on the society of these climate fluctuations (Konig, 2011).

Rainwater harvesting is defined in this chapter as atmospheric precipitations collected and stored usually in artificial reservoirs, known as cisterns (Angelakis, 2014). This rainwater is used for household purposes such as bathing or washing, washing dishes, laundering clothes, irrigation or other urban uses.

From the early civilizations, people in arid and semi-arid regions have relied on harvesting rainwater. Every settlement of the humankind basically depended on a sufficient water supply. This applies especially for arid and semi-arid climate conditions in the regions around the Mediterranean basin and especially in southeastern Greece, where water resources availability is extremely limited during the summer (Antoniou *et al.*, 2014). In this region, rainwater harvesting was practiced since the early human settlements, in order to increase water availability.

It is important to differentiate rainwater harvesting to supply a group of people with water and stormwater[1] management for flood control. Stormwater can be highly polluting and have dramatic consequences due to flooding. Rainwater is normally of good quality and, today, its harvesting typically concerns small-scale installations in individual houses, office buildings or industrial sites, including

---

1   Stormwater refers to the water resulting from rain draining into the stormwater system from roofs, roads, footpaths and other ground surfaces. It is usually channelled into local waterways. Stormwater carries rubbish, animal faeces, human faecal waste (in some areas), motoroil, petrol, tyre rubber, soil and debris. Initial runoff associated with storms can contain very high concentrations of enteric pathogens (disease-causing organisms) and contaminants (both chemical and physical).

agricultural greenhouses. Rainwater harvesting can however be part of a stormwater management strategy (e.g. green roofs, roof storage or mini dams, underground storage, aquifer recharge or open storage basins integrated in the landscape).

These last decades, large rainwater harvesting projects have been implemented on housing developments, industrial complexes and agricultural greenhouses, to reduce water costs (potable, wastewater and stormwater charges), as well as to reduce stormwater infrastructures. Water storage structures range from: (a) individual domestic rainwater tanks, (b) the collection and reuse of all precipitations on large industrial or agricultural sites, (c) community wetlands for treatment and storage, (d) aquifer recharge for storage and recovery to (e) large-scale dams.

Nowadays, appropriately treated rainwater has the potential for use within dwellings, offices, housing estates, industry, horticulture, gardens, etc. The final use of the rainwater will dictate the level of treatment that it will require. Where such use does occur, it is essential that appropriate safeguards are taken to prevent cross contamination of potable water supplies, damage to internal fixtures and fittings or harm to the environment (Angelakis *et al.*, 2012). The design and development of such water collection systems is an emerging technology encouraged by the need for water conservation and water taxes. It can be of great value where water is scarce, but in many circumstances it is still expensive and not necessarily beneficial to the environment. It is essential that any applications may be properly controlled to prevent risks to public health (Angelakis *et al.*, 2012).

There are examples of rainwater harvesting systems in many countries. Some of them were installed and operated for centuries. Rainwater harvesting has been practiced in Crete, Hellas, since the Neolithic times, ca. 7,000 – 3,200 BC (Angelakis and Spyridakis, 2013). Thereafter, during the Bronze Age (ca. 3,200 – 1100 BC), rainwater harvesting was driven by the necessities to make efficient use of natural resources, to make civilizations more resistant to destructive natural elements, and to improve the standards of life. At that time, Minoans (Crete, ca. 3,200 – 1100 BC) and an unknown civilization (ca. 2,600 – 1900 BC) in the Indus valley at Mohenjo-Daro, Harappa, and Lothal developed advanced water supply systems, including water cisterns, which were called epektathhkan in Europe and Asia (Mays *et al.*, 2012).

The scope of this chapter is to present, chronologically, the main achievements in harvesting of rainwater worldwide, including water supply technological principles and consumption by humans, extending from the earliest civilizations to the present. It is not an exhaustive presentation of what is known today about rainwater harvesting, treatment and use since the beginning of human quest for water supply systems. Emphasis is given to the places and periods of great achievements. A recent achievement of multi-purpose decentralized rainwater harvesting system at a high-rise building complex is introduced.

2. Prehistoric times

2.1. Minoan Era (ca. 3,200 -1100 BC)

The island of Crete, Hellas, was inhabited even before the early Neolithic period. Genetic markers in modern population indicate that the first Neolithic migrants arrived to Crete between 8,800 and 10,000 BC, from the Levant, the region in the eastern Mediterranean that today encompasses Israel and the West Bank, Jordan, Syria and part of southern Turkey (Paschou *et al.*, 2014). The first evidence of the use of metal artifacts consists of a copper axe found by Sir Arthur Evans in Kephala, Knossos (Strasser, 2010). Crete was permanently inhabited during the Bronze Age (ca. 3,200 – 1100 BC) by the Minoan civilization that flourished and reached its pinnacle as the first European civilization of the Aegean world (Alexiou, 1964). Among other evidences, this may be demonstrated by the advanced techniques used for collecting, storing, and transporting surface water, highlighting that Minoans had a good degree of understanding of the basic water management techniques (Koutsoyiannis *et al.*, 2008; Angelakis and Spyridakis, 2010).

Several examples of Minoan achievements in collecting and storage of rainwater have been reported (Koutsoyiannis *et al.*, 2008; Angelakis *et al.*, 2012). In Minoan Phaistos, Archanes, Zakros, Chamaizi, and Myrtos-Pyrgos, in contrary to Knossos, Tylissos, and other Minoan establishments, the water supply system was dependent directly on precipitation. Rainwater was collected from the roofs and yards of buildings in cisterns. At Phaistos, no wells or springs have been found. Special care was given to (a) cleaning the surfaces used for collecting the runoff water and (b) filtering in coarse sandy filters the water before it flowed into the cisterns in order to maintain the purity of water. The collected water was mainly used for washing clothes and for other cleaning tasks (Angelakis and Spyridakis, 1996). An element of the rainwater harvesting system in Phaistos is shown in Fig. 1. More on Minoan cisterns are referred in Mays *et al.* (2013).

Figure 1. Small water cistern with coarse sandy filter in the rainwater harvesting system in Phaistos. With permission of A. N. Angelakis.

2.2. Indus Valley civilization (ca. 3,300 -1300 BC)

During the Indus Valley civilization, the inhabitants of Mohenjo-Daro were masters in constructing wells and cisterns. It is estimated that about 700 wells have been built within their city (Kenoyer, 1998). The cities had strong walls to resist damages due to floods. One reason for this large number of wells and cisterns is that Mohenjo-Daro received less winter rain and was situated further from the Indus River than the other prominent cities of the Indus Valley civilization. Hence, it was necessary to collect and store rainwater for various purposes. An example of a cistern excavated in Moen-Jo-Daro is given in Fig. 2.

Figure 2. Different types of cisterns during the Indus Valley civilization: in Mohenjo-Daro (top) (Bisht, 2011) and in Dholavira (bottom) (Kenoyer, 1998).

Another very good example of water achievement during the Indus Valley civilization is the well-planned city of Dholavira, on Khadir Bet, a low plateau in the Rann in Gujarat (Kenoyer 1998). A large number of tanks were cut in the rocks to provide drinking water to the tradesmen who used to travel along an ancient trade route. Each fort in the area had its own water harvesting and storage system in the form of rock-cut cisterns, ponds, tanks and wells that are still in use today (see Fig. 2).

2.3. The Mycenaean civilization (ca. 1600 – 1100 BC)

In about 1450 BC, an unexplained event laid waste all the centres of Minoan Crete. Meanwhile, the Minoan civilization was overrun by the Mycenaean civilization from mainland Greece. As a consequence, the advanced Minoan hydro-technologies, especially water cisterns, spread to the Greek mainland (Angelakis and Spyridakis, 1996).

3. Historical times

3.1. Urban Rainwater Harvesting and Management in China

A large cistern, built during the Yangshao culture (from 5,000 BC to around 3,000 BC), was discovered at Lingbao City (Henan Province). It evidences that the earliest history of rainwater harvesting in China is dated back to ca. 5,000 years ago (Jing, 2001). China was an agricultural based country for thousands of years. The urban history started at around 2,000 BC. In that time, there were many kingdoms established in centre China, especially in the Yellow River basin. The building of their capital cities was the start of urbanization in China. It included urban water systems construction. Accordingly, rainwater harvesting was also considered in order to meet the needs of the population. In China, the purpose of rainwater harvesting was different for rural and urban areas. The rainwater harvesting in the rural areas were mainly practiced for irrigation and daily life. In the urban areas, rainwater harvesting was mainly considered for the rainstorm water management, storage of water for water supply and waterscape.

Urban rainwater harvesting was considered as a part of the systematic water system in a city. A complete model of the urban water system of Chinese cities was first formed at the Han Chan'an city, the capital city of Han Dynasty, at around 200 BC. This model influenced urban water system design and construction in subsequent dynasties of China until the early 19th century. As presented in Fig. 3, this model consisted of several components, including urban rivers, ponds, moats and drainage rivers (Yun Zheng, 2015). According to the ancient idea, the banks of a river, especially for the major rivers like the Yellow River, were strongly considered as the ideal place for the establishment of a city (Huai Chu, 2005). When a city was built near a river, it was convenient for water supply but, simultaneously, it also faces highly rainstorm risk. Therefore one of the most important functions of the urban water system was to manage the rainstorm water.

3.2. Etruscans (ca. 800 – 100 BC)

Possible hydro-technological connections between the Minoan civilization and the Etruscans have been reported (Angelakis *et al.*, 2013). The evolution of water science in Europe was characterized by discontinuities and regressions during the Dark Ages. However, Minoans probably "built bridges" with neighboring civilizations such as the Egyptians, Mycenaeans, Etruscans, and Classical Greeks (Angelakis *et al.,* 2013). Several water cisterns are known in the city of Perugia, in Umbria. One of the most interesting cisterns is in *Via Cesare Caporali*, accidentally discovered in 1989 during renovations of a building. This cistern is similar to those in Minoan Knossos and Archanes. In the town of Todi, also in Umbria, there are about 5 km of hypogeum tunnels and galleries, and more than 30 cisterns, dating from the Etruscan times.

3.3. Classical and Hellenistic Periods (ca. 480 - 67 BC)

During the Classical and Hellenistic periods, significant developments were made in hydraulics. They allowed the invention of advanced hydraulic and pneumatic instruments and devices (such as water lifting devices, hydraulic clocks, musical instruments, steam boilers and a reactive motor). All of these developments reflect a good understanding of the combined action of air and water pressure (Antoniou

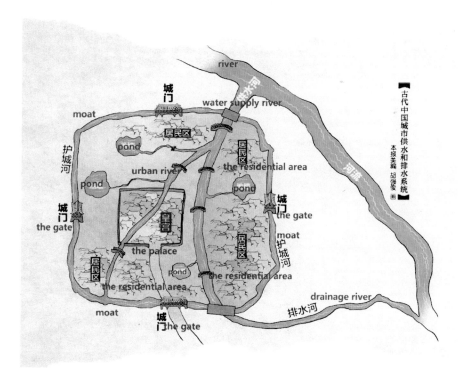

Figure 3. General form of an ancient urban water system in China.

et al., 2014). Also during the Classical and Hellenistic periods, pressure flow was applied on a large technological scale for water conveyance for first time in the humankind history.

Regarding rainwater harvesting during the Classical and Hellenistic periods, a characteristic example is the water supply system of the citadel at Pergamon, in western Anatolia (now Turkey). The first settlement of the town was on the top of a high hill. Its water needs were met by rainwater stored in a system of cisterns (ensuring secured water supply in the event of a war) and by a small spring at the foot of the hill. By 1993 AD, 149 such cisterns had been found, capable of supporting a population of about 7,900 inhabitants (Garbrecht and Garbrecht, 2005).

In the Hellenistic period, significant developments relevant to water supply and to hygienic lifestyle were achieved in several places of Hellenistic Hellas. During this period, impressive accomplishments were achieved in hydraulic works. Especially, cistern technologies of Minoans and Mycenaeans were further improved by building cisterns of rectangular cross-section as well as circular ones (e.g. in Lato, Dreros, Santorini, Amorgos, and Delos). In castle areas, cisterns were also totally or partly carved into rocks, as on the island of Rho (Antoniou, 2012). Several small-scale residential rainwater cisterns have survived, such as those in Santorini, Delos, Aegina (Fig. 4), Amorgos and Polyrrhenia. These were carved into rocks and were mainly pear-shaped. At least one layer of hydraulic plaster was applied to prevent water loss from leakage through the bottom and walls of the cisterns. The estimated capacity of such cisterns is about 10 m³.

In addition to these small-scale cisterns, much larger ones were excavated in rocky fortresses. Several examples show regular and well-designed shapes similar to the great rainwater cistern of the Theatre of Delos (Fraisse and Moretti, 2007).

Figure 4. Hellenistic cisterns: the main cistern (possibly originally covered) at Elanion sanctuary in the island of Aegina (left) and the slab-covered cistern of the sanctuary of Heraion at Loutraki Attika (right).

Figure 5. Nabataean rainwater fed cistern in Humeima, Jordan (left) and one of the cisterns of Masada, Dead Sea valley (right).

3.4. Nabataean and Hasmonean (ca. 87 BC – 150 AD)

The Nabateans built numerous cisterns for storage of rainwater in their city centres and scattered in the desert. Diodorus (II.48.2, XIX.94.6-9) refers to the high level of development of rainwater capturing devices and cisterns by the Nabateans, and their use of hidden cisterns in the desert in case of emergency. An extensive analysis of the water supply systems of Nabatean Bosra and Petra can be found in the works Mouton and Al-Dbiyat (2009) and Ortloff (2014). Nabatean cisterns were usually rectangular and plastered inside with grey waterproof cement. These cisterns were covered with slabs supported by pillars or separate arches, set into notches in the cistern walls (Fig. 5). Rainwater capture was either directly from wadis or, for the smaller cisterns in the mountains, by means of artificial ledges and gullies channelling rainwater from rock surface into the cisterns. Numerous examples of such cisterns can be found in Petra and Humaima, Jordan (Fig. 5). See also www.ancientwatertechnologies.com for examples of many Nabataean cisterns.

The Herodian fortresses in the Judean desert give examples of rainwater capture during the Hasmonean dynasty. These fortresses contain huge cisterns that were usually fed by aqueducts from wadis in the neighborhood, but also filled with rainwater during rare seasonal rainstorms. They are a highly specialized form of rainwater capture. Examples of such fortesses are the fortresses of Masada in Israel (Fig. 5, Netzer, 2001) and Machaerus in Jordan (Garbrecht and Peleg, 1994; Tsuk, 2011).

3.5. Roman period (ca. 67 BC - 330 AD)

In Roman times, the cisterns were constructed to provide water to families or workers (Mays, 2010; Viollet, 2000). They were masonry, built on ground level or underground, covered or not, with the inner side of the walls covered by a water repellent coating made of mortar (Haut and Viviers, 2012). Some cisterns were dedicated to collect rainwater and others were supplied with running water. The Roman aqueducts usually delivered water into large, often compartmentalised, cisterns (or set of cisterns) located as high as possible within the cities, to benefit as much as possible from the potential energy to distribute water. For instance, a detailed description of such large cistern complexes can be found in the work of Wilson (2001), about the distribution of water in several Roman cities in Tunisia.

Numerous remains attest of cisterns that were constructed, in Roman times, to collect rainwater, mainly to supply single houses. A well-known example of such a kind of system is the impluvium (Mays *et al.*, 2013). The impluvium is a square basin, typically a few dozen centimetres deep, in the centre of the atrium of a Roman house, aiming to collect rainwater from the roof (see Fig. 6). This basin was connected, for instance with a drain, to an underground cistern under the atrium. A nearby well allowed the inhabitants of the house to draw water from this cistern. Cisterns in such systems were usually small, due to the limited water catchment provided by surrounding roofs and courtyards. These cisterns were commonly rectangular with a barrel vault, while circular and carafe-shaped cisterns are also attested (Wilson, 1997).

Apart from such individual systems, that were dedicated to provide water for a single house, a lot of large-scale Roman hydraulic projects based on the use of rainwater collected in cisterns are referenced, in regions with low available surface water (for instance small islands) or at locations difficult to reach with an aqueduct (for instance hilltop settlements that can not be supplied by an inverted siphon).

Regarding islands, it is clear that rainwater was the only option if the island is too small to provide groundwater fed springs. Many islands in the Mediterranean had rainwater fed cisterns constructed during Roman times. Good examples of Roman cisterns are found on the islands of Karpathos, Greece, and Pandataria (modern Ventotene), Italy. Several large cisterns on Ventotene were fed by rainwater and interconnected by small aqueducts that fed a villa and the port area (De Rossi, 1993; De Rossi, 1998).

Obviously, settlements on isolated hills could not be supplied water by an aqueduct, even using inverted siphons. Therefore, these settlements had to rely on rainwater or on wells, using water-lifting devices. A striking example of such a settlement is the Housesteads Roman fort. This fort, on Hadrian's Wall, is one of the best-known monuments in northern England. It was built a few years after 122 AD, when the construction of the Hadrian's Wall started. According to Beaumont (2008), it appears that a conventional aqueduct could not have supplied the fort with water. However, it has been evaluated that, harvesting rainfall from the roofs within the fort, 800 men could have been supplied with water. Six cisterns can be observed at the fort. Five of them are approximately 1.1 m width, 2.6 m long, and have a depth of approximately 0.7 m. The sixth cistern is the largest and is located close to the well-preserved latrines in the southeast corner of the fort (see Fig. 6). This cistern is 3 m width, 4.6 m long and with a depth of 0.7 m. It was used to supply water to the latrines.

Two other illustrative examples of a large-scale Roman hydraulic project based on rainwater harvesting can be given. In Athens, Greece, there is a Roman cistern at the base of the Acropolis (Mays, 2010). A roof supported by columns covered this cistern. It is thought that this cistern could have been supplied with rainwater, collected either from the slope of the Acropolis or from the roof of adjacent buildings. This cistern probably delivered water to supply Roman baths. The town of Tiddis, Algeria, is situated on a steep hillside and was supplied by a large rainwater cistern on the hillside above the town, built in 251 AD (Wilson, 1997). Similar large cisterns existed at Bararus, Algeria (Hallier, 1987; Wilson, 1997).

Figure 6. Roman cisterns: Impluvium (water basin) in the centre of the Atrium of a former house, ancient Roman Pompeii, Campania, Italy (top). The drain connecting the impluvium to the underground cistern can be observed on the picture. Picture by Norbert Nagel / Wikimedia Commons. License: CC BY-SA 3.0. Latrines at the Housesteads Roman fort (bottom), flushed by water channels supplemented by a cistern located at the back of the latrines. Picture in the public domain.

Although most Roman cisterns were covered, large rectangular open cisterns, fed by floodwater from local wadis, are common in Roman times, particularly in the dry provinces. Such open cisterns are common in Tunisia and Algeria (Wilson, 1997) and in Jordan (Mouton and Al-Dbiyat, 2009).

It is worth noticing that it may be difficult for archaeologists to make the distinction between a cistern dedicated to collect rainwater and a cistern that was supplied with running water, due to the fact that archaeological hydraulic remains are seldom complete. For instance, several cisterns build in the southern part of the city of Apamea (Syria) were initially understood as being dedicated to collect rainwater (Balty, 1987). However, a recent analysis (Vannesse et al., 2014) has demonstrated that these cisterns were part of larger hydraulic systems (fountains) and that they were supplied with water through a connection with the aqueduct inside the city.

4. The Byzantine period and Venetian rule (330 – 1538 AD)

Byzantine Empire or Eastern Roman Empire, with Constantinople as the capital, are terms used to describe the Hellenic-speaking Roman Empire during the Middle Ages. During that period, the technologies applied for water supply of the cities were manly based on cisterns and wells. The surviving relevant Roman tradition was transmitted and applied to the water supply system of a large part of Constantinople. This system not only fed covered cisterns with running water, through aqueducts, but also open-air cisterns such as the *Xerokipion* (dry garden) and the *Aetius* cistern (Bogdanovic, 2008; Cinic, 2003). The total capacity of the underground cisterns in Constantinople was estimated equal to 200,000 m^3 and the total capacity of the open-air cisterns equal to 800,000 m^3 (Mays et al., 2012). Cisterns used for harvesting of rainwater were a dominant hydro-technology in several Byzantine cities and other settlements. Such a cistern is shown in Fig. 7. During the millennial existence of the Byzantine Empire, its influence spread widely into North Africa and the Near East. In fact, several Byzantine cisterns have been found in various parts of Hellas (e.g. in Mistra, Leontari Arkadias,

Figure 7. Middle Ages cisterns: Byzantine water cistern (of rectangular cross–section) in the Areti Monastery in eastern Crete (left) and Venetian cistern at the island of Grambousa in western Crete (right).

Monemvasia, Crete, several Aegian islands, Cyprus, and Athens) and even in small remote islands such as Amorgos. At the end of the Byzantine period (after ca. 1200 AD) several regions of the southern Europe (e.g. Crete, Cyprus, Peloponnesus, and the most of Aegean and Ionian islands) passed under the Venetian rule. Some of those regions were under Italian occupation until the 18th century. During that period, the rainwater harvesting technology was highly improved. A Venetian cistern in the small island of Grambousa (western crete) is shown in Fig. 7. This traditional hydro-technology is still in use in several Aegean islands, in eastern Crete, and elsewhere.

5. Pre-Columbian Americas

5.1. Xochicalco (ca. 650 – 900 AD)

After the disintegration of Teotihuacan's empire in the 7th century AD, foreigners from the Gulf Coast lowlands and the Yucatan Peninsula appeared in central Mexico. Cacaxtla and Xochicalco are two regional centres that became important with the disappearance of Teotihuacan. Xochicalco ("in the place of the house of flowers") was located on a hilltop approximately 38 km from modern-day Cuernavaca, Mexico, and became one of the great Mesoamerican cities in the late classic period (ca. 650 – 900 AD). There were no rivers or streams or wells to obtain water, so rainwater harvesting was the source of water. Rainwater was collected in the large plaza area and conveyed using drainage structures (see Fig. 8) into cisterns. From the cisterns, water was conveyed to other areas of the city using pipes. The collapse/abandonment of Xochicalco most likely resulted from drought, warfare, and internal political struggles (Mays et al., 2013)

5.2. Mayan civilization

The ancient Mayan civilization developed around 3000 years ago in Mesoamerica. The Maya lived in a vast area covering parts of present-day Guatemala, Mexico, Belize, and the western areas of Honduras and El Salvador. Maya settled in the last millennium BC and their civilization flourished until around 870 AD. The environment that the Maya lived in was less fragile than that of the semi-arid lands where the Ancestral Puebloans and Hohokam lived (Mays et al., 2013).

The Mayan civilization faced recurrent droughts before it collapsed due to climate deterioration. Haug et al. (2003) have shown that the collapse of the Mayan civilization occurred during the spatio-temporally extensive dry period in the region, interspersed by more severe droughts centred at about 810, 860, and 910 AD. Scarborough and Gallopin (1991) documented that rainwater collection and storage was a major source of water supply during the dry seasons. Cisterns were constructed in Tikal (see Fig. 8) to face the seasonal scarcity of water. Tikal was one of the largest lowland Mayan centres, located some 300 km north of present-day Guatemala City (Mays et al., 2013). The city was located in a rainforest setting with a present-day average annual rainfall of 135 cm. A number of artificial cisterns were built in Tikal, which became more and more important as the population increased.

According to Scarborough (2003), the most central precinct catchment at Tikal was 62 ha, which could collect more than 900,000 cubic meters of runoff (based upon 1,500 mm of annual rainfall) due to the impervious cover of the plaza and the plastered monumental architecture. The six central precinct reservoirs at Tikal could contain 100,000 – 250,000 cubic meters of water (Scarborough, 2003).

Figure 8. Rainwater harvesting cisterns: Xochicalco times (top) and Mayan times located in Tikal, Guatemala (bottom). With permission of L.W. Mays.

Three distinct types of cisterns are reported by Scarborough and Gallopin (1991): centrally located cisterns, residential cisterns, and margin cisterns. The terminology is essentially based on location of the cistern and its capacity to store water. Similar water collection and storage systems have been documented in other areas of South America (Pandey *et al.*, 2003).

In the northern part of the Yucatan, the Maya built chultans (bell shaped cisterns) from a built platform surface. These cisterns are functional similar to other cisterns such as those built by the Greeks, Romans, and Nabataeans (Mays, 2010; Mays, 2013; Mays *et al.*,2013).

6. Modern times

6.1. Present times (1899 AD – today)

In several parts of the world, modern water technologies started to be developed at the end of 19th and the beginning of 20th century. They were based on the technologies of the past as well as on deep wells, pumps, pipes, etc. It was continued with an advanced manner after the World War I, and even more after the World War II, i.e. the middle of the last century (Angelakis and Vavoula, 2012). The use of water cisterns for water supply was a common practice in several parts of the developed world. Cisterns to collect rainwater are still the main part of water supply systems in various arid and semi-arid regions of the world. In these regions, people face malnutrition and vitamin deficiency; water is so scarce that the most efficient way to provide it is to harvest rainwater.

6.2. Seoul's Star City: A rainwater harvesting benchmark for Korea

In recent years, seasonal climate extremes have intensified, resulting in huge socioeconomic damages. As an adaptation strategy for coping with climate extremes, an ancient concept of rainwater harvesting is getting revisited. Recently, researchers have reappraised the decentralized multi-purpose rainwater harvesting system (Rwhs) as a useful infrastructure to mitigate water-related disasters such as flooding, sudden water break and fire events, especially in highly developed urban areas (IWA, 2008).

The Star City Rwhs in South Korea is a successful case that is designed with an intention of alleviating water-related disasters. Star City a large commercial/residential complex consisting of a department store and four apartment buildings, each having between 35 and 57 stories. In total, there are 1310 apartments, meant to accommodate four to five thousand people. The catchment area comprises 6,200 m^2 of four rooftop areas and 45,000 m^2 of terraces and gardens throughout the complex. During the design stage, a 3,000 m^3 rainwater tank was introduced at the 4th floor of Building B, and divided into three tanks, 1000 m^3 each (IWA, 2008).

Several innovative concepts have been applied in implementing the rainwater harvesting system at Star City. The first is the concept of a multi-purpose system; the system at Star City serves the purpose of flood mitigation, water conservation, and emergency preparation. The second is the concept of proactive management of flooding; the Star City system has a remote control system for monitoring and controlling the tank water level. The three different tanks also store water separately according to water quality. The risk of flood can be controlled pro-actively with the remote control system by emptying or filling the tanks appropriately. The third innovative concept applied in this project was the city government's incentive program for the developer, so that government will allow more floor space to build to compensate the extra cost for rainwater harvesting system.

During the 7 years operation, some technical data are reported (Han and Mun, 2011; Mun and Han, 2012). This successful demo project convinced the city officials and lawmakers, and triggered to make a city ordinance and propose a national law for rainwater management.

7. Conclusions

From the early civilizations, people in arid and semi-arid regions have relied on collecting rainwater and storing it in reservoirs known as cisterns. Cisterns have been constructed in the entire region around the Mediterranean and the Near East since the third millennium BC. Not only were cisterns used to store rainwater; they were also used to store aqueduct water for seasonal variations. Cisterns during the ancient times have ranged from construction of irregular shaped holes (tanks) dug out of sand and loose rocks, and then lined with plaster (stucco) water proofing, to the construction of rather sophisticated structures such as those built first by the Minoan and the Indus valley civilizations (Mays, 2007).

A brief historical development of rainwater harvesting since the prehistoric times to the present times has been presented. These unique structures have allowed humans to live in arid and semi-arid regions for over 5,000 years. These hydraulic structures are certainly evidence of the social, political, and economic conditions, and most likely the military conditions, of the various periods of human history.

Rainwater harvesting continues to be practiced globally, and there is renewed interest in its revival, the system nonetheless has fallen to disrepair. Climate policy and water policy would require to be streamlined to promote that technology in the water-stressed regions of the world. Pandey *et al.* (2003) reported that neither the water policy nor the climate policy discussions appears to notice the worth of the rainwater harvesting, especially in urban areas where water resources are fast depleting due to rapid increase in population and unrestricted use of water. Historical studies on rainwater harvesting, collection, and storage technologies provide insights into possible responses of modern societies to the future sustainable management of water resources.

References

Angelakis, A.N. 2014. Evolution of Rainwater Harvesting and Use in Crete, Hellas, through the Millennia. Water 6: 1246-56.

Angelakis, A.N. and Spyridakis, S.V. 1996. The status of water resources in Minoan times - A preliminary study. In Diachronic Climatic Impacts on Water Resources with Emphasis on Mediterranean Region, Edited by A. Angelakis and A. Issar, Springer-Verlag, Heidelberg, Germany, p. 161-191.

Angelakis, A.N. and Spyridakis, D. S. 2010. Water Supply and Wastewater Management Aspects in Ancient Greece. Water Sci. and Techn., Water Supply, 10(4): 618-628.

Angelakis, A.N. and Spyridakis, S. V. 2013. Major Urban Water and Wastewater Systems in Minoan Crete, Greece. Water Sci. and Techn., Water Supply, 13(3): 564-573.

Angelakis, A.N. and Vavoula, G. 2012. Evolution of Urban Hydro-technologies in Crete, Greece Through the Centuries. In Protection and Restoration of the Environment XI, CD Proceedings and Book of Abstracts, 3-6 July 2012, Thessaloniki, Greece, p. 323.

Angelakis, A.N., Dialynas, M. G., and Despotakis, V. 2012. Evolution of Water Supply Technologies in Crete, Greece, Through the Centuries. In Evolution of Water Supply Through the Millennia, Edited by Andreas Nikolaos Angelakis, Larry W. Mays and Demetris Koutsoyiannis, IWA Publishing, London, UK, Ch. 9: 227-258.

Angelakis, A.N., De Feo, G., Laureano, P. and Zourou, A. 2013. Minoan and Etruscan Hydro-technologies. Water, 5: 972-987.

Antoniou, G.P. 2012. The architecture of the fortress on the Island of Rho in Dodecanese. In The architecture of fortifications in the Aegean and the medieval settlement of Anavatos of Chios, Edited by A. Kavadia and P. Damoulos, Committee for the Preservation of Anavatos, Chios, Hellas, p. 91-104.

Antoniou, G.P., Kathijotes, N., Angelakis, A.N. and Spyridakis, D.S. 2014. Historical Development of Technologies on Water Resources Management and Rainwater Harvesting in the Hellenic Civilizations. Inter. Journal of Water Resources Development, 14(08): 1-14.

Balty, J.C. 1987. Problèmes de l'eau à Apamée de Syrie (Water in Apamea). In Proceedings of L'homme et l'eau en Méditerranée et au Proche-Orient. IV. L'eau dans l'agriculture, Lyon, p. 9-23.

Beaumont, P. 2008. Water Supply at Housesteads Roman Fort, Hadrian's Wall: the Case for Rainfall Harvesting. Britannia, 39: 59-84.

Bisht, R.S. 2011. Harappan Hydro-Engineering and Water Management. Presented at ICTS Mini Workshop: Future of the past, November 22-26, 2011, Manglore, India.

Bogdanovic, J. 2008. Cisterns. Encyclopedia of the Hellenic world [in Greek], Constantinople.

Jin Huai Chu. 2005. City and Water in Ancient China: with case of old Capital Cities. The Journal of Hai He University, 7.

Cinic, N. 2003. Yerebatan cistern and other cisterns of Istanbul. Emda Export Ltd, Istanbul, Turkey.

De Rossi, G.M. 1993. Ventotene e S. Stefano : un'agile ma esauriente guida per la riscoperta storica, archeologica e naturalistica delle due isole e per una loro "rilettura" nel museo di Ventotene. Guidotti, Roma.

De Rossi, G.M. 1998. La Cisterna dei carcerati e l'approvvigionamento idrico in età romana nell'isola. Guidotti, Roma.

Fraisse, P. and Moretti, J.C. 2007. Le theatre, Vols. I, II Exp. ArchDelos XLII. De Boccard, Paris, France.

Garbrecht, J.D. and Garbrecht, G.K.H. 2005. Water supply challenges and solutions of the ancient city of Pergamon. In Proceedings of Oklahoma water 2005, Stillwater: Oklahoma Water Resources Research Institute, Oklahoma, USA.

Garbrecht, G. and Peleg, Y. 1994. The water supply of the desert fortresses in the Jordan valley. Biblical archaeologist, 57: 161-170.

Hallier, G. 1987. Les citernes monumentales de Bararus (Henchir Rougga) en Byzacène. Antiquités africaines, 23: 129-148.

Han, M.Y. and Mun, J.S. 2011. Operational data of the Star City rainwater harvesting system and its role as a climate change adaptation and a social influence. Water Science & Technology, 63(12): 2796-2801.

Haug, G. H., Gunther, D., Peterson, L. C., Sigman, D. M., Hughen, K. A. and Aeschlimann, B. 2003. Climate and the collapse of Maya civilization. Science, 299: 1731-1735.

Haut, B. and Viviers, D. 2012. Water supply in the Middle East during Roman and Byzantine periods. In Evolution of Water Supply Through the Millennia, Edited by Andreas Nikolaos Angelakis, Larry W. Mays and Demetris Koutsoyiannis, IWA Publishing, London, UK, Ch. 13: 319-350.

International Water Association (IWA). 2008. Seoul's Star City: a rainwater harvesting benchmark for Korea. Water, 21: 17-18.

Jing, L.L. 2001. The Cistern was existed at Yangshao Period. Xinhuanet. http://news.h2o-china.com/html/2001/02/1664983063814_1.shtml (Accessed at November 23, 2014)

Kenoyer, J.M. 1998. Mohenjo-Daro: An Ancient Indus Valley Metropolis. University of Wisconsin, Madison, USA.

Koutsoyiannis, D., Zarkadoulas, N., Angelakis, A.N. and Tchobanoglous, G. 2008. Urban water management in ancient Greece: Legacies and lessons. ASCE, Journal of Water Resources Planning and Management, 134: 45-54.

Konig, K.W. 2001. The Rainwater Technology Handbook. WILO-Brain, Dortmund, Germany.

Mays, L.W. 2007. Water sustainability of ancient civilizations in Mesoamerica and the American southwest. Water Sci. Technol. Water Supply, 7: 229-236.

Mays, L.W. 2010. Ancient Water Technologies. Springer Science and Business Media, Dordrecht, The Netherlands.

Mays, L.W., Antoniou, G. and Angelakis, A. N. 2013. History of Water Cisterns: Legacies and Lessons. Water, 5: 1916-1940

Mays, L.W. 2013. Use of Cisterns during antiquity in the Mediterranean region for water resources sustainability. Water Sci. Technol. Water Supply, 13: 735-742.

Mays, L.W., Sklivaniotis, M. and Angelakis, A. N. 2012. Water for Human Consumption through the History. In Evolution of Water Supply Through the Millennia, Edited by Andreas Nikolaos Angelakis, Larry W. Mays and Demetris Koutsoyiannis, IWA Publishing, London, UK, Ch. 2: 19- 42.

Mouton, M. and Al-Dbiyat, M. 2009. Stratégies d'acquisition de l'eau et société au moyen orient depuis l'antiquité (Water systems in Middle-East from antiquity). Institut Français du Proche Orient, Beyrouth, Lebanon.

Mun, J.S. and Han, M.Y. 2012. Design and operational parameters of a rooftop rainwater harvesting system: Definition, sensitivity and verification. Journal of Environmental Management, 93: 147-153.

Netzer, E. 2001. Das wasserversorgungssystem von Masada. Wasser im Heiligen Land Frontinus Suppl.III, 195-204.

Ortloff, C. 2014. Water engineering at Petra (Jordan): recreating the decision process underlying hydraulic engineering of the Wadi Mataha pipeline system. Journal of Archaeological Science, 44: 91-97.

Pandey, D.N., Gupta, A.K. and Anderson, D.M. 2003. Rainwater harvesting as an adaptation to climate change. Current Sci., 85: 46-59.

Paschou, P., Drineas, P., Yannaki, E., Razou, A., Kanaki, K., Tsetsos, F., Padmanabhuni, S.S., Michalodimitrakis, M., Renda, M.C., Pavlovic, S., Anagnostopoulos, A., Stamatoyannopoulos, J.A., Kidd, K.K. and Stamatoyannopoulos, G. 2014. Maritime route of colonization of Europe. In Proceedings of the National Academy of Sciences.

Scarborough, V.L. 2003. The Flow of Power, Ancient Systems and Landscapes. SAR Press, Santa Fe, New Mexico.

Scarborough, V.L. and Gallopin, G.G. 1991. A water storage adaptation in Maya lowlands. Science, 251: 658-662.

Strasser, F.T. 2010. Stone Age Seafaring in the Mediterranean, Plakias Region for Lower Palaeolithic and Mesolithic Habitation of Crete. Hesperia, 79: 145-190.

Tsuk, T. 2011. Water at the end of the tunnel. Touring Israel's ancient water systems, Tel Aviv, Israel (in Hebrew)

Vannesse, M., Haut, B., Debaste, F. and Viviers, D. 2014. Analysis of three private hydraulic systems operated in Apamea during the Byzantine period. Journal of Archaeological Science, 46: 245-254.

Viollet, P.L. 2000. L'hydraulique dans les civilisations anciennes (Hydraulics in ancient civilizations). Presse de l'Ecole des Ponts et Chaussées, Paris, France.

Wilson, A. 1997. Water Management and usage in Roman North Africa. PhD Thesis, University of Oxford, Oxford, UK.

Wilson, A. 2001. Urban Water Storage, Distribution, Usage in Roman North Africa. In Water Use and Hydraulics in the Roman City, Edited by Ann Olga Koloski-Ostrow, Kendall-Hunt Publishing Company, Dubuque, Iowa, USA, Ch. 7: 83-96.

Xiao Yun Zheng. 2015. Drainage in Ancient China: Historical Wisdom and the lessons. Accepted for publication in The Finnish Journal of Environmental History, 1.

Ancient Water Wisdom

Traditional water systems in India[1]

Vasudha Pangare and Ganesh Pangare

1. Introduction

India's rich diversity is not only reflected in its traditional water harvesting but also in its water management systems. Blessed with nearly all types of agro-climatic zones, from the cold desert to the hot desert and from mountains rising up to 8000 m to a coastline measuring more than 7000 km, India also has the highest rainfall in the world and the largest riverine island. In a way India is a microcosm of the world in terms of the diversity of natural resources and ecosystems. Traditional water harvesting and management systems in India were developed in order to function within these ecosystems and climatic conditions. Ancient Indians learned to harness water resources in ways that could meet their various needs and to also ensure that the harvesting of rainwater replenished the resources. This lengthy history of traditional water harvesting techniques and management systems can provide valuable lessons even today.

The present paper presents an overview of the traditional water management systems in India for drinking water, domestic use and irrigation. Moreover, examples of these systems demonstrate their significance and relevance to present times.

2. Traditional systems for drinking water and domestic use

Traditional water systems were based on the principles of conservation. In indigenous methods water made available from mountain streams, springs, shallow aquifers as well as harvested rainwater in tanks and ponds was used for drinking and domestic purposes. Traditional sources of water were often designated for drinking, bathing and washing, depending on the quality of the water. Water

Table 1 (next page). Traditional Water Harvesting Systems For Drinking Water and Domestic Use. Source: Pangare Ganesh, Pangare Vasudha, Das Binayak. 2006. "Springs of Life: India's Water Resources". New Delhi: Academic Foundation, World Water Institute and BIRDS.

---

1   The present paper is based on: Pangare Ganesh, Pangare Vasudha, Das Binayak. 2006. "*Springs of Life: India's Water Resources*". New Delhi: Academic Foundation, World Water Institute and BIRDS.

Traditional Water Harvesting Systems For Drinking Water and Domestic Use

Region	System of Water Harvesting	Type	Use	Technique
	Collecting rainwater	Chaal (Uttaranchal)	Animal consumption	Natural formation or depression found along mountain ridge tops saddled between two adjacent crests.
		Khal (Uttaranchal)	Animal consumption	Large natural lake which can store several thousand cubic meters of water.
	Collecting water from subterranean seepages or springs	Chuptyaula (Uttaranchal)	Animal consumption	Natural rudimentary structures found in the high-altitude areas.
	Collecting rainwater and water from subterranean seepages or springs	Naula/Baori (Uttaranchal)	Domestic water use	Shallow, four-sided stepped wells constructed in the form of an inverted trapezoid, walled on three sides and covered with a roof of stone slabs. Some are massive, ornate structures with rooms and platforms for bathing and washing clothes. Animals are prevented from entering the tank. The earliest functioning naula, the Badrinathji-ka-naula dates back to 7th century AD.
		Baori (Himachal Pradesh)	Domestic water use	Shallow step-well, a usually covered structure. The larger ones measure c.5 x 5m at the top, while smaller ones, called baoru, measure 2 x 2 m. They are walled to keep animals out and to prevent unclean water from entering. Now and again a trough is provided outside for animals.
		Nauns (Himachal Pradesh)	Bathing and washing clothes	Very large baoris are called nauns. They are usually uncovered structures.
Hill and mountain region (Himalayan regions)	Diversion channels from hill streams or glaciers	Dhara (Uttaranchal)	Drinking (also used for irrigation)	These are basically water fountains. Water from springs or subterranean sources is channeled through outlets, which are in the shape of either a simple pipe or various figurines e.g., animals, female forms etc. There are three types of dhara depending on the height above ground (a) sirpatia dhara: if one can drink the water standing upright (b) mudpatia dhara: if one has to bend over to drink (c) patvinyan dhara: if one has to sit down to drink. These dhara are all seasonal.
		Nahun (Himachal Pradesh)	Domestic consumption	Water fountains, usually square or oblong. They are enclosed along the sides and back, but open in front with flooring of two massive stone beams overlaid with flat slabs diagonally positioned.
		Chharedu (Himachal Pradesh)	Domestic consumption	Spring fountains wherein the spring water falls through a carved stone. It has a rectangular enclosure and a drain.
	Diversion channels from hill streams or glaciers leading to a storage tank	Panihar (Himachal Pradesh)	Domestic consumption	Cistern.
		Ponds (Jammu and Kashmir, Himachal Pradesh)	Domestic consumption	Rudimentary structures.
	Storage tanks/ponds collecting rainwater	Khola (Sikkim)	Drinking	Simple structures to collect the water Which is transported through bamboo poles to individual houses.
	Rainwater collected on rooftops	Tanks (Mizoram)	Domestic consumption	Horizontal rain gutters are placed along the sides of the sloping roof. The pipes are connected to a storage tank.

Region	Method	Name	Use	Description
Indo-Gangetic plains (mainly Punjab, Haryana, Uttar Pradesh, Bihar and West Bengal)	Tapping groundwater	Dugwells	Domestic consumption	Very common when accessing groundwater for domestic use.
	Collecting rainwater or tapping groundwater in storage tanks	Baoli	Domestic consumption	Step-well, either rock-hewn or with masonry work. Usually a square or oblong structure often provided with stepped stone embankments.
	Dam		Domestic consumption	Damming a natural spring.
	Diverting river water to storage tank	Dighi (Delhi)	Drinking	Square or circular reservoir connected to a canal and with steps for entering. Usually a *kahar* or a *mashki* was hired to draw water.
	Tapping groundwater	Baori (Rajasthan, Gujarat)	Drinking	Step-well, often elaborate structures with arches, sculptures and decoration. They are shallower than the wells. The largest part of the structure is built underground. A variety of structures exists depending on architectural styles.
	Tapping groundwater from aquifers	Jhalar (Rajasthan)	Bathing and religious rites	Rectangular structure with steps along three or all four sides.
		Tanka (western Rajasthan)	Drinking	Underground tanks. These circular holes were made in the ground, lined with fine polished lime and These often decorated with tile covering, which helped to keep the water cool. Such tankas were found in most houses. They are used as a last resource.
	Tapping groundwater from seep springs	Beri/Kui (Rajasthan)	Drinking and animal consumption	Shallow and narrow wells c.6 to 8 m deep, dug at *par*, a place where the flowing water accumulates and seeps into the earth.
		Toba (Rajasthan)	Drinking, animal consumption	Ground depression with a natural catchment area
Arid and semi-arid region (western, central and southern India)	Collecting rainwater from rooftop	Tanka (western Rajasthan)	Drinking	Rainwater falling on the sloping roofs was captured through a pipe into an underground *tanka*, sometimes as large as a spacious room. The first spell rain was usually not collected as this cleaned the pipes and roof.
	Collecting rainwater within artificially created catchments that drain water into artificial storage wells	Kund (western Rajasthan)	Drinking	Underground circular pits, c.3 to 4.5 m deep and wide, and plastered with lime and ash. They are usually covered with domical roof and provided with a pulley to lift water. They are made of locally available material or cement and constructed at the centre of a saucer shaped catchment area and mostly privately owned. The catchment is created by using sealing material e.g., pond silt, charcoal ash and gravel.
	Collecting rainwater in special structures in order to prevent mixture with saline ground water	Virda (Kutch)	Drinking	Shallow wells dug in low depressions called *jheels*. The structures reach down to the upper layer of fresh rainwater up to c.1 m above ground water.
	Collecting rainwater	Pond/lake/tank found in almost all arid/ semi-arid regions	Domestic consumption	Circular/square/rectangular structure either with elaborate masonry work or with rudimentary design.
	Collecting water in pits through diversion channels	The Andaman and Nicobar Islands	Domestic consumption	Shompen and Jarawa tribes use longitudinally spilt bamboo, placed along the slopes in order to collect rainwater drop by drop in pits called jackwells. A series of jackwells is connected through a network of bamboos so that overflow from one leads to another, ultimately leading to a large jackwell. The bamboo channels are also placed under trees in order to harvest rain through leaves.

Figure 1. Traditonal systems of water harvesting still supply water in many parts of the country, Adalaj Ka Vav - Step well, Gujarat. Photograph: Ganesh Pangare.

Figure 2. Traditional Water Lifting Device, Orissa. Photograph: Ganesh Pangare.

is regarded as sacred with regard to religious objectives. Water sources were also designated for animals. Table 1 presents an overview of the traditional systems for harvesting water for drinking and domestic use encountered in the three main zones: the mountain region, the arid and semi-arid region and the Indo-Gangetic plains. Two case studies, or examples of traditional water systems, are discussed below: the *qanat* system of Burhanpur (Madhya Pradesh) and the Uperkot Fort in Junagad (Gujarat).

2.1 Mumtaz Mahal's legacy: the Qanat of Burhanpur, Madhya Pradesh

Burhanpur is a small town on the banks of the Tapi River in Madhya Pradesh near the Maharashtra-Madhya Pradesh border, in the foothills of the Satpura mountain range. The town's historical significance stems from the fact that Mumtaz Mahal, wife of Emperor Shah Jahan for whom the Taj Mahal was built, first came to Burhanpur from Persia. The Empress died in Burhanpur and was buried here. It was only later that her remains were moved to Agra.

During the days of the Mughal Empire, Burhanpur was the bastion from where the Mughals controlled the southern parts of India. It was important to have a secure supply of water for the armies stationed there. Fearing that surface water could be poisoned, it was necessary to find an innovative way to access subterranean water.

At Burhanpur Mumtaz Mahal commissioned a Persian geologist, Tabkutul Arz to execute a *qanat* in order to supply water to the town. The *qanat* of Burhanpur was planned and constructed in 1615 AD and is the only one of its kind in India. *Qanats* are prevalent in Iran, Iraq, Afghanistan and parts of Central Asia. They are basically underground tunnels serving to bring groundwater to the surface by means of gravity along the contours. The *qanat* of Burhanpur measured more than 10 kilometers in length. The town's location was geologically perfect for tapping the subterranean flow that did not vary too much through the seasons.

During the period when it was in use, the *qanat* would supply *c.*10.000.000 liters of water per day. Today although a large part of the *qanat* has been destroyed, certain sections of the system still supply water to a small community consisting of *c.*5000 residents in the vicinity at zero cost.

2.2 Ancient system for today's needs: Uperkot Fort in Junagadh, Gujarat

The ancient fortified town of Junagadh is located at the foot of the Girnar Hills in Gujarat. The Uperkot Fort was built within this town in 319 BC. Junagadh has a tradition of collecting rainwater in underground structures called *tankas*. Several *tankas* could store sufficient water to last the household for up to 2 years. Junagadh has an ancient legacy in water management. The former rulers of Junagadh had built a series of water structures (e.g., step wells, water storage tanks) within the magnificent fort complex of Uperkot in order to cater to the needs of Junagadh town.

The Adi Chadi Bav, a step well, is an 8 m deep tank that still collects water flowing from the Girnar watershed. The fort's twelve tanks served to store water supplied to the population through a system of channels and pipes by gravity flow. Although the fort has been rebuilt and expanded many times by various rulers, and

Figure 3. Tank from where
water is supplied by gravity
to the town, Uperkot Fort.
Photograph: Ganesh Pangare.

even abandoned for several centuries, through the ages its ancient system of water
harvesting and water supply has survived. The system functioned so well that,
according to legend, the fort at one time withstood a twelve-year siege.

The ancient system can no longer fulfill the needs of the current population.
Nonetheless the system is still used by the local municipality in conjunction with
other sources of water supply. Water is lifted from the nearby Willingdon Dam
in order to augment the water in the tanks. Here is it treated and transported to
a storage cistern through the ancient system of gravity flow, and supplied to the
town every third day.

3. Traditional irrigation systems

Since traditional irrigation systems were developed to function within the ecosystem and climatic conditions within which they operated, different types of systems existed in different agro-climatic zones. Depending on the soil types, climatic variations and rainfall patterns, various types of irrigation systems and agricultural practices were followed in various parts of the country. Management systems and water usage were adapted to the ecology within which they existed, ensuring that water was not only used but also distributed wisely and efficiently.

In the mountain region, in the Himalayas, the focus was on (a) channeling seepage, spring water and glacial water directly into the fields or (b) collecting water from these in storage tanks and then channeling it into the fields. In the arid and semi-arid regions systems were developed (a) to capture rainwater in ponds, tanks and embankments, (b) to channel runoff from the catchment into fields or storage structures and (c) to lift water from wells or streams with mechanical devices operated by bullocks. In the Indo-Gangetic plains, inundation channels were applied in order to divert floodwaters to fields. Water was lifted from ponds, lakes and wells with the help of manual mechanical devices and rainwater was stored in embankments. In peninsular India, tunnels served to access subterranean watercourses. Masonry walls were utilised to raise the stream water and channel it to the fields.

Table 2 presents an overview of the traditional systems found in the three main regions: the mountain region of the Himalayas, the arid and semi-arid regions and the Indo-Gangetic plains. Two case studies, or examples of traditional irrigation systems, are described below: (a) the Apatani rice cultivation system found in the state of Arunachal Pradesh in the north-eastern region of the country, and (b) the tank irrigation systems of Sarangpur in the state of Chhattisgarh.

3.1 The Apatani system, Arunchal Pradesh

In the northeast of India, the Apatani tribe, with a population of $c.25,000$, lives on the Ziro plateau located $c.1500$ m above sea level in the lower Subansiri district of Arunachal Pradesh. This plateau lies between the Kamala, Khru and Panjor ranges in the Eastern Himalayas. The Apatani is the only tribe to have always practiced sedentary agriculture in a region where largely shifting cultivation is practiced. This in itself renders the system unique.

The Apatani follow a traditional form of rice cultivation, the knowledge of which is passed down from generation to generation. Women do almost all the work in the fields including irrigation. The rice fields are irrigated by means of an intricate system of channels and ducts which carry water from a series of streams flowing into the Kele River. This system depends upon streams originating from the mountains which join the river flowing through the plateau. The existence of these springs and streams closely depends upon the health of the catchment from which they hail. The catchment has a good forest cover which until now the community has preserved.

Traditional Irrigation Systems

Region	Systems of Irrigation	Type	Technique
Mountain irrigation systems (Himalayan regions)		*Dhara* (Uttaranchal)	Water from springs or subterranean sources is channeled out through outlets, which are in the shape of either a simple pipe or animals, females etc. Mainly used for drinking purposes, but *dharas* with larger flows are also used for irrigation.
	Diversion channels from hill streams or glaciers leading directly to fields	*Guhl* (Uttaranchal)/*Kuhl* (Himachal Pradesh)	Water is diverted from nearby mountain streams through small gravity flow channels traversing contours of mountain slopes. They are used for irrigating terraced fields.
		Bamboo drip (Khasi and Jaintia hills of Meghalaya)	Perennial hill streams are diverted down to plantations by an intricate system of bamboo channels in such a way that water drips at a slow rate to plants.
		Apatani system (Arunachal Pradesh)	Feeder channels from river or streams are connected to all plots of land by manipulating water flow through various types of barriers. The plots are divided by intricate design of earthen contour dams supported by bamboo frames. The *bunds* have inlets as well as outlets and plots are irrigated through proper functioning of these. They are used for rice cultivation.
	Diversion channels from hill streams or glaciers leading to storage tanks	*Zing* (Ladakh)	Small structure where the water from glaciers, guided through channels, is stored. As glaciers melt by evening, more water is available in the channels then compared to mornings.
		Zabo (Kikruma village, Nagaland)	*Zabo* means impounding water. Water harvesting ponds are dug out near the catchment area.
	Artificial reservoirs	*Chappris* (Himachal Pradesh)	Shallow dug ponds located on the hillsides where the slope tends to flatten out. These ponds are dug without any masonry work.
Arid and semi-arid irrigation systems (western, central and southern India)	Storage structures fed by rain or a stream	*Eris* and *Oranis* (Tamil Nadu)	Rectangular or square tanks.
		Kere (Karnataka)	Tanks built in a series whereby the outflow of one tank supplies the next one all the way down.
		Cheruvu (Andhra Pradesh)	
		Katas	A tank constructed by throwing a strong earthen embankment, slightly curved at both ends, across a drainage line.
	Collecting rainwater in catchment	*Khadin* (Jaisalmer district, Rajasthan)	The runoff from the catchment is stored in the lower valley floor enclosed by means of an earthen bund. The bund is provided with a spillway and a sluice at the lowest level. In winter, when water disappears due to seepage and evaporation, the area serves tois used cultivate wheat or chickpeas, which then does not need water.
	Diversion channels for capturing hill streams	*Pat* (Madhya Pradesh and Maharashtra)	Rock-cut or masonry channels.
	Dams for capturing rainwater	*Bandhara* (Maharashtra)	Earthen or masonry dams built across rivers and streams.
	Lifting groundwater from wells	*Kos* (Gujarat)	A rope and metal or leather bucket pulled by bullocks. It lifts 60 to 80 liters of water at a time and can irrigate ½ to 1 *bigha* of land during 6 hours of operation.

		Rahent (Gujarat, Maharashtra)	A Persian wheel or rahat worked by bullocks irrigating 1 bigha in a day.
		Pagpavthi (Gujarat)	Similar to a rahent, but manually operated. It is a slow and labourious process.
		Dhinkvo (Gujarat)	A manually powered lifting device. It consisting of a pot or a bucket suspended from a rope tied to the longer end of a wooden pole pivoted on a vertical support with a weight attached to the shorter end
Plains and flood plains irrigation systems (Indo-gangetic plains)	Inundation channels that divert floodwaters to fields	Jampois (Jalpaiguri, West Bengal)	Small channels from streams.
		Lat	A long, straight or covered embankment thrown across a plain on which rice is cultivated.
		Ahar-Pynes (Bihar)	An ahar is a rectangular catchment basin with three-sided embankments built at the end of a pyne: an artificial channel capturing rain waters.
	Lifting water from ponds, lakes, wells	Chua/Taavbalti/Dhenki (North Bengal)	A bucket is tied at one end of a pole to lift water from an open well.
		Thenda (Coastal Orissa)	A long bamboo pole with a bucket at one end and a weight/balance at the other end and lifts water from a well. It is operated by one or two men.
		Sena (Coastal Orissa)	A tray-like unit made of palm, which is held by a sling on two sides by two persons to lift water from a well or a pond.
		Jhalars (Punjab)	Shallow wells excavated on the banks of the streams from which water is lifted by means of a Persian wheel.
	Artificial storage reservoirs	Ahars (West Bengal)	A storage created by building earthen bunds, usually 2 to 3 m high with several outlets.
		Abi (Haryana)	A well, lined or kuchcha, is dug near the river bank and carried down to a level lower than its bed with its mouth exposed on the river side. A channel from the river leads water into the well worked by means of a rope and bucket.
	Rainwater stored in the fields by embankments	Haveli system (Madhya Pradesh)	Rainwater is held in embanked fields until sowing time. Water is let out as soon as the land is dry. The fields are sown after which the crops do not need to be watered.
Coastal irrigation systems (peninsular India)	Tunnels	Surangam (Kerala)	A horizontal well excavated in hard lateritic formation to tap a natural subterranean watercourse. Captured water is stored in a pit in front of tunnel. It is provided with vertical shafts if the tunnel is very long. Also used for domestic purposes.
	Dams	Oddu (Andhra Pradesh)	A strong masonry wall of lime or cement built across a stream or a river to raise water to a certain height and then divert it to fields.

Table 2. Traditional irrigation systems in India. Source: Pangare Ganesh, Pangare Vasudha, Das Binayak. 2006. "Springs of Life: India's Water Resources". New Delhi: Academic Foundation, World Water Institute and BIRDS.

Figure 4. Apatani women farmers working on the irrigation system. Photograph: Ganesh Pangare.

Figure 5. A bund and a water channel, Apatani System. Photograph: Ganesh Pangare.

Water is distributed through a management system that ensures an equitable irrigation to fields located in the upstream and downstream areas. Once the upper fields receive their share of water, the outlet channel is opened allowing the next set of fields to receive water. This method is followed until the final field is reached. However, in this process, it takes a while for the water to reach the tail end. During this time the lower fields have to remain without water. In order to overcome this problem, a separate channel at the head is created from the main stream through which water is diverted to fields located at the tail end. The community takes collective responsibility to maintain the systems. The women contribute the majority of the labour required for maintaining the channels.

During the 1950s, when the Agriculture Department of the State Government began to encourage the rice farmers to keep fish in special ponds, farmers thought it would be better to breed the fish in their rice fields instead. This led to an innovation in fish-rice farming within the Apatani system which the Apatani now followed extensively.

The significance of the Apatani system of rice cultivation is: it is a highly evolved indigenous system of rice cultivation that is highly productive, energy-efficient and economically and environmentally viable. Research has proved that the system is highly efficient and helps to preserve the ecosystem in which it is practiced. The farming system is still organic in nature and has not yet been influenced by modern farming techniques or the introduction of chemical fertilizers and pesticides. The preservation of the biodiversity in the area is closely linked to the practice of the Apatani rice farming system.

Along with rice, millet and maize are also cultivated. Bamboo and pine are planted around the fields. The fields are separated by 0.6 m high earthen dams supported by means of bamboo frames. These dams serve to hold water and soil in the fields. Millet is grown on these dams in order to strengthen them, as well as on dry hill slopes. The Apatani cultivate Amo and Mipa: the traditional varieties of rice. As the fields are located in valleys, the soil remains fertile thanks to the nutrient wash-out from the hill slopes. Fertility is also maintained due to the manure which is available from the waste occurring from the pisiculture practised in the rice fields, and from the manure of domestic animals. Refuge from homesteads is also used. In fact channels leading to the fields carry refuse along with rainwater from the habitation to the fields.

The system is however currently under threat from various sources. On numerous occasions loggers have tried to gain access to the forests which form the catchment of the irrigation system. In recent times the growing township of Hapoli located on the Apatani plateau poses a threat to the traditional system of irrigation. The town's sewage is being emptied into the river that irrigates the rice fields. Where in the past only the local village sewage would enter the irrigation system, now various contaminants do so. Steps need to be taken to address this problem.

3.2 Tanks of Sarhangarh, Chhattisgarh

Sarhangarh (meaning Bamboo), in Raigarh district of the state of Chhattisgarh was once an ancient kingdom of the Gond tribe. This kingdom, or region, as we need to call it today, has a 200-year-old cascade tank system consisting of thirty tanks. Jaswant Singh, one of the Gond rulers constructed the tanks in order to fulfill the irrigation and drinking water requirements of his kingdom. Among these tanks, the most popular are the 150 acres Mura *talab* and the Khara *bund* with a total catchment area of 4 square km. Rainwater is harvested in these tanks. The surplus water from these tanks flows to a drain. The surplus water from these tanks flows to a drain next to the palace moat, from which it flows through the Ghogna stream, or *nullah*, and then to the Mahanadi River. Over time, the conditions of the tanks deteriorated and they are no longer utilised for irrigation or drinking water purposes. The bunds are broken, silted and the channels clogged. The local municipal corporation of Sarhangarh town manages these tanks and has leased them out for fishing. Water needs are largely met by means of lifting groundwater. Several years ago, a major water crisis occurred in the region, largely due to the large-scale withdrawal of groundwater. The state government now decided to revive the tanks allowing them to again serve to fulfill the water needs of Sarhangarh.

The tanks of Sarhangarh are an example of a system of irrigation applied in many parts of the country for centuries. The Chandela and Bundela tanks which the Chandela rulers built in the Bundelkhand region of Madhya Pradesh and Uttar Pradesh during the 11th century still irrigate a large area in Bundelkhand. In the Tikamgah region, out of 109 irrigation works maintained by the irrigation

Figure 6. A traditional irrigation tank, Sarhangarh, Chattisgarh. Photograph: Ganesh Pangare.

department, eighty are Chandela tanks. Tanks are still widely used in Tamil Nadu, in the northern and coastal districts of Andhra Pradesh, in south-central Karnataka, in north and east Maharashtra, northern Madhya Pradesh, northeastern Uttar Pradesh, Bihar, Jharkand, Chattisgarh and Rajasthan. There are about 208,000 tanks in India. About 60 % of the area irrigated by means of tanks is concentrated in Tamil Nadu, Andhra Pradesh and Karnataka. These tanks were made to harvest rainwater and runoff with technical knowledge and skill. Land use patterns have changed, population pressures have increased but still these tanks work when protected and revived.

4. Conclusions

Traditional systems are time-tested, scientifically proven and adapted to the ecosystem within which they function. Such systems had significant characteristics: (a) the physical structure suited the terrain in which it operated, (b) water resources were used and managed as common property resources, and (c) community based institutions were set up and practices established ensuring that water was not only used and distributed fairly but also conserved wisely.

Today, traditional water systems are unable to meet the needs of the growing population. The prolific utilisation of borewells and the electrification of pumps have changed the way water is 'owned' and used. The basic concept of water as a common good on which the traditional water management systems functioned has undergone a change. Water availability within the ecosystem has become variable due to changing rainfall patterns and growing demand for water. Community managed systems have given way to state managed institutions.

In a rural society depending upon agriculture as the source of income, water is the dividing line between poverty and plenty. Most resource poor regions have fragile ecosystems, where farmers still depend upon time-honoured irrigation practices passed down through the generations. Certain practices have been modified in order to suit the present situation. Some are used in conjunction with modern irrigation systems.

As two-thirds of the total cropped area in the country is rainfed, and in need of assured irrigation, efforts to increase water security for agricultural production and for drinking and domestic use need to take into consideration the conservation and management aspects of the traditional systems, which are relevant even today. Policy interventions need to incorporate the learning and wisdom from these traditional systems.

Although the traditional systems by themselves cannot meet the water needs of today, the examples cited in the present paper indicate that if the traditional systems are revived and protected they can still meet part of the demand for water within the ecosystem within which they function. The *qanat* of Burhanpur still provides water to *c.*5000 people. The Sarhangarh tanks were revived so that water could be harvested in order to meet some of the needs of the town's population. Uperkot's traditional gravity flow system still supports the water supply utility of the town of Junagadh. The Apatani system of agriculture existing in a fragile ecosystem is economically and ecologically viable even today.

Traditional systems may or may not provide for today's water needs, but they are a living heritage and need to be preserved because of their natural, historical and cultural significance.

References

Pangare Ganesh, Pangare Vasudha, Das Binayak. 2006. *"Springs of Life: India's Water Resources"*. New Delhi: Academic Foundation, World Water Institute and Bharathi Integrated Rural Development Society.

Water and heritage in Angkor, Cambodia

The monuments, the ancient hydraulic network and their recent rehabilitation

Peou Hang

P.Eng., PhD., Hydraulics and Hydrology
Deputy Director General, the APSARA National Authority, Cambodia

Abstract

The Khmer people have managed water since the creation of Cambodia during the early Common Era (2nd century). Water management is a part of their daily life. The evidence in the Angkor region indicates that the innovative water technology they once applied, in many ways, still is cutting edge.

The Angkor region was the capital of the Khmer Empire for more than 500 years. Angkor was recognized as the 'Hydraulic City'. The reason for this: it is organized around an immense water management network, which supported food systems and transport of materials. There was some speculation but between 2004 and 2005 Cambodian hydrologist researchers discovered the strategic multi-purpose functioning of this water network.

From an engineering perspective, in the absence of a bedrock, the Khmer temples were constructed on an artificial sand layer requiring high groundwater levels in order to assure it not only remains wet but also strong enough to support and thus safeguard the temples/monuments. The moats around the key temples are visual indicators that the sand foundation is being kept wet. However water also had cultural and practical purposes.

Siem Reap is a modern touristic city located 5 km downstream of Angkor Park. This entire region uses groundwater. Due to the increasing number of tourists every year and the rapidly growing population, the demand for water primarily drawn from the groundwater has also increased dramatically. Water management for the Siem Reap-Angkor area is the most critical issue with regard to safeguarding the monuments and for sustainable development. Therefore the challenge is to satisfy the needs of water for daily use, while the stability of Angkor temples standing on the sand layer and linked to the groundwater is ensured.

The APSARA Authority and Local authorities have immediately adopted a variety of precautions and solutions concerning effective water management. Firstly, the water source for the future expansion of the water supply in Siem Reap is the Western Baray and the Tonlé sap Lake. Secondly, the groundwater is recharge by the rehabilitation and refilling of the ancient man-made reservoirs.

The Water Management Department of the APSARA Authority has conducted the necessary theoretical, preparatory and practical work in order to rehabilitate the ancient Angkorian hydraulic systems permitting the restored cultural landscape and general environment to recover their essential roles in safeguarding the monuments. Much has been learned and is still being learnt about just how advanced the hydraulic engineering was and how it was able to meet multiple needs.

In terms of disaster mitigation the rehabilitation of Ancient Hydraulic System proved its capacity of preventing floods across the entire region (the Angkor temples, airport and Siem Reap city) in 2012 and 2013. Local communities also benefit from increased water availability during the dry seasons, which enhances food security and economic opportunities. As the world seeks ways to mitigate climate changes, water management is seen as the priority. Rehabilitation of this Ancient Hydraulic System places Siem Reap in an enviable position, but it significant planning and ongoing management are required in order to meet demands with regard to water.

This long and challenging program has been implemented with the technical and financial resources of the APSARA Authority. Moreover, it has restored the most important ancient system with regard to the moats of the temples of Angkor Wat, Angkor Thom, Preah Khan, to the moat and the reservoir of the site of the Banteay Srei, the Western Baray, the Northern Baray and the Sras Srang (Royal Basin) as well as the restoration of 37.87 km of ancient canals and dikes associated with the water management and flood control as to Angkor Park, the international airport and Siem Reap city.

Keywords: *Angkor, Hydraulic, Khmer, ancient hydraulic network, baray, water management, world heritage, flood, groundwater*

1. Introduction

The site of Angkor covering more than 40,000 ha and containing 112 villages was inscribed as a World Heritage Site in 1992. After this inscription, Siem Reap attracted more and more tourism requiring a large quantity of water resources to ensure this development.

From the existing hydraulic system in Oc-Eo (O Keo) of the 2nd century located in southern part of Vietnam today and Angkor Borei of the 5th century (Vann Molyvann, 2008), we can see the evolution of technology in water management system. It consists of a canal (more than 80 km long) between the harbour city of O Keo and the inland capital of Angkor Borei (Steak and Sovath, 2001). The concentrate hydraulic system is found in the Angkor region. The Khmer mastery of water engineering in ancient times is shown in a range of Angkor's hydraulic structures (e.g., ancient reservoirs (*baray*), moats, laterite spillways, laterite bridges, ponds, canals, dikes). During the 1950s and 1960s Bernard-Phillip Groslier (of the École d'Extrême-Orient – EFEO) recognizes Angkor as a 'Hydraulic City' because it is organized around an immense water management network (Groslier 1979). The system has been remapped by Pottier (Pottier, 1999) and later on in by means of the Geographical Information System (GIS), but the functioning of this water network was not yet revealed. Only from 2004-2005 did the Khmer researcher find out how it functions to then rehabilitate it.

This article will demonstrate the importance of water resources as to safeguarding the temple and the increasing of the tourism in the region requiring large amounts of water. At the same time the entire region (temples/monuments, villages, airport and Siem Reap city) was threatened by floods every year since 2009. How can the APSARA National Authority establish a compromise between safeguarding the monuments and the sustainable development of the Siem Reap-Angkor region?

2. Conception of a temple construction

The soil in central plain of Cambodia cannot support heavy loads. In order to build stone temples such the Angkor Wat, Bayon, Ta Prohm and Preah Khan, the best technique had to be found. Khmer engineers at the time discovered the physical properties of sand and water and realized they could combine these two elements when building: sand, once wet, can support a heavy load. The discovery of this technique led them to locate the places where this theory could be applied. Studies indicate that the Angkor region is the best location, as underground water is close to the ground surface (Acker, 2005). The immediate presence of underground water was then utilized in order to completely fill the sand layer under the monument ensuring its stability. To assure the sustainability of the ground water when supporting the temples, the Khmer ancestors introduce water into their culture. We demonstrate only two main points (Thousands of Lingas, moat) without discussing the other ceremonies practiced by local people every day.

The ancient Khmers knew the vital role played by water resources as to safeguarding the Angkor region and learned how to preserve water. This is why this vital resource is celebrated within the tradition, culture and spirit of the Khmer people. Several of these customs are still celebrated today.

2.1 The sacred water of Mount Kulen

Khmer ancestors carved the Siem Reap River of Thousand Lingas into the river beds of Mount Kulen and Kbal Spean (Fig. 1). Here these rivers source, before they flow into Siem Reap and the Angkor site plain. At Banteay Srei they come together to form the Siem Reap River. The water flowing from the 'Thousand lingas' has become sacred and has served in the major ceremonies (e.g., coronations, cremation ceremony) of the Khmer Kingdom since the 9th century. During a coronation, the sacred water of Mount Kulen is used to bless the future King. This tradition is still practiced as with the coronation of Norodom Sihamonie in October 2004, utilizing sacred water from Kulen Mountain (http://news.bbc.co.uk/2/hi/asia-pacific/3963945.stm). The Khmer population believes in the power of this sacred water, applying it to cure diseases or during blessings to bring luck (http://www.legrandtour.fr/fr/ module/ 99999648/729/extrait-les-lingas). However, the real goal of the sacred water from Mount Kulen is (a) to underline to the population the need to protect water resources, the region's life-blood, and (b) to maintain the sustainability of this resource, which is essential for the conservation and development of the Siem Reap region. Therefore, the water source provided by Mount Kulen will be lost if deforestation continues and the environment is destroyed.

Figure 1. Sacred water - the Thousand Lingas in Kbal Spean (Kulen mountain chain).

2.2 The moats

Prior to constructing a temple, the natural soil was removed and replaced with sand requiring water for resistance. Of course, this sand layer linked to groundwater. In order to make temples sustainable in case of any variation in underground water, the moat system was adopted. Thus, each temple in the central plain of Cambodia is surrounded with moats (fig. 2). They play a pivotal role collecting runoff water from the temple during the monsoon and recharging the layer of sand underneath the temple.

Figure 2. The moat of the Angkor Wat temple.

The Khmer ancestors understood that if the safeguarding of water was conveyed as a message or ordered (law) by means of applying technical reasoning, this would not be sustainable. Considering water not only as a form of life-blood but also as the basis for a system of beliefs, the recommendations may have lasted. Next, in order to ensure that the sustainable water in the moat supported the temple, the engineering approach was transformed into an aspect of religion. In the Khmer tradition moats are regarded as the Ocean and the temple as Mount Meru (the dwelling of the Gods).

3. Water Management as to the development of the Siem Reap region

After inscribing the site of Angkor on the World Heritage Site List in 1992, the Siem Reap/Angkor region has become the largest tourism site in the country and a powerhouse of tourism development which for Cambodia has become one of the main pillars of economic growth. The majority of tourism is of a cultural nature. Nowadays Cambodia's income from tourism is more than 16% of the GDP, implying that visitors to the region will continue to increase every year.

The growing number of tourists every year and the needs of a water supply as to the daily use of the entire region has caused a remarkable increase concerning the demand for water. The entire region uses underground water linked to the stability of the monument as mentioned in the previous section. In this regard, the Water Management for Siem Reap-Angkor is the most sensitive issue with regard to the Sustainable Development and Safeguard monuments in order to ensure the stability of Angkor temples standing on the layer of sand linked to the groundwater which can recharge naturally and quickly with the presence of trees, but the upstream and the top of Kulen Mountain is deforested.

In order to ensure the compromise between the development of tourism and the safeguarding of the temple, the government of Cambodia is setting the long term policy to stop the increase of pumping underground water and take water surfaces such as the Western Baray (56.000.000 cubic meters) in 2015 and the Tonlé sap Lake in 2019. Without waiting the long time solution and in order to ensure the development of tourism, the APSARA National Authority has adopted two solutions since 2004: (a) the reforestation in the entire region in order to increase the recharge of underground water (Hang, 2005). However it will take a long time for those trees grow up and play a role and (b) to rehabilitate ancient reservoir (*baray*, moat, basin) in order to immediately recharge the underground water (see section 4).

Nowadays, we face not only the problem of water resources as to the water supply in the region but also the flood which has threatened tourism every year since 2009. In search of the best ways to protect the temples, airport and the city of Siem Reap from the floods, the Department of Water Management of APSARA National Authority has conducted necessary projects as to analyzing as well as field investigating by means of theoretical and practical research. The goal is to (a) rehabilitate the ancient Angkorian Hydraulic System, (b) permit the restoration of not only the Cultural Landscape but also the Environment and (c) recover their essential role of safeguarding monuments. This long and challenging program has been implemented with technical and financial resources within the APSARA National Authority. It especially consisted of comparing of the analysis and preliminary findings with exceptional data provided by the upheavals following the floods of 2009, 2010 and 2011 (Hang, 2013). This solution will described in section 5.

4. Rehabilitation of ancient hydraulic structures

As mentioned above the recharge of underground water is most important as to maintaining the stability of the monuments/temples. The general concept of the preservation of the safeguarding of world heritage is the rehabilitation of the ancient water structure, if possible allowing its system to function as in ancient times. Many years of research have been carried out in order to understand these complex systems built in the course of the development of the Angkor region. Only between 2004 and 2005 did we comprehend the entire system of water management of the Khmer Empire. Everyone knows that, if the region is to continue to be a city for long time, the main requirement is the presence of a water resource in order to supply the people inhabiting the entire region.

The main task to be achieved before the rehabilitation of the ancient hydraulic structures is to analyze the flow from the upstream limit of the watershed towards the outlet of the Kulen Plateau until it spills into the Tonlé sap Lake, by means of three watersheds: Stung Pourk in the west, the Stung Siem Reap in the centre and Stung Roluos in the east (Fig. 3). It appeared that the Stung Pourk and Stung Roluos are natural waterways whereas the Stung Siem Reap is an ARTIFICIAL waterway from Bam Penh Reach (a laterite spillways connecting the Pourk River and the actual Siem Reap River).

More than 10 years of applied research on the ancient hydraulic system of Department of Water Management of APSARA, the department achieved the restoration of some structures that built during the Khmer Empire of Greatness Angkor (Fig. 4) by hydraulics engineers as mentioned below.

4.1 The Sras Srang

This royal basin royal was dug during the middle of the 10th century and modified in the course of 13th century by King Jayavarman VII. This basin has been dry from April 2004 on. The reason for this is: is does not have the system to fill it. The sources of water are rain and groundwater linked to the Eastern Baray through underground and/or groundwater. As the Eastern Baray has fallen dry and water table has descended, the Sras Srang also dries up during the dry season. In March 2005, the Water Management Department set up a new system in order to fill the Sras Srang by taking water from the Phnom Bok reservoir (Roluos River) through the Eastern Baray.

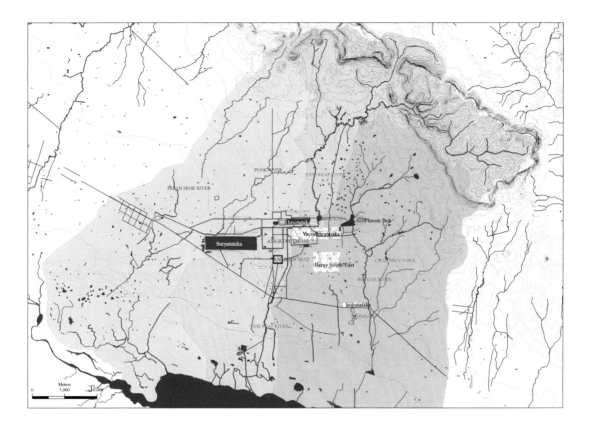

Figure 3. The watersheds of the Roluos (East), Siem Reap (centre) and Pourk (West).

4.2 The Temple of Banteay Srei

Its moat and small *baray* (located north of the shrine) were rehabilitated in 2009 after the restoration of the temple by Switzerland. Two water structures were built on the southern dike in order to ensure the overflow from the *baray* and the irrigation of the rice fields located south of the *baray* which is filled with water during the entire year. It can be supplied to the moat of Banteay Srei via an underground flow. Once the *baray* is filled with water the entire year, the local community can benefit from the presence of water for fishing and community tourism such a boat tour on the *baray*. The APSARA-NZAid project (NZAid: the New Zealand Agency for International Development) supports the local community in order to setup these activities. This community project was been inspired by the Northern Baray project (see below).

4.3 The Moat of Angkor Thom

Only 3 km of the southwestern moat contains water. The southeastern moat only contains water during the rainy season. In 2010, the Water Management department carried out an archeological survey at the eastern part of the temple of Angkor Thom (the Victory and Death Gates) in order to connect the eastern moats

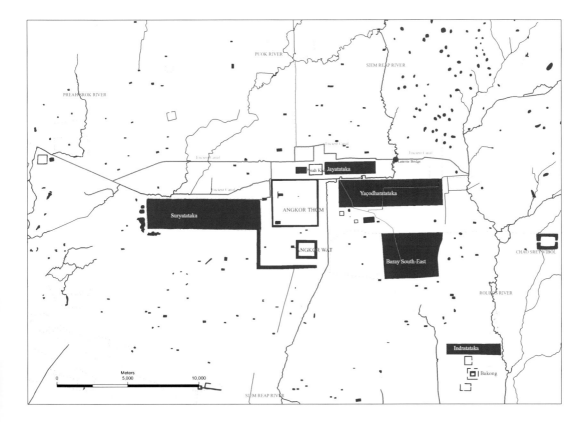

Figure 4. The ancient hydraulic structure and hydraulic network in Angkor Region.

with the northern and southern moats. Resulting from this work, the southeastern moat (3 km long) contains water during the entire year (dry and rainy seasons). In 2012, with the restoration work linked to the rehabilitation of the Western Baray and the ancient hydraulic network in order to optimize the water management, the entire moat measuring 12 km can flood. This moat can store nearly 2.000.000 cubic meter of water.

4.4 The Angkor Wat

Prior to the feeding system of Angkor Wat its moat consisted of an ancient canal running from the southwestern moat of Angkor Thom with a canal behind Balloon through Sras Trapeang (to the west of the road in front of Angkor Wat). This system takes at least 2 weeks to bring water from Siem Reap River to the moat of Angkor Wat. It cannot raise the water level in the moat as in ancient times. In 2010, the rehabilitation of the canal of Sampeou Loun and the moat of Phnom Bakheng connected to the southeastern moat of Angkor Thom in order to feed the moat of Angkor Wat in a short time with a maximum water level as ancient times. This system allowed a rising of the water level in the moat of more than 1.3 m higher than the maximum level of the previous feeder system had been.

4.5 The Jayatataka

The Jayatataka, or the Northern Baray, measures 3600 by 930 m. It has a storage capacity of 5.000.000 cubic m as to the first phase. For the second phase the storage was increased up to 10.000.000 cubic m by means of raising the dikes. Built during the 12th century (AD 1181) by King Javaraman VII, it started to dry up in the course of the 16th century. This new invention of water engineering technology in Khmer Empire of the 12th century consisted of filling the Northern Baray with water by means of a network of dikes and canals in order to collect runoff water and raise the water level allowing it to flow into this *baray*. The dike and canal system begins from the northwestern dike of the Northern Baray and turns four times in 90 degrees before going straight towards the north until the foot of Mount Kulen. These large canals (60 m wide) are used by local people as rice fields because no water has flowed through them in the past 500 years. Several villagers built their house in this runoff water collection system of the Northern Baray.

Prior to our 2004-2005 research as to this feeding system of the Northern Baray, it was very complicated to understand how this *baray* was filled. Research carried out among local people indicated that the dikes, founded on the site north of the *baray* of Jayatataka is called 'The Ancient Royal Road to the Mountain', From experience, however, it cannot be a royal road because: (a) it turns in 90 degrees which is not the case with a 12th-century road; (b) it has only one canal along the dike. In ancient times and even today in the plains of Cambodia roads are built by excavating the soil from both sides in order to become drainage canals later. However, these dikes have only one large canal and the other side has a natural ground level.

These reasons lead to the conclusion that 'dikes and a canal system to collect runoff water' applies to the Northern Baray.

All the *barays* in the Angkor region have their inlet of water at the northeastern corner. However, during the rehabilitation of the Northern Baray, it is necessary to move the inlet structure to the connection point between the feeder system and northern dike. This choice avoids flooding the local people residing within the system of water collection of this *baray*. Moreover, the ancient canal is dredged (cleaned) only 20 m instead of 60 m in order to retain the number of rice fields of local people.

The restoration work commenced after approval by the ICC-Angkor (the International Coordinating Committee for the Safeguarding and Development of the Historic Site of Angkor) in June 2007. The southern broken dike of the *baray* of Jayatataka at Kraing Kroch (East), the original outlet near the shrine of Preah Khan and thirteen points on the runoff water collection system were repaired. Next the *baray* of Jayatataka collected 700,000 cubic meters during the first rainy season (in 2008), 2,980,000 cubic meters in 2009, 3,678,000 cubic meters in 2010, and more than 5,000,000 cubic meters in 2011, 2012, 2013 and 2014. The local community comes to fish in this *baray* every day. The APSARA Authority assists the villagers of Phlong and Leang Dai in setting up a community business on the 'Natural Circuit at North Baray' (Baray Reach Dak Community Tour). This provides them with an income by means of guiding tourists in the natural circuit surrounding the *baray* and to the flooding forest inside the *baray* on a local boat (Hang, 2014). This local community project has been duplicated at the temple of Banteay Srei.

This *baray* did not serve irrigation purposes as the other *baray* in the region, but to supply the city of Angkor Thom, Preah Khan and the Neak Pean hospital with water.

4.6 The Neak Pean

The Neak Pean is an island temple (376 x 320 meters) in the Northern Baray resembling a mébon (i.e., a temple in the middle of a *baray* used to survey the water level) of other *barays*, but it has another function: a hospital applying medicinal plants. The temple has five basins which, in recent times, were dry all year round

Figure 5. The Neak Pean and its basins.

except for the central basin which contained water for only a few months during the rainy season. However, since the Northern Baray has been refilled, these five basins are again filled with water and are full all year round. The water from the Northern Baray infiltrates the large central basin. Next when the water reaches the spillway level located in the small chapel positioned between the central basin and the smaller basins, it starts to overflow and fills the smaller basins (Fig. 5). This movement of water into the five basins linked to the Northern Baray provides one of the best illustrations of the hydraulic system in the Angkor World Heritage property, indicating that the ancient Khmer applied the techniques of infiltration and exfiltration (underground flow) in order to recharge the groundwater, moat and basins (Hang, 2014). This process allows the water to become clear and clean.

4.7 The Preah Khan

The Preah Khan is one of the main shrines King Jayavarman VII built towards the end of the 12th century. As with other temples, it has its own moats. However, the moat of the Preah Khan did not have a canal system to provide surface water and fill the Srah Srang as in ancient times. It contains water only for a small part and not the entire year. Since the Northern Baray contains water, this moat is also full of water during the entire year. This indicates not only the connection between the Northern Baray and the temple of Preah Khan via the underground water communication but also the effect of the rise of the water table from the recharge of the Northern Baray to the underground. In 2011, the connections were made between the western moat and the others in order to assure the same water level in each moat surrounding the temple during the rainy season.

4.8 The West Baray

The West Baray, built by King Suryavarman I during the 11th century, measures 8 x 2.2 km and can store more than 56.000.000 cubic meters. The main role of this Baray is to recharge the ground water and to assure the irrigation by means of canals in the southwest (Pottier, 2001). In 1957, in order to fill the West Baray it was necessary to dig a canal and a spillway to bring the water from the Siem Reap River at the northeast corner of the Angkor Thom. This canal runs inside the moat of Angkor Thom (i.e., the north and northwestern moat) for c.4.5 km and connects to a canal parallel to the access road to the Takave Gate (i.e., the western gate) of Angkor Thom. A map of this system was published in an 1941 article by Goloubew). These canals caused this part of the moat as well as the eastern part of the West Baray to fall dry. Certain researchers then believed that the falling dry of the eastern part was caused by sedimentation.

In 2010, the Water Management department of the APSARA Authority discovered the original feeding system of western Baray. In it one ancient pound called Tropeang Khchorng' (the desedimentation basin located at northeastern corner of Baray) and and ancient canal (running in a N-S direction) originating from the northwestern corner of the moat of Angkor Thom. In 2011, the APSARA reopened the original inlet canal of West Baray in order to absorb the flood and therby protect the villages. In 2012, the APSARA rehabilitated the entire feeding system capable of feeding the West Baray in a short time with the original capacity of 56.000.000 cubic meters. Nowadays the West Baray is connected to the flood management system described below in section 5.

5. Rehabilitation of the 12th-century Hydraulic System

The 12th-century hydraulic system comprises the water network located in the northern part of the temples of Angkor Thom, Preah Khan and Ta Som. This system is the combination of the natural Pourk, Rolous and Stung Preah Srok Rivers, canals (including the Siem Reap River), dikes linking the waterways and the ancient reservoirs (as described in section 4). These networks are able to allow water engineering to optimize the entire water management in the Angkor region.

Since 2009 the entire region is facing floods during rainy season which has an impact on the temples/monuments, villages and the city of Siem Reap (as to tourism as well as local residents). The APSARA Authority is able to manage the flow in order to protect the temples/monuments as well as certain villages, but not yet the city of Siem Reap. In 2011, Siem Reap was flooded on five occasions when, for instance, the Old Market (the centre of Siem Reap) could not even be accessed by means of a pickup vehicle. Several million dollars were required in order to repair the infrastructure of the province of Siem Reap. In 2012, the government requested the APSARA Authority to find a solution to protect not only Angkor Park and the upstream region but also the city of Siem Reap against flooding. As indicated in the present article, the policy of the APSARA Authority is to reuse the ancient hydraulic system.

We need to go back to the history and look into the record of the city of Angkor during ancient times in order to find out how one was able to face to this challenge by means of their complex hydraulic system. After our research, no inscription encountered on Khmer Empire territory mentioned a flood or a drought in the Angkor region. Otherwise the Khmer people should have a memory of disaster and have transferred that information to the next generation or included in a legend. If those problems never happened in the past, it implies that the water management system in ancient time is the best means of optimizing water resources. The moats of Angkor Wat and Srah Srang falling dry in 2004, as well as the floods of 2009, 2010 and 2011 are caused by the fact that the ancient system did not function for a long time.

Comprehending the overall organization of the Angkorian Hydraulic System consisting of rivers, *barays*, moats, canals, pounds and dikes, the way in which the water flow was ensured thereby highlighting channels and their connections can be identified in the field. This discovery led us to understand that the level of the North Baray, in the northeast, included a canals and dikes running from east to west and an ancient laterite bridge (on Siem Reap River) consisting of a multiple arc form which could serve to control the flow and discharge. With this distribution node, and through the channels, we managed to distribute water in three directions (see Fig. 6) instead of sending it all through the Siem Reap River:

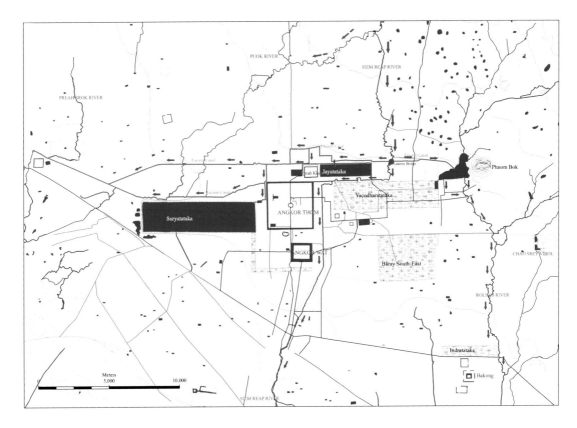

Figure 6. Flow direct through 12th-century hydraulic system (after rehabilitation).

the moat of Angkor Thom (2.000.000 cubic meters), the moat of Angkor Wat (1.500.000 cubic meters and the waterway to the Siem Reap River flowing to the south, whereas the Stung Roluos River flowed to the east and the Stung Pourk River as well as the Stung Preah Srok River emptied into the North Baray (storing 5.000.000 cubic meter) and the West Baray (storing 56. 000.000 cubic meter).

In 2012, the main part of this system has been rehabilitated. That is the reason why the cities of Angkor and Siem Reap was able to avoid the flood during rainy seasons of 2012, 2013 and 2014. Without this work the city of Siem Reap will face to be flooded at less four times. This result has been confirmed that the Millennium Hydraulic System cannot only optimize Water Resources Management but also control flooding.

Until 2014, the APSARA Authority had rehabilitated more than 37.87 km of the 52 km of the 12th-century system. The remain part concerns the ongoing rehabilitation with precaution to the archeological survey and the impact of the local people who is utilize this part of canal or reside within the system.

6. Conclusion

Prior to 2004-2005, the Angkor hydraulic system did not work. It had just discovered its function and had started its rehabilitation. The evidence and result of the rehabilitation of the ancient hydraulic system proved its capacity and efficiency as to the sustainable use of natural resources and the prevention of a natural catastrophe. We are insured that the era of Angkor's prosperity, this imperial capital had an efficient form of hydraulic engineering, both coherent and systematic.

Khmer ancestors have warned by introducing the most important technical of maintenance of system into the religious aspect and teach Khmer people how to live in harmony with the nature and environment. Therefore the rehabilitation of Angkor hydraulic system implies we can sustain it for future generations.

The proposal to upgrade this system with new technology is required in order to assure the future management of water. Innovative steps in order to combine the Millennium hydraulic system of Angkor with new technology will assure the best water management in the region.

Acknowledgements

I want to express my gratitude to Professor Azedine Beschaouch for his advice, his time and his generous support. Without him the rehabilitation of Jayatataka (North Baray) would never started, implying that the Angkor hydraulic system would probably never have been rehabilitated. I also would thank also my colleague Mr. Jady Smith for his assistance in APSARA-NZAid project which benefitted local communities residing within the hydraulic system. My special thanks goes out to all the staffmembers of the Water Management Department of APSARA Authority with whom I cooperated intensely during last 10 years in order to realize these projects.

Bibliography

Acker, Robert. 2005. Hydrology and the Siting of Yasodharapura. Phnom Bakheng Workshop on public interpretation. Organized by the World Monument Fund (WMF) in Siem Reap, December 4-6, 2005. Published by the Centre for Khmer Studies (www.khmerstudies.org), Siem Reap, Cambodia, pp. 73-86.

Goloubew, V. 1941. L'hydraulique urbaine et agricole à l'époque des Rois d'Angkor. Extrait du Bulletin économique de l'Indochine. Année 1941 – fascicule I.

Groslier, Bernard-Philippe. 1979. 'La Cité hydraulique angkorienne: Exploitation ou surexploitation?'. Bulletin de l'École Française d'Extrême-Orient, 66, pp. 161-202.

Hang, Peou. 2014. Sacred water: rediscovering the ancient hydraulic system of Angkor and traditional knowledge of water management and engineering systems. International Journal of Intangible Heritage. Vol. 9, pp. 17-25.

Hang, Peou. 2013. 'The Angkorian Hydraulic System' in: World Heritage, No. 68. Special issue: World Heritage in Cambodia, June 2013, pp. 22-25.

Hang, Peou. 2009. Project: Rehabilitation of Jayatataka (North Baray), Department of Water Management, APSARA (Authority for the Protection and Management of Angkor and the region of Siem Reap), Cambodia, July 2009, p. 31.

Hang, Peou. 2008. Water Resource Management for Angkor Park and Siem Reap Region. Angkor: Living with Heritage – Heritage Values and Issues Report. Godden Mackay Logan Pty Ltd., August 2008, Australia, pp. 139-146.

Hang, Peou. 2005. Forest Management in Angkor Park, Phnom Bakheng Workshop on public interpretation. Organized by the World Monument Fund (WMF) in Siem Reap, December 4-6, 2005. Published by Centre for Khmer Studies, Siem Reap, Cambodia, pp. 93-99.

Pottier, Christophe. 1999. Carte archéologique de la Région d'Angkor. Zone sud, PhD, Université Paris III –Sorbonne Nouvelle (UFR Orient et Monde Arabe), Paris.

Steak, Miriam T. and Bong, Sovath. 2001. Recent research on emergent complexity in Cambodia's Mekong. Indo-Pacific Prehistory Association Bulletin 21. Melaka Papers, Vol. 5. Pp. 85-98.

Vann, Molyvann. 2008. Cités du Sud-Est Asiatique, Le Passé & Le Présent. Thèse pour obtenir le grade de docteur de l'Université de Paris 8.

Water and World heritage

Anne Lemaistre

UNESCO Representative in Cambodia

Where there is water, there is life. This tautological evidence explains the fact that human settlements in all their forms are associated with the indispensable presence of water: sources, springs, rivers, canals...all civilizations are shaped and look for the most appropriate answers in order not only to face the constraints of their environment but also to get the best of it. The necessary water management, its excess or scarcity justified the myriad technological innovations and new forms of social organization to confront these challenges. This is where human ingenuity has sparkled.

Water has acquired a sacred status over thousands of years and its use is accompanied by rituals, music, songs, and prayers. The industrial world, more pragmatic, has utilized water more systematically: irrigation systems, transportation, power generation…

In order to illustrate this, cultural World Heritage sites and cities, internationally recognized protected areas inscribed on the World Heritage List because of their Outstanding Universal Value, reflect the multiplicity of cultures in their relation to water as well as to the technological evolutions of human civilization: irrigated terraces, water mills, water gardens and hydraulic cities still amaze us.

In the same way, natural World Heritage sites also celebrate the beauty of the water left in its natural state, very often spectacular, outstanding waterfalls, lakes rich in biodiversity and the seabed…

Natural World Heritage Sites

Of these 197 Natural World Heritage Sites, inscribed because of the natural values, eighty-five are linked to water in all its diversity: rivers, streams, fjords, rocky coasts, towering cliffs, lakes, waterfalls, wetlands and marine sites, designated thanks to their remarkable biodiversity or ecosystem values, importance as natural habitats, exceptional natural beauty, or importance as outstanding examples of major stages of the earth's history. Only a small number have been selected in order to illustrate the most representative example of their category.

Rivers: The Three Parallel Rivers of Yunnan, China

The Three Parallel Rivers of Yunnan (China) are the Yangtze, Mekong and Salween which run approximately parallel, from north to south, through steep gorges which, in places, are 3,000 m deep and bordered by glaciated peaks more than 6,000 m high. The fifteen protected areas contain an outstanding diversity of landscapes (e.g., deep-incised river gorges, luxuriant forests, towering snow-clad mountains, glaciers, alpine karst, reddish sandstone landforms (*Danxia*), lakes and meadows over vast vistas. Located in the convergent regions of the three world's major biogeographic realms, the Three Rivers are located in an epicentre of Chinese biodiversity and harbour the richest biodiversity among the temperate areas of the world.

Waterfalls: The Iguazu Water, Argentina-Brazil

The semicircular waterfall at the heart of this site is *c*.80 m high and 2,700 m in diameter. It is situated on a basaltic line spanning the border between Argentina and Brazil. Consisting of many cascades producing vast sprays of water, it is one of the most spectacular waterfalls in the world. The surrounding subtropical rainforest houses over 2,000 species of vascular plants and is home to the characteristic wildlife of the region: tapirs, giant anteaters, howler monkeys, ocelots, jaguars and caimans.

Marine sites: The Great Barrier Reef, Australia

The Great Barrier Reef was inscribed as the first Marine World Heritage site in 1981. Until 2010 it remained the largest World Heritage site protecting 344,400 square km of marine waters, with the Galapagos Islands being the second largest World Heritage Site at 140,665 square km, of which 135,000 square km consist of marine waters. Now the Phoenix Islands Protected Area (408,222 square km) and Papahanaumokuakea National Marine Monument (362,061 square km, United States) are the first and second largest World Heritage sites. Recent sites inscribed because of their marine values include the Lagoons of New Caledonia (France) and Socotra Archipelago (Yemen). Other World Heritage Sites protecting significant marine biodiversity and marine ecosystem processes, and among the top 40 largest World Heritage sites, include Shark Bay (Australia), Islands & Protected Areas of Gulf of California (Mexico), Banc d'Arguin National Park (Mauritania), the Natural System of Wrangel Island (Russia), the Wadden Sea (Germany and the Netherlands) and Malpelo Fauna and Flora Sanctuary (Colombia).

The Great Barrier Reef is the world's most extensive coral reef ecosystem that has evolved over millennia. This site of remarkable variety and beauty located on the north-east coast of Australia contains the world's largest collection of coral reefs, with 400 types of coral, 1,500 species of fish and 4,000 types of mollusk. It also holds great scientific interest as the habitat of the dugong ('sea cow') and the large green turtle, which are threatened with extinction. Collectively these landscapes and seascapes provide some of the most spectacular maritime scenery in the world.

Figure 1. The waterfall in Iguazu National Park, Argentina-Brazil.

Figure 2. The Great Barrier Reef, Australia.

Threats: The outstanding qualities of these natural sites cannot be celebrated without recalling the enormous efforts required daily in order to not only conserve them but also to combat the numerous dangers they face. Marine World Heritage Sites, for example, face pollution, habitat loss, over-fishing, invasive species, uncontrolled development and climate change. Climate change and associated increased sea temperatures also threaten coral reefs from bleaching and the functioning of other marine ecosystems.

Cultural sites

The Water Cities: Angkor, Cambodia; The Old Town of Lijiang, China; Venice and Its Lagoon, Italy; Amsterdam, Netherlands

Angkor, Cambodia

Angkor, in Cambodia's Northern Province, is one of the most important archaeological sites of Southeast Asia. It extends over *c.*400 square km and consists of temples, hydraulic structures (basins, dykes, reservoirs, canals) as well as communication routes. Angkor was the centre of the Khmer Kingdom for several centuries. With impressive monuments, ancient urban plans and large water reservoirs, the site is a unique concentration of features testifying to an exceptional civilization. Temples such as Angkor Wat, the Bayon, Preah Khan and Ta Prohm, exemplars of Khmer architecture, are closely linked to their geographical context as well as being imbued with symbolic significance. The architecture and layout of the successive capitals bear witness to a high level of social order and ranking within the Khmer Empire. Angkor is therefore a major site exemplifying cultural, religious and symbolic values, as well as containing high architectural, archaeological and artistic significance. Angkor has been described as a 'hydraulic city' by Bernard-Philippe Groslier, French archaeologist-*cum*-conservator at Angkor during the 1960s. He demonstrated that the Khmers built large reservoirs called *barays* (2 x 8 km), to ensure optimal storage of water for cultivating rice. With the help of gravity, the *barays* collect the maximum amount of water onto a large surface in order to create permanent rice fields. During the monsoon seasons, the *baray* would fill with water, allowing for rice cultivation during the dry season. These methods sustained a rice production which has allowed the expansion of the Empire.

The Old Town of Lijiang, China

The Old Town of Lijiang, which is perfectly adapted to the uneven topography of this key commercial and strategic site, has retained a historic townscape of high quality and authenticity. Its architecture is noteworthy for the blending of elements from several cultures that have come together over many centuries. Lijiang also possesses an ancient water-supply system of great complexity and ingenuity still functioning effectively today. The traditional water system, called 'the three wells' is still in use: the first well for drinking, the second for cleaning vegetables and the third for washing clothes.

Figure 3. The Old Town of Lijiang, China.

Venice and Its Lagoon, Italy

Founded in the 5th century AD and spread over 118 small islands, Venice became a major maritime power in the 10th century. The entire city is an extraordinary architectural masterpiece in which even the smallest building contains works by several of the world's greatest artists such as Giorgione, Titian, Tintoretto, Veronese and others.

In this lagoon covering 50,000 square km, nature and history have been closely linked since the 5th century when Venetian populations, in order to escape barbarian raids, found refuge on the sandy islands of Torcello, Jesolo and Malamocco. These temporary settlements gradually became permanent. Moreover the initial refuge of the land-dwelling peasants and fishermen evolved into a maritime power. Over the centuries, during its entire period of the expansion, when obliged to defend its trading markets against the commercial undertakings of the Arabs, the Genoese and the Ottoman Turks, Venice never ceased to consolidate its position in the lagoon.

Venice and its lagoon landscape is the result of a dynamic process illustrating the interaction between people and the ecosystem of their natural environment over time. Human interventions show not only high technical but also creative skills in the realization of the hydraulic and architectural works in the lagoon area. Venice and its lagoon form an inseparable whole of which the city of Venice is the pulsating historic heart as well as a unique artistic achievement. The influence of Venice on the development of architecture and monumental arts has been considerable.

Amsterdam, the Netherlands

The Amsterdam Canal District illustrates exemplary hydraulic and urban planning on a large scale by way of the entirely artificial creation of a large-scale port city. The gabled facades are characteristic of this middle-class environment. The dwellings bear witness to the city's enrichment through maritime trade as well as the development of a humanist, tolerant culture linked to the Calvinist Reformation. During the 17th and 18th centuries, Amsterdam was seen as the realization of the ideal city that served as a reference urban model for numerous projects in new cities around the world.

The Water Gardens

The ancient Persian paradise gardens have not only been the source of inspiration for public or private gardens but have also influenced the art of garden design as far as in India with the Taj Mahal and Europe with Palace Water Gardens.

The Persian Paradise Gardens, Iran

They exemplify the diversity of Persian garden designs that evolved and adapted to different climate conditions while retaining principles rooted in the times of Cyrus the Great, the 6th century BC. Always divided into four sectors, with water playing

Figure 4. Amsterdam, Netherlands.

Figure 5. The Persian Paradise Gardens, Iran.

an important role for both irrigation and ornamentation, the Persian garden was conceived to symbolize Eden and the four Zoroastrian elements of sky, earth, water and plants. These gardens date back to various periods since the 6th century BC and also feature buildings, pavilions, walls as well as sophisticated irrigation systems.

The Tomb Water Gardens: Taj Mahal, India

The Taj Mahal, an immense mausoleum consisting of white marble was commissioned in Agra between 1631 and 1648 by the Mughal emperor Shah Jahan in memory of his favourite wife. It is considered the jewel of Muslim art in India and one of the universally admired masterpieces of the world's heritage. It was the first architectural expression of a Persian paradise garden brought by the Mughals to the Indian Subcontinent, fulfilling diverse functions with strong symbolic meanings. Known as the *charbagh*, in its ideal form it was laid out as a square subdivided into four equal parts. The symbolism of the garden and its divisions are noted in mystic Islamic texts describing paradise as a garden abundantly filled with trees, flowers and plants. Water also plays a key role in these descriptions and has been reinterpreted. In Paradise, four rivers source at a central spring or mountain, and separate the garden by flowing towards the cardinal points. They represent the promised rivers of water, milk, wine and honey.

Major waterworks, which brought water to the Taj garden from the Yamuna River by means of an aqueduct supported on arches, are situated outside its western wall and still preserve their original design as do wells, reservoirs and fountains.

Palace Water Gardens: the Bergpark Wilhelmshöhe, Germany

Descending a long hill dominated by a giant statue of Hercules, the monumental water displays of Wilhelmshöhe were begun by Landgrave Carl of Hesse-Kassel in 1689 around an east-west axis and developed further into the 19th century. Reservoirs as well as channels behind the Hercules Monument supply water to a complex system consisting of hydro-pneumatic devices that supply the site's large Baroque water theatre, grotto, fountains and 350 m long Grand Cascade. Beyond this, channels and waterways wind across the axis, feeding a series of dramatic waterfalls and wild rapids, the geyser-like Grand Fountain which reaches a height of 50 m, the lake and secluded ponds that enliven the Romantic garden created in the 18th century by the Elector Wilhelm I. The huge size of the park and its waterworks along with the towering Hercules statue constitute an expression of the ideals of absolutist Monarchy whereas the ensemble is a remarkable testimony to the aesthetics of the Baroque and Romantic periods.

Hydraulic Engineering Systems

The water is used to render services. Irrigation as to agriculture and transportation were the traditional usages of pre-industrial societies. Later on, mines and factories applied the power of water allowing machines to function.

Amongst the hydraulic engineering systems we can distinguish:

- Irrigation systems
- Transportation systems
- Water power systems

Irrigation Systems: The Dujiangyan Irrigation System – China

The construction of the the Dujiangyan irrigation system began during the 3rd century B.C. This system still controls the Minjiang River and distributes its waters into to the fertile farmland of the Chengdu Plains. Mount Qingcheng is the birthplace of Taoism. This is celebrated by means of a series of ancient temples.

The Dujiangyan Irrigation System has maintained a natural water flow by directing it in different directions for various uses without building any dam. This system consists of a watershed dividing the river in two: the inner city as to irrigation and outer river as to flood discharge. During the rainy season, excess water runs into the outer river thus preventing flooding. It also serves as a filter for sand and stones. This system has been operating at low cost and in a highly reliable manner for some 2,250 years. It is indeed a miracle in the history of water control.

Figure 6. The Dujiangyan irrigation system, China.

Transportation Systems: Canal du Midi, France; La Louvière, Belgium

Canal du Midi, France

This 360 km long network of navigable waterways linking the Mediterranean and the Atlantic through 328 structures (locks, aqueducts, bridges, tunnels, etc.) is one of the most remarkable feats of civil engineering in modern times. Built between 1667 and 1694, it paved the way for the Industrial Revolution. The care its creator, Pierre-Paul Riquet, took as to the design and the way it blends with its surroundings turned a technical achievement into a work of art.

La Louvière, Belgium

The four hydraulic boat-lifts on this short stretch of the historic Canal du Centre are industrial monuments of the highest quality. Together with the canal itself and its associated structures, they constitute a remarkably well-preserved and complete example of a late 19th-century industrial landscape. Of the eight hydraulic boat-lifts built at the end of the 19th and the beginning of the 20th century, the only examples in the world which still exist in their original working condition are these four lifts on the Canal du Centre.

Water Power Systems: Shustar, Iran; The Upper Harz Water Management System and the mines of Rammelsberg, Germany; The Derwent Valley Mills, United Kingkom

Shustar, Iran

Shushtar, a historical hydraulic system, inscribed as a masterpiece of creative genius, can be traced back to Darius the Great in the 5th century B.C. It involved the creation of two main diversion canals on the river Kârun one of which, the Gargar canal, still provides water to the city of Shushtar via a series of tunnels supplying water to mills. Forming a spectacular cliff from which water cascades into a downstream basin, it then enters the plain situated south of the city. Here it has enabled the planting of orchards and farming over an area of 40,000 ha known as *Mianâb* (Paradise). It contains an ensemble of remarkable sites including the Salâsel Castel, the operation centre of the entire hydraulic system, the tower where the water level is measured, dams, bridges, basins and mills. It bears witness to the know-how of the Elamites and Mesopotamians as well as of a more recent Nabatean expertise and Roman building influences.

The Upper Harz Water Management System and the mines of Rammelsberg, Germany

The Upper Harz mining water management system, located south of the Rammelsberg mines and the town of Goslar, has been developed over a period of *c*.800 years in order to assist in the process of extracting ore for the production of non-ferrous metals. Its construction was first undertaken during the Middle Ages by Cistercian monks, and it was then developed on a vast scale from the end of the 16th up until the 19th century. It consists of an extremely complex but perfectly coherent system of artificial ponds, small channels, tunnels and underground drains. It enabled the development of water power to be applied in mining and metallurgical processes. It is a major site with regard to mining innovations in the western world.

Derwent Valley Mills, United Kingkom

The Derwent Valley in central England contains a series of 18th and 19th-century cotton mills and an industrial landscape of high historical and technological interest. The modern factory owes its origins to the mills at Cromford, where Richard Arkwright's inventions were first put to an industrial-scale production. The workers' housing (associated with this and the other mills) remains intact illustrating the socio-economic development of the area.

Major conservation issues are:

*   Water infiltration and humidity
*   Lack of maintenance
*   Pollution and waste (e.g., mud consisting of urban waste purification, manure, slaughterhouse waste, non-biodegradable industrial waste)
*   Discontinuity of traditional agricultural practices
*   Destruction or modernization of the canals

Conclusions

Thanks to its amazing diversity and astonishing beauty, World Heritage is appreciated for its extraordinary aesthetic qualities. But not only…. Heritage sites are also icons of societal pride and identity, symbols of reconstruction in devastated countries and opportunities for social cohesion. In addition, heritage in its relation to water encapsulates knowledge, know how, symbolic uses and appropriate technological responses for societies adapting to their environment. Heritage in this context illustrates the technological evolution of the humankind in order to better manage water scarcity or excess. Heritage linked to water reveals the human ingenuity that has provided and provides essential service functions even today and may be relevant to the future of humankind.

Beautiful tropical islands in the Caribbean Sea

Human responses to floods and droughts and the indigenous archaeological heritage of the Caribbean

Corinne L. Hofman and Menno L.P. Hoogland

This paper was written during Hurricane Gonzalo (Category 1) in October 2014, when we were stranded on St. Maarten (Martin) on our way to Saba

Abstract

Caribbean communities have been exposed to the challenges of water ever since the occupation of the archipelago 7500 years ago. Alternating periods of drought and extremely wet climatic conditions, the threat of tropical storms, hurricanes, major wave events like tsunamis, and the continuous menace of sea level fluctuations have led the indigenous peoples of the Caribbean to adapt their insular way of live. Today these challenges, in addition to other catastrophes and the risks of earthquakes and volcanic eruptions, alongside human interferences (e.g., construction activities, sand mining and looting) form serious threats to the indigenous archaeological record. This paper focuses on the evidence of such catastrophic events and the responses from the indigenous communities in terms of water management by means of a number of archaeological case studies from across the Caribbean.

Introduction

Inhabitants of the Caribbean islands have been exposed to the challenges of water ever since the occupation of the archipelago 7500 years ago. This tropical region features annual cycles characterized by alterations of dry and wet climatic conditions. In addition to natural events and risks of tropical storms, hurricanes, tsunamis and sea level fluctuations (involving large quantities of water as well as often disastrous floods, landslides and erosion), the Caribbean island communities, specifically those located on the low limestone islands, are also continually threatened to be confronted with severe droughts. These phenomena, together with other calamitous events (e.g. earthquakes, volcanic eruptions) stimulated the first inhabitants of the insular Caribbean to respond, anticipate and adapt their ways of life. This paper discusses evidence of catastrophic events and water management in the archaeological record across the Caribbean. Today, natural disasters and risks, in addition to cultural interferences (e.g., large-scale constructions for the tourist industry and economic development, agriculture, sand mining and looting), present a serious menace to the indigenous archaeological record, with the danger of losing essential parts of the global heritage and world history.

The Caribbean islandscape

Situated largely on the Caribbean Plate, in the Caribbean Sea, the Caribbean archipelago comprises more than 7,000 islands, islets, reefs, and cays of rock, sand or coral, scattered over an area of 2,754,000 km² (Fig. 1). Although general processes underlie the formation of the Caribbean, individual islands may have extremely varied geological and ecological histories. The Lesser Antilles comprise three main island groups of which the Windward Islands and the Leeward Islands includes more than twenty major islands as well as countless smaller ones. They are characterized by the fact they consist of limestone and have volcanic origins (Knippenberg 2006; Van Soest 2000). Being continental islands, Trinidad and Tobago are considered to be more related to the mainland of South America, as are the various offshore islands along the Venezuelan littoral. Of these, Margarita, Cubagua and Coche belong to the State of Nueva Esparta, whereas Los Aves, Los Roques, La Orchila, La Blanquilla, Los Hermanos, and Los Testigos are part of the Federal Dependencies of Venezuela. Together with Bonaire, Curaçao and Aruba they belong to the so-called Southern Antilles. The Greater Antilles consist of Puerto Rico, Hispaniola (Dominican Republic and Haiti), Jamaica and Cuba. The Bahamas Archipelago and the Turks and Caicos Islands, finally, are situated in the Atlantic Ocean north of Cuba, and not in the Caribbean Sea. The diverse geological

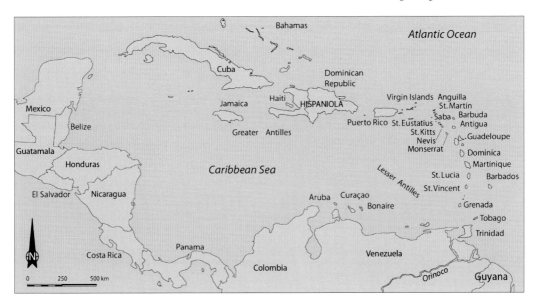

Figure 1. Map of the Caribbean.

makeup of the Caribbean islands has ultimately led to a discontinuous distribution of natural resources, which may have stimulated craft specialization on the part of the indigenous communities with easy access to the materials involved. This diversification in the availability of scarce resources must have been a stimulating factor in the creation and maintenance of inter-community exchange networks across the region. Moreover, it served as a safety net in times of climatic stress and natural catastrophes.

Vulnerable environments

Islands are very fragile and vulnerable environments (Fosberg 1963). In particular, this applies to the Caribbean islands due to their key position within the North Atlantic Climate System (see Cooper 2012a). Indigenous peoples from the mainland of Central and South America ventured out to the islands on expeditions across the Caribbean Sea as early as c.7500 years ago before settling there permanently (Hofman et al. 2011). In the Caribbean and elsewhere in the world, island colonists have been very active in altering their new environment and domesticating the landscape from the moment of their arrival by means of intentionally, establishing 'transported landscapes' or accidentally by 'portmanteau biotas', introducing new plant and faunal species from the mainland as well as from other islands (Kirch 1997, 2000; Terrell et al. 2003; Watlington 2003; Fitzpatrick and Keegan 2007). The climatic conditions island communities were faced with (including not only changes from dry to wetter periods but also the risk of floods and landslides caused by tropical storms, hurricanes or extreme wave events like tsunamis) would certainly have impacted their ways of life and the socio-cultural as well as political dynamics across the region over time (Blancaneaux 2009; Delpuech 2004; Fitzpatrick and Keegan 2007).

Environmental alterations and activities (e.g., slash-and-burn and slope agriculture) must have strongly influenced the islands' original biotopes. This would have (a) challenged the agricultural potential and availability of resources and (b) led to landslides and processes of erosion during storms. Certain notable changes in the region between periods with excessively wet and dry climatic regimes occurred during the Holocene (e.g. Curtis and Hodell 1993; Curtis et al. 2001; Keegan 1995; Higuera-Gundy et al. 1999; Hodell et al. 1991; Malaizé et al. 2012). Over time the insular inhabitants adapted to these climatological fluctuations (Delpuech 2004; Cooper and Peros 2010). Paleo-environmental data from several sites in the Caribbean have provided us with general insights into the climatic conditions during the pre-colonial period (Beets et al. 2006; Malaizé et al. 2012; Siegel et al. 2005). A period of drought with hurricanes characterizes the entire Archaic Age, from 4300 BC on, followed by a less dry spell and a decrease of the number of hurricanes during the Ceramic Age. A major drought was again recorded between AD 700 and 900. Moreover, a shift with respect to the preceding centuries can be observed in terms of settlement locations and density as well as strategies of environmental exploitation. Carbon and nitrogen isotopic carbon and nitrogen studies on the shells of terrestrial molluscs (*Bulimulus guadaloupensis*) from the archaeological site of Anse à la Gourde (Grande-Terre, Guadeloupe) demonstrate that the climatic conditions were extremely variable during the Ceramic Age. Wet periods were witnessed around AD 100, 200, 400, and 800 to 1400 whereas dry periods occurred between AD 200 and 400, AD 800 and 1000, and again around AD 1600 (Beets et al. 2006; Delpuech 2004). The snail-shell carbon isotope values changed significantly after AD 1000, probably indicating a vegetational response to the wetter conditions of that time (Beets et al. 2006; Malaizé et al. 2012).

Safety nets: extensive networks of mobility and exchange

The available archaeological evidence suggests that Caribbean prehistory featured a continuous to-ing and fro-ing of individuals and groups of people, originating from various areas in coastal South America, the Isthmo-Colombian area and littoral Central America. With a range of environmental, socio-political, economic, ideological motives, they moved at both micro- and macro-scales through the island archipelago (Hofman et al. 2007, 2010; Hofman and Bright 2010; Hofman and Carlin 2010; Rodríguez Ramos 2010). From the onset of island occupation, the Archaic and later Ceramic Age communities maintained local and regional networks of mobility and exchange in which people, goods and ideas moved between the islands and across the Caribbean Sea. Processes are involved which we would recognize as colonizing migration, cross-community mobility, residential mobility, including post-mortem mobility, resource and seasonal mobility, and inter-community mobility such as feasting, raiding and exchange (e.g. Bellwood 2004; Curet 2005; Hofman et al. 2007; Keegan 2006; Kelly 1995; Manning 2005; Moch 2003; Moore 2001). These networks were also important safety nets in times of harshness and climatic challenges, especially because of the large diversity in settlement locations (e.g. coastal, inland, hill tops, proximity to caves, resources and exploitation possibilities) enhancing the diversification within the networks and strengthening the existing social ties. When the Europeans arrived in the Caribbean in 1492, extensive indigenous networks existed of which the colonizers certainly took advantage in order to rapidly expand across the Caribbean Sea and the rest of the Americas (Hofman and Carlin 2010). Although the indigenous inhabitants must have transmitted their local knowledge to the Europeans concerning the way in which to handle the climatic hazards they were confronted with, the Europeans introduced their own lifestyles which were not always suited to the local conditions (see also Cooper 2012a,b).

Floods

Sea level fluctuations

Sea level variations especially affected human occupation on the low lying limestone islands of the Caribbean archipelago (Cooper 2010; Cooper and Peros 2010; Delpuech 2004; Delpuech et al. 2001; Fitzpatrick 2010). Following the regular sea level rise and coastal geomorphological changes during the Early Holocene, a shoreline stabilization is noticed after c.5000-4500 BP (Delpuech 2004; Delpuech et al. 2001). Data on historical sea level changes in the Caribbean are scarce. Kemp et al. (2011) present us with a reconstruction of the sea level curve over the past 2100 years. Based on salt marsh sedimentary sequences from North Carolina, it can eventually serve as a proxy for the sea level changes in the Caribbean. According to Kemp et al., the sea level was stable from *c*.100 BC until AD 950. During the following 400 years the sea level rose *c*.0.6 mm per annum. In around AD 1350 a period of a stable or slightly falling sea level started, lasting until the second half of the 19th century. Stratigraphic data extracted from a 9-m-deep core in a mangrove area on the shore of Guadeloupe, however, suggest that the sea level rose *c*.1.8 m in the Grand Cul-de-Sac area during the past millennium. This was caused by local tectonic activity in the context of a general subsidence of the eastern part of Grande-Terre (Feller et al. 1992). Large areas of land were submerged, including the islets of Petit Cul-de-Sac Marin located between the islands of Grande-Terre

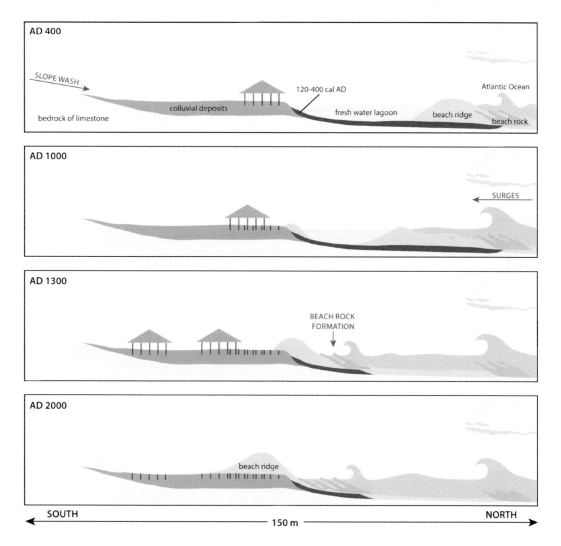

Figure 2. The Erosion and formation processes of new beach ridges and the shift of the Amerindian settlement location at the site of Anse à la Gourde (Guadeloupe) between AD 400 and 2000. Drawing by Menno L.P. Hoogland

and Basse-Terre. This possibly obscured any evidence of archaeological sites in this area, as was the case in many other island coastal regions. The eastern portion of Grande-Terre has been particularly affected by a sea level rise and related changes of the coastline over the past 1 or 2 millennia (Delpuech et al. 2001).

The Ceramic Age site of Anse à la Gourde is situated on the peninsula of La Pointe des Châteaux (eastern Grande-Terre, Guadeloupe). The site was inhabited from the 6th until the 15th century AD in four successive occupation phases and evidence change in settlement location over time because of perpetual sea level rise and coastal erosion (Fig. 2). It seems that, each time the higher elevations were chosen to settle after periods of storms, extreme precipitation rates as well as a subsequent erosion and a breakdown of protective coastal barriers were induced. Ostracod samples gathered locally from various *salinas* demonstrate they are excellent recorders of climate change in the region. Stable oxygen isotope analysis combined with floral and faunal data provide us with ample evidence for changes in precipitation and evaporation during the period of deposition. Ostracods are invariably the organisms that occur most frequently. They belong to the species *Cyprideis similis* and *C. edentata* that are particular to *salinas* (Beets et al. 2006). The shift of the reef barrier towards the interior has been related to a sea level rise which necessitated not only a gradual retreat of human habitation towards the interior but also the search for higher settlement grounds (Beets at al. 2006; Hofman et al. 2001; Hofman et al. 2014). During the earliest occupation phase at Anse à la Gourde, a reef barrier existed with a low salinity lagoon behind grown with mangrove. The earliest habitation of the site, between *c*.AD 400 and 600, was situated on the shore of this brackish water lagoon, between 50 and 100 m south of the Atlantic littoral. In *c*.AD 800 a rise of sea level resulted in the breakdown of the coastal barrier as well as a progressive salinity of the lagoon. The occupants of the settlement moved towards the interior and established themselves on the newly formed elevated dunes. This process perpetuated over the centuries with the village moving further inland as a response to the continuous coastal erosion.

Major wave events like tsunamis

Major wave events like tsunamis are not frequent and difficult to assess in the archaeological record (see also Morton et al. 2006). However, to prehistoric populations the impact of a major tsunami would have been physically and cosmologically devastating. Major tsunamis such as the 1755 example resulted from a major earthquake on the coast of Portugal. In the Lesser Antilles it reportedly created waves of up to 7 m on for instance the island of Saba, which rarely occurs (Barkan et al. 2009; Lander et al. 2002). The majority of tsunamis have probably been induced by means of relatively weak undersea earthquakes in the Caribbean vault. A tsunami is characterized by several high-energy, long-period waves with spacing between wave crests of 5 up to 20 minutes. These waves spread in almost straight lines near the coastline and cause large run-ups which vary at a scale of tens of kilometers as a function of coastal bathymetry (Ioualalen et al. 2007; Scheffers et al. 2005, 2009). Sediment from below the storm wave base, the shore face, beach, and landward by-pass zone is taken up by these waves and transported forwards in suspension. Once distributed over a broad region this sediment falls out of suspension when the flow decelerates (Scheffers et al. 2005, 2009). Scheffers (2002) and Scheffers et al. (2006) mention a significant tsunami event at *c.*4200 BP as well as three further tsunami periods at 3100, 1500 and 500 BP, all probably affecting the southern Caribbean islands of Curaçao and Bonaire. The earliest dates are contemporary with the first Archaic Age occupation on Curaçao at Rooi Rincon and Spaanse Water, and Gotto Lake at Slagbaai on Bonaire (Haviser 1987; Hoogland and Hofman 2013). It is presumed that major wave events like tsnuamis significantly altered the coastal mangrove environment and destroyed coral reefs. This would have had repercussions as to human survival and have encouraged communities to adapt their living space to inland bays e.g., on the leeward side of the islands. However, such sites were never identified on these coasts, perhaps because they are covered by thick tsunami deposits (Scheffers et al. 2005, 2009).

The site of Anse Trabaud is located in the southeastern part of Martinique and dates from between the 7th and 14th century AD. The area is particularly vulnerable to storm events (Safface et al. 2002; Schleupner 2007, 2008). The settlement is situated on a tombolo which comprises a number of successive beach barriers and connects a small island with the mainland of Martinique. Between the tombolo and the mainland a shallow laguna has formed with mangrove vegetation. The

Figure 3. Excavation unit 10 at the site of Anse Trabaud. The deeply buried refuse layer containing organic materials (see insert) and pottery belongs probably to a house structure built at the edge of the mangrove.

stratigraphy of the excavation units in the mangrove area evidences it is covered with a thick layer of sediments deposited during storm events and tsunamis (Fig. 3). The indigenous inhabitants of Anse Trabaud adapted to the gradually rising sea level by moving to the outer and higher beach barriers over time. The earliest evidence of occupation dates to AD 600-900 and presumably consisted of stilt houses built within the mangrove area. The area is currently buried under 2 m of mangrove mud mixed with sand, allowing conservation of organic materials (e.g. wood, calabash). The material remnants mainly consist of very large ceramic plates and bowls which were only slightly trampled but entirely blackened by the mangrove mud (Hofman 2012).

Tropical storms and hurricanes

Tropical storms and hurricanes are common natural phenomena in the Intra-Americas Sea (see also Cooper 2012a; Delpuech 2004; Fitzpatrick 2010). The islands of the eastern Caribbean are situated along the course of low pressure systems which develop on the coast of Africa. Next they cross the Atlantic Ocean and gradually turn into tropical storms and eventually hurricanes which frequently occur in the area positioned between Grenada in the south of the Lesser Antilles and the Bahamas to the north (Fig. 4). Within this region the Leeward Islands and Puerto Rico are particularly vulnerable. Stratigraphic evidence revealing rapid sedimentation at the Late Ceramic Age site of Rendezvous Bay on Anguilla suggests that the pre-colonial inhabitants of that site must have dealt with hurricane events (Watters and Petersen 1993). Indications for storm events also exist for the pre-colonial record of Puerto Rico (Clark et al. 2003; Siegel et al. 2005). During the last 100 years approximately 1000 tropical storms and about 200 hurricanes of

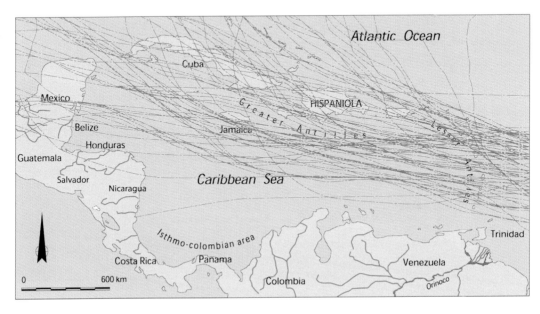

Figure 4. Map of the Caribbean with the hurricane tracks recorded by the National Oceanic and Atmospheric Administration (USA) in the months of August. Map by Menno L.P. Hoogland.

Categories 2–5 occurred in the Intra-Americas Sea region (Scheffer et al. 2005). The island of St. Martin for example witnessed seven direct hits between 1995 and 2014. Hurricanes have inflicted severe damage to the archaeological record of the Lesser Antilles (Delpuech et al. 2001; Fitzpatrick 2012; Hofman et al. 2012; Siegel et al. 2013). During and after a hurricane the wind force induced waves cause considerable erosion of the coastal barriers (e.g. beaches, dunes) due to the continuous impact of breakers. Their number per hour can reach up to 350 (Scheffers et al. 2005). The precipitation accompanying these storms not only results in slope wash but also in the formation of drainage channels. Existing channels may well widen or change their course. Precipitation rates have been measured up to levels of 127 to 254 mm as to hurricanes moving at a speed of *c.*10 km per hour. With slower moving systems the precipitation levels may reach 380 mm or more with extremes measuring between 650 and 1250 mm (http://www.wpc.ncep.noaa.gov/tropical/rain/tcmaxima.html).

A constant rainfall accompanied by massive gusts of up to 250 km per hour or even higher for a hurricane now labelled as Category 5, thunderstorms, and meters high waves and floods demand not only specific social responses but also the adaptation of settlement location, house construction and shelter facilities such as caves. On mainland Venezuela, along the middle Orinoco, a long tradition of mound building has been recognized. These artificial mounds had to protect people against floods (Roosevelt 1980). In the Lesser Antilles artificial habitation mounds have not been documented. However, on these islands as well as the Greater Antilles, the preferred settlement locations during pre-colonial times comprised the leeward slopes of mountains or the higher parts of flat areas, which may well have been chosen in order to protect communities against storm events and associated floods. Good examples hereof are to be found in the late pre-colonial settlement locations of Los Buchillones (north-central Cuba), Kelbey's Ridge (in the northeastern part of the island of Saba) and El Flaco and Los Ballatases in the northwestern Dominican Republic (Cooper 2012a; Hofman and Hoogland 2015; Hoogland 1996; Pendergast et al. 2003; Jorge Ulloa Hung, personal communication, 2013).

Hurricane-proof shelters have been documented at the settlement site of Golden Rock, St. Eustatius, located in the *Cultuurvlakte*, a plain in the middle of this island with a surface area of 20 km². It is situated between an old volcanic landscape in the northwest and the more recent volcano The Quill in the southeast (Versteeg and Schinkel 1992). The site is dated between AD 400 and 900. Fourteen structures have been identified of which five small houses, three large residential structures (*malocas*) with windbreaks and smaller elongated, rectangular or other constructions. The largest *maloca* measures 19 m in diameter and has central posts dug up to 3 m into the volcanic tuff and lapilli deposits in order to make sturdy constructions. A row of lighter posts carrying the roof and forming the wall of the *maloca* surrounds this circular inner structure. Windbreaks were attached to the houses, offering protection to the entrances and the activity areas near the house against the prevailing northeast trade winds and heavy rains. The basic house structure is clearly hurricane-proof. Moreover, it can be repaired rapidly after a disaster as only the light construction elements (e.g. roofing, walls) would have to be replaced (Cooper 2012; Samson et al., in press).

A similar pattern has been found at the site of El Cabo in the southeastern Dominican Republic which revealed approximately fifty structures, thirty-one of which were circular houses measuring between 6 to 10 m in diameter. The main posts of the individual structures were dug deep into the bedrock providing a strong support to the roof-bearing posts with an outer wall construction made of alternating large and smaller posts. The structures were finished with thatched roofs consisting of palm leaves and walls of woven twigs. A similar practice of digging posts into the bedrock is encountered at the Anse à la Gourde site on Guadeloupe. The layout of the houses at this site, with two concentric rows of posts, resembles the structures documented at the site of El Flaco in the northwestern Dominican Republic. In the latter case, there is also clear evidence of the repairing and replacement of posts. The houses at El Flaco are located on man-made platforms on a leeward slope in the foothills of the Cordillera Septentrional. The sloping areas of the settlement location provide an excellent drainage during tropical rain storms. Other structures identified at the site of El Cabo included windbreaks resembling those found at the Golden Rock site on St. Eustatius. They were not only used to mitigate strong gusts but also to provide sheltered areas to work in and around the houses (Samson et al., in press). Caves often serve as shelters in places often affected by tropical storms and hurricanes such as the *farallones* near El Cabo (see also Cooper 2012a). Present-day rural communities in the area also refer to the caves as places of refuge in times of threatening natural disasters. The Los Buchillones site (north-central Cuba) dates to AD 1250-1500 and features houses on stilts. The mahogany posts are dug up to 1.70 m into a lagoon deposit. The houses consist of two concentric circles and offer a sound resistance to hurricanes. Thanks to the application of stilts these structures were protected against floods as well as the local gradual rise of the sea level (Cooper 2012a,b; Pendergast et al. 2003).

Droughts

In extremely arid environments such as certain limestone islands and during a severe drought, ingenious water procurement and management systems were put in place. They included ditches (*rooien*) in order to irrigate the Southern Antilles, pot stacks for procurement of water on the many arid islands and *Lobatus gigas* containers to collect rainwater in the Los Roques Archipelago located off the coast of Venezuela.

Natural and artificial gullies

The ditches or *rooien* (i.e., small natural gullies which fill with water during spells of rain) found around the site of Tanki Flip on Aruba date to the Ceramic Age and most likely represent ancient water management systems. The site was first occupied in *c*.AD 950/1000. None of the available radiocarbon dates indicate a period of settlement after AD 1400, suggesting that the hamlet was abandoned before any European colonisation (Bartone and Versteeg 1997:110-113). Ceramic Age settlements tend to occur near one or more gullies. Furthermore, gullies may facilitate travel and communication across the island. At the site of Tanki Flip, several man-made examples were discovered, indicating a north-south orientation. These artificial gullies connected the naturally occurring west-to-east oriented *rooien* (Raymundo Dijkhoff, personal communication, 2010). Gullies have been discovered at the Aruban Santa Cruz site too. They presumably served as natural irrigation systems for horticulture, characterizing the local *cacicazgos* (i.e., a hierarchical form of socio-political organization) of the Caquetio Amerindians as described in contemporaneous European documents. The gullies were discovered in a part of the Santa Cruz site where few other features such as postholes related to any habitation have been documented (Harold Kelly, personal communication, 2014). They were most likely related to an agricultural area

Pot stacks

The availability of water would have been the limiting factor to permanent habitation on many of the small, arid limestone islands, in particular during periods of severe drought as recorded in several instances during the pre-colonial occupation of the Caribbean (see also Hinds et al. 1999). A possible solution would have consisted of the use of pot stacks along the beaches of sandy bays (Fig. 5). On the island of Barbados many such stacks comprising large, bottomless pots have been found. They have also been reported from Carriacou, St. Vincent, Mustique, Guadeloupe, and Puerto Rico (Bullen and Bullen 1972; Hackenberger 1988; Hinds et al. 1999; Hofman et al. 1995; Schultz 1998). The stacked pots served as ceramic well casings and their use as water procurement systems is uncontestable. These stacked pots are placed at the base of the dunes. The water table of fresh underground aquifers

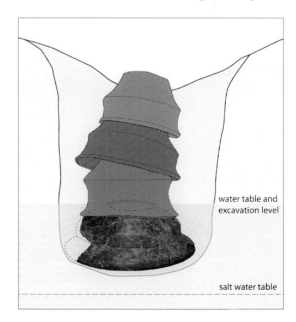

Figure 5. Reconstruction of a pot stack used as fresh water well at the site of Morel, Guadeloupe. The lower bottomless vessel was encountered under the present-day water table during the 1995 excavations at Morel. Reconstruction by Menno Hoogland after example from Barbados.

water table and
excavation level

salt water table

is situated *c*.1 m below the surface of the beach, floating on the salty seawater. Freshwater flowing down from the hilly areas in the interior is tapped by means of shallow wells. In order to construct a well, several inverted, bottomless pots are positioned on top of each other. Large pot bases and griddle fragments, stones and cobbles served as packing materials, supporting the sides and the opening (Schultz 1998). At the site of Heywoods on Barbados, wood was found at the base of certain wells suggesting this material formed part of the well structure (Hinds et al. 1999). Stacks are also known from beyond the insular Caribbean, notably the Maya area in Guatemala (Ashmore 1984) and coastal Ecuador (Martinez and Pavon 1989). The freshwater lenses are particularly vulnerable to the impacts of storm events and a sea level rise, implying that the pot stack system would not have functioned during these extreme weather conditions (Bowleg and Allen 2013).

Queen Conchs as rain water containers: an indigenous practice?

In Cayo Sal Island (Los Roques Archipelago) about 100 adult Queen Conch (*botuto* or *Lobatus gigas*) shells were found placed in an upside-down position, one alongside the other and arranged in a rectangular area of 2×2.5 m (Fig. 6). This was not a pre-colonial feature, but according to elderly local fishermen (Felipe Salazar, Loy Gómez, personal communication, 1983 to A. Antczak) it served 19th-century fishermen from Bonaire to collect rain water. This method is, in fact, highly effective. In an experimental test it was established that between four and five shells can collect as much as 1 litre of water during 30 minutes of heavy rain. In 1986 larger scatters of upside-down shells were located in the area of a 19th-

Figure 6. Queen Conch (Lobatus gigas) shells arranged by 19th-century fishermen to collect rain water on Cayo Sal Island, Los Roques Archipelago, Venezuela. Photograph: A. Antczak.

century lime kiln on Isla del Faro (Las Aves Archipelago). The indigenous peoples visiting these islands may have applied this ingenious way of obtaining potable water. To date, however, no direct evidence of such a practice has been found within any ethnohistoric or archaeological contexts (Antczak and Antczak 2006; Antczak et al. 2008).

Discussion

Contemporary challenges to the indigenous archaeological heritage

Key problems related to site preservation and visibility as a result of storm events, sea level rise and local tectonic activity (e.g. subduction and uplift in northern Haiti or the Cul-de-Sac Marin in Guadeloupe) are severe erosion, landslides, or sedimentation which are all fairly common on the Caribbean islands (Cherry et al. 2012; Delpuech 2004). Hurricanes or other storms may have affected shorelines by means of submerging, covering, or erasing coastal sites (e.g. Crock and Petersen 2001; Davis 1982; Delpuech 2004; Keegan 1995; Litman 2001; Perdikaris 2011; Watters 2001; Watters et al. 1992). Areas of former habitation may have been altered or completely disappeared due to coastal erosion or sedimentation (Delpuech 2004; Delpuech et al. 2001; Scheffer et al. 2005). At coastal sites such as Morel (Guadeloupe) we recorded a change in coastline accompanied by a severe loss of a portion of the archaeological deposits. This loss has been measured to have been 50 m between 1940 and 1990 (Hofman et al. 1999) (Fig. 7). The site

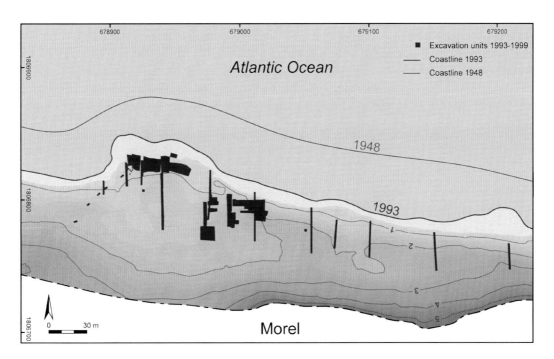

Figure 7. The location of the excavation units 1993-1999 and the reconstruction of the coastal erosion at Morel (Guadeloupe) by means of aerial photographs taken in 1948 and 1993. Drawing by Menno L.P. Hoogland.

of Lavoutte on St. Lucia is subject to heavy erosion due to a retreating coastline on the one hand and slope wash on the other hand, whereby archaeological materials are exposed. Hurricane Dean in 2007 has severely damaged this site resulting in the exposure of numerous human remains which have undergone extensive rescue excavations in 2009 (Hofman and Branford 2009; Hofman et al. 2012; Siegel et al. 2013). Other examples hereof include the Grand Bay site on Carriacou (Fitzpatrick 2010) or the Late Ceramic Age site of Godet on the southeastern coast of St. Eustatius which is at risk of being lost in the immediate future due to heavy erosion (Gilmore et al. 2011).

It is also possible that entire islands will be submerged in the foreseeable future (Delpuech et al. 2001: 103). In more inland areas, sedimentation may have conserved, but also obscured sites. Extreme wave events like tsnunamis also have had a serious post-depositional impact on the indigenous archaeological record. This often forgotten phenomenon nonetheless contributes to a strong misrepresentation of the past. A good example hereof is the island of Bonaire. Here a succession of tsunami events from 4500 BP on has been recorded by means of the coral deposits located on the east coast (Scheffers et al. 2005). The coastal geomorphic environment of Anegada alludes to similar features (Davis and Oldfield 2003). These phenomena significantly affect the current visibility and distort the archaeological reality (Delpuech et al. 2001). The almost complete absence of any Archaic Age sites on the Windward Islands, on several of the Virgin Islands, on Jamaica and the Bahamas may be the result hereof too.

Concluding remarks

Waterlogged sites in mangrove areas possess a huge heritage value thanks to the preservation of wood and other perishable materials. Sites such as Los Buchillones (Cuba), Morel (Guadeloupe), and Rivière Salée as well as Anse Trabaud on Martinique are exemplary for the Caribbean region (Hofman et al. 1999; Hofman and Hoogland 2012; Pendergast et al. 2003). Recent construction activities, agriculture and sand mining accelerate the destruction process and stimulate coastal erosion (Siegel et al. 2013). For instance, at the site of Morel on Guadeloupe mining for sand formed a regular business. Its location is extremely vulnerable to tropical storms and hurricanes. Consequently, the process of coastal erosion has been detrimental here. After a hurricane, this site became a well-frequented *supermarché de l'archéologie*, where private collectors shopped for the most stunning indigenous works of art. The urge to implement laws regarding cultural heritage protection is imminent on numerous Caribbean islands in order to prevent any further loss of the unwritten and as yet undocumented history of the first Antilleans (Siegel et al. 2013). Moreover, climatic threats are a permanent concern to the current inhabitants of the Caribbean and the small-island states (Hiwasaki et al. 2014; Ion-Beptiste and Yacou 2007). Undoubtedly, the impact of natural catastrophes will affect the island communities in all their aspects. 'If a targeted coastal protection and careful planning of future infrastructure are not anticipated, island communities will struggle to adapt to the tide of environmental change' (http://intasave-caribsave.org/climate-change-caribbean-pacific).

Acknowledgements

We are indebted to Willem Willems for inviting us to participate in this volume. We have hugely enjoyed working with him in the NEXUS1492 project where, as a co-PI, he was in charge of the heritage project. Numerous natural as well as human impacts threaten the Caribbean indigenous archaeological record. Laws in order to protect it are sparsely implemented. The ERC-Synergy NEXUS1492 project (funded by the *European Research Council / ERC grant agreement n° 319209*) aims to contribute to the safeguarding of the indigenous archaeological heritage in the geopolitically diverse islandscape of the Caribbean in collaboration with local stakeholders.

We are grateful to Andrjez and Marlena Antczak for providing us with information on the queen conch water containers and Harold Kelly for the data concerning the gullies for irrigation on the Santa Cruz site, Aruba.

Finally, we would like to acknowledge Dr. Arie Boomert for editing the original English text and to the two anonymous reviewers for their useful comments.

References

Antczak, A., J. Posada, D. Schapira, M.M. Antczak, R. Cipriani, and I. Montaño. 2008. A History of Human Impact on the Queen Conch (*Strombus gigas*) in Venezuela. In *Early Human Impact on Megamolluscs*, eds. A. Antczak and R. Cipriani, 49-64. BAR International Series 1865. Oxford: Archaeopress.

Antczak, M.M., and A. Antczak. 2006. *Los Ídolos de las Islas Prometidas: Arqueología Prehispánica del Archipiélago de Los Roques*. Caracas: Editorial Equinoccio.

Barkan, R., U.S. ten Brink, and J. Lin. 2009. Far field tsunami simulations of the 1755 Lisbon earthquake: Implications for tsunami hazard to the U.S. east coast and the Caribbean. *Marine Geology* 264: 109-122.

Bartone, R.N., and A.H. Versteeg. 1997. The Tanki Flip Features and Structures. In *The Archaeology of Aruba: The Tanki Flip Site*, eds. A.H. Versteeg and S. Rostain, 23-126. Oranjestad: Archaeological Museum Aruba and the Foundation for Scientific Research in the Caribbean Region.

Beets, C.J., S.R. Troelstra, P.M. Grootes, M.J. Nadeau, K. van der Borg, A.F.M. de Jong, C.L. Hofman, and M.L.P. Hoogland. 2006. Climate and pre-Columbian settlement at Anse à la Gourde, Guadeloupe, north-eastern Caribbean. *Geoarchaeology: An International Journal* 21(3): 271-280.

Bellwood, P. 2004. *First Farmers: The Origins of Agricultural Societies*. Oxford: Blackwell Publishing.

Blancaneaux, A.F., 2009. *Contribution à l'étude de la disparition de la culture saladoïde aux Petites Antilles: Corrélation préhistorique possible entre climat et culture*. Unpublished PhD dissertation, Université des Antilles et de la Guyane and Université Paris I, Pantheón Sorbonne.

Bullen, R.P., and A.K. Bullen. 1972. *Archaeological Investigations on St. Vincent and the Grenadines, West Indies*. American Studies Report 8. Orlando: The William Bryant Foundation.

Cherry, J.F., K. Ryzewski, and T.P. Leppard. 2012. Multi-period landscape survey and site risk assessment on Monserrat, West Indies. *Journal of Island and Coastal Archaeology* 7(2): 282-302.

Clark, J.J, J. Walker and R. Rodríguez Ramos. 2003. Depositional history and evolution of the Paso del Indio site, Vega Baja, Puerto Rico. *Geoarchaeology* 18: 625-648.

Cooper, J. 2010. Modelling mobility and exchange in precolumbian Cuba: GIS led approaches to identifying pathways and reconstructing journeys from the archaeological record. In *Journal of Caribbean Archaeology, Special Publication 3*, eds. C.L. Hofman and A. J. Bright, 122–137.

Cooper, J., and M. Peros. 2010. The archaeology of climate change in the Caribbean. *Journal of Archaeological Science* 37(6): 1226-1232.

Cooper, J. 2012a. Fail to prepare then prepare to fail: rethinking threat vulnerability and migration in the pre-Columbian Caribbean. In *Surviving Sudden Environmental Change: Answers from Archaeology*, eds. J. Cooper, and P. Sheets, 91–114. Boulder: University Press of Colorado.

Cooper, J., 2012b. Building resilience in island communities: A paleotempestological perspective. In *Climate, landscapes, and civilizations,* eds. L. Giosan, D.Q. Fuller, K. Nicoll, R.K. Flad, and P.D. Clift, 43-50. Florida: American Geophysical Union.

Crock, J.G., and J.B. Petersen. 2001. Stratified sites and storm events: The formation and destruction of beach sites in Anguilla, West Indies. In *Proceedings of the 19th Congress of the International Association for Caribbean Archaeology*, eds. L. Alofs and R.A.C.F. Dijkhoff, vol. 1, 204-213. Oranjestad: Publications of the Archaeological Museum Aruba 9.

Curet, L.A. 2005. *Caribbean Paleodemography: Population, Culture History, and Sociopolitical Processes in Ancient Puerto Rico.* Tuscaloosa: University of Alabama Press.

Curtis, J.H., M. Brenner and D.A. Hodell. 2001. Climate change in the circum-Caribbean (Late Pleistocene to Present) and implications for regional biogeography. In *Biogeography of the West Indies: Patterns and Perspectives*, 2nd ed., eds. C.A. Woods and F.E. Sergile, 35-55. Florida: CRC Press.

Curtis, J.H., and D.A. Hodell. 1993. An isotopic and trace element study of ostracods from Lake Miragoane, Haiti: A 10,500 year record of paleosalinity and paleotemperature changes in the Caribbean. *Geophysical Monograph* 78: 135–52.

Davis, D. 1982. Archaic settlement and resource exploitation in the Lesser Antilles: Preliminary information from Antigua. *Caribbean Journal of Science*, 17: 107–121.

Davis, D., and K. Oldfield. 2003. Archaeological reconnaissance of Anegada, British Virgin Islands. *Journal of Caribbean Archaeology* 4: 1-11.

Delpuech, A. 2004. Espaces naturels et territoires amérindiens dans la Caraïbe orientale. In *Late Ceramic Age Societies in the Eastern Caribbean*, eds. A. Delpuech and C.L. Hofman, 3–16. Oxford: British Archaeological Reports, BAR International Series 1273.

Delpuech, A., C.L. Hofman, and M.L.P. Hoogland. 2001. Amerindian settlements and archaeological reality in the Lesser Antilles: The case of Grande-Terre, Guadeloupe. In *Proceedings of the 19th International Congress for Caribbean Archaeology*, eds. L. Alofs and R.A.C.F. Dijkhoff, vol. 2, 99–120. Oranjestad: Publications of the Archaeological Museum Aruba 9.

Feller C., M. Fournier, D. Imbert, C. Caratini, and L. Martin. 1992. *Datations ^{14}C et palynologie d'un sédiment tourbeux continu (0-7 m) dans la mangrove de Guadeloupe (F.W.I.). Résultats préliminaires.* In *Evolution des littoraux de Guyane et de la zone caraïbe méridionale pendant le quaternaire*, ed. P. Marie-Thérèse, 193-202. Paris, Symposium PICG 274/OSTROM, Paper presented at the colloquium.

Fitzpatrick, S.M. 2012. One of the shoals of giants: Natural catastrophes and the overall destruction of the Caribbean's archaeological record. *Journal of Coastal Conservation* 14(1): 1-14.

Fitzpatrick, S.M., and W.F. Keegan. 2007. Human impacts and adaptations in the Caribbean Islands: An historical ecology approach. *Earth and Environmental Science Transactions of the Royal Society of Edinburgh* 98(1): 29-45.

Fosberg, F.R., ed. 1963. *Man's Place in the Island Ecosystem: A Symposium.* Hawaii: Bishop Museum Press.

Gilmore G., M.L.P. Hoogland, and C.L. Hofman. 2011. *An Archaeological Assessment of Cul-de-Sac (The Farm), St. Eustatius.* Unpublished Report, St. Eustatius/Leiden University.

Hackenberger, S. 1988. An abstract of investigations by the Barbados Museum 1986. *Journal of the Barbados Museum and Historical Society* 38(2): 155-162.

Haviser, J.B. 1987. *Amerindian Cultural Geography of Curaçao.* Amsterdam: Foundation for Scientific Research in Surinam and the Netherlands Antilles.

Higuera-Gundy, A., M. Brenner, D.A. Hodell, J.H. Curtis, B.W. Leyden, and M.W. Binford. 1999. A 10,300 ^{14}C record of climate and vegetation change from Haiti. *Quaternary Research* 52: 159–70.

Hinds, R., M. Bennell, and M. Hill Harris. 1999. Excavations at Heywoods. *Proceedings of the 17th Congress of the International Association for Caribbean Archaeology*, ed. J.H. Winter, 122-135. New York: Rockville Center.

Hodell, D.A., J.H. Curtis, G.A. Jones, A. Higuera-Gundy, M. Brenner, M.W. Binford, and K.T. Dorsey. 1991. Reconstruction of Caribbean climate change over the past 10,500 years. *Nature* 352: 790-793.

Hofman, C.L. 2012. Anse Trabaud commune de Sainte-Anne, Martinique: Reconstruction d'un village amérindien. Son insertion dans le réseau d'échanges Antillais entre 600 et 1200 après J.-C. *Rapport de prospection thématique avec sondages.* Unpublished report, Leiden University.

Hofman, C.L., A. Boomert, A.J. Bright, M.L.P. Hoogland, S. Knippenberg, and A.V.M. Samson. 2011. Ties with the "Homeland": Archipelagic interaction and the enduring role of the South American mainland in the pre-Columbian Lesser Antilles. In *Ties with* the *"Homeland": Archipelagic Interaction and the Enduring Role of the South American Mainland in the pre-Columbian Lesser Antilles,* eds. L.A. Curet and M.W. Hauser, 73-85. Tuscaloosa: University of Alabama Press.

Hofman, C.L., and E.M. Branford. 2011. Lavoutte revisited, preliminary results of the 2009 rescue excavations at Cas-En-Bas, St. Lucia. *Proceedings of the 23rd Congress of the International Association for Caribbean Archaeology,* ed. S.A. Rebovich, 690-700. Dockyard Museum, Antigua.

Hofman, C.L., and A.J. Bright, eds. 2010. Mobility and exchange from a pan-Caribbean perspective. *Journal of Caribbean archaeology, Special Publication* 3.

Hofman, C.L., A.J. Bright, A. Boomert, and S. Knippenberg. 2007. Island rhythms: The web of social relationships and interaction networks in the Lesser Antillean Archipelago between 400 B.C. and A.D. 1492. *Latin American Antiquity* 18(3): 243-268.

Hofman, C.L., A.J. Bright, and M.L.P. Hoogland. 2006. Archipelagic resource mobility: Shedding light on the 3000 years old tropical forest campsite at Plum Piece, Saba (Northern Lesser Antilles). *Journal of Island and Coastal Archaeology* 1(2): 145-164.

Hofman, C.L., A.J. Bright, and R. Rodríguez Ramos. 2010. Crossing the Caribbean Sea: Towards a holistic view of pre-colonial mobility and exchange. In *Journal of Caribbean Archaeology, Special Publication* 3, eds. C.L. Hofman and A.J. Bright, 1-18.

Hofman, C.L., and E.B. Carlin. 2010. The ever dynamic Caribbean: Exploring new approaches to unraveling social networks in the pre-colonial and early colonial periods. In *Linguistics and Archaeology in the Americas: The Historization of Language and Society,* eds. E.B. Carlin and S. van de Kerke, 107-122. Leiden/Boston: Brill.

Hofman, C.L., A. Delpuech, and M.L.P Hoogland. 2014. *Espaces Amérindiens: Archéologie en Grande-Terre de Guadeloupe.* Le Moule, Guadeloupe: Musée Edgar Clerc, Catalogue d'exposition.

Hofman, C.L. and M.L.P. Hoogland 2015. *Investigaciones arqueológicas en los sitios El Flaco (Loma de Gayacanes) y La Luperona (Unijica). Informe preliminar.* Boletin del Museo del Hombre Dominicano. Santo Domingo.

Hofman, C.L., M.L.P. Hoogland, and A. Delpuech. 1999. New perspectives on a Huecan Saladoid assemblage on Guadeloupe: The case of Morel I. In *Archaeological Investigations on St. Martin (Lesser Antilles). The sites of Norman Estate, Anse des Pères and Hope Estate. With a contribution to the "La Hueca problem",* eds. C.L. Hofman and M.L.P. Hoogland, 303-312. Leiden University, Archaeological Series 4.

Hofman, C.L., M.L.P. Hoogland, and A. Delpuech. 2001. Le site de l'Anse à la Gourde, St. François, Guadeloupe. Fouille programmée pluriannuelle 1995-2000. *Rapport de synthèse.* Leiden University/DRAC.

Hofman, C.L., M.L.P. Hoogland, D.A. Weston, L.E. Laffoon, H.L. Mickleburgh, and M.H. Field. 2012. Rescuing the dead: Settlement and mortuary data from rescue excavations at the pre-colonial site of Lavoutte, Saint Lucia. *Journal of Field Archaeology* 37(3): 209-225.

Hofman, C.L., J. Ulloa Hung, and L.F.H.C. Jacobs. 2007. Juntando las piezas del rompecabezas: Dándole sentido a la cronología cerámica del este de la República Dominicana. *El Caribe Arqueológico* 10: 104-15.

Hoogland, M.L.P., and C.L. Hofman. 2013. *Archaeological Investigations at Spaanse Water, Curaçao.* Unpublished report, Leiden University.

Hoogland, M.L.P., C.L. Hofman, and R.G.A.M Panhuysen. 2010. Island dynamics: Evidence for mobility and exchange at the site of Anse à la Gourde, Guadeloupe. In *Island Shores, Distant Pasts: Archaeological and Biological Approaches to the Pre-Columbian Settlement of the Caribbean,* eds. A.H. Ross and F.M. Fitzpatrick, 148-162. Gainesville: University Press of Florida.

Hiwasaki, L., E. Luna, and R. Syamsidik Shaw. 2014. *Local & Indigenous Knowledge for Community Resilience: Hydro-Meteorological Disaster Risk Reduction and Climate Change Adaptation in Coastal and Small Island Communities.* Jakarta : UNESCO.

Ion-Baptiste, P., and A. Yacou. 2007. *Les risques majeurs aux Antilles: Approche culturelle et prévention sociale.* Karthala-Clerc, Guadeloupe.

Keegan, W.F. 1995. Recent climatic and sea level fluctuations in relation to West Indian prehistory. *Proceedings of the 16th Congress of the International Association for Caribbean Archaeology,* ed. G. Richard, 95-104. Basse-Terre, Guadeloupe.

Keegan, W.F. 2006. Archaic influences in the origins and development of Taíno societies. *Caribbean Journal of Science* 42: 1-10.

Kelly, R.L. 1995. *The Foraging Spectrum: Diversity in Hunter-Gatherer Lifeways.* Washington, D.C.: Smithsonian Institution Press.

Kemp, A.C., M.A. Buzas, B.P. Horton, and S.J. Culver. 2011. Influence of patchiness on modern salt-marsh foraminifera used in sea-level studies (North Carolina, USA). *Journal of Foraminiferal Research* 41:114-123.

Kirch, P.V. 1997. Introduction: The environmental history of Oceanic islands. In *Historical Ecology in the Pacific Islands,* eds. P.V. Kirch and T.L. Hunt, 1-21. New Haven, Connecticut: Yale University Press.

Kirch, P.V. 2000. *On the Road of the Winds: An Archaeological History of the Pacific Islands before European Contact.* Berkeley: University of California Press.

Knippenberg, S. 2006. *Stone Artefact Production and Exchange Among the Northern Lesser Antilles.* PhD dissertation, Leiden University.

Lander, J.F., L.S. Whiteside, and P.A. Lockridge. 2002. A brief history of tsunami in the Caribbean Sea. *SCI Tsunami Hazards* 20: 57–94.

Litmann, C.B. 2001. Quaternary sea level change in the Caribbean: The implications for archaeology. In *Proceedings of the 19th International Congress for Caribbean Archaeology,* eds. L. Alofs and R.A.C.F. Dijkhoff, vol. 1, 59–65. Oranjestad: Publications of the Archaeological Museum Aruba 9.

Loualalen, M., J. Asavanant, N. Kaewbanjak, S.T. Grilli, J.T. Kirby, and P. Watts. 2007. Modelling the 26 December 2004 Indian Ocean tsunami: Case study of impact in Thailand. *Journal of Geophysical Research: Oceans* 112(C7): 1-21.

Malaizé, B., P. Bertran, P. Carbonel, D. Bonnissent, K. Charlier, D. Galop, D. Imbert, N. Serrand, C. Stouvenot, and C. Pujol. 2011. September. Hurricanes and climate in the Caribbean during the past 3700 years BP. *Holocene* 21(6): 911-924.

Manning, P. 2005. *Migration in World History.* New York: Routledge.

Moch, L.P. 2003. *Moving Europeans: Migration in Western Europe since 1650*. Bloomington: Indiana University Press.

Moore, J.H. 2001. Evaluating five models of human colonization. *American Anthropologist* 103(2): 395-408.

Morton, R.A., B.M. Richmond and G. Gelfenbaum. 2006. *Reconnaissance Investigation of Caribbean Extreme Wave Deposits – Preliminary Observations, Interpretations, and Research Directions*. Open-File Report 2006-1293. U.S. Department of the Interior, U.S. Geological Survey.

Pendergast, D.M., E. Graham, R.J. Calvera, and M.J. Jardines. 2002. The house in which they dwelt: The excavation and dating of Taino wooden structures at Los Buchillones, Cuba. *Journal of Wetland Archaeology* 2(1): 61-75.

Perdikaris, S. 2011. *Paleoenvironmental investigations in Barbuda, WI*. Paper presented at the 24th International Congress for Caribbean Archaeology (Session Caribbean Human Ecodynamics), Martinique. Université Antilles-Guyane, Martinique.

Rodríguez Ramos, R. 2010. *Rethinking Puerto Rican Precolonial History*. Tuscaloosa, Alabama: Alabama University Press.

Roosevelt, A.C. 1980. *Parmana: Prehistoric Maize and Manioc Subsistence Along the Amazon and Orinoco*. New York: Academic Press.

Safface P., J.V. Marc, and O. Cospar. 2002. *Les cyclones en Martinique: Quatre siècles cataclysmiques*. Matoury, Guyane Française: IBIS Rouge.

Samson, A.V.M. 2011. The wise woman built her house upon the rock: Architectural resilience in the Greater Antilles, Turks and Caicos, and Virgin Islands. *Proceedings of the 24th International Congress for Caribbean Archaeology*, ed. B. Bérard, 421-431. Université Antilles-Guyane, Martinique.

Samson, A.V.M, C.A. Crawford, M.L.P. Hoogland, and C.L. Hofman, in press. *Dialogue between archaeology and humanitarian shelter: Resilience in pre-Columbian house-building and repair*. Human Ecology: an inter-disciplinary journal.

Scheffers, A. 2002. Paleotsunamis in the Caribbean: Field evidences and datings from Aruba, Curaçao and Bonaire. *Essener Geographische Arbeiten*, 33: 181.

Scheffers, A., S.R. Scheffers, and D. Kelletat. 2005. Paleo-tsunami relics on the Southern and Central Antillean Island Arc (Grenada, St. Lucia and Guadeloupe). *Journal of Coastal Research*, 21: 263–273.

Scheffers, S.R., J.B. Haviser, T. Browne, and A. Scheffers. 2009. Tsunamis, hurricanes, the demise of coral reefs and shifts in prehistoric human populations in the Caribbean. *Quaternary International* 195(1/2): 69-87.

Scheffers, S.R., A. Scheffers, D. Kelletat, U. Radtke, K. Staben, and R.P.M. Bak. 2006. Tsunamis trigger long-lasting phase-shift in a coral reef ecosystem. *Zeitschrift für Geomorphologie*, 146: 59–79.

Schleupner, C. 2007. Spatial assessment of sea level rise on Martinique's coastal zone and analysis of planning frameworks for adaptation. *Journal of Coastal Conservation* 11(2): 91-103.

Schleupner, C. 2008. Evaluation of coastal squeeze and its consequences for the Caribbean island Martinique. *Ocean and Coastal Management* 51(5): 383-390.

Schultz, C.S. 1998. The Carriacou Hypothesis: Bottomless stacked pots, a study in Amerindian fresh water procurement. *Proceedings of the 16th International Congress of the Association for Caribbean Archaeology*, ed. G. Richard, 217-228. Basse-Terre, Guadeloupe.

Siegel P.E., C.L. Hofman, B. Bérard, R. Murphy, J. Ulloa Hung, R. Valcárcel Rojas, and C. White. 2013. Confronting Caribbean heritage in an archipelago of diversity: Politics, stakeholders, climate change, natural disasters, tourism and development. *Journal of Field Archaeology* 38(4): 376-390.

Siegel, P.E., J.G. Jones, D.M. Pearsall, and D.P. Wagner. 2005. Environmental and cultural correlates in the West Indies: A view from Puerto Rico. In *Ancient Borinquen: Archaeology and Ethnohistory of Native Puerto Rico*, ed. P.E. Siegel, 1-54. Tuscaloosa, Alabama: University of Alabama Press.

Smith, F.H. 2009. Review of "Above Sweet Waters: Cultural and Natural Change at Port St. Charles, Barbados, c.1750 BC – AD 1850", by P.L. Drewett and M.H. Harris. *New West Indian Guide/Nieuwe West-Indische Gids* 83(3/4): 333-335.

Terrell, J.E., J.P. Hart, S. Barut, N. Cellinese, A. Curet, T. Denham, C.M. Kusimba, K. Latinis, R. Oka, J. Palka, M.E.D. Pohl, K.O. Pope, P.R. Williams, H. Haines, and J.E. Staller. 2003. Domesticated landscapes: the subsistence ecology of plant and animal domestication. *Journal of Archaeological Method and Theory* 10(4): 323-368.

Van Soest, M. 2000. *Sediment Subduction and Crustal Contamination in the Lesser Antilles Island Arc*. PhD dissertation, Free University of Amsterdam.

Versteeg, A.H., and K. Schinkel. 1992. *The Archaeology of St. Eustatius: The Golden Rock Site*. Publication of the St. Eustatius Historical Foundation 2/Publication of the Foundation for Scientific Research in the Caribbean Region 131.

Watlington, F. 2003. The physical environment: Biogeographical teleconnections in Caribbean prehistory. In *General History of the Caribbean*, vol. 1: *Autochthonous Societies*, ed. J. Sued-Badillo, 30–92. London: UNESCO-Macmillan.

Watters, D.R. 2001. Preliminary report on the correlation of Archaic Age localities with a paleoshoreline on Barbuda. In *Proceedings of the 19th International Congress for Caribbean Archaeology*, eds. L. Alofs and R.A.C.F. Dijkhoff, vol. 1, 102–109. Oranjestad: Publications of the Archaeological Museum Aruba 9.

Watters, D.R., J. Donahue, and R. Stuckenrath. 1992. Paleoshorelines and the prehistory of Barbuda, West Indies. In *Paleoshorelines and Prehistory: An Investigation of Method*, eds. L.L. Johnson and M. Stright, 15–52. Boca Raton: CRC Press.

Watters, D.R., and J.B. Petersen. 1993. Preliminary report on the archaeology of the Rendezvous Bay site, Anguilla. *Proceedings of the 14th International Congress of the Association for Caribbean Archaeology*, eds. A. Cummins and P. King, 348-359. Bridgetown, Barbados.

Woodroffe, C.D. 2003. *Coasts: Form, Process and Evolution*. New York: Cambridge University Press.

Pacific Islands on the brink of submergence

Rising seas in an age of climate changes

John A. Peterson

University of Guam
jpeterson@uguam.uog.edu

Abstract

The western Pacific Ocean is a vast sea of islands scattered about the largest ocean on earth. Volcanic seamounts rise above the water along the deepest trenches in the earth's oceans. Studies of archaeological landscapes over the past 6,000 years in the western Pacific Ocean gives us geophysical data to interpret sea level change of as much as two meters above present. At the same time, these landscapes have archaeological data toward understanding adaptive human settlement and subsistence during this period of dynamic colonization of the region from Asia and Island Southeast Asia. Human seafarers first explored the region around 3,500 years ago at a time when sea levels were changing worldwide and new shorelines were being exposed. Sea levels around the globe have ranged from 60 meters above present to 130 meters below present over the past 120,000 years. 2,000 to 5,500 years ago they rose nearly two meters above present, and in the course of that rise and fall created the coral reef atolls of the central and western Pacific Ocean. The low islands provided a mosaic of settlement opportunities for maritime peoples in the region, and contributed to a resilient ocean-going lifeway for the past 2,000 years. Now, the region is facing a rise of 1-2 meters over the next 50 years that will drown these islands. Archaeological and ethnographic studies demonstrate the relatively recent settlement and the emergence of a distinctive early Micronesian Village based on sophisticated navigational knowledge, a dispersed matrilineal clan system that enabled wide-ranging settlement, and a 'transported landscape' of cultigens and hybridized varieties. Coastal studies demonstrate that prior sea level changes may have been punctuated and dramatic. This may portend similarly sudden shifts over the next 50-100 years that will be catastrophic for the Micronesian lifeway as well as destructive of the islands themselves. Migration *from* the islands rather than *among* the islands is the likely course of the next few decades. Sea level change molded landscapes creating possibilities and constraints in the past, and now threaten to do so for the near future. Landscape Archaeology studies can help illuminate both the physical changes and adaptive human responses. Perhaps these lessons will provide understanding toward guiding future human responses in the region.

Introduction

School children in the Marshall Islands of the Pacific Ocean in eastern Micronesia (Figure 1) are given a lesson in environmental education from the vantage point of a canoe sliding above sandy shoals offshore from the capital city of Majuro. Beneath them is the ghostly form of a former island that had risen above the seas 50 years ago with coconut trees (personal communication, Tony de Brum, 2013). In the past five decades high tides have already begun to cover low islands and have made many others uninhabitable from brackish water intrusion into the fresh water lenses and drowning of gardening patches in the island centers. In the next five decades most low Pacific Islands may be submerged completely. The low atoll islands formed from collapsing volcanic seamounts that form an arc around the former caldera. As they were sinking, at the same time the sea has risen from as low as 130 meters in the last full glacial period, 22,000 years ago. As temperatures climbed, glaciers melted and the sea rose to nearly two meters above present sea level in the period from 5,500 to 2,000 years ago. During that time the low atoll islands of the Pacific formed coral reefs atop the calderas. As sea level declined to modern levels, the coral reef platforms were above water by two meters and gradually anchored coconut and other tropical island vegetation. By 2,000 years ago they were fully emergent and habitable by maritime peoples who began to settle them after that time. Today these islands are at risk from sea level that may rise as much as one to two meters in the next 50 years, and perhaps even more catastrophically over the next 100 years (IPCC 2013). This dramatic change is the consensus prediction of climate scientists studying human-induced climate change. The people of the Marshall Islands and others in the Pacific are migrating to higher islands and to the US Mainland, where already many Marshall Islanders reside in northern Arkansas where they are employed by chicken processing plants. Archaeological investigations in Guam, Saipan, and throughout the western Pacific assess the geomorphic evidence of sea level rise and punctuated fall from 5,500 to 3,000 to 2,000 years ago, as well as the history of human settlement that began about 3,500 years ago in the islands and then accelerated and expanded around 2,000 years ago when atolls emerged above sea level and offered thousands of habitable islands for settlement. Studies of the Togcha site in Guam, the Susupe site in Saipan, and the Charterhouse site in Tumon Bay, Guam document the occupational history of the region in the face of prior climate change and offer a model for future vulnerability and pathways for resilience for the very near future of the islands. Recent investigations in shoreline contexts have contributed to models of shoreline evolution as well as human settlement from as early as 3,500 years ago on high islands, and after 2,000 years ago on low islands. Recent observations

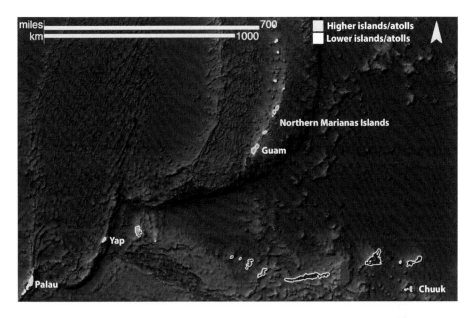

Figure 1. Area locator map (http://upload.wikimedia.org/wikipedia/commons/b/b0/
Micronesian_Cultural_Area.png).

of high spring tides, encroaching brackish water in aquifers, and flooding during heavy seas and extreme weather demonstrate that residency is threatened and that likely within decades these fragile islands and their cultures will be extirpated.

Several small and independent projects have formed the basis for interpretations drawn for this paper, beginning with discoveries at the Pago Village on the east coast of Guam where a large land development provided an opportunity to examine the village as well as its surround. Two other projects, one in Saipan to the north of Guam at the Susupe Marsh, and another at Togcha Bay south of Pago provided evidence from buried terrain for punctuated rather than gradual terrain evolution that might serve as a model for future impacts from climate change. Extreme storm events, rapid sea level change, and generally increasing aridity might be the future norms in an uncertain climate future. The record of the past few thousand years illustrates the often rapid and dramatic landscape events that shaped the present and that will likely shape the future settlement of the region.

The Early Micronesian Village

The low islands of Micronesia are scattered throughout the western Pacific atop ancient volcanic ridges and collapsed calderas. When sea level was nearly two meters above present, shallow coral reefs formed along the rims of the calderas in the Marshall Islands and among the outer islands of Chuuk and Yap. As sea level declined episodically over the next few millennia, land surfaces two meters above present sea level emerged and formed substrates for vegetation and, later, human habitation. The first pioneering plants were ocean borne and brought by birds, but on the arrival of humans plants with economic importance were introduced such as coconuts, breadfruit, taro, yams, and likely also swidden grains like millet and rice. Anderson described this as a 'transported landscape' that included varieties that constituted the *habitus* for island dwellers and village lifeways (Anderson 2005).

The high islands of the western Pacific had been emergent for millions of years, but it was only after 2,000 years ago that the low islands or atolls were above water level. As sea levels dropped nearly two meters to modern levels, atolls were exposed and began to accumulate material from the lagoons that washed and blew upslope and formed beach sand ramps above the coral reef skeleton (Dickinson 2014). These eventually protected lenses of fresh water that 'floated' above brackish intrusive seawater and provided the fresh water needed for subsistence and taro farming. Rainfall fed these Ghyben-Herzberg lenses, providing freshwater in a delicate balance of resources for habitation.

Following exposure the islands became part of an extensive network or mosaic of settlement opportunities for maritime navigators (Petersen 2009). Matrilineal clan organization provided a framework for cooperation in the region, whereby navigators would be welcomed to kin settlements, and affiliated kin-based villages occasionally sheltered whole communities who were displaced by typhoons and other disasters. The system was also supported by development of new hybrid breadfruit varieties as the *Artocarpus altilis* variety from New Guinea that was transported into Polynesia was crossed with *Artocapus mariennensis* to produce salt tolerant, short season, and seedless varieties that were highly adapted to low island terrain. This along with a village agroforestry environment including also banana, coconut, *Noni*, and other perennials was supplemented with taro and yams (Petersen 2009; Peterson 2009).

Navigational Knowledge

Micronesia is a vast Pacific Ocean speckled with islands. As Micronesians say, the sea connects them rather than separates them. There is no question that the deep knowledge of maritime navigation was the mechanism linking these disparate islands that covered an area as vast as the continental United States, over 2,000 by 1,000 miles in area. Rock art in the Ritidian caverns on Guam has preserved a map of stellar knowledge to be shared among navigators, and many navigators use a stick frame device as a teaching tool for young navigators. The lore is transmitted orally and includes not only daily solar observations and nightly stellar observations, but also reading of ocean currents and swells (Goetzfridt 1982). One navigator, Manny Sikau, a master of the craft, described moments during an 800 mile voyage from an atoll in Chuuk to Guam. When the swells were faint he had to lie out on the outrigger and dangle his scrotum beneath him to pick up the rhythm of the swells that would carry him to Guam (Sikau, personal communication, 2008). When the Hokulea was reconstructed in Hawaii to explore seafaring traditions among Hawaiians, the sponsors recruited a navigator from the outer islands of Yap to teach them the craft. Mau Piailug from Satawal joined the Hokulea project and shared the Micronesian knowledge of navigation for the successful 1976 voyage from Hawaii to Tahiti (Finney 2003).

Archaeological Landscapes

Guam and the Marianas are known from the historical record from relatively early Spanish contact. Ferdinand Magellan's sea-wracked expedition nearly foundered on its shores after many weeks at sea without provisions. They stayed briefly, determined to cruise on toward the China trade and the Moluccas' spices. By the late 17th century a permanent if fitful Jesuit mission was established and numerous Spanish accounts describe the people, the island, and their lifeways.

Moore (2005) reviews the literature from Spanish and other exploration of Guam and the Marianas, as well as investigations of agricultural fields and cultigens in Guam and the Marianas. The most informative account is from Juan Pobre who lived in Rota in 1602, and reported that 'a variety of roots and tubers was planted in plots located in the hills some distance away from the coastal villages, and people living on the coast traded or exchanged fish for the agricultural products grown by people living in the interior' (Driver 1989:21). Upland taro and other yams, including Dagu (*Dioscorea alata*) were also grown on these plots.

Following Spanish introduction sweet potato (*Ipomoea batatas*)(Moore 2005:104) was also grown. American and French visitors commented that yams and taro were planted extensively in local as well as remote patches of arable land, and also that wild yams, including a variety of spiny yam, were found in 'dry areas with deep soil'(Moore 2005:105). Yams were often piled in fields for storage. Moore argues that stone piles or mounds found in fields may have served as a platform for this storage feature. Agricultural fields have not been well-documented in Guam and the Marianas or throughout Micronesia. Most appear, however, to be expedient swidden fields. Mounding is a common practice. This produces fine tilth to enhance tuber growth. Stone is often found on fields either as mulches or as platforms for yams and sweet potatoes. Low density charcoal, pottery and marine shell is also commonly reported. These may have been used either as mulch or as soil additives to improve tilth and fertility.

In Pago Bay on Guam a large area archaeological project allowed us to examine an extended horticultural landscape around a core village area (Carson and Peterson 2010). The village occupied a low bench above the sea on a gentle hillslope away from the base of a steep cliff behind the village. An area roughly 10 acres in size, in a narrow strip at the base of the steeper slope, was identified as a potential agricultural field. The field area has a gentle slope of 3-5%, and is variably from 30 to 80 m wide. Dozens of rock features were found scattered throughout the field. These consisted of fist-sized stones in windrows roughly 3-4 m wide and 5-8 m long. The stone features were ovate in shape. The stones were unconformably above the A Horizon of the Guam-Saipan complex soil terrain.

Surface erosion from exposure of topsoil and also from increased storm runoff from occasionally denuded slopes uphill have degraded the terrain of the agricultural field. It is difficult to determine the extent of soil loss but appears to have been moderate to severe in some areas. Even so, several inches of arable soil remains today, and was probably appreciably more before modern development of the site. The stone mounds appear to be slightly pedestalled, indicating resistance to sheet erosion. This also suggests that the use of the field was probably not recent, but rather was within the era that thickened-rim latte period sherds were being deposited on the fields.

A radiocarbon sample was collected from 25-35 cm below ground surface from top of Bt (argillic) Horizon in the soil. The collection location was about 70 ft above sea level, 100 m inland, and on a 5-7% slope. The sample was collected from a 1 by 1 m excavation unit exposure profile. A series of paleoenvironmental samples for pollen, phytolith, and starch residue analyses was also collected from this profile. The radiocarbon age (Beta-249673) was of bulk carbon in a one-liter sample of soil matrix. The conventional age of 2110 ± 40 calibrated most likely in the range of 210-30 B.C.

This age reflects the average age of the soil at depth and is a useful estimate of the period of soil formation. It does not date the archaeological use of the field. The high 13C/12C ratio (-20.8 ‰) suggests C4 pathway or carbon derived from arboreal sources. This could either have been naturally decaying trees or burned trees or midden clearing of natural fires. In any case, it is probably not related to the period of agricultural use of the field which appears to be much later in the late latte period, ca. 500 ybp.

Soil formation in the period ca. 2,000 ybp is suggestive of equitable climate during that period. This estimate conforms with expectations from other sources and other paleoclimate proxies. This will be discussed later in the analysis of soil paleoenvironmental samples collected from the Pago River floodplain. Paleoenvironmental sampling of the fields was done in 10 cm levels. Seven samples from the profile were analyzed along with scrapings from three sherds just below ground surface.

In November 2008 National Park Service staff from Historical Preservation Offices in Micronesia visited MARC and Guam to assist with field archaeological studies and crosstraining. Roque Magofna, Tommy Leon Guerrero, and Diego Camacho conducted 1 x 1 m unit excavations in the agricultural field site in upper Pago Bay. Without prompting or foreknowledge, Diego Camacho identified the terrain of the field as typical of *gaddo'* farming in Saipan. He pointed to the depth of the soil in a roadcut exposure, to the relatively level slope, and placement at the base of a steeper slope as typical of good terrain for yam farming.

After seeing the rock mounds and the field, Roque Magofna and Tommy Leon Guerrero offered that their grandparents had used rocks and hibiscus leaves (*Hibiscus tiliaceae*) as soil building materials. Mixing the rock and leaves improved tilth and promoted fatter yams while the leaves also contributed fertility. Occasional burning of the fields contributed charcoal and easily incorporated plant nutrients such as phosphorous and potash that was liberated by the burning.

Mud samples were collected from a backhoe trench excavated 100 meters from the Pago River wetland, and 100 meters from its confluence with Pago Bay. The samples were collected from 100 to 250 cm below ground surface. These strata were all wet, mucky dark organic soil. There did not appear to be intact structure, and examination of pollen, phytoliths, and starch residues as well as the radiocarbon ages of the deposits demonstrate that the entire column was repeatedly mixed and disturbed. Nonetheless, this disturbance appears to have been within the period A.D. 1000–1200.

Radiocarbon ages of two samples from 120 cm and 250 cm depth were in the same age range. At 120 cm depth the conventional age was 930 ± 40 (calibrated A.D. 1020-1190) (Beta-253678). The conventional age of the sample at 250 cm depth was 850 ± 40 (calibrated A.D. 1040-1280) (Beta-253677). The 13C/12C ratio suggests C4 pathway, or carbon from arboreal forest (-25.2 and -25.5 ‰ respectively).

Results of pollen, phytolith, and starch residue analyses were revealing of a mangrove – estuarine environment from the period A.D. 1000-1200 in samples from 120, 150, 200, and 250 cm depth. Breadfruit, taro (pollen, raphides, and tissue), mangrove, coconut, *lycopodium* (fern), pandanus, sedges, and grass pollen were found in most of the samples. All samples had abundant charcoal particles.

The uppermost sample from 100 cm had a very recent radiocarbon age of 107.9+/- 0.4 pMC, indicating the material was living in the last 50 years. Horrocks found a pollen type of *Fabaceae* which he interpreted as a very recent introduction, possibly *Verbenaceae*. The radiocarbon age and the intrusive species indicate that from 100 cm and upward the soil was rapidly cumulic and recent.

Contextual, morphological, soils, radiocarbon, and paleoenvironmental data support the observation that agricultural fields were developed for farming of *gaddo'* yams in the upper Pago Bay settlement. The setting at the base of the steeper slopes leading upward to Yona is a unique catchment for runoff rainfall and soil nutrients and sediments. The results of the paleosediment studies in both the agricultural field and near the Pago Bay wetland demonstrate the diverse and varied subsistence agricultural base of Chamorro residents of Pago Bay (Figure 2). The wetland environment and upstream habitat in the Pago River supplied arboricultural foods such as breadfruit, coconut, and, of course a variety of mangrove species of marine shellfish and fish. Disturbance of upstream habitat demonstrated by abundance of charcoal and grass pollen indicate a managed landscape. Taro was grown in the Pago River and also possibly in freshwater near the estuary. More attention needs to be given to riverine catchments in Guam to identify taro pondfields or enhancements in the channel that promote slack water for taro cultivation. The evidence from this project indicates that taro was present in that environment. In contrast, the dry uplands in the agricultural field supported yam domestication, at least in the later contact period or immediate post-contact era. Horrocks found European cheno-am pollen even in the lowest deposits in the agricultural field (30-40 cm depth) indicating mixing in the soil column, but also demonstrating post-Contact use and disturbance of the soil. The radiocarbon, soils, and paleoenvironmental evidence support a diverse range of cultigens in the local environment as well as possibly two periods of equable climate, in the periods 2,000 ybp and also A.D. 1000 to 1200. These accord with regional expectations, and would have been beneficent periods for soil development as well as subsistence horticulture and agriculture.

Climate change and its effects on rainfall, sea level, winds and weather have had a salutary effect on the islands, especially since 2,000 years ago when many atolls were emergent above falling sea levels. New land was exposed for farming,

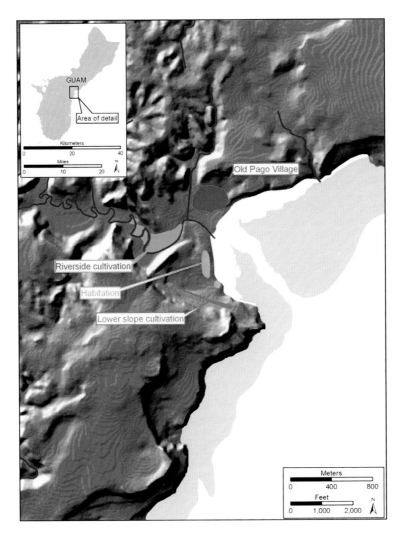

Figure 2. Pago Bay showing village, yam fields, taro pondfield terrain, and coastal resource zone (adapted from Carson and Peterson 2010).

new islands were formed to connect settlements scattered across the Pacific, and beneficent weather patterns led to formation of stable soils throughout the last two millennia. Coastal conditions changed throughout this period as well, with sea level draw-down exposing large areas of former coral reef and lagoon habitat. Mangrove swamps that favored the brackish water in river mouths were stranded and diminished in area, along with the molluscan and other food sources that nourished previous settlements. The shift toward more land-based subsistence could have been a response to a decline in marine molluscs in the reef lagoons and (Carson 2014). Likely pelagic species were less abundant also as mangrove habitat serves as the nursery of deeper ocean fish. Mangrove forests respond very slowly to perturbation and draw-down of sea level would have had long-lasting effects along the coastal zones of Micronesian islands. Previous climate change in the past few thousand years has clearly controlled settlement and subsistence in the western Pacific with a variety of often complex and contradictory effects.

Coastal landforms and Punctuated Changes

The general picture over the past 6,000 years is of sea level that overtopped modern levels at the end of a long-term sea level rise from late full glacial conditions 22,000 years ago, to relatively more rapid sea level rise through 8,000 years ago, resulting in a stable high-stand of 1.8 meters above present sea level for a period of approximately 3,000 years ago, until ca. 4,200 years ago, when sea level appears to have fallen from its maximum, to 3,000 years ago, when it may have fallen as much as a meter, to a period of about 2,000 years ago when sea level appears to have fallen another one meter, to a period of about 1,000 year ago when sea level appears to have risen about one meter, then fallen again about 5-700 years ago during a period of apparently catastrophic climate events and impacts on both upland and coastal terrain.

The western Pacific was impacted by eustatic changes in sea level for hundreds of thousands of years, rising to 6 meters above present in the last interglacial period, then falling to 130 meters below present sea level during the last full glacial period, about 22,000 years ago; then rising dramatically again up to 5,500 years ago, then falling again in bursts about 3,000 and 2,000 years ago. Present indicators are that sea level is rising again worldwide in response to climate change. In the islands of the western Pacific this has been especially significant as the low islands, consisting of coral atolls, were emergent only after 2,000 years ago at present sea level, and were submerged during the period of high still stand 2,000 to 5,500 years ago (Dickinson 2000; 2003; 2014).

Changes in sea level had a dramatic impact on human settlement of the western Pacific. Sundaland, for example, in what is now Island Southeast Asia, shrunk from an extensive landmass connecting the region to islands with vastly greater shoreline. This change occurred over the last 20,000 years, but was most pronounced in the last 8,000 years. Islands that were linked by land were now connected by sea and were awash in a 'sea of islands.' Human adaptations to the region included the invention of outrigger canoes with lateen sails that were highly effective at traversing these seascapes; transported landscapes of domesticated plants and animals provided the resource base for extensive and dispersive settlement; and matrilineal and matrifocal social organization provided the structure for rapid and highly successful sea migration beginning 3,000 to 3,500 years ago in the region. The Mariana Islands were settled around 3,400 years ago; the Lapita florescence in near Oceania began about the same time and then spread eastward over the next few hundred years.

Landscapes in Guam have been documented that provide evidence for these changes. In Tumon Bay on Guam a relict shoreline with an organic drape was discovered about 70 meters from the present shoreline (Figure 3). The radiocarbon age of the organic drape was found to be calibrated AD 120 – 350 (Beta-239574),

Figure 3. Relict shoreline ramp. Algal mat on ramp dated to AD 120-350 cal.

demonstrating progradation from this relict beach no earlier than 2,000 years ago. The terrain model for Tumon Bay shows the relict foreshore to the right at AD 100 – 350, with a later, Latte Period, settlement on the emergent shoreline in the era AD 1100 – 170. The high stand line in this graphic should be adjusted upward above the AD 100 – 300 beach.

Radiocarbon ages from the Tumon Bay document these transitions from dates of Latte Period archaeological deposits at the top of this figure, the relict foreshore (4th and 5th from the top, charcoal dates), and also from dates of *Halimeda* spp algae that have carbonate tests that form a flaky, coarse-grained sand if relatively recently deposited before burial from other sediments in the reef lagoon (Peterson and Carson 2009). These two dates are therefore dating the period of formation of the reef lagoon and help to bracket the shoreline.

Recent coring studies at Lake Huguangyanmaar in South China provide paleoenvironmental proxy data that is applicable as anti-correlational data for modeling climate change in the western Pacific. The cores show varves with titanium deposition from wind-blown soils eroded from northern continental Asia. These were deposited during dry, cold conditions in the north but were anti-correlational to periods of strong East Asian monsoons. Beneficent and wet conditions in the north correlated with golden ages in north China; wet, extensive southwest monsoons in the western Pacific correlate with periods of migration and climate stability in the western Pacific (Liu et al. 2000, Yancheva et al. 2007).

These shoreline models for Guam demonstrate the effects of changing eustatic sea level on the Pacific Islands during periods of global change reflected in the Huguangyanmaar core sequence. Another set of paleoenvironmental markers for the region is paleosols. Pedogenesis would have been favored during long periods of wet monsoon and relatively equable conditions. The southwest monsoon furthers these conditions in the region.

In Guam, dating of paleosols mirrors these periods of climate stability documented in the Huguangyanmaar sediments. At a soil underlying the yam field at Pago Bay, as discussed earlier, the age of the soil was around 2,000 years ago, with calibrated ages in the early years of this warm, wet period, around 210 to 340 B.C (Carson and Peterson 2010). Another paleosol was found in the upper shoreline terrain of Ypan, Guam, and also dates from that period. Another paleosol found exposed in a backhoe trench in the floodplain of the Pago River has been documented in the range of 1,000 to 1,200 years ago, coeval with another warm, wet period known worldwide as the little climatic optimum, or LCO. At Togcha River near Talafofo, Guam, results of radiocarbon dating of paleosols developing ca. 2,000 years ago were documented in a chronostratigraphic sequence in southeastern Guam. The Huguangyanmaar Lake data correlates very closely with the paleosol ages from Guam, as well as with the shoreline data from sea level change.

People who settled the expanse of the western Pacific 3,500 + years ago apparently surfed these good periods with a westerly Asian Warm Pool and a stable southwest monsoon, as evidence of human settlement in the region attest. Significant change in populations and culture occurred in or around these periods, ca 3,400 years ago, 2,000 years ago, 1,200 to 1,300 years ago, and 1,000 to 800 years ago. Archaeological evidence also supports a migration in the period 2,000 years ago when atolls in Micronesia and elsewhere in the tropics would have been emergent and habitable. These movements probably began to circulate westward and northward with more interaction in the western Pacific from Polynesia and the Solomons into the eastern Carolines. New migrations or contact with the Philippines over several periods are also evident in the archaeological record.

Two recent archaeological projects in Guam and in Saipan illustrate how archaeological data can be very robust for interpreting the character of climate change. At Susupe Lake on Saipan analysis of an archaeological excavation unit and of core samples collected from the lake contributed to an interpretation of rapid climate change and sea level changes and impacts in an isolated embayment (Figures 4-6) . Lake Susupe is presently a freshwater marsh located a few hundred

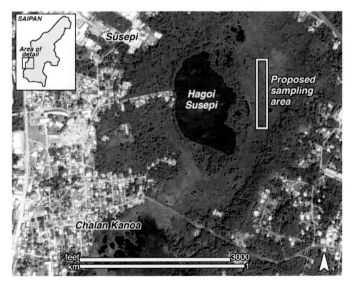

Figure 4. Susupe Marsh on Saipan, Northern Mariana Islands.

meters from the ocean, but at one time, nearly 1000 years ago, it was open to the sea and was brackish water mangrove habitat. Prior to that it was alternately fresh and brackish water as sea level fell and rose, flooding the freshwater lake. A previous study conducted by Athens and Ward (1999) documented the middle and late Holocene paleoenvironmental history of the lake. In their interpretation the changes were gradual and very longterm. Current investigations illustrate the dramatic and punctuated character of both sea level and climate change in the region.

In the course of analyzing sediment cores from wetlands on Guam and the Marianas, Athens presented the finding that charcoal began appearing in the core samples in strata that he identified as 4,000 to 4,400 ybp (Athens and Ward 1999; 2005). This charcoal, he reasoned, was from fires that could not have been from natural sources, as the pollen data from his cores confirmed that the potential natural vegetation of Guam was tropical forest. Therefore fire implied human intervention. However, recent investigations of charcoal in archaeological sites demonstrate that charcoal in the range less than 60-200 microns, as Athens reported from the pollen slides analyzed in his project, are most likely aerosol and possibly from hundreds of miles distant (Théry-Parisot et al.2010). If this was the case, then possibly the 4,000 years old charcoal was consistent with a severe period of drought in Eastern Asia. This was proposed by Liu and Feng (2012) consistent with paleoclimatic data as well as significant cultural changes during the buildup to the earliest period of urban and proto-state settlements in China. Walled towns, paddy-rice farming, and shared ceramic styles emerged following this period of extended aridity. The aerosol charcoal found in sediments 1,500 miles eastward in the Mariana Islands could have been blown from mainland Asia during this period. Global climate change processes in the broader region had significant impacts on Guam even at great distance.

Periodic drought has profound impacts on island landscapes from local as well as distant events. In the core records from Susupe very distinct breaks in sediment can be seen (Figure 5). The excavation unit that was placed near the shores of the modern marsh illustrate this disjunctive deposition and radiocarbon ages demonstrate that changes can be sudden and dramatic. A prolonged drought, for example, followed by a typhoon, is especially erosive as the dry soil cannot absorb the moisture and is easily eroded. Storm surges likewise can transport lagoonal materials onshore and form deep sudden deposits; at the same time mass wastage from upslope can redeposit materials rapidly over lower terrain. Recent excavation at Lake Susupe above the southwest shore documents beach rock dating to ca. A.D. 1200 at an elevation '3-5 feet' above mean sea level, buried under 70 cm of poorly consolidated slump that appears to have undergone incipient pedogenesis, also dating to A.D. 1200-1300 (Figure 6). These radiocarbon ages demonstrate rapid and deep deposition. According to Athens model for linear interpolation, these deposits should have been 4.3 – 4.8 meters below the lake surface of Lake Susupe. Rather, they are from the lake surface elevation up to 50 cm above. (Peterson and Acabado 2012). The calcium carbonate beach rock formation within a meter of the present ground surface is evidence of an earlier shoreline formation at this

Figure 5. Continuous core samples from Athens core at Susupe Marsh showing unconformities in deposition in the sediments.

SUSUPE SOUTHWEST PROFILE

0 - 20cm bgs

Course unsorted calcareous gravel and pebbles in fine dark gray clay (7.5 Y/R 3/3)
• Thick VST Latte period sherds
• Basalt net sinker
• Anadara shell
• Apple snail
• Japanese bottles - late pre-war
• U.S. mess kit next to unit on ground surface

20 - 40cm bgs

Lighter yellow/tan clay,
C Horizon of soil (7.5 Y/R 6/6) contacted at 30cm, continuous with dark gray clay A Horizon.

40 - 70cm bgs

C Horizon, as above.

70cm bgs

Calcrete, beach rock.

RADIO CARBON AGES

Beta - 317068
(organic sediment)

cal AD 1295 - 1404
Bulk soil carbon,
30 - 40cm bgs

Beta - 310769
(organic sediment)

cal AD 1224 - 1297
Bulk soil carbon,
50 - 60cm bgs

Beta - 317067
(organic sediment)

cal AD 1295 - 1404
Organic sludge in niche on beach rock

Beta - 317066
(carbonate)

cal AD 1291 - 1442
Calcrete - from top of beach rock

Beta - 317070
(marine shell)

cal AD 611 - 858
Anadara on beach rock

Figure 6. UOG-NPS shovel test trench in the vicinity of Lake Susupe.

elevation that is now perched well above the sea level at which it formed two millennia earlier.

The Togcha Shoreline on Guam: a late Holocene record

The punctuated and dramatic impacts of climate change are also illustrated by a project conducted in southeastern Guam near the Togcha River (Figures 7-9). This small data recovery excavation provides an excellent frame for study of the entire known period of human settlement on Guam, from the earliest associated with the high still-stand ca. 5500-3000 ybp represented by the fine-grained beach sand deposits at the base of the unit; through a period of progradation with seaward retreat of the shoreline, but intermittent storm surge depositing large clasts on the upper beach strand. This latter period included a period of soil formation representing some stability in the upper beach zone, but still subject to intense storm surge deposition. Finally, a long period of stability appears to have ensued wherein overbank flooding of the Togcha contributed the majority of sediments in the form of highland soils that were degrading, possibly from human disturbance of the upland terrain for swidden farming.

In this excavation a fine-grained carbonate sand was found at the base of the unit dating to the period 3200 ybp. Beneath sand an *Anadara* shell (brackish water mollusk) dated to 3400 ybp, demonstrating earlier mangrove habitat in the vicinity that was then covered by the fine-grained beach sand. A red-slipped pottery sherd lay immediately above the fine beach sand, indicative of the period of human occupation that has been documented at early sites throughout the Mariana Islands. Above the fine sand is a zone of deposition of much larger clasts indicating rapid burial of the shoreline, perhaps by storm surge in one storm

Figure 7. Togcha Bridge location on Guam.

event. Higher levels show that the river began to control this local environment by overbank deposits and formation of a cumulic soil that formed a paleosol, dating to as early as 2400 ybp. This coincides with a period of stable weather conditions in the western Pacific that was sufficient to lead to long-term pedogenesis, and also coincides with the global trends documented at the Huguangyanmaar core in southern China that documents coeval trends on the East Asia mainland. Along with its support for parallel climatic events throughout the region, the Togcha deposits also point to the often punctuated character of change. Climate change is not necessarily a long, gradual process.

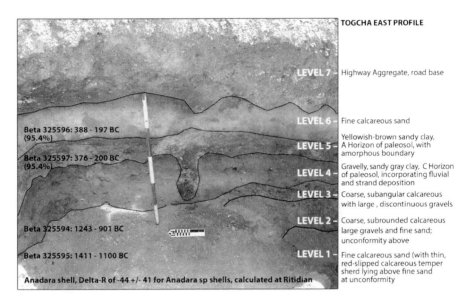

Figure 8. Togcha Bridge excavation profile and radiocarbon dates.

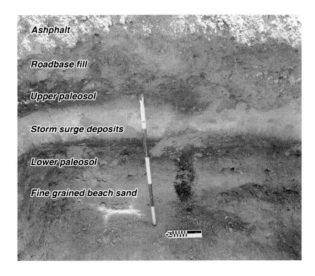

Figure 9. Interpretive profile of guardrail installation at the Togcha Data Recovery Unit.

The knowledge obtained from current investigations demonstrates that the impacts of climate change are often dramatic and punctuated, and that they are interactive with other components of the environment. For example, intense rainfall, storm surge from typhoons, sea level and periodic tidal currents may interact and produce greater impacts on coastal terrain. If periodic drought from increased ambient air temperatures decreases infiltration of precipitation, the effects of intense rainfall are increased also. The anticipated effects of climate change are therefore synergistic and a combination of effects may be more damaging than any one of them alone.

Esta: Contemporary Change, Predictive Models

The western Pacific has been impacted by the effects of climate change throughout the late Holocene and the period of human settlement in the region. This is demonstrated by the studies of village landscapes, marsh deposition, and shoreline evolution discussed above. The processes follow global trends (IPCC 2013, Yancheva et al. 2007) with demonstrable local impacts. While atmospheric trends may be regional, sea level rise is eustatic around the globe. Its impacts and processes are well-documented from the Arctic to the western Pacific, with local differences based on geoid processes in the bulge of oceanic waters responding to geological pressures (Dickinson 2003; Nunn 2007; Tornqvist, and Hijma 2012). In the western Pacific, for example, the range of sea level rise in the China Sea and along the China coast was more pronounced and in the range of several meters (Rolett et al. 2011, Mitrovica and Milne 2002) while in Guam it was closer to the global, or eustatic, average of 1.8 meters from about 6000 to 2000 years ago. The punctuated character of sea level draw-down is also evident from global data, but is seen very dramatically in landforms excavated in Guam.

The settlement of Oceania in the vast western Pacific consisted of small parties of navigators sailing upwind against the prevailing trade winds, then downwind to home. They were travelling in a period of relatively stable weather and climate, following a period of climate distress in the region 4,000 years ago. Steady exploration over centuries led to landfalls in the Marianas around 3,500 years ago, and in the southern Pacific in the Solomons around 3,000-3,200 years ago. However, around 3,000 and especially after 2,000 years ago settlement intensified and began to appear on atolls that had been submerged before these episodic periods of emergence 3,000 and 2,000 years ago. The earliest documented settlement on low islands or atolls is after 2,000 years ago. For the past two millennia they have been home to maritime people who first adapted to the changing coastal and marine resources of the region, but who eventually brought with them a 'portmanteau' or 'transported landscape' that led to village gardens with taro and yam and breadfruit and coconut to expand their diets and their use of the landscape. These landscapes and current sea level have been relatively stable for the past 1,000 years, but as global temperatures increase atmospheric climate will change and sea level will rise again. Since 1950 average global surface temperature has risen 0.8 degrees Centigrade; the significant changes in sea level over the past 6,000 years responded to changes in the range of ocean-surface cooling of 0.5-2.0 degrees Centigrade (Montaggioni et al. 2006). Recent climate models predict such changes by 2100 or possibly as early as 2050 A.D (IPCC 2013). The extreme predictions that include scenarios of ice mass collapses in West Antarctica or Greenland are in the range six meters of very sudden sea level rise globally.

Climate change forecasts for the western Pacific have a high degree of uncertainty (IPCC 2013), largely because the region affects other major global patterns and because of a lack of data from the region. Warmer air temperatures however in the range of 1-2 degrees centigrade, Sea Surface Temperatures increasing by a similar amount, and higher acidity from absorption of carbon dioxide are the likely effects within the next 50 years. Expanding mass from rising temperatures along with glacial melt may increase sea level by as much as 1-2 meters during this period, and extreme weather events will likely magnify the impact of greater sea levels. Rainfall may increase, and most of this will be in big events like typhoons. These heavy rains contribute to significant erosion leading to sedimentation of coral reefs. Rising sea levels, increasing acidity and turbidity, and warming seas will lead to the demise of coral reefs worldwide. Bleaching events are already catastrophic, and are increasingly devastating; by 2030 coral polyps may be unable to produce calcium carbonate to build colonies because of rising acidity in marine environments. These dire predictions are supported by a wealth of research worldwide, and foretell a

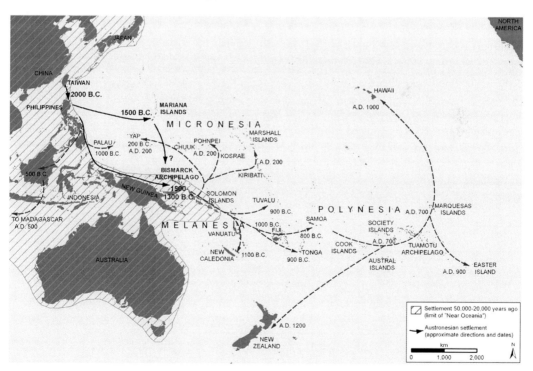

Figure 10. Chronology of Oceanic settlement migration in western Pacific, from Carson and Kurashina, 2012, article in "World Archaeology". Low islands settlement post-dated 200 A.D., or nearly 2,000 years ago after draw-down of sea level made islands habitable.

catastrophic future for the region. By 2050 most of the low islands of Micronesia may be uninhabitable, and by 2100 they may be mostly submerged.

Of course, small islands are not the only settlements at risk from rising sea level. All coastal residents worldwide will face inundation, storm surge, and intrusion of brackish water as well as eventual submergence of coastal terrain. This is not an idle speculation, but is demonstrated by the historical changes that have been preserved and can be seen in the landscapes of western Pacific islands. The effects are possibly more pronounced however, as the area also is affected by regular changes in sea level and storm activity from ENSO and Inter-tropical Convergence zone patterns. Already islanders on Kiribati in the southern realm of Micronesia have arranged a lease of an offshore Fijian Island as a refuge. Migration to Guam from the low islands of Yap and Chuuk is increasing steadily, and Guam is ill-prepared to absorb the social support needs for these migrants. Marshall Islanders are migrating to Hawaii and to northwest Arkansas where they have found employment in chicken processing factories. As Tony deBrum, Minister of Environment for the Marshall Islands recounts, one in eight frozen chickens sold in America is touched by a Marshall Islander (personal communication, 2013).

Preservation of the islands is possibly beyond us, but preservation of culture, language, and social networks may still be possible, perhaps using some of the same adaptive practices such as extended and dispersed matrilineal clan networks that sustained these Pacific cultures for millennia. As Marshall Islanders and others on low islands throughout the world protest that they did not make these problems, nonetheless the industrial societies that are largely responsible will have to be prepared to accommodate their migrating populations. The first world however, will be facing equally intransigent and monumental adjustments to the effects of climate change, possibly in the form of patterns of continental drought. As climate change observers like Stewart Brand (2009) and James Lovelock (2009) predict, it might be oceanic islands that in the long run hold the greatest opportunity for cultural and physical survival. While the low islands will sink, the high islands with volcanic uplifts might hold the seeds for human survival as *refugia* from catastrophic climate change.

References

Anderson, Atholl. 2005. Subpolar settlement in South Polynesia. Antiquity 79:791-800.

Athens, J. Stephen and Jerome V. Ward. 1999. Paleoenvironment, Vegetation and Landscape Change on Guam: The Laguas Core, Chapter V in Archaeological Inventory Survey of the Sasa Valley and Tenjo Vista Fuel Tank Farms, Piti District, Territory of Guam, Mariana Islands, by Boyd Dixon, J. Stephen Athens, Jerome V. Ward, Tina Mangieri, and Timothy Reith, pp. 121-151. Report prepared for Dept. of the Navy, Pacific Division, Naval Facilities Engineering Command, Pearl Harbor, Hawaii. International Archaeological Research Insitute, Inc.

Athens, J. Stephen and Jerome V. Ward. 2005. Holocene Paleoenvironment of Saipan: Analysis of a Core from Lake Susupe. Prepared for Division of Historic Preservation, Department of Community and Cultural Affairs, CNMI, Saipan, by International Archaeological Research Insitutie, Inc., Honolulu.

Brand, Stewart. 2009. *Whole Earth Discipline: An Ecopragmatist Manifesto*, Viking Adult, New York.

Carson, Mike T. 2014. *First Settlement of Remote Oceania: Earliest Sites in the Mariana Islands*. Springer, New York.

Carson, Mike T. and Kurashina, Hiro. 2012. Re-envisioning long-distance Oceanic migration: early dates in the Mariana Islands. *World Archaeology* 44(3):409-435.

Carson, Mike T. and John A. Peterson. 2010. Archaeological Research at the Laguna Pago Bay Resort, Lots 155 NEW, 164 NEW, and 164-4, Yona Municipality Guam. Prepared for Pago Bay Resort, L.L.C. and the Guam Historical Preservation Office.

Dickinson, William. 2000. Hydro-isostatic and tectonic influences on emergent Holocene paleoshorelines in the Mariana Islands, western Pacific Ocean. *Journal of Coastal Research*, 16, 735–746.

Dickinson, William. 2003. Impact of mid-Holocene hydro-isostatic highstand in regional sea level on habitability of islands in Pacific Oceania. *Journal of Coastal Research*, 19, 489-502.

Dickinson, William. 2014. Beach Ridges as Favored Locales for Human Settlement on Pacific Islands. *Geoarcheology* Volume 29, Issue 3, pp. 249-267, May/June.

Driver, Marjorie. 1989. Fray Juan Pobre in the Marianas 1602. *Miscellaneous Series 8*. Micronesian Area Research Center, University of Guam, Mangilao.

Finney, Ben. 2003. *Sailing in the Wake of the Ancestors: Reviving Polynesian Voyaging*. Honolulu: Bishop Museum Press, Honolulu.

Goetzfridt, Nicholas. 1982. *Indigenous navigation and Voyaging in the Pacific*. Greenwood Press, New York.

Hunter-Anderson, R.L., and Darlene Moore. 1994. *Archaeology in Manenggon Hills, Yona, Guam. Volumes I-IV. Prepared for MDI Guam Corporation, LeoPalace Resort, Yona, Guam.* Micronesian Archaeological Research Services, Guam.

IPCC. 2013. Fifth Assessment Report. Climate Change 2013: The Physical Science Basis. http://www.ipcc.ch/report/ar5/wg1/

Lightfoot, dale R., and Frank W. Eddy. 1994. The Agricultural utility of Lithic-Mulch gardens: Past and present. *GeoJournal* 34:425-437.

Liston, Jolie. 1996. *The Legacy of Tarague embayment and Its Inhabitants, Andersen Air Force Base, Guam, Volume I: Archaeology.* Report prepared for Andersen Air Force Base Guam.

Liu Jiaqu, Lu Houyuan, J. Negendank, J. Mingram, Luo Xiangjun, Wang Wenyuan, and Chu Guoqiang. 2000. Periodicity of Holocene climatic Variations in the Huguangyanmaar Lake. Chinese Science Bulletin, vol. 45, No. 18:1712-1717.

Lovelock, James. 2009. Lovelock, James (2009). *The Vanishing Face of Gaia: A Final Warning: Enjoy It While You Can.* Allen Lane, London.

Mitrovica, J.X. and Milne, G.A. 2002. On the origin of late Holocene sea-level highstands within equatorial ocean basins. *Quaternary Science Reviews* 21:2179-2190.

Moore, Darlene R. 2005. Archaeological Evidence of a Prehistoric Farming Technique on Guam. Micronesica 38:93-120.

Nunn, P.D. 2007. Holocene sea-level change and human response in Pacific Islands. *Earth and Environmental Science, Transactions of the Royal Society of Edinburgh* 98:117-125.

Peterson, Glenn. 2009. *Traditional Micronesian Societies: Adaptation, Integration, and Political Organization in the Central Pacific.* University of Hawaii Press, Honolulu.

Peterson, John A. and Stephen B. Acabado. 2012, *Protocols for Assessing Vulnerability of Historic Resources at the WAPA and AMME National Parks in Guam and Saipan.* Report for the U.S. National Park Service, Washington, D.C.

Peterson, John A and Mike T. Carson. 2009. 'Mid- to Late Holocene Climate Change and Shoreline Evolution in Tumon Bay, Guam.' John A. Peterson and Mike T. Carson, Pacific Science Inter-Congress and Proceedings, (March).

Rolett, B.V., Zheng, A., and Yue, Y. 2011. Holocene sea-level change and the emergence of Neolithic seafaring in the Fuzhou Basin (Fujian, China). *Quaternary Science Reviews* 30:788-797.

Théry-Parisot, Isabelle, Lucie Chabal, and Julia Chrzavzez. 2010. Anthracology and taphonomy, from wood gathering to charcoal analysis. A review of the taphonomic processes modifying charcoal assemblages, in archaeological contexts. *Palaeogeography, Palaeoclimatology, and Palaeoecology* 291(2010):142-153.

Tornqvist, T.E. and Hijma, M.P. 2012. Links between early Holocene ice-sheet decay, sea-level rise and abrupt climate change. *Nature Geoscience* 5:601-606.

Yancheva, G., R. N. Norbert, M. Jens, et al. 2007. Influence of the intertropical convergence zone on the East Asian monsoon. *Nature* 445:74-77.

Young, Fred J. 1988. *Soil Survey of the Territory of Guam.* US Department of Agriculture Soil Conservation Service. US Government Printing Office, Washington, DC.

Sand and water – and their effect on the pyramids of Meroe in the Sudan

Alexandra Riedel

QMPS-DAI-Cooperation project
Friedrich Hinkel Research Center
German Archaeological Institute Berlin
Alexandra.Riedel@dainst.de

Abstract

The royal cemeteries of Meroe in Sudan incorporate impressive pyramidal graves of the Kingdom of Meroe. Three large groups of small, steep pyramids are located east of the Royal City, the former capital of the Meroitic Kingdom. All in all, more than 1000 graves, including approximately 140 pyramidal superstructures, can be found in the so-called northern, southern and western cemeteries of Meroe.

To today's visitors the site offers a picturesque scene consisting of reddish-yellow sand dunes sprinkled on top with black stones and groups of dark, massive pyramids, but this image is a recent one. Only since the 1960s has sand accumulated in the area of the royal cemeteries, covering the surrounding plains and creating dunes between the pyramidal graves. The combination of wind and dunes causes enormous erosion at the original surfaces of the ancient monuments. In one case, observations have confirmed the loss of 90 % of the reliefs on a chapel wall during a period of only 6 years.

Whereas it seems there is too little water for any natural vegetation to prevent the site from accumulating sand dunes, even this moderate amount of rainwater causes structural damage to the pyramids. As the tops of the majority of the pyramidal structures are absent, water penetrates into the inner rubble core, weakening the stability of these ancient Meroitic remains.

The pyramids of Meroe are accordingly confronted with drifting sand, an enormous sand abrasion and damage due to rainwater. Even though the problems are old and well- known, there is no simple solution. The current situation in Meroe demands not only innovative and comprehensive investigations but also a thorough analysis of the situation as a preparation for the initiation of adequate counteractive measures.

The pyramids of Meroe

The Royal Cemeteries of Meroe are among the most prominent and famous remains of the Meroitic period in Sudan. Three large groups of pyramids can be found to the east of Meroe City, the former capital of the Meroitic Kingdom. All in all, more than 1000 graves, among them approximately140 pyramidal superstructures, are situated in the so-called Northern, Southern and Western Necropolis (Map 1). They include the burials of Meroitic kings, queens, princesses, members of royal families, high-ranking officials and individuals dated to between *c.*250 BC and 350 AD (Hinkel 2000: 12). In 2011 the site of Meroe, including the royal cemeteries, together with the sites of Musawwarat es-Sufra and Naqa, were inscribed in the World Heritage List as the 'Island of Meroe'.

The impressive tombs of the Kingdom of Meroe consist of burial chambers cut into the bedrock, a staircase leading down towards them, and a superstructure above. Whereas sand covers all the underground features, the superstructures dominate and have always dominated the cemetery fields – the pyramids with small chapels on one side.

The Meroitic pyramids are rather small and steep when compared with the huge constructions one may think of with their Egyptian neighbours in mind. Their inclinations vary slightly at *c.*70°. They measured up to 30 m high. Different

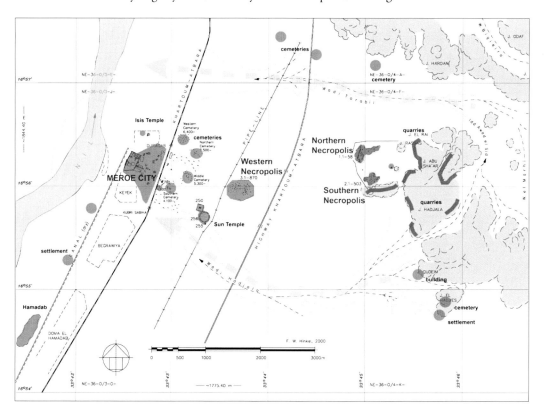

Map 1. Map of the area of Meroe with the main archaeological sites (Alexandra Riedel based on Friedrich Hinkel 2000: Fig. 1).

construction details attest different designs. The cladding stones are worked either as smooth surfaces or steps; the corners are often emphasized by a kind of corner lesene. Certain pyramids even rest on small platforms. In any case, the top stone of the construction seems to have been specially modelled and may have been the base for a certain kind of sculpture (Hinkel 2000: 18). On the east side, a chapel resembling a small Meroitic temple was added. It consisted of a single room; its entrance is marked by means of a small pylon. In several cases porticos with columns and low screen walls or an additional courtyard were constructed in front of the chapel. The pyramids and chapels were probably surrounded by a temenos wall (i.e., a wall enclosing a holy precinct) as certain remaining traces indicate.

The main construction material for all superstructures was local sandstone. Burned brick and rubble stones were used, too, increasingly at the end of the 1st century AD. As to the pyramids a rubble core was cladded with sandstone or brick masonry. The remains of coloured lime plaster confirm that the entire structure was once plastered and painted. Black-brown, red and yellow colours have been found as well as fragments of painted stars (Hinkel 2000: 18). Furthermore, the walls of the pyramid chapels were often decorated with striking reliefs. On the inner walls the majority hereof illustrate funerary scenes. On the outside the remaining pylons are often adorned with relief decorations, showing for instance motifs of the king and queen defeating their enemies. Additional graffiti can be found all over the chapel as wall as the pyramid walls dating from ancient Meroitic times to early and contemporary visitors.

The problem caused by sand and wind

Today the royal cemeteries offer a picturesque scene consisting of reddish-yellow sand dunes sprinkled with brownish-black stones and groups of dark, steep pyramids on top, but this image is a new one. Early photographs of this area taken in c.1900, for instance, by R. Buchta (c.1880), J.H. Breasted (1906) or G.A. Reisner (1920-22),[1] present us with quite a different view (Fig. 1a). In these pictures the north and south cemeteries are situated on a small ridge. Bedrock and rubble stones cover the hills. Toppled sandstone blocks and debris from the destroyed pyramid tops and chapels surround the monuments. The lower plains show relatively dense, savannah-like vegetation consisting of grass and low bushes.

The situation at the pyramids could have been described in a similar way until the 1960s. Only in the following decades did sand start to accumulate in the royal cemeteries and assume alarming proportion. Already in 1986 the archaeologists Hoffman and Tomandl pointed to the desertification of the site (and of other sites in the region such as Musawwarat es-Sufra and Naqa). A comparison of photographs dated between1970 and 1986 impressively shows the changing

---

[1] See the photograph of Buchta in: Zach, M.H. 2014. Die frühesten Fotografien meroitischer Altertümer. In: A. Lohwasser and P. Wolf, eds. Ein Forscherleben zwischen den Welten. Berlin: Der antike Sudan, pp. 405–413.; photographs by Breasted: < http://oi.uchicago.edu/collections/ photographic-archives/1905-1907-breasted-expeditions-egypt-and-sudan>; photographs by Reisner in: Reisner, G.A. 1923. The Pyramids of Meroe and the Candaces of Ethiopia. Museum of Fine Arts Bulletin, Vol. 21, No. 124: 11–27.

a

b

Figure 1. The Meroe northern cemetery. a: The Meroe northern cemetery - 1906. Photo from the Chicago University Breasted Expedition to Egypt and the Sudan (P. 2830, Courtesy of the Oriental Institute of the University of Chicago) – permission needed from Oriental Institute; b: The Meroe northern cemetery - 2008 (photograph by Pawel Wolf, 2008).

condition at the pyramids. Whereas in the earlier pictures one can see still the stony hills and vegetation in the plains, sand surfaces dominate the largest part of the scene in 1986 (Hoffman and Tomandl 1986: 60–61, 93, 105). Friedrich Hinkel[2] – a German architect working at these cemeteries between 1976 and 2004 – described the same phenomenon using aerial photographs dated from 1966 and 1978 (Hinkel 2000: 16, colour plates X–XI).

---

2   Friedrich Wilhelm Hinkel (1925-2007) was an East German architect working for the National Corporation for Antiquities and Museums in Sudan. His activities concentrated on the documentation and preservation of Sudanese Cultural Heritage, with a special focus on the royal pyramids at Meroe from the 1970s onwards. In 2009 his comprehensive archive of documentations was transferred to the German Archaeological Institute by his heirs.

Nowadays, visitors encounter the 'picturesque' situation described above: both small and huge sand dunes move through the pyramid fields (Fig. 1b). The sand accumulates at the flanks of the hills, around the pyramids and chapels. It completely covers the remains of small tombs creating a thin veneer all over the plains.

Yet the sand itself is not the main problem. The sand in combination with the wind causes major destruction. The windblown sand leads to enormous erosion at the original surfaces of the ancient monuments. It is a mechanical action whereby each grain of sand abrades the construction, resulting in a loss of original material – resembling the process of sandblasting. Making things even worse, the accumulation of sand at the pyramid fields is not comparable to a steadily progressing burial of the monuments, which would provide a certain protection. Rather, the dunes move through the cemeteries filling, for instance, parts of a chapel in autumn and exposing it again in spring, depending on the wind direction and air turbulence. As this process recurs every year abrasion becomes a serious problem as to the conservation of this extraordinary heritage (Fig. 2).

Currently the most obvious destruction can be observed with the sandstone blocks of the chapels and with the corners of the pyramids. Especially the reliefs (e.g., on the decorated outer or inner walls of half collapsed chapels) are exposed to the harsh conditions and endangered. The rate of destruction as to the chapel reliefs is alarming (Fig. 3a, 3b). In one case Friedrich Hinkel noted the abrasion of c.90% of the inner wall relief in a northern cemetery chapel (BEG N 6) during a

Figure 2. The Relief-decorated courtyard and chapel (BEG N 11); (photo by: Alexandra Riedel, 2009).

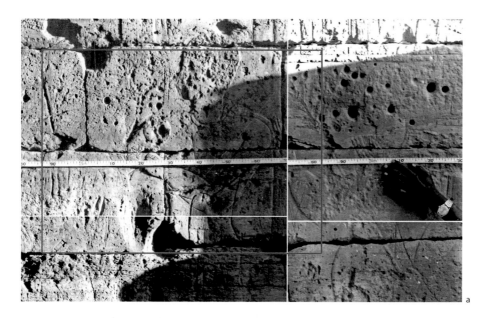

Figure 3. a: Montage of four pictures from a photo documentation of the inner north wall of chapel BEG N – 1981; the red frame marks the area of a 1997 photo (below) (photographs by Friedrich Hinkel, 1981; German Archaeological Institute, D-DAI-Z-Arch-FWH-F-KB-sw-342-20, D-DAI-Z-Arch-FWH-F-KB-sw-342-22, D-DAI-Z-Arch-FWH-F-KB-sw-342-34, D-DAI-Z-Arch-FWH-F-KB-sw-342-42); b: Photo documentation of the inner north wall of chapel BEG N – 1997 (photograph by Friedrich Hinkel, 1997; German Archaeological Institute, D-DAI-Z-Arch-FWH-F-DIA-10237).

period of only 6 years, between 1989 and 1995 (Hinkel 2000: 16). An opening in the chapel roof and a missing door were probably the reasons for this specific loss. Numerous other examples of ongoing destruction are obvious, but have not been documented or analysed as yet.

The local stone mainly used for the construction of the tombs is relatively soft sandstone and often called Nubian sandstone. Its colour is reddish-yellow but now and again it appears to be almost white. As with most Meroitic architecture the pyramids and their chapels were originally plastered with a hard lime plaster. This implies that the construction was covered by means of a protective layer, which was lost over the years. Having been exposed to the weather for centuries, the local sandstone has generated a brownish-red, hardened surface layer containing iron/manganese/clay minerals. This patina results from natural or artificial aging and can be found on the majority of the sandstone hills of this region too. In arid regions it is referred to as 'desert varnish'. However, the continuing abrasion by windblown sand since the 1960s destroys the hardened surface and grinds grooves into the soft stone material, as is visible with the brighter stone parts. This abrasion basically outruns the generation of a patina. The degree of erosion not only depends on the amount of sand and the wind velocity, but also on (a) the wind direction, (b) wind turbulences and (c) the position of parts of the monuments in relation to the sandy terrain, since the effect of the abrasion is significantly reduced with the increasing distance from the ground.

Reasons and causes for the invasion of sand

The struggle with the accumulating dunes has a long history in northern Sudan. Various archaeological excavations along the Nile provide evidence as to the filling of houses and areas with sand, the covering of abandoned buildings, or the temporary abandonment of settlements due to the invasion of sand. Well-known examples from Kawa, Meinarti, Amara and Old-Dongola go back to ancient times. Nowadays modern settlements, agriculture as well as excavation sites still fight the same problem as sand drifts in from the Sahara every season (Munro et al. 2012: 140–143).

Whereas the examples mentioned are from the area located between the first and fourth cataract of the Nile, Meroe is situated further south in the so-called Butana. The documentation of the monuments and their damage underlines that the extensive accumulation of sand was a minor problem at the Meroe cemeteries until the 1960s. The original lime plaster and a stone patina has protected the sandstone of the pyramidal tombs for c.2000 years very well. The major destruction at the antique monuments resulting from abrasion appears to be a recent phenomenon caused by the influx of sand and changing environmental conditions.

Today the Meroe region can be described as an arid to semi-arid region in the Sahel – the southern fringe of the Sahara – with sandy and stony plains, vegetation consisting of grass and bushes, several wadis and mountains. The settlements are situated along the Nile and surrounded by agriculture, with the area devoted to cropland increasing thanks to improved irrigation. Further inland small groups of semi-nomad pastoralists are settling in the vicinity of wadis and deep wells. Except for the Nile and these wells there are no permanent water sources. Vegetation in the Butana depends on the seasonal rainfall occurring between May and October.

Degradation or desertification of the Butana has been described and discussed for more than 6 decades. Already in the 1950s investigations showed changes in the vegetation. Subsequent detailed studies have proved land degradation. Climatic changes, changes in the nature of husbandry and human intervention in the natural landscape have been discussed as influences. Climate-induced changes and the consequences of human transformations are often difficult to distinguish due to their complex interplay. A causative factor is certainly the several dry periods witnessed in the course of the 20th century, which culminated in two devastating droughts in 1984/85 and 1990/91. The variability of rainfall increased. In certain years rain completely failed to appear. A second significant causative factor is human impact. In addition, the increasing population of Sudan and the fact that parts of the former nomadic population have started to take up permanent residence both lead to intensified land use. Agricultural areas expand. The inland is more and more used for animal husbandry especially around the few permanent water sources. The latter development, in particular, results in overgrazing around settlements and wells, along rivers and wadis. Major human intervention in the landscape such as the construction of dams along the Nile and Atbara induces resettlement and changes in the water supply, adding to the complex list of causative factors. The result is degradation of the plant cover in the Butana. The amount of vegetation as well as the variety of species is dramatically reduced. The degree hereof depends on local conditions. In certain areas investigations showed degradation to such an extent that the uppermost layers of the soils erode, resulting in a severe loss of the regeneration potential of the plant cover (see Akhtar-Schuster: XII–XV, 12–23 and Wolf 1995: 10–12)[3].

The decrease of vegetation in the Butana affects the accumulation of sand dunes. On the one hand, sand drifting in from other areas (e.g., the Sahara) is no longer stabilized by means of a dense plant cover. On the other hand, deflation increases in the Butana itself. Formerly covered soil starts to erode and is redeposited, adding to the quantity of drifting sands. The observed accumulated sand dunes at Meroe are a consequence of these processes.

New investigations and an analysis of satellite data suggest a general 'greening' of the Sahel since the 1980s. The rainfall and the quantity of seasonal vegetation have increased. This trend is not uniform, but rather shows regional differences. Again, local conditions and other factors such as human intervention seem to influence the vegetation (Hutchinson et al. 2005: 535–537). Furthermore, one has to keep in mind that a 'recovery' of areas such as the Butana cannot be expected

---

3   There have been several investigations into the desertification, environmental degradation, analyses of rainfall in the Butana. Unfortunately the region of Meroe was not the focus of these investigations. For further information, see: Akhtar, M., Mensching, H.G. 1993. Desertification in the Butana. *GeoJournal*, 31.1: 41–50.; Elagib, N.A., Mansell, M.G. 2000. Climate impacts of environmental degradation in Sudan. *GeoJournal*, 50: 311–327; Elhag, M.M., Walker, S. 2010. Environmental Degradation of Natural Resources in Butana Area of Sudan. In: Zdruli, P. et al., eds. Land Degradation and Desertification: Assessment, Mitigation and Remediation. Dordrecht: Springer, pp. 171–178.

due to soil erosion and changes in existing vegetation. A period of regeneration accompanying improved climatic conditions can result in new plant cover, which may have the same 'greenness', but the species composition will differ.[4]

A certain trend towards increasing vegetation can also be observed in the Meroe region. The consequences of this development for the royal cemeteries and the accumulation of sand dunes in the Butana remain to be seen. As the effects are unpredictable and the return of a dry period is certain, preservation work at the pyramids and practicable concepts in order to tackle the problem of sand abrasion are absolutely essential.

The right amount of water

Whereas it seems there is too little water for natural vegetation in order to adequately prevent the site from accumulating dunes, even this moderate amount of rainwater causes structural damage to the pyramids. In certain years the seasonal rain leads to flooded areas in the region of Meroe. The water fills wadis and plains, on occasion washing away bridges, houses or parts of the highway. The heritage sites of the Meroe region are endangered too. Excavation trenches are flooded, fragile mud structures deteriorate, burned brick and stone constructions are exposed to rising moisture or salt crystallization – just to present but a few examples of the problems.

At the pyramid fields rainwater washes out pits and holes in the ground creating cavities and voids in the structure of the pyramids and chapels. The water undermines foundations causing damage and structural instability. It penetrates into the walls or the vaults of the chapels whenever a proper top stone or roofing is missing and washes out water channels, which could lead to a collapse and the loss of original fabric. Last but not least, as the tops of most of the pyramidal structures are absent, water penetrates into the inner rubble core of the pyramids too, weakening their stability.

Whereas the first two problems are challenging because of the sheer number of tombs, the penetration of rainwater into the core of the pyramids is probably the most demanding. The steep construction of the pyramids causes an inner soil pressure of the rubble filling, which has to be supported by the sandstone cladding. The ashlar masonry of the cladding operates like a retaining wall against the inner filling, comparable to an earthen hill or dam. The exposed filling material presents us with natural slope angles up to 45°. Considering that the inclination of the pyramids measure c.70°, the difference illustrates the stresses and bending moments introduced onto the sandstone cladding walls. The effects of the inner soil pressure are quite obvious: pyramid walls buckle and become distorted, cracks are visible. If the stresses exceed the load capacity of the walls, the masonry collapses. Nowadays the majority of the pyramids already show structural damage caused by inner soil pressure or have bending walls. The penetration of rainwater into the rubble core filling, the washing out of material or the generation of cavities could add stresses to the fragile structural stability and lead to the further collapse of pyramid walls.

---

4   The 'Greening' of the Sahel was discussed in a Special Issue of the Journal of Arid Environments, Volume 63, Issue 3, pp. 533–670 (November 2005).

Possible interventions

The pyramids of Meroe are confronted with drifting sand, extensive sand abrasion and damage due to rainwater. Even though the problems have been known for some time, there is no simple solution. The damages originate from factors ranging from local structural issues to regional natural and climatic changes. Former investigations and preservation measures at Meroe concentrated on specific local phenomena and counter actions. As to a sustainable development and preservation of the site it seems a more holistic approach is required, including local and regional perspectives. Accordingly the current situation in Meroe demands not only innovative, comprehensive investigations but also a thorough analysis of the situation as a preparation for adequate counteractive measures.

A starting point should be the exploitation and examination of previous work at the site. Especially the archive of the late Friedrich Hinkel, containing substantial documentations including photographs and architectural drawings of the pyramids, constitute an essential basis for all future work at the pyramids of Meroe. It allows, for instance, comparative analyses of damages of the last 40 years. In addition to documentation and research, Hinkel's work focused on preservation work. For example, between 1976 and 1988, he reconstructed fourteen chapels in order to preserve their remains and especially their striking wall reliefs (Hinkel 2000: 21). His knowledge of the monuments and an evaluation of his preservation work is a valuable resource with regard to the development of a future conservation concept. As Hinkel's work was not continued after 2004 it is necessary to complete the existing documentation.

In order to achieve a comprehensive understanding of the site and the challenges of its preservation new investigations by scientists schooled in a wide range of specialisations are required, as for example the problem of sand illustrated. The accumulation of dunes and the abrasion of the sandstone constructions, for instance, are a result of complex mechanisms. A single local action cannot discontinue them, because environmental changes such as the desertification or degradation of the Butana are regional phenomena. The entire area, including all the archaeological sites, is affected. Here the causes and effects need to be clarified on a regional level to form a first step toward defining and setting common objectives, together and in cooperation with, for instance, agriculture and forestry agencies, local communities and environmental protection initiatives.

On the local scale of the Meroe site comprehensive investigations and the development of long term concepts should be the second step. The northern and southern cemeteries are situated on ridges in front of the eastern mountain range whereas the western cemetery lies in a small plain located between the hills and Meroe city on the Nile. Further northwards the mountain range continues westwards as far as the Nile. In this way all three pyramid fields are enclosed by mountains in the east and north and the Nile in the west; two wadis adjoin in the north and south. Even though the general causes for the influx of sand are known, the local situation requires additional investigation. Research in other areas of northern Sudan showed that the sources of the sand and the sand drift differ. Whereas, for instance, most winds are from the north, wind directions from the southwest occur in the Meroe region as well. Accordingly, the influx of sand can come from several directions at different times of the year; the amount of sand transported can also vary (Munro et al. 2005: 149–153). For the area of Meroe and especially for the site of the pyramids detailed investigations have not been carried out so far. Questions need to be asked and answered, for instance: (a) where is the sand coming from?, (b) is the sand a product of the erosion of the sandstone mountains or does it drift in from the Butana plains?, (c) what are the dominant wind directions at the site? and (d) how do the mountains and the elevation of the terrain affect the main wind directions, and do they create turbulence? Only a thorough analysis of the local setting will allow the development of an adequate concept to influence the existing situation to the desired positive extent. The objective is to reduce the influx of sand by means of stabilising or reducing dunes upwind. The installation of precisely placed vegetative belts and/or the fostering of indigenous vegetation in the wadis and adjacent plains could be possible interventions. Keeping in mind that the area surrounding the site is used for animal husbandry and farming, all activities need to involve the local communities.

Additionally a third step could include the immediate local activities at the pyramid fields. The actual removal of accumulated sand – executed with reasonable care – provides a quick and effective method to reduce the degree of abrasion for a certain period of time. Furthermore, initial preventive conservation measures at the chapels and pyramids should be initiated in order to avoid or minimise further damage. Simple interventions (e.g., the closing of the chapels or the temporary covering of endangered reliefs on the outer walls) could preserve important parts of monuments until the sand abrasion is minimized.

The sustainable preservation of the pyramids of Meroe is a complex challenge. In order to ensure any improvement a holistic approach is needed including an interdisciplinary approach as well as regional and local perspectives. Specialists (e.g., restorers, structural engineers, archaeologists, architects, heritage managers, tourism planners, geographers, geologists) should be integrated. Moreover, the example of the pyramids demonstrates that cultural heritage, especially as it is influenced by climatic changes and changes of landscape, cannot be understood with a focus on the individual monument only. Cultural heritage is rather a part of historic landscapes much larger in scale than modern buffer zones. Consequently the preservation of a cultural heritage needs to consider the surrounding natural landscape as well as its impact on the site.

Outlook

In 2013 the Qatar-Sudan Archaeological Project[5] (QSAP) started as a joint initiative of both countries with the objective of promoting the rich archaeological heritage in the Republic of the Sudan. The project registered in Sudan as a NGO under the name 'The Nubian Archaeological Development Organisation' covers

---

5   For information on the Qatar-Sudan Archaeological Project and the Qatari Mission for the Pyramids of Sudan, see http://www.qsap.org.qa/en/about-us> and <http://www.qsap.org.qa/en/about-us/sudan-pyramids>.

the funding of forty archaeological missions, the rehabilitation and construction of museums as well as the building of two mission camps. Embedded in QSAP is Qatar's own archaeological mission with a focus on the ancient pyramid cemeteries of the Kingdom of Kush – the Qatari Mission for the Pyramids of Sudan (QMPS) with its director HE Sheikh Hassan bin Mohamed bin Ali Al-Thani (Vice Chair of Qatar Museums - QM). The main activities of Qatar's mission will be devoted to the tombs of Meroe and the three pyramid fields. Its objectives are archaeological research, preservation of the monuments and development of sustainable site management and tourism. Integrated into the overall concept of QMPS a subproject shall be initialized in order to reduce the abrasion of monuments at the site by means of reducing the accumulation of sand in the core area. Irrigated vegetative belts are considered to trap drifting sands; as the supply is diminished, the deflation of sands at the site could then exceed influx. Furthermore, the QMPS has invited the German Archaeological Institute in Berlin to contribute to the Qatari Mission for the Pyramids of Sudan. Already in 2014 the digitalisation of the Friedrich-Hinkel-Archive started as a first cooperation project in order to establish a profound basis for the planned work at the pyramids.

At Meroe preliminary activities and investigations have started in 2014, too, including a first assessment of conservation problems at the pyramids themselves and a meeting of all stakeholders in order to establish common strategic objectives for the development of the site. The Qatari Mission for the pyramids of Sudan is about to begin. In 2015 (a) a review of previous work, (b) a comprehensive documentation, (c) a thorough condition assessment at the pyramid fields, (d) the preparation of a research plan and (e) the development of conservation policies are planned. The selection of an interdisciplinary team of Sudanese and international specialists is underway in order to master the complex tasks. In sum, the Qatari Mission for the Pyramids of Sudan intends to holistically approach the development of the pyramid sites of Sudan together with all stakeholders and the local communities not only to learn more about the Sudanese Heritage but also to conserve it for future generations.

References

Akhtar-Schuster, M. 1995. *Degradationsprozesse und Desertifikation im semiariden randtropischen Gebiet der Butana / Rep. Sudan.* Göttingen: Göttinger Beiträge zur Land- und Forstwirtschaft in den Tropen und Subtropen 15.

Hinkel, F.W. 2000. The Royal Pyramids of Meroe. Architecture, Construction and Reconstruction of a Sacred Landscape. *Sudan and Nubia,* 4: 11–26.

Hoffmann, I., Tomandl, H. 1986. *Unbekanntes Meroe.* Wien-Mödling: Beiträge zur Sudanforschung, Beiheft 1.

Hutchinson, C.F., Herrmann, S.M., Maukonen, T., Weber, J. 2005. Introduction: The 'Greening' of the Sahel. *Journal of Arid Environments,* 63 (3): 533–670.

Munro, R.N., Ibrahim, M.A.M., Abuzied, H., El-Hassan, B. 2005. Aeolian sand landforms in parts of the Sudan and Nubia. Origins and impacts on past and present land use. *Sudan and Nubia,* 16: 140–154.

Wolf, P. 1995. Bemerkungen zum Schutz der Denkmäler von Musawwarat es Sufra vor Wind- und Sanderosion - Teil 1: Mechanismen und Schäden der Erosion. *Mitteilungen der Sudanarchäologischen Gesellschaft zu Berlin e.V.,* 3: 10–19.

Preserving New York City's waterfront industrial and maritime heritage through resilient and sustainable development

New York City's coastal development

Kate Daly

"Preserving New York City's waterfront industrial and maritime heritage through resilient and sustainable development"

New York City's coastal development

Like coastal cities around the world, New York City is reinventing its shoreline. In a city where residents had previously been isolated from much of the city's degraded shorelines, the 21st century has seen a concentrated effort to reconnect New Yorkers with their waterfront, as part of an ambitious plan for urban sustainability. The transformation of the water's edge, often through the development of residential and recreational uses, necessitates a reconsideration of the waterfront industrial buildings that played an important role in the city's economic ascendancy in the 19th and 20th centuries, but now reflect complicated legacies of contamination and obsolescence. As New York reshapes its shoreline to address residential development pressure, brownfield clean-up, and the risks of climate change, heritage conservation is an essential planning tool that must be part of any sustainable vision for the urban waterfront.

The waterways surrounding Manahatta were trading routes for the Lenape people long before the Dutch established the trading colony of New Amsterdam nearly 400 years ago. A natural deep water harbor at the confluence of two rivers set the stage for the growth of a city that became one of the most important ports and industrial centers in the United States.[1] In the 18th and 19th centuries, the waterfront surrounding Manhattan's harbor was divided into piers, warehouses, and other maritime and trade uses that fostered the economic growth of the city (figure 1). The completion of the Erie Canal in 1825 connected New York City's shipping ports to agricultural producers upstate and in the Midwest, and assured

---

1   The Lenape called the island Manahatta, which means "hilly island." The waterways commonly referred to as rivers are more accurately an estuary (the Hudson River) and a tidal strait (the East River).

Figure 1. Topographical map of the City of New York, Egbert L. Viele, ca. 1874, detail, showing outline of lower Manhattan's original shoreline and later landfill (Library of Congress Geography and Map Division).

New York's preeminence. As the City grew, demand for developable land increased. Beginning in the early 19th century, tens of thousands of acres of tidal marsh and underwater land were developed, effectively stripping the coastline of its natural buffer zone (figure 1). Today lower Manhattan is 33 percent larger than it was upon the arrival of the Dutch.[2]

In Brooklyn in the 19th century, as tidal marshes were filled in and piers and warehouses constructed, shipbuilding, sugar, and storage becoming the major economic engines for the rapid development of that city's waterfront. Shipping and maritime industries flourished in proximity to deep water ports, most notably the Atlantic Basin in Red Hook and the Brooklyn Navy Yard, and over time light and heavy manufacturing industries lined the adjacent shorelines. These industries contributed to the thriving trade economy of the United States into the first half of the 20th century.

By the mid-1950s, industrial sectors including manufacturing, wholesale trade, and transportation accounted for 56 percent of the New York City's private employment. By 2008, that figure had dropped to 18 percent. As a result of transportation innovations in the second half of the 20th century, including the replacement of traditional bulk shipping with cargo container shipping and the expansion of interstate highways, manufacturers no longer needed to locate their factories and warehouses adjacent to coastal shipping ports. This development, coinciding with capital flight south and then overseas, led to the decline of manufacturing throughout the East Coast of the United States.[3]

With the waning of local manufacturing, many areas of New York City's waterfront fell into disuse and disrepair. The story of the city's industrial past, and a critical phase of the United States's water-dependent Industrial Revolution, is still evident in New York City's waterfront landscapes. The shoreline industrial sites that remain leave a complex legacy—the buildings are typically not designed or equipped to meet the needs of 21st-century industries, and in many cases are sited within the floodplain on land contaminated by past heavy industrial uses.

---

2   93,800 acres, or almost half the current acreage of New York City, of marshland and underwater land were developed between 1800 and 1980. Steinberg, *Gotham Unbound*, 395. Hudson, *Cities on the Shore*, 97.

3   "Vision 2020: New York City Comprehensive Waterfront Plan," 50-51.

New York City's industrial heritage

In the late 20th and early 21st centuries, some industrial sections of New York City's coastline were converted to public parks and residential use, part of the city's efforts to reconnect with its shoreline by integrating an economically productive waterfront with the recreational uses and environmental protections that foster sustainable, mixed-use areas actively used by residents and tourists. The City of New York has addressed the evolving uses and growth of the waterfront through various plans, including a "Comprehensive Waterfront Plan" in 1992, followed by the 2011 "Vision 2020: New York City Comprehensive Waterfront Plan." New York City's historic industrial waterfront buildings reflect the city's development across centuries, but must respond to the future, and the challenges, opportunities, and potential conflicts the intersection of flood management, economic development, and historic preservation will bring. This will necessitate what has been called "fluid urbanism," a renewed awareness of the delicate ecological balance between the demand for housing and recreation along the city's shoreline and the impacts of climate change.[4]

Although the City's official plans all acknowledge preservation, heritage tourism, and adaptive reuse as important elements in any strategic waterfront development, there is no comprehensive plan for the preservation and recognition of industrial and maritime heritage, no equivalent to Germany's "Route der Industriekultur," or the Erie Canalway National Heritage Corridor, which transects New York State. Some of New York City's industrial waterfront heritage has been preserved through adaptive reuse or thanks to the absence of development incentives that could encourage demolition. The New York City Landmarks Preservation Commission has successfully protected several formerly industrial neighborhoods, including DUMBO and Fulton Ferry in Brooklyn, and the South Street Seaport, SoHo, TriBeCa, Gansevoort, and West Chelsea in Manhattan. A small number of individual industrial buildings have also been recognized for their architectural and historical significance, including the iconic former Domino Sugar refinery on the East River.

Domino Sugar Refinery, Brooklyn

The former Domino Sugar plant on the Brooklyn waterfront is a notable example of a successful effort to preserve some vestige of the borough's significant manufacturing history amidst development pressures. Sugar refineries played a large role in the growth of Brooklyn's economy in the 19th century. By mid-century, Brooklyn produced half the nation's supply of sugar and had become the greatest sugar-refining center in the world.[5] The story of the sugar trade in Brooklyn is a narrative of complex trade ties between north and south, and the U.S. and the

---

4   Joseph, *Fluid New York*, 3, 9.
5   Burrows and Wallace, *Gotham*, 660-661.

Caribbean. The trade in sugar created a particularly brutal plantation economy in many islands of the Caribbean, and was an integral component of the Atlantic triangular slave trade.[6]

The Havemeyer [later Domino] plant was established by the mid-19th century in the Williamsburg neighborhood of Brooklyn, taking advantage of a waterfront location to receive shipments of raw sugar directly via steamship and freight car. The sugar refinery remained in active use until 2004, when the decommissioned site was sold to a non-profit development group after a controversial rezoning of the industrial Williamsburg neighborhood to allow for high-rise residential construction. The large, ca. 1884 Filter, Pan & Finishing House portion of the refinery complex was designated a protected local landmark, amidst competing demands for preservation of more historic buildings at the site and community requests for the construction of affordable housing. The complex changed hands again in 2012, and is now slated for conversion to commercial, residential, and retail use. Plans for the restoration and adaptive reuse of the protected historic building were challenging, due to the past industrial uses of the building, which was filled with multi-story heavy equipment. The building's location directly on the East River also necessitated flood protection mechanisms in anticipation of sea level rise and increased storm severity, including raising the waterfront plaza and building ground floor level ten feet above the flood plain, and altering the historic window configurations to accommodate the altered floor levels and the new use.

Climate change as a threat to industrial and maritime heritage

The inclusion of industrial heritage in the City's waterfront revitalization efforts is essential, but in the 21st century the threat to these historic buildings goes beyond development and demolition. As a city surrounded on all sides by water, with 520 miles of shoreline, New York is one of the U.S. cities most susceptible to hurricane hazards like wind and flooding. It is estimated that up to one-fourth of New York City's land will fall within the floodplain by mid-century. Industrial buildings, many sited directly on the waterfront within the floodplain, are particularly exposed. The historic buildings that comprise New York City's industrial waterfront heritage will need to adapt to this risk if they're to survive into the future.

Since 1821, 13 hurricanes have directly struck or affected New York City; six of them of them have occurred since 1995. The economic imperative to protect its shoreline drove much of the City's ambitious plan for fortifying resources within the floodplain well before a devastating hurricane struck the City in October 2012. In 2007, the City of New York released "PlaNYC: A Greener, Greater New York," a long-term sustainability plan. In addition to plans to reduce the City's greenhouse gas emissions, PlaNYC included resiliency initiatives to protect the

---

6   Raw sugar was supplied to Brooklyn refineries from America's southern states and from the Caribbean, where it was primarily harvested by slaves. Slavery ended in the United States in 1865, but continued in Cuba, the world's largest exporter of raw sugar, until 1886. "Havemeyers & Elder Filter, Pan & Finishing House Designation Report," 2.

City's infrastructure from the anticipated consequences of climate change. The plan included updates to the building code to make new buildings more flood resistant and plans for restoring wetlands to recapture stormwater, introducing bioswales to City streetscapes, and planting one million trees throughout the City.

Hurricane Sandy made landfall on 29 October 2012, and was an unprecedented natural disaster for New York City in terms of size, damage, and the number of people affected. Forty-three New Yorkers lost their lives and entire communities were devastated. The storm caused $19 billion dollars in damage and flooded an area that included nearly 89,000 buildings. The storm and its aftermath destroyed or rendered unsound hundreds of buildings and damaged thousands more. In lower Manhattan's South Street Seaport historic district tidal floods up to seven feet deep inundated entire streetscapes of landmarked 19th-century buildings, while in Brooklyn the DUMBO historic district, a 19th-century manufacturing district on the shore of the East River, experienced extensive flooding and storm damage on the ground floors of industrial loft buildings.

Contested industrial landscapes

The South Street Seaport and DUMBO historic districts both encompass industrial or maritime streetscapes that were established as a result of their proximity to the waterfront and have over time through deliberate public or private planning efforts been transformed into thriving, high-rent commercial and residential neighborhoods. But in some other neighborhoods of New York formerly industrial sites remain contested landscapes, with tensions between the inevitable development pressure and the desire to preserve industrial uses and historic buildings. Whereas many post-industrial U.S. cities are grappling with how to re-populate or revitalize abandoned building stock, in New York City the threat to post-industrial sites is primarily that of demolition to make way for new high-end residential buildings. In Manhattan, areas like the Meatpacking District and West Chelsea retain much of their historic industrial architecture thanks to their protection as local historic districts, but have lost many of their ties to manufacturing or commercial uses, and have been transformed into upscale residential areas. While real estate development pressure in Manhattan made these transformations in some ways a foregone conclusion, the challenge of how formerly industrial neighborhoods could be developed in an equitable and balanced way is still unresolved in some industrial areas of Brooklyn, and in 2007 the non-profit preservation advocacy group the National Trust for Historic Preservation identified the Brooklyn Industrial Waterfront as a heritage area in danger of disappearing.

Alternative strategies for preserving industrial heritage

For many sites, local landmark designation is not the appropriate preservation tool, and creative approaches are necessary in order to protect industrial heritage. Challenges include the conflict between the preservation of historic sites and development pressure or community demands, a dearth of flexible preservation tools for preserving buildings that may lack high-style architectural significance but are part of a vernacular industrial tradition, and the challenges that climate change poses for waterfront historic resources.

Areas where local landmark designation may not be a feasible strategy for preservation, due to more vernacular styles, alterations to historic fabric over time, and serious flood management challenges, include the waterfront Red Hook and Gowanus neighborhoods of Brooklyn. Both areas had strong ties to industry and shipping well into the early 20th-century, and subsequent disinvestment and abandonment have shaped their character. In both neighborhoods, the pressure of economic development threatens historic resources. These historic, waterfront neighborhoods make for interesting case studies of the adaptive reuse challenges and opportunities the industrial building typology presents.

Gowanus, Brooklyn

The historic Gowanus neighborhood in Brooklyn presents unique challenges to both economic development and heritage conservation, including issues relating to the abandonment and deferred maintenance of large-scale industrial buildings, environmental conditions, and flooding. Whether and how redevelopment efforts will recognize and preserve this brownfield-filled industrial heritage corridor's historical built fabric has not yet been determined.

Until the 1840s, the Gowanus area of Brooklyn was still largely farmland, and Gowanus Creek was a tidal estuary flowing into Gowanus Bay, in New York Harbor. As the City of Brooklyn grew, the creek was transformed into a canal to facilitate the area's industrial development. Well before the canal's completion in 1869, new foundries, shipyards, gas manufacturing plants, coal yards and factories were built along the waterfront, and the area was transformed into a heavily trafficked urban industrial center (figure 2). The streets adjacent to the waterfront developed into residential rowhouses and the area's industry provided for the livelihoods of thousands of local residents. By the late 19th century gas plants, tanneries, mills and chemical plants lined the banks of the Gowanus Canal, but the decline of domestic shipping by water in the late 20th century led to dwindling jobs, population and manufacturing in the area.

The legacy of years of industrial pollution eventually prompted a controversial 2010 Superfund designation by the U.S. Environmental Protection Agency, which characterized the canal as one of the most toxic waterways in the United States. At the same time, the mixed-use neighborhood's historic streetscapes and proximity to desirable residential neighborhoods have in the past 10 years generated greater interest in large-scale development along the canal, despite the challenges presented by brownfield conditions and vacant industrial buildings. Leading up to the Superfund designation, development pressure increased, with an effort, later stalled, to rezone the neighborhood to allow for large-scale residential developments. That rush to develop was slowed by the Superfund designation, with its $500 million price tag and 10-year remediation period. The Gowanus neighborhood is grappling with other environmental issues as well. Gowanus lies within a floodplain, and during Hurricane Sandy in October 2012 the canal

Figure 2. Gowanus Canal, Brooklyn. Photographs by the author.

overflowed into the surrounding streets. The City is exploring concepts for storm surge barriers on the Gowanus Canal to prevent and mitigate flooding.

The neighborhood is at a critical juncture. It must balance the preservation of unique historic streetscapes, manufacturing uses, and active industrial sites with the changes necessary for economic revitalization and the activation of underutilized sites. Although the historic industrial landscape is an important part of Gowanus's identity and sense of place, historic preservation hasn't been at the forefront of community efforts until this year, when a community group nominated the entire neighborhood for listing as an Urban Industrial District on the U.S. National Register of Historic Places. The State Historic Preservation office declined to advance the nomination in light of opposition from property owners in the area, who were concerned about increased regulation, and questioned how realistic it is to preserve historic features like canal embankments that will be replaced as part of the Superfund cleanup.

One alternative approach to local landmark designation or National Register listing could be the creation of a National Heritage Corridor, like the Erie Canal National Heritage Corridor. These listings are honorific, but could bring greater public attention to the important industrial history of the area. There is also a potential opportunity for a nexus between those interested in preserving historic buildings and efforts to revitalize and preserve existing urban manufacturing uses. These two constituencies are not automatic allies, and a partnership would need to be built.

Red Hook, Brooklyn

When the Dutch colonized Brooklyn and settled Gowanus in 1636 they also established an outpost further south, in Red Hook. By the 1850s Red Hook was home to one of the busiest ports in the world, Atlantic Basin, and was a terminus for the Erie Canal. But the transition to containerized shipping led to an economic downturn in the second half of the 20th century, and the once thriving industrial neighborhood lost jobs and businesses and struggled with crime and decaying building stock.

The 1990s brought limited reinvestment in the neighborhood, with a cruise ship pier, a chain supermarket housed within the prominent 19th-century Red Hook Stores waterfront warehouse building (figure 3), and controversial plans for an IKEA superstore. IKEA proposed locating a 300,000 square foot furniture store on the waterfront, at the site of the ca. 1866 Red Hook Graving Dock No. 1, one of the largest dry docks in the U.S. still in active use and located within the Red Hook Significant Maritime and Industrial Areas, a designation intended to preserve the historic maritime industries in the neighborhood. Negotiations with the City and community in 2004 resulted in an approval of the IKEA big box retail store and pier, with the maintenance of some portion of existing piers for continued use by a local barging operation.[7] The approval included the demolition of historic shipyard buildings and the loss of the Red Hook Graving Dock.

The neighborhood's isolated geography, with water on three sides and no nearby subway station, and the designation of some areas as industrial business zones, has limited residential development as compared to other nearby Brooklyn neighborhoods, and this has served to protect many of the area's historic 19th-century storage, manufacturing, and rowhouse buildings. One of the most pressing threats to this historic maritime area is its location within the coastal floodplain. The neighborhood was evacuated in advance of Hurricane Sandy, and the storm's 14-foot storm surge caused extensive damage to low-lying businesses and homes.

---

7   "Vision 2020," 52.

Figure 3. Ca. 1860s Red Hook Stores warehouse, now the Fairway Building, Red Hook, Brooklyn. Photograph by the author.

In light of the serious flooding dangers in this historic waterfront community, proposals were solicited in 2013 as part of the Rebuild by Design competition, a regional initiative of the US Department of Housing and Urban Development and the Presidential Hurricane Sandy Rebuilding Task Force. Many of the competition submissions focused on fostering sustainable, resilient waterfront development that acknowledges the importance of Red Hook's maritime history and industrial sectors.

As in Gowanus, in Red Hook there has been to date little attention to using formal heritage conservation tools to protect the vernacular streetscapes, however private individuals have undertaken the restoration of several important 19th-century warehouse buildings, and there are local efforts to commemorate the area's history. The Red Hook Waterfront Museum, housed aboard the ca. 1914 floating Lehigh Valley Railroad Barge #79, educates visitors about the neighborhood's maritime past, and the importance of preserving Red Hook's industrial and maritime heritage. In addition, in an effort to salvage and display some vestige of the maritime livelihood it was displacing, IKEA developed Gantry Pier at the IKEA Waterfront Plaza, where installations of industrial artifacts and historic markers attempt to illustrate the area's maritime history. The retention and display of industrial artifacts to allude to an industrial past that has since been cleared away is an approach used with varying degrees of success in other recreational parks in New York.

Industrial landscapes and artifacts

The question of what to do when historic buildings have been cleared or altered beyond recognition, but some demand exists for memorialization of the industrial heritage that shaped a particular landscape, is a challenging one. One example in New York City illustrates how references to an industrial past can be incorporated into a waterfront recreational park.

Gantry Plaza State Park, Long Island City, Queens

> *"Gantry Plaza State Park is a 12-acre riverside oasis that boasts spectacular views of the midtown Manhattan skyline, including the Empire State Building and the United Nations. Enjoy a relaxing stroll along the park's four piers or through the park's manicured gardens and unique mist fountain. Along the way take a moment to admire the rugged beauty of the park's centerpieces - restored gantries. These industrial monuments were once used to load and unload rail car floats and barges; today they are striking reminders of our waterfront's past. With the city skyline as a backdrop and the gantries as a stage, the park's plaza is a wonderful place to enjoy a spring or summer concert."*[8]

Designed by landscape architect Thomas Balsley, Gantry Plaza State Park was created as part of the 74-acre Queens West Waterfront Development, which will ultimately include residential, commercial, hotel, and retail developments alongside schools and parks. The gantries from which the park gets its name were first constructed in 1876, during a period when the waterfront Hunters Point area of Queens served as a central point for oil refineries and manufacturing plants taking advantage of riverfront transportation networks. By the mid-20th century, industrial activity at Hunters Point began the same decline seen in other waterfront industrial neighborhoods around New York City. The empty manufacturing buildings and railyards that remained were ignored for many decades until New York's development boom reclaimed the land for contemporary uses. Today the site, with its mixed redevelopment and painted gantries standing tall alongside redesigned piers, offers one model for the transformation of waterfront industrial zones, and is notable as one of the first New York City parks designed to maintain the visibility of the shoreline. The park is similar to IKEA's Gantry Pier in that artifacts, the gantries, are deployed to tell the story of the historic industrial sites that previously lined the waterfront.

One question raised by the incorporation of these artifacts into a recreational space is how the historic vestiges of the industrial landscape are interpreted by visitors, especially in the absence of interpretive text or curation. Unlike the now famous High Line in Manhattan, where an industrial remnant became the foundation and defining component of a contemporary landscape design that incorporates the fabric of the historic elevated steel viaduct, the industrial artifacts in Gantry Plaza State Park are isolated sculptural objects (figure 4).

---

8   New York State Office of Parks, Recreation & Historic Preservation, Gantry Plaza State Park. http://parks.ny.gov/parks/149/details.aspx#sthash.JDBwxGmI.dpuf. Accessed August 18, 2014.

Figure 4. Gantry Plaza State Park, Long Island City, Queens. Photograph by the author.

Ruinscapes created through deindustrialization commemorate two historical moments: the past use of the site and its role in the industrialization of the shoreline, and the subsequent deindustrialization that defined many waterfront neighborhoods in the second half of the 20th century. Isolated industrial ruins within a park setting may offer a picturesque, aesthetic experience that prompts no awareness of or connection to the complex histories of the site. Elisabeth Chan notes, "The ruins of industry make marginalized environments apparent with their disorder, evidence of decay and traces of waste left behind. In contrast, the park containing ruins appears cleaned and in a state of healing…A park with industrial ruins has a character that can take on a themed quality, in which the notion of ruins defines the park more than the notion of industry."[9] The non-functional gantries in Gantry Plaza State Park serve as a dramatic backdrop for a waterfront landscape design, but with little connection to the surrounding development, and no historical markers to contextualize these vestiges of the area's industrial past, they ultimately serve as evocative industrial archaeology rather than a mechanism to connect New Yorkers with their city's not so distant industrial past.

Linking heritage preservation to economic development

Maintaining a balance between commemorating an industrial past and providing economic development opportunities for the future is a challenge that has played out in different ways throughout New York City. Whereas in some waterfront

---

9   Chan, "What Roles for Ruins?", 26.

industrial neighborhoods only artifacts or sole buildings have been preserved, there are also successful examples of continued industrial use serving as an agent of heritage conservation.

Brooklyn Navy Yard

The Brooklyn Navy Yard represents a rare and successful example of a waterfront historic site that has leveraged some of its historic resources as assets in the creation of a sustainable urban industrial park. Recently added to the U.S. National Register of Historic Places, the 300-acre Navy Yard was built by the Federal government in 1801 as a shipbuilding and repair facility, and remained in active use until 1966. It was subsequently purchased by the City of New York and has been the locus for intensive investment to revive local manufacturing, with a focus on sustainable practices within the management of the Yard itself and in the businesses who invest there. The Brooklyn Navy Yard Development Corporation has used public subsidy and private investment to maintain the historic graving docks and restore some of the site's historic piers and buildings using sustainable design practices, in the process attracting new manufacturing businesses and creating a Green Manufacturing Center. During Hurricane Sandy, floodwaters up to five feet high caused $50 million in damage to dozens of businesses at the waterfront complex, and the Navy Yard continues to implement stormwater management practices to mitigate the historic site's future vulnerability to flooding. Although decades of neglect under previous owners led to the loss of several historic resources, the Brooklyn Navy Yard is nonetheless a model for public subsidies leveraging private investment to cultivate a historic industrial area into a sustainable complex that retains its historic uses while adaptively repurposing its historic assets.

Water and heritage in New York City

New York City's industrial waterfront heritage must respond to the future, and the challenges and opportunities the intersection of flood management, economic development, and historic preservation will bring. This paper has presented a few representative examples from two of the city's five boroughs. Each of the sites described has been or is now a contested landscape, where both development pressure and the encroachment of the water that initially fostered the establishment of industry along the shoreline threaten to undermine the preservation of the area's historic built environment.

As the City implements its waterfront, sustainability, and resilience plans, the reinvention of the waterfront must not forego the opportunity for a re-envisioning of the historic industrial sites that helped to build the city's economies and shaped its waterfront landscapes for centuries. International examples, such as the Tate Modern in London and 798 Art Zone in Beijing exemplify the intersection of culture, heritage and economic development that can flourish in former brownfield sites, while local models like the Brooklyn Navy Yard illustrate the possibilities for retaining manufacturing uses amidst a thriving, historic, and sustainable urban industrial park. New York City's future waterfront development must allow for imaginative proposals that respect our industrial past and incorporate this heritage into the development of sustainable, resilient and integrated mixed-use cityscapes.

Sources

Bone, Kevin (ed.). 2003. *New York Waterfront: Evolution and Building Culture of the Port and Harbor*. New York: The Monacelli Press.

Burrows, Edwin G., and Mike Wallace. 2000. *Gotham: A History of New York City to 1898*. New York: Oxford University Press.

Chan, Elisabeth Clemence. 2009. "What Roles for Ruins?: Meaning and Narrative of Industrial Ruins in Contemporary Parks." *Journal of Landscape Architecture: JoLA*, 20–31.

City of New York. 2013. *PlaNYC. A Stronger, More Resilient New York*. New York: NYC Special Initiative for Rebuilding and Resiliency.

Hudson, Brian J. 1996. *Cities on the Shore: The Urban Littoral Frontier*. London; New York: Thomson Learning.

Joseph, May. 2013. *Fluid New York: Cosmopolitan Urbanism and the Green Imagination*. Durham: Duke University Press Books.

National Oceanic and Atmospheric Administration (NOAA). 20100. *Adapting to Climate Change: A Planning Guide for State Coastal Managers*. Silver Spring, MD: NOAA Office of Ocean and Coastal Resource Management.

New York-Connecticut Sustainable Communities Consortium. 2013. *Coastal Climate Resilience: Urban Waterfront Adaptive Strategies*. New York: HUD Sustainable Communities Regional Planning Grant and the City of New York.

New York City Department of City Planning. *Vision 2020: New York City Comprehensive Waterfront Plan*.

Postal, Matt. 2007. "Havemeyers & Elder Filter, Pan & Finishing House Designation Report" (LP-2268). City of New York.

Steinberg, Ted. 2014. *Gotham Unbound: The Ecological History of Greater New York*. New York: Simon & Schuster.

Heritage values of water and sea defense in Recife

Challenges for a local governmental approach

Evelyne Labanca Corrêa de Araújo

Brazilian Architect and Urban Planner;
Technical Analyst at the SEBRAE Pernambuco

Abstract

This paper aims to not only broaden the understanding but also to outline the challenges experienced by a municipal government concerning the definition and management of the heritage values of water and sea defence in Recife, Brazil.

Recife began its history almost 500 years ago. It was part of a Portuguese colony, initially a natural port and fishing village until the Dutch arrived. Instead of building a port to serve a city, Recife actually came into being the other way around: the Dutch built a city to serve the port (Castro, 1948), and water played a substantial role in its urban development. However, this condition has now become a relevant risk due to inadequate management of water and sea defence practices through the centuries in association with the climate change and expected rise of the oceans. This paper thus argues that a proper recognition of the heritage values of water and sea defence in Recife as an asset to be conserved. This challenging task for the local government can help overcome the risks the city is facing at the moment.

However, the present paper does not exhaust the notion of heritage value of water and sea defence in Recife. However, it does intend to (a) support the debate on this issue, (b) guide future studies and, especially, (c) inspire any local action as to a better definition as well as with regard to the management of the city's cultural continuity.

Therefore, after brief methodological and theoretical considerations, an analysis of the role played by water regarding the city's development is presented, divided into three parts. Firstly, an introduction points out the main critical issues concerning the current relationship between water and heritage. Next, an overview of this relationship as to the city's development from the 16th to the 21st century onwards not only increases our understanding but also outlines the main issues concerning local action. Finally, a critique of the key strategies currently adopted by the municipality is presented as the local governmental approach timidly tries to reconstruct the relationship between water and heritage as part of a climate change policy. Even though the challenges with regard to the definition of its heritage values and management as to any cultural continuity are far from overcome, efforts are made based on assessments and plans that intend to benefit from the water and sea defence identity as well as the historical practices.

Keywords: *water and sea defence – heritage values – urban development – cultural continuity.*

The objective and problem

The objective of this paper is to broaden the understanding and outline the challenges a municipal government faces as to the definition and management of the heritage values of the water and sea defence in Recife, Brazil. Presented as an interesting case-study into water and heritage issues, Recife is one of the oldest Brazilian cities. Its urbanization has always been highly impacted by the waters of rivers, streams and the Atlantic Ocean that frames its landscape.

It is stated on the subject of water and the Dutch:

> *"No element is as intrinsic to the Dutch cultural identity as water. A look at maps of the Netherlands spread over the centuries is enough to realize how defining water is for this delta."* Tracy Metz and Maartje van den Heuvel (2012).

If the words 'Dutch' and 'Netherlands' were to be replaced by 'Recife' this observation would still ring true. Water and sea defence framed not only the local landscape but also shaped Recife's entire cultural and urban development process. This relationship became a heritage itself. Established as an important international seaport and trade centre since the Brazilian colonial period, water is intrinsic to the city's culture and identity. That was one of the main reasons for the foundation of this settlement by the Portuguese in 1537 on an alluvial plain located at the mouth of the Capibaribe River. Johan Maurits van Nassau-Siegen chose it to be the political and cultural hub of the Dutch Empire in Brazil during the 17th century (Castro, 1948).

Recife began its history as a natural port and fishing village originally built by the Portuguese. When the Dutch arrived, instead of building a port to serve a city, Recife came into being the other way around. The Dutch built a city to serve the port, taking advantage of it. Water played a substantial role in its urban development through time (Castro, 1948). However, due to inappropriate management and sea defence practices through the centuries, water and the sea have become a relevant risk to the city's cultural continuity.

Recife is particularly vulnerable to climate change as its territory on average lies 2 m above sea level. It is one of the twenty most endangered coastal cities in the world due to the expected rise of the oceans in accordance with the 5th Assessment Report of the Intergovernmental Panel on Climate Change (Stocker and Dahe, 2013). Along with these risks, pressure upon historically water related areas is created by the Real Estate market, endangering a traditional water-friendly fabric that has materialized the cultural message through time. These areas are transformed into new, high-rise and gated communities as well as into touristic facilities, wearing away the material evidences of this history (Instituto Pelopidas Silveira, 2014).

Recife also illustrates the situation of small and medium-sized historical settlements in the developing world. With more good ideas than money available, yet with relevant social and management problems lingering, these cities must deal with the task of paying the debts of the past and, at the same time, strongly invest in their future. However, this often endangers any heritage in the name of progress. In the case of Recife, the challenge is far from overcome. That is exactly where a more effective definition and management of the heritage values of sea defence could play an essential role in the city's cultural continuity. As water has been a major framework within the city's historical development process since the very beginning, its correct recognition and management can help to improve the responses to these threats.

The method

As a classical single case-study investigation based on Yin (2005), the challenges as to the definition and a local government's approach concerning the heritage value of seawater defence in Recife are discussed here by focusing on an analysis outlining the role that water played throughout the city's historical process. This is carried out in order to (a) allow further works to deepen the subject and (b) reorient local government policies and plans in order to consider this a key issue with regard to the city's culturally oriented urban development.

Prior to an analysis, the main theoretical aspects were reviewed, especially those regarding the heritage value and the significance as a cultural process, in order to guide the investigation. In addition, the historical and current cartography were examined to help understand the urbanization process, verifying the presence of water on the city's territory through time. Finally, the local government's main plans and policies were analysed not only to reveal the connection between the challenge at hand but also the water and sea defence heritage value as key subjects in local action.

The structure of the analysis was based on a simple description of the 5 centuries of dialectic relation between urbanization and water. This analysis comprised: (a) a brief introduction pointing out the main current critical issues concerning the relationship between water and heritage, (b) an overview of this relationship as to the city's development from the 16th to the 21st century increasing the understanding and outlining the main issues needing local action, and (c) a final critique concerning the key strategies currently adopted by the municipality is delivered as the local governmental approach timidly tries to reconstruct the relationship between water and heritage as part of a climate change policy. Even though the challenges to any definition and management of its heritage values are far from overcome, efforts are made based on assessments and plans that intend to benefit from water and sea defence identity as well as historical practices.

Important theoretical aspects

This paper does not exhaust the notion of the heritage value of sea defence in Recife. Its purpose is (a) to contribute to the debate on this notion, (b) guide future studies on its improved definition and management as to Recife's cultural continuity, and (c) help other small and medium-sized cities in a similar situation with this task. What can we understand by the heritage value of sea defence in this case? In order to broaden the discussion, certain important theoretical backgrounds are considered here.

Riegl (1999) brought the understanding that the notion of monuments was the one that could satisfy material and spiritual needs of mankind, thus becoming a cultural heritage. That is to say, it has no value on its own except for the value mankind gives to it by means of a cultural process. In accordance with Jokilehto (2006), heritage value can be understood as a social association of qualities to things being produced '*through cultural-social processes, learning and maturing of awareness*' (Jokilehto, 2006). The Burra Charter (2013) tackles the notion of cultural significance as synonymous to cultural heritage significance and cultural heritage value, this significance possibly changing over time and with use. It brings '*aesthetic, historic, scientific, social or spiritual value for past, present or future generations*', cultural significance being completely embodied in the place itself, in its setting, in its use, and in the various associations and meanings (Burra Charter, 2013).

The reef barrier and the waterfront constitute a main fabric, as interpreted by the Burra Charter, materializing the sea defence heritage and revealing values through the relationship the city has built with water over this fabric as a cultural-social process. Moreover, it is also constantly built by it. As this fabric is locally shaped, the conservation of the heritage value of sea defence in Recife relies heavily on a local governmental approach. From Alois Riegl's definition of values (1999) to the Burra Charter contributions on defining cultural significance (2013) and the Statement of Amsterdam relating to water and heritage (2013), it is clear that a road must be travelled before the heritage value of sea defence in Recife can receive proper recognition.

Following these directives, Randall Mason (in de la Torre, 2002) suggests the following steps when integrating value assessments with planning processes: (a) creating a statement of significance, (b) matching the values to the physical characteristics of the site, (c) analyzing threats as well as opportunities, and (d) policy making and action planning. In Mason's view, these steps should not be taken as a linear process as they may overlap. In Recife's case, the creation of a statement of significance in order to maintain a cultural continuity is nowadays challenging due to the threat posed by the appeal of waterfront areas for the real estate market, paradoxically associated with the risk of sea rise due to climate change. In this context, managerial strategies have attempted to focus on land development control as well as climate change mitigation policies in order to combine any mitigation of the mentioned risks with the opportunity of reorienting the ongoing policies towards a culturally oriented process.

Another aspect highlights the need to '*communicate relevant information on water management as both risk to and essential part of heritage* (…) *through collaboration with the cultural sector and use of multiple communication channels including policy briefs and new media*' (Statement of Amsterdam, 2013). This investigation plays a double role: while serving as a directive for a future statement of significance, it also discloses the water and heritage-related approach, helping to not only increase awareness but also to share the importance of this relationship with the city's future. After all, assessment of values in Recife's case attributed to water and sea defence are the main initiatives as to shaping decisions and increasing conservation efforts.

The analysis

The relationship between water and heritage addressed here is a starting point for relevant strategies based on the historical and social significance as to the city's present and future generations. Getting to know and understand the historical process is thus the base for furthering the discussions on preparing a statement of significance evolving directly from the values attributed to the case of Recife.

Recife is one of the first colonial settlements and the earliest state capital in Brazil. Founded in 1537 as the port of Olinda, it is now one of the country's most important cities. Occupied by the Dutch between 1630 and 1654, it became one of the most prosperous cities of the Americas (Zancheti, 2006). Capital of the state of Pernambuco, Recife is located in Brazil's Northeast Region. Its 1.5 million habitants consist of a 100% urban population distributed across 219 km²[1]. Recife is intersected by more than 50 km of rivers and approximatively 100 streams and canals which are originally part of a floodable mangrove area, surrounded by 60 m high argyle hills vulnerable to landslides.

Current critical issues

Learning to deal with the sea has always been a matter of survival for Recife as it was literally framed by water. Its original territory was an isthmus (i.e., a narrow piece of land positioned between a continuous sandstone reef barrier) the estuary and huge mangrove areas spreading out across an extensive alluvial marine floodplain, as illustrated by Golijath in 1648 (Menezes, 1988). According to Oliveira (1942), the sea was the main sculptor of the city's territory when it created the sandstone reefs that naturally defended the floodplain from its waters. Charles Darwin who was familiar with these reefs doubted the existence on our planet of a natural structure that seemed to be so artificial (Oliveira, 1942).

The relationship between water and heritage has been dialectic since the dawn of Recife's existence. Due to the city's natural conditions constraining any occupation, in recent decades, the centripetal forces of urban growth have replaced low density neighbourhoods by means of high buildings. The rich and the poor share the habit of putting pressure on these fragile areas, landfilling them in order

---

1   All data from the Government of Pernambuco (2013).

Figure 1. "De haven van Pharnambucq", C. B Golijath – 1648. Source: Atlas Histórico Cartográfico do Recife (1988).

to make room for high-rise condominiums, shopping centres and slums, especially stilt houses locally known as *palafitas* (Alves, 2009).

All this has squeezed Recife between the impacts of urbanization on one side and the present impacts of climate change at the sea on the other side. Two-thirds of its territory lies at an average of 2 m above sea level. Although this has been a known threat since recent decades, only in the 21st century has awareness started to play a role in the local government's strategy for action. An important part of this awareness was the understanding of the role that played over the centuries in building a cultural identity.

A historical overview

The reef

The relationship between water and sea defence heritage in Recife has been evident since its origin as a small settlement with row houses built during the 16th century. The former fishing village was named after the Portuguese word for 'reef' referring to the barrier reef situated along most of its Atlantic coast. Suitable for a natural seaport and sufficiently deep for large ships, it became one of the most strategically positioned and economically dynamic settlements of the entire Portuguese colonial period in South America. Recife was at that time part of Olinda, the main settlement located at a higher point of the site. The Portuguese chose this position because of its strategic combination of a hill for the village and especially the natural seaport, through which they brought slaves from Africa and exported sugarcane, wood, and other goods. The barrier reef, the port, and the natural sea defence infrastructures enabled this settlement to thrive (Castro, 1948; Oliveira, 1942; and Zancheti, 2006).

The settlement

During the 17th century, the Dutch West India Company took over most of Brazil's Northeast Region. As part of a colonization of the Americas, Recife turned into *Mauritsstad*[2], the capital of Dutch Brazil, independent and more important than Olinda. As one of the main settlements of the so-called 'new world', it then included the first botanical garden, zoo, and synagogue in the Americas. The incoming rulers introduced their waterfront culture and practices. Wharves and sugar mills were built in order to improve the settlement's economic potential. Inland channels and waterways were designed to overcome water as a limitation for expansion. With the Dutch, the sea defence began to form the centre of the planning issues. Portuguese fortresses were destroyed and rebuilt according to Dutch designs and defence techniques. The first bridges were constructed. Settlements were expanded to newly dry lands as commercial hubs in order to deal with sugar production. During the 24 years of Dutch domination *Mauritsstad* emerged highlighting planning applying water practices by means of the design and construction of significant works. Around the middle of the century the Portuguese had occupied *Mauritsstad*, not only expelling the Dutch but also by and large destroying the culture of dealing with water (Castro, 1948; Menezes, 1988; Instituto Pelopidas Silveira, 2013; Sa and Vasconcelos, 2011).

The economy

Returning to the Portuguese, during the 18th century economy flourished by means of river navigation. Embankments were built beside the coastline and began to simply push the historical settlement and urban activities away from the sea. Along with numerous Roman Catholic churches, new suburbs sprawled hereby developing one of the largest problems of Recife to the present day: the increase of wastewater and the loss of water planning practices (Castro, 1948; Menezes, 1988 and 2014; Instituto Pelopidas Silveira, 2013; Sa and Vasconcelos, 2011).

The urbanization

The 19th century was the era of urbanization. Great public works (e.g., theatres, avenues) were built and urban activities expanded. Two main rivers intersect the city (the Beberibe and Capibaribe Rivers), along with more than 100 natural canals. Recife then became known as the Venice of Brazil thanks to the massive presence of water courses in its urban landscape. Although the inner port was still

---

2   Named after Governor Johan Maurits van Nassau-Siegen, ruler of Dutch Brazil.

active, providing all kinds of goods to the population, coastal navigation played a main role in the city's economy. The port was expanded. However, the increasing population and the new living quarters also implied that sewage pollution was dumped directly into the urban waters, increasing the stilting of the water courses. The successive land filling in the course of the centuries further endangered the critical condition of Recife's urban environment (Menezes, 1988 and 2014; Instituto Pelopidas Silveira, 2013; Sa and Vasconcelos, 2011; Empresa Municipal de Manutenção e Limpeza Urbana, 2014).

The denial

Recife developed into a metropolis during the 20th century, growing rapidly towards locations where once sugar mills were found in a conurbation process, consolidating an ambiguous waterfront culture. On the one hand, the turn of the century was a time of denial. Inside the city's centre, the Port of Recife was enlarged by means of destroying a great deal of the urban structure dating from the 17th and 18th century. The more recent settlements turned their backs to the polluted urban waters. Poverty began to occupy the rivers and canals by means of stilt houses. Slums were literally built on water. Two major floods affected more than 66% of the city during the 1970s with significant human and material loss. Paradoxically, towards the end of the century, the land value on the waterfront increased because of privileged views. Moreover, the real estate brought pressure upon the historical areas, replacing water-friendly built heritage with gated, high-rise communities. On the other hand, an inadequate management and use of water was still problematic. Sewage compromised the quality of life. Public works altered sinuous river beds. Channels and estuaries were landfilled hereby influencing tidal movements, increasing floods, as well as the erosion of plots of land by means of the sea and riverbanks (Menezes, 1988 and 2014; Instituto Pelopidas Silveira, 2013 and 2014; Sa and Vasconcelos, 2011; Empresa Municipal de Manutenção e Limpeza Urbana, 2014).

The challenge

Silting of the water courses and land sealing as yet continue during the 21st century, along with an urbanization process under the dilemma of preserving *versus* renewing the city's urban structures. All this has contributed to an increase in the risks of floods especially whenever frequent tropical rain is combined with high tides. The time honoured fishing village has turned into a global village providing us with the opportunity to learn from its history what to do and what to no longer do, as a matter of survival. The challenge is to not only look at the past in order to understand the relationship between water and heritage through the centuries but also to rehabilitate this relationship (Instituto Pelopidas Silveira, 2013; Sa and Vasconcelos, 2011; Empresa Municipal de Manutenção e Limpeza Urbana, 2014; Secretaria de Meio Ambiente e Sustentabilidade / ICLEI-Local Governments for Sustainability, 2014).

	16th	17th	18th	19th	20th	21st
	THE REEF	THE SETTLEMENT	THE ECONOMY	THE URBANIZATION	THE DENIAL	THE CHALLENGE
WATER	Estuary and mangrove	Channels and waterways	Waste water	Sewage	Sewerage	Rehabilitation
			River navigation	Coastal navigation	Land filling	Land Sealing
	Natural port	Wharves	Embankments	Inner port	Port enlargement	Stilting
BUILT HERITAGE	Sugar	Sugar mills	Suburbs	Quarters	Real estate	Preservation X Renewal
	Row houses	Fortresses and bridges	Churches	Public works	High rise	
	Fishermen village	*Mauritsstad*	Town of Recife	City of Recife	Metropolis of Recife	Global village

Table 1. The synthesis of the dialectic relationship between water and urban heritage in Recife, between the 16th and the 21st century. Source: Elaborated by the Author (2014).

This historical overview reveals two main issues to be discussed here. On the one hand, if the city was established because of (and framed by) water as well as consequent sea defence practices and structures, the areas originally occupied by the water-related activities and water itself form the physical fabric that retains their heritage values through time. They should be treated as cultural heritage in order to conserve and improve the notion of cultural continuity. On the other hand, the main factors regarding their original location and the factors guiding the city's progression, or growth, as brilliantly dealt with by Castro (1948), were all based on water as a key element. In the initial periods, waterways were also an element to be defended against. The reason for this: sea and rivers merged into the alluvial plain and needed to be controlled by way of urbanization. They were also a condition to be overcome. The city expansion denies the need for any proper water-related planning and management (e.g., the suppression of mangrove and landfilling of floodable areas). This all reduces the room for water over time.

In order to eliminate any doubts, a comparative analysis of the cartography registers over time shows that this reduction was drastic. In the beginning, Recife's trajectory water surface was significantly large enough to enable the Dutch to choose such a reduction. It has decreased by a factor of more than seven in the course of 5 centuries. In 1648, the water occupied c.64.45 km² to drop to 21.18 km² in 1876. In 2007, according to the municipal database, the water surface comprised 9.09 km².

The urbanisation process of Recife leaves no room to reconfigure water as the larger feature in its landscape i.e., the city cannot simply give back the room it took throughout the years in a not so friendly way. However, that very same reason for its location factors can, and should, be treated as a cultural heritage to be preserved. Above all, the sea defence was a testimony here. The reason for this is:

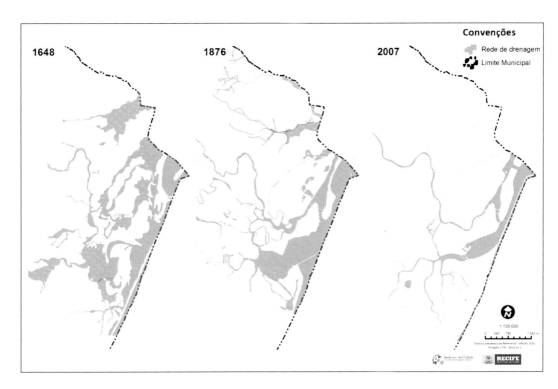

Figure 2. The reduction of the water surface in Recife through the centuries. Source: Pelopidas Silveira Institute for the City of Recife (2015).

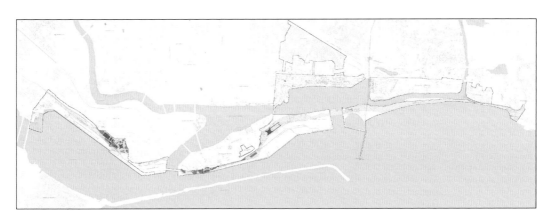

Figure 3. The potential archaeological water and sea defence areas in the main waterfront of Recife. Source: Projeto Recife-Olinda (2005).

the value was beginning to be built upon the cultural significance as addressed in the Burra Charter (2013).

The main zones with the attribute of physically retaining any heritage value as a testimony of the waterfront transformation over time are presented here. Outlined in Fig. 3 as potential archaeological areas, they are identified as part of the studies of a major project supervised by the City Halls of Recife and Olinda, and the State Government of Pernambuco in 2003-2005, but discontinued by the current governors. The problem is: the current initiatives carried out by the local government timidly address the need to deepen the recognition and the appropriate management of the heritage value of water and sea defence in Recife.

The local governmental main approaches in relationship with the heritage values of water and sea defence in Recife

Regarding the necessity to better address the heritage value of water and the sea defence in Recife, a critique of key strategies currently adopted by the municipality has been composed. Focusing on a local level, the dangerous situation caused by climate change and the expected rise of the oceans has been the municipality's main concern. It has driven Recife to realize the need to rethink its future. Recife is taking this opportunity to plan a sea defence and resilience based on reshaping the relationship between water and heritage, hereby gradually repositioning its urban development course. The challenge is to (a) reconstruct this fruitful relationship (b) improve the cultural continuity and (c) enhance the significance established in the city's foundation during the Dutch period of domination as previously discussed.

In this way, important partnerships are carried out by the municipality rendering the actions taken more effective. Innovative and integrated management structures are implemented. Urban land use, spatial planning laws and instruments are beginning to be revised. Innovative policies have been designed, all aimed at improving urban sustainability.

The main core of this transformation is a major initiative entitled the Urban Low Emission Development Project – Urban-LEDs (Secretaria de Meio Ambiente e Sustentabilidade/ ICLEI, 2014). It is mainly a low-carbon development strategy, a partnership between the City Hall of Recife and ICLEI – Local Governments for Sustainability. This agreement, signed in 2013, allowed Recife to become the first city in the North and Northeast Regions of Brazil to measure the produced amount of greenhouse gases. Reduction goals have been established in order to gradually reduce the emissions until 2020.

Under the Urban-LEDs Project's major plans, spatial planning instruments and interventions are being reoriented in order to include low-carbon perspective and importance of the historic rehabilitation of urban water management. A municipal climate change policy is also designed and implemented (Secretaria de Meio Ambiente e Sustentabilidade, 2014a), guided in part by concepts of environmental conservation and resilience, and control of greenhouse gas emissions.

Figure 4. A view of the historic centre of Recife with high-rise buildings on ancient water and sea defence areas. Source: City Hall of Recife (2014).

The evaluations carried out under the Urban-LED Project have observed that the current Master Plan is very permissive as to the development without defining any social, heritage and environmental payback. On the contrary, it stimulates urban sprawl with unsustainable patterns of densification, putting pressure on urban water systems and the last existing green areas. In response, as part of the *Recife Education and Public Management Project* (City Hall of Recife/World Bank), the muncipality is engaged in designing a major land use and regulation plan, consisting of revising the city's main spatial planning instruments. The goal, in part, is to qualify any urban development and increase the heritage and urban water system protection.

One of the most important initiatives, however, is a specific Master Plan for the management of urban waters (Empresa Municipal de Manutenção e Limpeza Urbana, 2014). It is driven by principles e.g., multidisciplinarity, the adoption of hydrographic basins as planning units, an emphasis upon economically and environmentally sustainable solutions, the harvest and control of stormwater, the reduction of sealing, the inhibiting occupation of lowland and fragile areas, the increase of flood reservoirs instead of the canalization of water courses. All this is integrated into the Recife land use and regulation plan. The strategy is to act in large, medium and small water courses, from rain gutters and ordinary infrastructures to rivers and channels, gradually moving from dealing with water as a problem to treating it as a potential urban asset for sustainability. The main goal of this plan is to start planning with water practices again, a normal method during the 17th century but gradually lost over time. More than an infrastructural action

Figure 5. A view of the old military and port facilities at Cais José Estelita during the Ocupe Estelita. Source: Midia Ninja (2014).

instrument, this Master Plan concerning urban waters management would help to restore the historic continuity in Recife when it comes to water and sea defence.

Making everything work together is not easy. Political issues interfere on numerous occasions. It is not unusual to have moments of conflict and to misunderstand that the values of sea defense are dynamic and need to be constantly built as cross-cut subjects in other plans and actions. In this way, the municipality has created a transdisciplinary committee in order to integrate local and regional stakeholders from the public and private relevant sectors called the Climate Change Committee. An effort has been made to position the members in order to achieve the same goal as it has not only the task to align concepts but also to review policies and action plans which various institutions have designed for the city.

In the end, most initiatives underline the historic relationship between water and heritage in Recife in a residual way. No specific heritage-guided plan or committee has been developed. This increases the fragility of the issue. It usually ends up relying on the sensibility of occasional managers that reorient (when possible) activities in order to embrace heritage values, especially those concerning water and sea defence in Recife.

However, an interesting phenomenon to wit a social movement called Direitos Urbanos (meaning Urban Rights) has emerged in Recife in 2012. This internet-based community movement was founded in 2002 and comprises more than 30.000 followers of all ages and backgrounds. One of its main purposes is: fight for the cultural continuity and conservation in Recife. It started a massive campaign in May 2014 related to the heritage values of water and sea defence against a major real estate project located on a 1.1 km² site known as Cais Jose Estelita. The area represents one of the last examples of a military and port occupation of the waterfront under Dutch domination during the 17th century which is still almost intact. The strategy of this campaign involves (a) studies and cooperating with Occupy movements and (b) stimulating a constant engagement of the population in social media groups and frequent meetings.

The group and its supporters are managing to replace the notion of heritage for a wider public in Recife, often going against economic interests. Its fight for the preservation of the Cais Jose Estelita has now disseminated worldwide and is known as #OcupeEstelita. Among other subjects, this internet-based movement has managed to refresh discussions on heritage values in a way never seen before in Recife.

Final words

As Zancheti (2006) mentioned, conservation and urban development are two sides of the same coin. There is no conservation or cultural continuity without any urban development as it requires social resources that do not generate benefits on their own. In addition, the construction of heritage values (i.c., water and sea defence) is necessarily a long, complex and multi-faceted process. Therefore, defining these values not only in a scientific or governmental approach, but also in a social approach comprises a way for them to survive and enhance over time. All studies and policies will not suffice without any public awareness and engagement. This can be called cultural continuity.

Speaking of heritage values of water and sea defence, inspired by the time honoured and current Dutch water management strategies, Recife needs to work on new paradigms. Instead of only containing rivers, stilting and sealing the land, these paradigms must seek to '(...) maximize opportunities to make nature an ally in the strife to stabilize water levels and prevent floods. (...) this new paradigm is accompanied by slogans such as space for rivers, living with water and building with nature' (de Boer and Bressers, 2011).

As declared in the Statement of Amsterdam (2013), attractive, resilient and sustainable cities fully integrate their heritage management, water technology, urban and spatial planning and public engagement. In the case of Recife, the challenge is far from being overcome albeit important moves are being made towards this goal. This is exactly where the values of sea defence heritage along with an integrated assessment as to action planning can play an essential role concerning urban development.

Learning to tackle sea defence over the past centuries shows that the relationship between water and heritage has turned itself into a cultural heritage. Values shaping it rely in particular on the historic, aesthetic, scientific and social significance for present and future generations. However, only the people of today have the power to make the decisions in order to guarantee any cultural continuity. When properly recognized and managed as such, the heritage value of a sea defence can be of great benefit when increasing resilience and helping to protect other forms of heritage in a more integrated and sustainable manner.

The local poet named Carlos Pena Filho once said that Recife is "*half stolen from the sea and half from the imagination of men*" (in Dias, 2011). The present article has provided a brief overview of the way in which this happened through time, its impacts, what is being carried out in order to manage this relationship between water, the sea and the city, and between water and heritage i.e., the main challenges for a local governmental approach. After all, Recife cannot stand still while ignoring that the same water and sea that shaped its territory as well as its history is now trying to take its half back.

References

Alves, Paulo Reynaldo Maia. 2009. *Valores do Recife: o valor do solo na evolução da cidade.* Recife: Fundarpe.

Araujo, Evelyne L.C. 2013. *Key issues on urban land use and development planning in Recife, Brazil.* Internal Report. Recife: Instituto Pelopidas Silveira.

Batista Filho, Gerson. 2010. Entre os rios e o mar, o descaminho das águas na RMR. In: Monteiro, Bernardo Silva; Vitório, Afonso (Org.). *A interação entre o setor de consultoria e universidades na produção do conhecimento técnico em Pernambuco: coletânea de artigos técnicos.* Recife: Sinaenco.

Castro, Josue de. *Fatores de localização da cidade do Recife.* 1948. Brasil: Imprensa Nacional.

Dias, Julio Cesar Tavares. 2011. Poeta da Cidade: o Recife na poesia de Carlos Pena Filho. In V Colóquio de História – Perspectivas históricas: historiografia, pesquisa e patrimônio. Recife: UniversidadeCatólica de Pernambuco. http://www.unicap.br/coloquiodehistoria/wp-content/uploads/2013/11/5Col-p.915-928.pdf. Accessed 15 March 2013.

Direitos Urbanos. 2012. https://www.facebook.com/groups/direitosurbanos/ Last access 13 January 2015.

Empresa Municipal de Manutenção e Limpeza Urbana. 2014. *Plano Diretor de Drenagem Urbana do Recife.* Recife: Prefeitura do Recife.

Governo de Pernambuco, Prefeitura do Recife, Prefeitura de Olinda. 2005. Projeto de Requalificação Recife Olinda.

ICOMOS Australia. 2013. The Burra Charter: The Australia ICOMOS Charter for Places of Cultural Significance. http://australia.icomos.org/wp-content/uploads/The-Burra-Charter-2013-Adopted-31.10.2013.pdf. Accessed 12 December 2014.

ICOMOS Netherlands. 2013. *The Statement of Amsterdam – ICOMOS Conference on Water & Heritage "Protecting delta: Heritage helps!"* http://www.icomos.nl/media/Water_and_Heritage/Final_Statement_Protecting_Deltas_Heritage_Helps.pdf. Accessed 20 September 2014.

Instituto Pelopidas Silveira. 2013. *Atlas de Bolso de Planejamento Urbano do Recife – versao preliminar.* Recife: Prefeitura do Recife.

Instituto Pelopidas Silveira/ The World Bank. *Plano de Ordenamento Territorial do Recife.* Internal Report/ Terms of Reference. Recife: Prefeitura do Recife.

Jokilehto J. 2006, World Heritage: Defining the outstanding universal value. City & Time 2 (2): 1. [online] URL: http://www.ct.ceci-br.org. Accessed 3 October 2014.

Menezes, Jose Luiz da Mota (org). 1988. *Atlas Histórico Cartográfico do Recife*. Recife: URB/Fundação Joaquim Nabuco - Editora Massangana.

Menezes, Jose Luiz da Mota (org). 2014. *Pontes do Recife: a construção da mobilidade*. Recife: Bureau de Cultura.

Metz, Tracy and van den Heuvel, Maartje. 2012. Water and the Dutch. Rotterdam: NAi Publishers.

Museu da Cidade do Recife. 2014. *Base cartográfica*. Recife: Prefeitura do Recife.

Oliveira, Valdemar de. 1942. *Geologia da planície do Recife: contribuição ao seu estudo*. Recife: Oficinas gráficas do Jornal do Commercio.

Sa, Lucilene Antunes Correia Marques and Vasconcelos, Thatiana Lima. 2011. *A Cartografia Histórica da Região Metropolitana do Recife*. In 1° Simposio Brasileiro de cartografia histórica "Passado e presente nos velhos mapas: conhecimento e poder. https://www. ufmg.br/rededemuseus/crch/simposio/VASCONCELOS_THATIANA_E_SA_ LUCILENE_ANTUNES.pdf. Accessed September 2014.

Secretaria de Meio Ambiente e Sustentabilidade. 2014. *Política de Sustentabilidade e de Enfrentamento das Mudanças Climáticas (Lei Nº 18.011/2014)*. Recife: Prefeitura do Recife. http://www.legisweb.com.br/legislacao/?id=269646. Accessed 2 June 2014.

Secretaria de Meio Ambiente e Sustentabilidade. 2014. *Sistema Municipal de Unidades protegidas – SMUP (Lei Nº 18014/2014)*. Recife: Prefeitura do Recife. http://www. legisweb.com.br/legislacao/?id=270178. Accessed 2 June 2014.

Secretaria de Meio Ambiente e Sustentabilidade/ ICLEI-Local Governments for Sustainability. 2014. *I Inventário das emissões de gases de efeito estufa na cidade do Recife*. Internal Report. Recife: Prefeitura do Recife.

Secretaria de Meio Ambiente e Sustentabilidade / ICLEI-Local Governments for Sustainability. 2014. *Projeto Urban-Leds: Plano de Baixo Carbono do Recife*. Internal Report. Recife: Prefeitura do Recife.

Stocker, T. and Dahe, Qin. 2013. *Climate change 2013: The physical science basis*. http:// pt.slideshare.net/IPCCGeneva/fifth-assessment-report-working-group-i. Accessed 2 June 2014.

Torre, Marta de la. 2002. *Assessing the Values of Cultural Heritage: Research report*. Los Angeles: The Getty Conservation Institute. http://www.getty.edu/conservation/ publications_resources/pdf_publications/pdf/assessing.pdf . Accessed November 2014.

Yin, Robert K. 2005. Estudo de caso: planejamento e métodos. Porto Alegre: Bookman.

Zancheti, Silvio M. 2006. Desenvolvimento versus conservação urbana em Recife – um problema de governança e gestão pública. In *Reabilitação urbana de centralidades metropolitanas: reflexões e experiências na América Latina do século 21*, eds Cesar Barros and Evelyne L. C. Araujo, 49-65. Recife: Zoludesig.

Hazard vulnerability and management of cultural heritage in the context of water-related hazards in the Republic of Korea

Hae Un Rii[a], Hyo Hyun Sung[b] and Jisoo Kim[c]

a. Professor, Dept. of Geography Education, Dongguk University
b. Professor, Dept. of Social Studies Education, Ewha Womans University
c. Graduate student, Dept. of Social Studies Education, Ewha Womans University

1. Introduction

Water-related hazards have been major issues with the cultural heritage of Korea. Due to the geographical location of the Korean peninsula between the Eurasian continent and the Pacific Ocean in the mid-latitude, a concentration of precipitation during the summer characterizes the climate of Korea. Intensive rainfall between June and July, called *Jangma*, marks the rainy season. Typhoons now cross the Peninsula with strong winds and heavy rainfall. The *Jangma* and typhoons have caused floods and resulted in countless examples of damage and loss of cultural heritage every year (Fig. 1). In order to reduce such hazards and protect human life and property, large-scale structures (e.g., dams, weirs, etc.) have been built along the rivers of Korea. Meanwhile changing river channels and massive

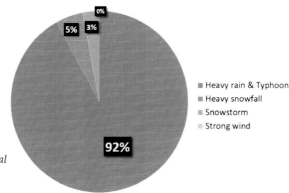

Figure 1. The total amount of damage caused by various natural hazards in Korea between 1992 and 2012.

dredging have accompanied the constructing of dams and weirs. These man-made alterations have comprised another variable that has exposed cultural heritage sites to danger.

The conservation of cultural heritage should be requisitely protected from such impacts in that the loss and damage of cultural assets are inestimable on account of a panhuman value consisting of originality and historical meaning in the people's mind. Damage to the cultural heritage by natural hazards is directly related to the damage to historic, ethnic and national symbolism. Being a type of damage that can never be recovered, it is therefore important to recognize which vulnerability and impacts of the hazards are present and where, when, and how they occur, and which solutions exist in order to resolve any current or possible future issues in Korea. Vulnerability can be defined as the degree of level that a certain system is affected by the changing climate, extreme meteorological events, etc. according to the IPCC Third Assessment report in 2001. This concept includes climate exposure as an external stress and a disturbance as well as sensitivity and adaptability as the internal states of a system. It thus essentially concerns the natural and the anthropogenic factors of a certain hazard. As to the greater concern for the water-related hazards in Korea, the issues of disaster management with regard to the cultural heritage should be reviewed within the concept of vulnerability, concerning the interrelationship between distinct characteristics of the Korean climate as the external stress and inappropriate management of water systems as internal state.

The present study aims to review the issues regarding water-related disasters affecting the cultural heritage within the Korean context. The issues were examined in two direct and detailed aspects: natural and anthropogenic effects, although these effects are coupled in the real world. In terms of natural aspects, flood hazards and cultural heritage were reviewed under the climatic features of Korea. Man-made interventions in rivers affecting the cultural heritage were introduced in terms of the anthropogenic aspect. Policy issues and efforts in order to improve the conservation of the cultural heritage were also reviewed.

2. The natural aspects of water-related hazards on the cultural heritage

2.1 The climatic environment of Korea

The Korean peninsula, on which Korea is situated, features a monsoon season as it is located on the east coast of the Eurasian Continent. Because of the locational factor, albeit it in the same latitude as the west coast of the Eurasian Continent, it is hotter in summer followed by the North Pacific high and colder in winter due to the Siberian high (Lee 2000, 3-4; Kwon, et al. 2004, 58-62). The annual precipitation of Korea is *c.*1300 mm, mostly concentrated between June and September i.e., nationally: 1.6 times the global average of 807 mm. Moreover, the coefficient of the river regime, the rate of variability of the highest to lowest discharge per annum, lies between *c*.300 and 400 mm. This implies there has been high risk of drought and flood hazard in Korea, although it could depend on the level of the adaptive strategy in local scale (MCT 2006, 10).

The total precipitation of the Korean peninsula tends to be concentrated in the summer season because of typhoons and the frequent rainfall during two wet seasons, the *Jangma* and the *Late Jangma*. The *Jangma* starts in mid-June when a stationary front is formed between the subtropical oceanic air mass of the North Pacific and the polar air mass (Lee 2000, 127-128). From mid-June, when it reaches the southern part of the Peninsula until it moves northward, to late July between 50% and 70 % of the annual precipitation occurs in the form of a steady downpour (Lee 2000, 132). After the *Jangma*, a heavy convective rainfall often occurs in the hot weather of the North Pacific high pressure system. Another wet season, the *Late Jangma*, sets in around late August to early September. The subtropical high pressure system weakens and the polar pressure system high strengthens during this season as the front zone comes down on the peninsula, causing another heavy rainfall (Lee 2000, 128-130). Moreover, several tropical low pressure systems in the form of typhoons strike with heavy rain between July and October. Approximately three typhoons visit the Peninsula annually especially between July and September. Typhoons bring a sudden downpour for *c*.4 days within a 150 km radius in average, triggering floods and landslides. In a topographical environment such as Korea where 70 % of the territory is mountainous, the effect of a typhoon is easily combined with an orographic effect. Now and again it is connected to the timely rain front during the *Jangma* season. Its impact is often amplified toward an extremely high precipitation in the wider area (Lee 2000, 128; NRICH 2007, 76).

The wet season and typhoons cause frequent heavy rains which inevitably lead to floods during the summer. For this reason cultural heritage sites are often flooded too. Heavy rainfalls not only cause direct damage such as flooding a heritage site, but can also be a source of indirect damage bringing about other forms of disaster. For example, a stone heritage may be cracked from the bottom to the top due to the unstable ground. This may happen as a result of change in the ground e.g., erosion or unequal subsidence due to continuous rainfall (NRICH 2007, 288). Landslides caused by heavy rainfall may also lead to serious damage to cultural properties in mountainous areas. For instance, the Ihawjang House, designated a Historic Site, a private residence of Syngman Rhee the first President of the Republic of Korea, was damaged by a landslide after the heavy rainfall of 400 mm per hour in 2011. In the case of typhoons, strong winds are a powerful external force when destroying heritage sites: it inflicts great damage to structures already weakened due to intense rainfall (NRICH 2007, 74).

The influence of intense rainfalls and typhoons has become more extreme recently. According to research on climate change, the annual precipitation of Korea has been rising (NRICH 2010, 42; Lee et al. 2011b, 243). Especially the amount of precipitation during the wet season i.e., between July and August, has shown a sharp rise in the entire Korean peninsula (Park et al. 2008, 329; Lee et al. 2011b, 243). More intense rainfall over a shorter period of time increases the danger of flooding (NRICH 2010, 24). Typhoons also show differences. The annual precipitation caused by typhoons has risen more than 40-90%. In Gyoungsangbuk-do, the southeastern province of the Korean peninsula, the annual precipitation induced by typhoons between 1973 and 1982 was 61.36 mm per year. However, it has increased to 104.93 mm per year between 1994 and 2005. (NRICH 2008a, 417). The maximum precipitation per day during the typhoon period shows a significant increase as well. The average of the daily maximum precipitation during the 1973-1982 typhoon period was 43.95 mm per day, whereas between 1994 and 2005 it measured 78.49 mm per day (NRICH 2008a, 417). Since 1994, within this context, landslides and the like in the mountainous areas have increased as has flooding in the low lying areas (NRICH 2007, 294).

2.2 The flood risk analysis on the cultural heritage of Korea

Under the threat of floods and storm hazards to the cultural heritage, the Korean government and related academics have recently paid attention to the conservation of cultural heritage as well as of human life and property as a main target of flood protection plans. Several research projects have focused on the impact of storms and floods to heritage sites since 2006. It was initiated by related government authorities and research institutes such as the Cultural Heritage Administration and the National Research Institute of Cultural Heritage of Korea.

According to the results of research, the damage to the cultural heritage of Korea was mainly due to heavy rainfall and typhoons. In the case of the heritage consisting of stone, the proportion of water-related damage such as floods due to heavy rainfall and typhoons was measured to be over 30% (NRICH 2008b, 31). Wooden heritage was also damaged mainly due to flooding after heavy rainfall and typhoons (NRICH 2008b, 30). A survey of local government officers and experts in charge of heritage management revealed that floods were considered the most devastating factor as to cultural heritage (NRICH 2008b, 60).

Within this context, a national institute has conducted a flood hazard assessment for several historic sites since 2010 applying hydrologic modeling under simulated heavy rainfall. It was predicted that any cultural heritage in heavily urbanized areas, such as the Temporary Palace at the Hwaseong Fortress in Suwon City, might

Figure 2. The temporary Palace at the Hwaseong Fortress and the flood inundation map of the site with a 100-year return period of rainfall scenario (Cultural Heritage Administration of Korea; NRICH 2009).

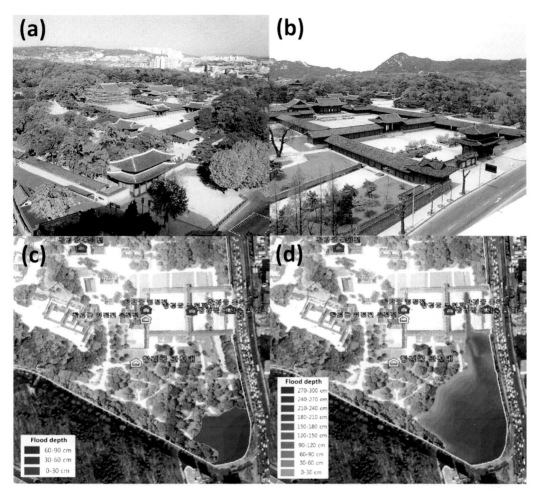

Figure 3. Top: (a) the Changdeokgung Palace and (b) the Changgyeonggung Palace near the central business districts of Seoul. Bottom: the flood inundation maps of a 500-year return period depending on (c) the 1-hour duration and (d) the 3-hour duration rainfall (Cultural Heritage Administration of Korea; NRICH 2011).

Figure 4. The Gyeongbokgung Palace near the central business districts of Seoul and the flood inundation map of the 180-minute duration rainfall with a 200-year return period (Cultural Heritage Administration of Korea; NRICH 2012).

Figure 5. Jongmyo Shrine near the central business districts of Seoul and the flood inundation map of the 180-minute duration rainfall with a 200-year return period (Cultural Heritage Administration of Korea; NRICH 2012).

experience flooding caused by sewer overflow rather than river inundation due to the insufficient capacity of the drainage system (Fig. 2) (NRICH 2009, 261). The Changdeokgung Palace and the Changgyeonggung Palace, royal palaces dating from the Joseon Dynasty (14th to 20th century) in Seoul, could experience floods around the outlet part of the palace basin due to the same reason (Fig. 3) (NRICH 2011, 122-187). The Gyeongbokgung Palace and the Jongmyo Shrine, a nearby royal palace and shrine, were under flood risk, too, which could be caused by the backflow of sewers due to a bottleneck effect in the drainage system (Fig. 4 and 5) (NRICH 2012, 218-221). Floods and storm hazards might impair the cultural heritage more seriously in tandem by means of deterioration and cracks. These are identified as the most significant factors that magnify any existing or probable damage by means of natural hazards (NRICH 2008b, 34). If the cultural heritage was exposed to acute short-term hazards, these conditions would potentially result in more disastrous impacts on the properties.

The sensitivity of heritage against deterioration or natural hazard may depend on the features and characteristics of the particular cultural heritage (e.g., age, type, material, structure, etc.). Therefore, it is worth associating the specific features and characteristics of cultural heritage sites with the hazard vulnerability. According to research on various examples of hazard sensitivity as to the cultural heritage of Korea, many heritage sites designated as a *Scenic Site* and an *Important*

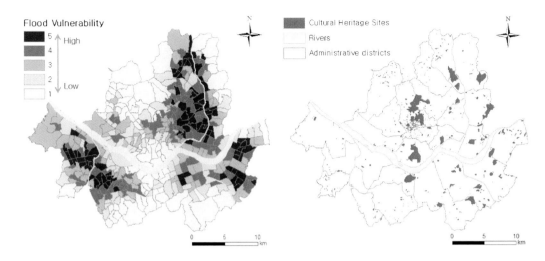

Flood Vulnerability
- 5 High
- 4
- 3
- 2
- 1 Low

Cultural Heritage Sites
Rivers
Administrative districts

Figure 6. The flood vulnerability levels and cultural heritage sites in Seoul, Korea (Kim and Sung 2014).

Folklore Cultural Heritage showed a relatively high level of hazard sensitivity towards heavy rain and typhoons (CHA 2012a, 59). With regard to the type of heritage, architectural heritage sites related to *religion/faith* and *housing/residence* showed a high sensitivity towards heavy rain and typhoons as well as towards heavy snowfall (CHA 2012a, 60).

Another study identifies more specific results as to heritage sites related to flood vulnerability in Seoul (Fig. 6). It revealed that 20% of heritage sites are located in the areas with a high flood vulnerability level, concentrated on the downstream areas of three specific tributaries of the Han River (Kim and Sung 2014). As to the type of heritage sites, many *Government office sites* are located within high flood vulnerability level areas, whereas the majority of the *Buddhist temples, temple sites* and *ceramic kiln sites* are located within areas with a low vulnerability. It was identified that heritage sites have their own location determined by means of classification. In the case of *Government office sites* the central government agency sites dating from the Joseon Dynasty are generally speaking located spatially close to the palace on the abruptly changing slope and lowlands, which is prone to flooding. Regarding *Buddhist temples* and *temple sites*, their location determinants are based on "*Pungsu*"; a basic concept from Fengshui but modified to Korean topography as well as mountainous landscape in the pre-modern period. *Ceramic kiln sites* were by and large located at the foot of mountains in order to acquire firewood more easily and to keep embers burning for a long time, thus inevitably positioned in a high altitude, low flood-vulnerability area. The features of cultural heritage increase or decrease the vulnerability of the heritage to a certain natural hazard (Kim and Sung 2014). Therefore these studies present us with the insight: it is important to consider which features and characteristics a certain cultural heritage has regarding flood prevention measures.

3. The anthropogenic aspects of water-related hazards on the cultural heritage

3.1 The artificial river improvement and its impact on cultural heritage

In order to minimize the high flood risk caused by rainfall distribution concentrated in the summer, Korea has implemented plans for improving rivers as part of land development schemes since the 1970s. The focus of the plan is flood control, putting emphasis on flood prevention and securing agricultural as well as industrial water. It includes the operation of organizing the width of river and the depth of river bed. In the course hereof a large-scale dredging is carried out. Maintenance for the stabilization and fixation of waterways also takes place during this stage, in which concrete banks and not only dikes are built uniformly but channels are straightened. Many reservoirs, dams and water gates have been implemented in order to control the water supply during the dry period. In this way all sorts of structures (e.g., dams, weirs, dikes, etc.) could be built. Meanwhile the hydrographic characteristics of the channels and the shape were changed artificially.

For example, a rock-carved Buddha allegedly from between the 10th and 11th century was damaged by drilling and blasting while constructing the Nak-Dan Weir in the Nakdong River. Indirect impacts also do harm to the cultural heritage such as through erosion of the material caused by the raised humidity due to an increase in the number of foggy days as a result of the change in environment. As to dam construction, outdoor heritage or archeological evidences may be newly found. Their existence and present condition is recognized when undertaking a surface survey of the cultural properties on submergence-prearranged areas. In order to conserve the cultural heritage, a cultural heritage complex is built nearby to which newly found heritage artifacts are moved and then reconstructed. In this process, the cultural properties lose the authenticity and historical context they possessed at the original location.

As one of the case of the river maintenance plan, the Four Major River Restoration Project implemented on a large scale was continued as follows regarding the impacts on the cultural heritage caused by artificial action on water-related matter.

3.2 The extensive river improvement and the cultural heritage: the case of the Four Major Rivers Restoration Project

3.2.1 The four Major Rivers Restoration Project and the newly discovered cultural heritage

The Project on the Four Major Rivers is a grand-scale river maintenance plan as to the four major rivers in Korea: the Han, Geum, Nakdong and Yeongsan Rivers. This plan has been implemented over 5 years: between February 2008

Figure 7. The newly
constructed weirs during
the Four Major Rivers
Restoration Project (MLTM
2012b, 2).

Figure 8. The cross section of
the weir (MLTM 2012a, 88).

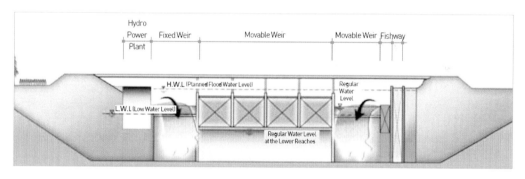

and February 2013. It serves to prevent any flood damage, securing water for the dry season, and improving the quality of the water (4 Rivers Guide 2014). The establishment of weirs, dams and reservoirs, reinforcement of banks, and the installation of water pollutant management facilities were carried out within the scope of the Four Major River Restoration project. Especially, a large-scale riverbed dredging was executed at the mainstream of these four rivers in order to improve the discharge capacity and lower the flood stage. Sixteen multifunctional weirs were built in order to secure water resources (Fig. 7 and 8).

A large amount of historic remnants and sites were found during the surface survey of the cultural heritage in the construction section. The surface survey on the four rivers was carried out over 294 km² around designated, undesignated,[1] and buried heritage sites, distributed within 500 m of the bank (CHA 2011, 206). As a result, 1651 cultural properties were found in total, of which 1482 items were undesignated and buried heritage and 169 were designated heritage (CHA 2011, 206). Major historical sites newly found in the investigation include shell mounds, tombs, fortress, kiln sites, temple sites, etc. These findings date from the prehistoric age up to the Joseon Dynasty.

As to further actions after the surface survey, excavations were carried out with regard to the buried heritage during the investigation if needed. As to the designated heritage, actions have been taken in order to conduct an examination of the construction impact on the heritage and modification of the present construction plans (CHA 2011, 206).

3.2.2 The impact of the Four Major Rivers Restoration Project on the cultural heritage

So many heritage sites were discovered throughout the surface investigation into the cultural heritage by the Four Major River Restoration Project. It did indeed produce a positive aspect: abundant and various archaeological evidences were gained nationwide. However, numerous conflicting opinions have been raised regarding whether the impact on the heritage preservation around the river is merely positive, suggesting too that adverse impacts have also been mentioned at the Audit and Inspection in 2013.

According to the result of this inspection, carried out after the project was completed, serious flaws were found in the procedure of the project (BAI 2013, 8-35). First of all, c.6 km² was left out of the investigation and no excavation was carried out in the 2.6 km² where preservation measures and excavation were ordered. As to the construction section overlapping the cultural heritage sites, data on 1.5 km² of the area where heritage properties were distributed were absent in the report. Moreover, despite the duty of heritage expert supervision during the construction wherever any heritage sites are distributed, the construction was carried out without an expert along a section measuring up to 127.8 km² (BAI 2013, 29-35). It is difficult to avoid the possibility that newly discovered heritage could have been destroyed before any sufficient research was carried out. The reason for this: adequate measures were not undertaken in order to preserve such areas while the construction was underway.

Moreover, suspicions concerning adverse impacts of the project on cultural heritage sites through environmental change have been brought up in certain media. For example, a possibility has arisen that the change of hydraulics caused

---

1   In Korea, the heritage classification consists of: (a) the State-designated heritage, (b) the City/province-designated heritage, (c) the Cultural heritage material, (d) the Registered cultural heritage, and (e) the Undesignated cultural heritage. See, the Cultural Heritage Administration homepage <http:// english.cha.go.kr/english/new/index.action>.

Figure 9. The destroyed Waegwan Bridge (CHA 2013).

Figure 10. The collapsed section of the Gongsanseong Fortress (CHA 2014).

by the construction might have influenced cultural property overhanging the river such as a bridge. In summer of 2011, the Waegwan Bridge, designated as *Registered Cultural Heritage* located on the Nakdong River, was destroyed. The Namji Railroad Bridge, another heritage located on the same river, was identified to be at risk of collapsing with its pier dropping 30 cm to the ground (Fig. 9) (Choi 2011b). It turned out that they were at risk of collapsing due to the increase of the Nakdong River's water level and velocity caused by heavy rainfall (CHA, 2013, 8). However, an opinion was raised that the risk of collapsing was due to the dredging operation during which no reinforcement for the bridges were created.

This would have caused the erosion at the bridge supports due to the enhanced velocity of the water (Choi 2011a; Kim 2011b). Another example shows that the construction could have influenced the ground environment near the river where the heritage is located. For instance, a partial section of the Gongsanseong Fortress on the banks of the Guem River, registered as a *Historic Site*, collapsed during the torrential downpour of September 2013 (Fig. 10). Certain media have reported that the collapse could be fundamentally due to the deepened riverbed after the dredging operation of the project so that the increased hydraulic pressure and the flow weakened the lower part of the ground (Lee 2013).

Furthermore, the construction of hydraulic structures might affect the deterioration of heritages located around the riverside due to a regional climate change. In general the construction of dams and dikes influences the local climate. Many researches have proved the increase of relative humidity and foggy days in surrounding areas after a dam or weir has been built (Lee 1981, 20; Hong 1982, 28; Yang 1994; Jeon et al. 2002, 163-165). The overall increase of humidity hastens the chemical and biological weathering on a cultural heritage, which can also affect the structure. Take the example of the Yeoju Weir, situated within 1 km from Yeongneung and Nyeongneung. Here two royal tomb sites dating from the Joseon Dynasty are located on the banks of the Namhan River's midstream. This place has inherent natural aspects of damp ground and has been frequently reinforced with molding during the Joseon Dynasty (The Annals of the Joseon Dynasty 2014). However, it seems that foggy days or fog density could be increased and that climatic elements (e.g., temperature, humidity) may change due to the constant supply of water vapor from man-made reservoirs (Kim 2010; Park 2010). In addition, the dredged channel and the weir may increase the water table level, which would cause marshes or floods around the Nyeongneung area (Kim and Lee 2010, 240-241).

4. Issues regarding the management system and the policy on water-related hazards

Of the many impacts on the cultural heritage of Korea, the present issues regarding the management system and the policy on natural hazards are addressed in this chapter.

4.1 Overview on the management system and policy of water-related hazard on cultural heritage

Regulations regarding the disaster management for cultural heritage sites of Korea are mainly established in the 'Cultural Heritage Protection Act'. The primary articles related to the disaster prevention of the cultural heritage are the Articles 14 and 85. Article 14 (Prevention of Fire, Disasters, etc.), as a principal provision related to preventing disasters as to cultural heritage, regulates the policy on the prevention of fire and disasters, guidelines to correspondence and installing fire and theft prevention facilities. Article 85 designates a 'Disaster Prevention Day for Cultural Heritage' in an effort to raise public awareness concerning

Designator	Designation Type						
Administrator of Cultural Heritage Administration	STATE-DESIGNATED HERITAGE						
	National Treasure	Treasure	Important Intangible Cultural Heritage	Historic Site	Scenic Site	Natural Monument	Important Folklore Cultural Heritage
	REGISTERED CULTURAL HERITAGE						
Governors of Province/City	CITY/PROVINCE-DESIGNATED HERITAGE						
	Tangible Cultural Heritage	Intangible Cultural Heritage	Monument				Folklore Heritage
	CULTURAL HERITAGE MATERIAL						

Table 1. The management system of the cultural heritage according to the Cultural Heritage Protection Act (No.11037).

the disaster preparedness as to cultural properties. It was enacted in response to the Sungnyemun's collapse due to a fire on 10 February 2008. On this day, the implement plans and measures of the national and municipal governments (e.g.,safety checks of cultural heritage sites, disaster drills) are tested in order to build up the public and managers' capacity when dealing with disasters as to any cultural heritage (Jang 2011, 282).

Depending on the designator, as shown in Table 1, the management system of the cultural heritage consists of two categories: (a) the state-designated heritage and *Registered Cultural Heritage*, designated and managed by the head of Cultural Heritage Administration and (b) a city or province-designated heritage and *Cultural Heritage Material*, designated and managed by the governor of the province (Ryu 2013, 185-187). Disaster management with regard to the cultural heritage is managed by the Cultural Heritage Risk Management Division under the Policy Bureau of the Cultural Heritage Administration by means of planning policies in order to prevent disasters thereby not only developing the safety supervision and disaster prevention system but also the guidelines for the disaster correspondence, etc. (Cultural Heritage Administration 2014). The safety measures, instructions and systems established by the central government are implemented in provinces and cities under the jurisdiction of cultural heritage.

With regard to the heritage related policy, the Korean government has suggested a future direction of policy and strategy since 2002 when the long-term master plan concerning the preservation, management and utilization of cultural heritage was announced. Since then, the government has presented annual plans as to carrying out the main work. A five-year master plan (2012-2016) as to the conservation policies of cultural heritage has been implemented, see Fig. 11 (CHA 2012b, 5).

Out of many, the 'Establishment of integrated system for the cultural heritage disaster management' and the 'Establishment of the Cultural Heritage Disaster Prevention Research Center' were included as specific tasks and action plans concerning the 'Capacity building for safety management and preservation of cultural heritage' (CHA 2012b, 108-119). As a result, from 2012 on, a specific annual plan has been established and implemented in order to achieve this goal.

Policy Goals	Promotion of the accessibility to culture Promotion of the conservation, management and utilization of cultural heritage Sustainable development through the harmony of development and preservation Reasonable regulation and protection of private property right Strengthening of international prestige of Korean cultural heritage	
Main Tasks	Protection of the historic and cultural environment	Utilization and industrialization of the heritage value
	Capacity building for safety management and preservation of cultural heritage	Promotion of the research and education on cultural heritage
	Systemization of the heritage management and maintenance	Encourage for the International exchange of cultural heritage
	Development of archive for cultural heritage in state-of-the-art technology	Inscription and management of World heritage

Figure 11. The Policy Goals and Main Tasks of 2012-2016 Master Plan on the Cultural Heritage of Korea (CHA 2012b, 5).

After the 2008 Sungnyemun Fire, the social significance of safety management regarding disasters as to cultural heritage has been recognized in Korea. For this reason, regulations on the safety management of the cultural heritage have been enhanced from 2008 on. Considerable progress has been made especially with regard to the wooden heritage by means of an intensive installation of safety facilities and guards (Ryu 2013, 198-199). However, various institutional and organizational boundaries need to be addressed.

First of all, certain institutional boundaries concern the prevention of water-related hazards. Article 14 of the Cultural Heritage Protection Act, the core provision for the hazard management on cultural heritage, is focused on the prevention of fire and theft, whereas no specific regulations are set for other disasters (e.g., flood, storm damages): the more characteristic disasters to which Korea is prone (Kim 2013). As there are no records or statistics dealing with the damage caused by natural hazards to cultural property, it is difficult to determine the substantial measures (Kim 2013).

Organizational limitation regarding the measures against water-related hazards as to cultural heritage includes the absence of field supervision organizations and specialists. A main administrative management body has been specified with regard to the disaster management of the cultural heritage. However, no specialists or organizations are exclusively responsible for various risks and hazards that could happen to cultural heritage sites in the field (Han 2008, 195; Ryu 2013, 195-196).

4.2 Efforts to improve the management system and policy on water-related hazards

Korea has seen continuous efforts, facing the problems mentioned above, in order to improve the preparedness and response to disasters inflicted upon the cultural heritage. It can be categorized as an effort concerning regulation improvement and the development of concrete countermeasures.

As to the efforts towards regulations and policies, the Cultural Heritage Administration has worked on a policy study in order to enhance and amend regulations as to the security of cultural heritage sites (Kim 2013). The 'Five-year master plan (2012-2016) for preservation, management and utilization of cultural heritage' has foregrounded not only the enhancement on safety management but also the preservation capacity of cultural heritage. As one of the policy's main tasks it deals with (a) the establishment of an integrated management system as to cultural heritage disasters, (b) the amendment of regulations related to disaster prevention, (c) the designation of an advisory committee and supervisor of disaster prevention, and (d) the development of manuals and educational programs.

Furthermore, as to disaster prevention, especially flood hazards, investigations in order to identify the present situations and development of protection system against disasters are being undertaken. In 2008 a survey was carried out among governmental institutions, municipal administrators and specialists related to the issue of defining the actual condition of the present disaster management system and the present state of the cultural heritage damages inflicted by disasters. According to this survey, over 70% answered that the present quality of the disaster prevention system is below average. A technical development of the safety procedure was chosen as a priority to be improved as to the prevention of disasters on the cultural heritage (NRICH 2008, 61-79). The possibility of a certain bias as to the survey results due to the outrage of people over the disaster handling during the 2008 Sungnyemun Fire could have existed. This survey result drew nationwide attention to the disaster management as to the cultural heritage. Next several national plans for the development of a disaster management system were consistently implemented such as the systematic flood risk assessment.

Several flood management systems have been installed at Korea's leading historic locations: the Changgyeonggung Palace, the Gyeongbokgung Palace and the Jongmyo Shrine (NRICH 2011, 255-263; NRICH 2012, 225-228). These systems mainly integrate the disaster records of each heritage site, the earthquake hazard and the flood risk depending on the rainfall scenario, to then display such information on the internet. Additional integrated disaster management systems as to the architectural heritage have been installed on historic sites (NRICH 2013, 275-281). This system displays the database for each heritage site as well as the disaster records and the risk assessments related to flood and earthquake on the V-World 3D Map Service. It also includes prevention manuals for each disaster, stage, and subject so that it can deliver a suitable manual to the person in charge when estimates the type and the scale of the approaching hazard. As a part of the National Disaster Management System, this system can be operated internationally by means of providing technological support as to the disaster prevention simulation of the architectural heritage (NRICH 2013, 282)

5. Conclusion

This study has reviewed the issue of a water-related hazard and the cultural heritage of Korea. It was divided into two major aspects with more direct impacts on hazard triggers, albeit interrelated. As a result, the natural and human impacts were studied, especially as to issues relating to hazard vulnerability, policies and institutional management of cultural properties against any water-related hazard. The climatic characteristic of annual precipitation concentrated in the summer has created fundamental water-related impacts on the cultural heritage of Korea, causing numerous floods and landslides. The changing pattern of the climate such as an intensified rainfall poses a greater threat to the durability of cultural properties. Moreover, the anthropogenic river improvement is another factor resulting in adverse impacts on the conservation of cultural heritage sites. The construction of hydraulic structures has changed the hydrologic environment around river areas, which leads to the deterioration and erosion of heritage properties nearby. River improvement containing such a strong artificiality has affected the management of cultural heritage sites near rivers, arising as another water-related issue as to the protection of heritage sites. Cultural heritage sites are vulnerable to direct physical impacts (e.g., explosion shocks, submergence, erosion) as well as indirect impacts e.g., local climatic and geomorphological changes occurring in the process of constructing hydraulic structures.

Although many historic structures are inherently somewhat resistant to floods, they are gradually becoming vulnerable to various hazards as the natural environment changes and risk factors increase in Korea. In this context, the following issues should be considered in the future:

a. an analysis of the internal risk factors of cultural heritage in terms of vulnerability or risk assessment is needed. Today's study on the prevention of water-related hazards on cultural heritage focused on external factors such as damage of the flood due to intensive rainfall in Korea. However, internal risk factors (e.g., material, structure, construction era of a cultural heritage) should not be discounted because a specific trait of a cultural heritage can amplify the external impact of disaster,

b. the patterns of changing climate should be considered a potential risk factor. Climate change is shown through the increased intensity of various meteorological phenomena in Korea. This disturbs the original local climate and geomorphological processes of the area where cultural heritage sites are located to directly accelerate or stimulate natural hazards which may lead to more difficult situations as to the protection of the cultural heritage.

c. more integrated studies on disasters need to be carried out. For example, heavy rainfall triggers flooding as well as simultaneous landslides. Therefore a more comprehensive analysis of the composite factors of disasters as to a simple natural meteorological event must be prioritized.

d. as the protection of cultural heritage against an anthropogenic water-related hazard, the environmental impact assessment on a detailed practical level should be processed prior to the constructions. The environmental impact assessment has obviously been conducted. It was however somehow difficult to draw any detailed improvements and countermeasures in an actual application.

In sum, in situations where risk factors of damage to cultural heritage sites increase due to the change of the natural environment as well as artificial influences, it is necessary for the government of Korea to focus on a more comprehensive frame as to the management and preservation of cultural heritage.

Current regulations and management systems regarding the cultural heritage protection in Korea do not address the impacts of flood or other hazards at a practical level as to the disaster prevention of cultural heritage. In order to improve this situation, several attempts have been made to develop and improve technology-oriented disaster prevention systems for cultural heritage sites. These endeavours comprise positive contributions towards the protection of cultural heritage against floods and typhoons.

In addition to the development of technology-oriented disaster prevention systems, the preparedness for the cultural heritage as to water-related hazards can be recommended by the pre-disaster phase, the during a disaster phase and the post-disaster phase. In the former phase, institutional supports and plans should be established within the regulations and policies securing budget, facilities, equipment and human resource. They should take concrete shape as to the actual implementation of (a) required facilities, (b) a technology-based monitoring and disaster prediction system, (c) the equipment of manuals, (d) the evaluation of existing disaster prevention system and (e) a clear statement of the main stakeholder regarding the liability for disaster prevention, supervision, education and training, etc. In the during a disaster phase, emergency measures should be implemented under supervision of the disaster control centre and an effective communication line should be arranged. In the post-disaster phase, a detailed trigger and the process of a hazard should be analyzed and archived in order to prepare for future disasters. All of these aspects should be laid in the solid legal foundation of disaster management as to the conservation of a cultural heritage. Broad, in-depth analyses and evaluations of anthropogenic impacts as well as of natural hazard impacts should be composed on the prediction, response and restoration and sustainable management of water-related hazards.

Bibliography

Board of Audit and Inspection of Korea (BAI). 2013. *Audit and Inspection Report for buried heritage inspection and protection during the Four Major River Restoration Project. October 2013*. The Board of Audit and Inspection of Korea.

Choi, Ho-Young. 2011a. Nakdong Bridge in danger of collapse… 'Other bridges are in danger range as well'. *CBS Nocut News*, August 23.

Choi, Sang-Won. 2011b. Four Rivers bridge crisis. *The Hankyoreh*, August 23.

Choi, Sang-Won. 2011c. Namji Railroad Bridge at risk of collapse due to the Four River Restoration Project?. *The Hankyoreh*, August 22.

Cultural Heritage Administration (CHA). 2008a. *2008 Program for cultural heritage management*. Cultural Heritage Administration of Korea.

Cultural Heritage Administration (CHA). 2008b. *2008 Reply to written inquiries on Audit and Inspection to Kang, Seung Kyoo*. Cultural Heritage Administration of Korea.

Cultural Heritage Administration (CHA). 2011. *Requested materials for Audit and Inspection for Cultural Heritage Administration*. Cultural Heritage Administration of Korea.

Cultural Heritage Administration (CHA). 2012a. *Comprehensive plan on conservation of cultural heritage for climate change adaptation*. Cultural Heritage Administration of Korea.

Cultural Heritage Administration (CHA). 2012b. *2012-2016 Five-Year Master Plan for conservation, management, and utilization of cultural heritage*. Cultural Heritage Administration of Korea.

Cultural Heritage Administration (CHA). 2013. *Prevention of disasters for cultural heritage 2013*. Cultural Heritage Administration of Korea.

Han, Beum-Deuk. 2008. Improvement of cultural heritage disaster management: the case of Sungnyemun's Collapse in Fire. *Journal of Korea Contents Association* 8(10): 189-196.

Hong, Sung-Gil. 1982. Increase of the fogs in Andong due to the construction of Andong Reservoir. *Journal of Meteorological Society* 18(2): 26-32.

Jang, Ho-su. 2011. *Revision of Cultural Heritage Studies: Theory and Method*. Seoul: Paeksan.

Jeon, Byung-Il, Kim, Il-Gon, and Lee, Young-Mi. 2002. A change of local meteorological environment according to dam construction of Nakdong-River: 1. Meteorological data analysis before and after dam construction. *Journal of the Environmental Sciences* 11(3): 161-168.

Jo, Jung-Hun. 2011. Angry residents due to the collapse of Waegwan Bridge. *Ohmynews*, June 26.

Kim, Derk-moon. 2013. Current status and challenges of cultural heritage at risk in Korea. *Paper presented at the International symposium for the safety management of cultural heritage at risk. Seoul, Korea*. September 12.

Kim, Jisoo. 2013. Urban flood vulnerability mapping for Seoul, Korea. Master's thesis, Ewha Womans University.

Kim, Jisoo, and Sung, Hyo Hyun. 2014. Management of cultural heritage from natural hazard under climate change. *Paper presented at ICO-FORUM, Seoul, Korea*. November 20.

Kim, Jisoo, and Sung, Hyo Hyun. 2014. Possible threat on cultural heritage by flooding in Seoul. *Proceedings of the International Geographical Union Regional Conference in Krakow, Poland.* August 18-22.

Kim, Jongik, and Lee, Taegwan. 2010. A Literature Review on the Effect of Yeoju Weir toward the Local Area Environment in the 4th part of Han-River Restoration Plan. *Journal of Nakdonggang Environmental Research Institute* 14: 235-247.

Kim, Ki-Nam. 2011a. Collapsed old Waegwan Bridge. *The Kyunghyang Shinmun*, June 26.

Kim, Ki-Sung. 2010. Yeoju weir may harm the royal tomb… would cancellation of the world cultural heritage occur? *The Hankyoreh*, April 22.

Kim, Sun-Kyung. 2011b. Citizens claim 'the old Namji Bridge is in danger of collapse because of the dredging from the Four Major Rivers Restoration Project'. *Yonhap News Agency*, August 23.

Korea Ministry of Government Legislation (KMGL). Cultural Heritage Protection Act. Act No. 11037. Article 14, Article 85.

Kwon, Won Tae, et al. 2004. *The climate of Korea.* ed. Hyo-sang Chung. Korea Meteorological Administration and National Institute of Meteorological Research.

Lee, Hyoun-Young. 2000. *The Climate of Korea.* Seoul: Bobmunsa.

Lee, Jin-Young, Hong, Sei-Sun, Yang, Dong-Yoon, and Kim, Ju-Yong. 2011a. The locational characteristics of cultural sites found in South Korea. *Journal of the Korean Association of Geographic Information Studies* 14(2): 14-27.

Lee, Chong Bum. 1981. Change of fog days and cloud amount by artificial lakes in Chuncheon. *Journal of Korean Meteorology Society* 17(1): 18-26.

Lee, Kyoungmi, Baek, Hee-Jeong, Cho, Chun-Ho, and Kwon, Won-Tae. 2011b. The recent (2001-2010) changes on temperature and precipitation related to normals (1971-2000) in Korea. *Geographical Journal of Korea* 45(2): 237-248.

Lee, Si-Nae. 2013. Collapse of Gongsanseong Fortress in Gonju, South Chungcheon, possibly because of the Four Major Rivers Restoration Project?. *Money Today*, September 16.

Ministry of Construction and Transportation (MCT). 2001. *Water Vision 2020.* Ministry of Construction and Transportation of Korea.

Ministry of Government Administration and Home Affairs (MGAHA). 2002. *Disaster Report 2001.* Ministry of Government Administration and Home Affairs - The Central Disaster and Safety Countermeasures Headquarters.

Ministry of Land, Transportation and Maritime Affairs (MLTM). 2012a. *The Four Rivers Restoration Project.* Ministry of Land, Transportation and Maritime Affairs.

Ministry of Land, Transportation and Maritime Affairs (MLTM). 2012b. *The River Revitalization of Korea: The Four Rivers Restoration Project.* Ministry of Land, Transportation and Maritime Affairs.

National Emergency Management Agency (NEMA). 2012. *Disaster Report 2011.* National Emergency Management Agency.

National Research Institute of Cultural Heritage (NRICH). 2007. *Development of disaster prediction system for stone relics*. National Research Institute of Cultural Heritage.

National Research Institute of Cultural Heritage (NRICH). 2008a. *Development of disaster damage mitigation technology for stone and wooden culture assets*. National Research Institute of Cultural Heritage.

National Research Institute of Cultural Heritage (NRICH) 2008b. *Research planning on the disaster mitigation of architectural heritage*. National Research Institute of Cultural Heritage.

National Research Institute of Cultural Heritage (NRICH). 2010. *Flood and seismic risk assessment for Buyeo historic areas*. National Research Institute of Cultural Heritage.

National Research Institute of Cultural Heritage (NRICH) 2011. *Flood and seismic risk assessment for Seoul historic areas*. National Research Institute of Cultural Heritage.

National Research Institute of Cultural Heritage (NRICH) 2012. *Evaluation method of flood and earthquake risk for main regional architectural heritage*. National Research Institute of Cultural Heritage.

National Research Institute of Cultural Heritage (NRICH) 2013. *Construction of seismic risk, flood risk assessment and management system for architectural heritage in historical city*. National Research Institute of Cultural Heritage.

Park, Changyong, Moon, JaYeon, Cha, Eun-Jeong, Yun, Won-Tae, and Choi, Youngeun. 2008. Recent changes in summer precipitation characteristics over South Korea. *Journal of the Korean Geographical Society* 43(3): 324-336.

Park, Se-Yeol. 2010. 'The tomb of Sejong the Great waterlogged, due to the Four Major Rivers Restoration Project, may be dropped from the world cultural heritage'. *Pressian*, October 5.

Ryu, Ho Cheol. 2013. Cultural heritage management system and improvement of the limits - focused on establishing the tangible cultural heritage on-site management organization. *The Institute for Korean Culture* 54: 183-214.

Yang, Moon-Seuk. 1994. *Characteristics of fog occurrence in Chungju area before and after construction of Chungju multipurpose dam*. Master's thesis, Kongju National University.

Yum, Ji-Eun. 2013. 'Collapse of Gongsanseong as a result of the approval of Four Major Rivers Restoration Project'. *News 1 Korea*, October 13.

Yun, Je-Min and Lee, Young-Suk. 2013. Historic Site 'Collapsed... suspicious impact of the Four River Project'. *News 1 Korea*, September 15.

Cultural Heritage Administration. 2006. http://www.cha.go.kr/. Accessed 4 January 2015.

Doopedia. 2015. http://www.doopedia.co.kr/. Accessed 3 January 2015.

Four Rivers Guide. 2011. http://www.riverguide.go.kr. Accessed 17 November 2014.

National Institute for Korean History. The Annals of the Joseon Dynasty. http://sillok.history.go.kr/. Accessed 14 November 2014.

Park, Chan-min. 2013. A study of safety management and disaster response for architectural heritage. http://img.kisti.re.kr/originalView/originalView.jsp. Accessed 20 November 2014.

Flood Protection for Historic Sites – Integrating Heritage Conservation and Flood Control Concepts

Experiences in Germany

Heiko Lieske, Erika Schmidt and Thomas Will

Technische Universität Dresden

Abstract

Cultural heritage has always been exposed to the risks and threats of natural disasters. Whereas preventive mitigation strategies are predominantly aimed at protecting the population and its material assets, their practical measures have side effects: they pose new risks or may even do harm to the environment and to the often fragile structures and landscapes which constitute our built heritage. Now, however, the intangible values of cultural heritage are being increasingly recognized by cities and regions, though, defying quantification, they cannot be easily weighed against material values or against the cost of mitigation projects (Quarantelli 2003). In a nationwide comparative study conflicts and compromises between safety and authenticity, protection and preservation, have been addressed and practical approaches discussed (Lieske, Schmidt and Will 2012). This study is outlined in the following.

Keywords: *cultural heritage conservation, structural flood risk reduction, urban river rehabilitation, urban waterfronts.*

The inevitable conflict

Due to global climate change with its risk of increased flooding in many parts of the world (Jongman and Brenden 2014, Flood Insurance 2014) and ground-breaking advancements in hydraulic sciences and technology, hydraulic engineering and inner-city flood protection are facing entirely new and challenging opportunities, risks and areas of conflict. River cities are specific risk habitats due to the concentration of people, material and intangible values affected by flooding. Conventional protection measures have so far been focused on the construction of dams, reservoirs and flood walls. Recent advantages in hydrological modelling

(Wilson and Atkinson 2010) as well as public debate and political discourse, including European legislation (WFD 2000), have shifted the emphasis onto non-structural measures (e.g., disaster management plans, designation of flood plains excluded from development, early warning systems) and, as a priority, onto flood prevention by providing retention in catchment areas (Schanze et al. 2008. Ebnöther and Thurnherr 2008, Furrer 2008, Mileti 1999, Spennemann and Look 1998, Stovel 1998). The effect of this latter policy, however, is usually limited. The reason for this is: it is subject to a number of natural and anthropogenic conditions that often cannot easily be altered (Lieske 2012, Schanze et al. 2008, ELLA 2006). Structural measures in or close to the areas threatened by flooding therefore seem in many cases indispensable despite their possible side effects.

Flood risk reduction in urban areas requires special and often innovative approaches (Lawrence 2012, Kongjian, Zhang and Li 2008, Langenbach 2007). Urban settlements are places not only of concentrated activity and capital but also of condensed history and meaning. Architectural and garden monuments, sites of interest and liveliness, as well as consolidated socio-spatial relations make for human environments that should not be subjected to profound structural alterations. Meanwhile, waterfronts in settlements – once places for shipping, sewage disposal, trade and industry, then subject to neglect over much of the 20th century – are now receiving high public appreciation (Water 2007, Guccione 2005, Tourbier and Schanze 2005).

Up to now, the conflicts between heritage conservation concerns and safety requirements have rarely been considered in the planning and construction of protection systems or in related fields of research (an early but rare exception is Heyenbrock 1987). However, along with a recent, rapidly growing political and research interest in risk management, issues of environmental side effects of flood protection are increasingly being dealt with. Occasionally questions concerning the compatibility of flood protection and heritage conservation have been raised (Drdácký et al. 2011, Crouch 2009, Meier, Petzet and Will 2008, Taboroff 2002, McLane and Wüst 2000).

A nationwide comparative study

When our interdisciplinary team was given the opportunity to conduct a nationwide comparative study on heritage conservation and urban development confronted with large-scale flood protection schemes, we focused on two problem areas:

- Processes and policies: Which procedures are being implemented for the planning and construction of flood protection schemes? To what extent is the public involved in these processes? What effects do these procedures and processes have on the consideration of cultural heritage and urban qualities?

- Physical planning: Which hydraulic and architectural constructions are being used in the various projects; what are the design principles? What effects do these construction and design solutions have on the cultural heritage and on urban qualities?

More than fifty schemes in various parts of Germany were identified, whereof the most significant – twenty-two in number – were studied in further detail. In each of these cases, a survey, including comprehensive literature and archival research, was made of recent and historic hydraulic projects. In situ investigations covered architectural analyses, surveys of the local heritage stock, and guided interviews with authorities, planners and other experts. The public debate, as reflected in newspaper reports, was also taken into account, although not systematically analysed. The results are presented in detailed case studies, in a critical comparative commentary and in recommendations for authorities, planners and politicians (Lieske, Schmidt and Will 2012).

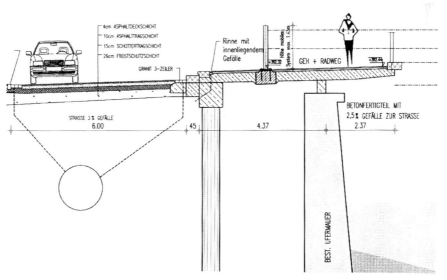

Figure 1. The city of Neuburg (Danube River). a: A waterfront view with raised protection level; b: The cantilevered waterfront promenade.

Figure 2. The city of Wasserburg (Inn River), a landscaped dike.

With regard to the impact on historic fabric and spatial structure, we identified the following types of intervention:

- Unobtrusive protection measures (Fig. 1, 2)
- Mobile elements above surface level (Fig. 3a)
- Stationary protection up to railing height (Fig. 4)
- Higher structures forming visual barriers (Fig. 3b, 5)
- Large-scale restructuring with considerable damage to heritage sites

The schemes which have been analysed not only demonstrate various conflicts but also that flood protection structures can be designed to merge successfully into the valuable fabric of historic towns and landscapes. They offer lessons on how to (a) achieve flood protection with minimal detriment to cultural heritage and (b) increase the attractiveness as well as the economic power of a place and generate surplus value as to the quality of life for its citizens.

In Germany the procedure concerning flood protection planning and its implementation are extensively regulated by law, as exemplified in the case studies. They illustrated that good results, in terms of minimal detrimental impact on the fabric or the appearance of protected monuments, were achieved when more interests and expertise than legally required were included in the decision making early on. However, this required corresponding political determination and additional money.

Good results in reconciliation of flood protection with heritage conservation were achieved when (a) appropriate time was taken for thorough research into the local conditions for flooding as well as into the condition and values of the endangered monuments, (b) various options for protection could be tested by dynamic modeling as well as experimentally in a flow channel, (c) hydrologists, engineers and conservators used all procedural possibilities in order to negotiate

Figure 3. The city of Dessau (Elbe and Mulde Rivers), the historic garden 'Luisium' (World Heritage Site Wörlitz Gardens). a: A temporary water-filled tube solution serving to raise the protection level of the historic dike and lock its openings; b: An obtrusive stationary sheet pile wall on top of a historic dike, impairing the view of the park folly.

a balanced solution, seriously considering and integrating other, non-structural options of risk reduction and (d) the design expertise of urban planners, architects or landscape architects was called in early on. For example, the aligning of a planned defense structure was in some cases initially worked out solely by hydraulic experts, with little or no concern for urban and architectural or landscape qualities. When, after the negative impact of such plans became visible, architects were called in,

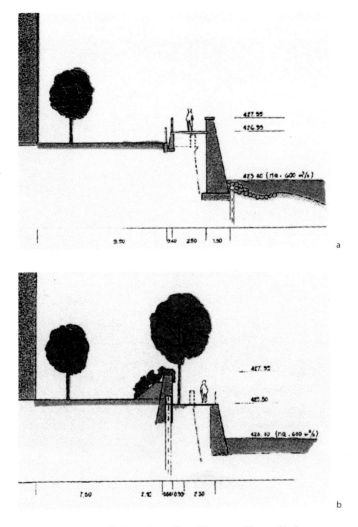

Figure 4. The city of Wasserburg (Inn River). a: The preliminary planning proposal for a flood protection wall; b: The segmented and embellished two-level solution reducing the impact on the historic waterfront.

they had to start the process of approaching the optimal alignment anew, bringing in an entire set of additional aspects that significantly influenced the overall success of an urban flood risk reduction structure.

Structures for flood protection often cause far-reaching changes, if not debasement, of people's neighbourhoods. Their attitude towards possible interventions seems to be highly influential. In some cases protection measures have been conceived immediately after a destructive flooding, when intimidated inhabitants demanded absolute protection right away. Hasty action taken under such pressure without adequate regard to other interests brought about structures of poor aesthetic quality and was extremely detrimental to neighbouring heritage

Figure 5. The city of Wörth (Main River), a flood wall integrated in the historic city walls.

sites – in some cases even to monuments of the highest value. On the other hand, good results were achieved and conflict was observed to be minimal in cases where the public had been fully informed, from the beginning, about preliminary research into the flood risk and the endangered heritage values. In these cases, the public had also been included in the discussion on various qualified protective measures. There is even one place presented in our study where the citizens renounced structural flood protection in favour of an unspoilt historic cityscape. Whether the observed coincidence of good or bad results according to conservation standards with different procedures may be regarded as an outcome of 'influence' which the procedures might have had, remains to be studied with socio-empirical methods. Such research was not included in the scope of our comparative study.

Flood protection as a catalyst for urban development

The scale, cost and persistency of large-scale flood protection structures suggest they should be conceived as comprehensive steps in urban development. Our comparative study showed that integrative planning procedures, similar to those applied in urban rehabilitation projects, provide opportunities to combine up-to-date flood protection with the preservation of urban heritage as well as a general upgrading and stabilization of historic river cities. Places near the water can not only be saved from natural disasters but can also obtain urban environmental improvements, for instance, when flood protection creates opportunities to convert abandoned industrial sites into highly valued neighbourhoods and urban open space, or to rediscover, redesign and re-evaluate urban waterfronts for public access and benefit. Finally, with a general upgrade of inner-city waterfronts, stimulated by means of hydraulic schemes, property values are very likely to increase. Given the importance of flood protection for the future of a community located next to a river and considering all its side effects, the extra effort of integrative planning is an investment that more than pays off.

International discussion

In June 2014 we held the international colloquium 'Flood Protection for Historic Sites. Integrating Heritage Conservation and Flood Control Concepts' at the Technische Universität Dresden to present the approach, findings and recommendations worked out in the study and to encourage discussion on these topics by experts from other countries (see www.flood-heritage-2014.de). Speakers and participants from seventeen nations and a wide array of professional fields addressed conditions and experiences from various geographic, political, economic and cultural contexts. Contributions to the conference will be published by ICOMOS Germany in 2015. As an immediate outcome of the conference, participants adopted the Dresden Declaration on Flood Protection for Historic Sites:

ICOMOS
Deutsches Nationalkomitee

Dresden Declaration on Flood Protection for Historic Sites

Adopted at the International Conference "Flood Protection for Historic Sites. Integrating Heritage Conservation and Flood Control Concepts", Dresden, 13-14 June 2014

Whereas

- most urban areas and many historic sites evolved along waterways or coastlines and are therefore especially flood-prone,
- flood events by all accounts will occur more frequently and costs of flood damage are expected to substantially increase
- and therefore a significant loss of cultural resources, character and economic vitality of cities has to be expected,

we therefore proclaim:

Increased efforts to reduce the threats of flooding are needed in order to preserve river cities and landscapes with their special qualities as valuable environments for future generations.

Flood mitigation projects have to ascertain and take into consideration the special values and vulnerabilities of historic sites from the beginning. Protective measures must not compromise or destroy the very assets that they are intended to protect. The quality of public space and its architectural and natural elements, the strong relationship between the built environment and nature (and water in particular), attractiveness for inhabitants and visitors based on the historic and aesthetic richness of towns and landscapes and the built cultural heritage – in short, the so-called "soft factors" that lend a place its identity and character – have long turned into hard arguments in the competition among cities. Listed historic monuments, which may not be compensated for by substitution or replacement, have to be given particular consideration.

Flood protection must be understood and practiced as an integral part of a comprehensive spatial planning process, with special consideration given to the individual conditions and qualities of historic sites. This includes public discussion of goals at an early stage, development and evaluation of realistic alternatives as well as the utilization of synergies between urban and flood protection planning.

In order to keep flood-prone historic settlements and sites competitive and to protect their quality of life the conference participants recommend the following

Action Programme for Flood Protection of Historic Sites:

1. It is recommended that communities identify historic sites that are subject to flooding. Their cultural values as well as the damage to be expected should be comprehensibly analyzed and documented and measures appropriate for their protection should be defined.

2. Based on the above evaluation, integrated development concepts for the protection of historic cities and cultural heritage sites against flooding should be prepared under public participation at an early stage and in close cooperation with different interest groups and stakeholders.

3. The relevant standards and regulations should be applied to historic towns with circumspection and flexibility. In the course of weighing values from case to case, deviations from standards and with that a certain remaining risk should be accepted. The organizational measures for flood protection and the responsibilities of communities, owners and users are to be included in the overall assessment.

4. Concepts of the Action Programme shall combine cultural, ecologic, spatial, structural and social aspects of flood risk management, forming an integral part of urban land use and development planning.

5. An interdisciplinary team of independent experts who are not involved in the local planning process should be consulted for advice in planning and evaluating projects.

For the participants and the Scientific Advisory Board: *Thomas Will, Heiko Lieske, Erika Schmidt, Technische Universität Dresden – Jörg Haspel, President, ICOMOS Germany, Berlin – Rohit Jigyasu, President, ICOMOS-ICORP, Tokyo/New Delhi – Bernhard Furrer, ICOMOS Switzerland, Bern – Dirk Carstensen, Technische Hochschule Nürnberg – Hagen Eyink, Federal Ministry of Environment, Nature Conservation, Building and Nuclear Safety, Berlin – Randolph Langenbach, US/ICOMOS, Oakland/Cal. – Hans-Rudolf Meier, Bauhaus-Universität Weimar – Joachim Tourbier, Philadelphia – Pali Wijeratne, President, ICOMOS Sri Lanka, Colombo*

References

Crouch, Tony. 2009. Facing the River. In: Earth Wind Water Fire. Environmental Challenges to Urban World Heritage, ed. Uli Eidenschink: 66-68. Regensburg.

Drdácký, Miloš, Luigia Binda, Insa Christiane Hennen, Christian Köpp, Luca G. Lanza and Rosemarie Helmerich (eds.). 2011: Cultural Heritage Protection against Flooding, Prague.

Ebnöther, Reto and Stefan Thurnherr. 2008. Loss of Cultural Property through Natural Disasters – Prevention through Risk Management: An Approach. In: Meier, Petzet and Will 2008: 41-52.

ELLA. 2006. Preventive Flood Management Measures by Spatial Planning for the Elbe River Basin. European Union INTERREG IIIB ELLA Project. Available from http://www.landesentwicklung.sachsen.de/download/Landesentwicklung/ELLA_EN.pdf.

Flood Insurance – Waves of Problems. 2014. *The Economist, 410*, Number 8877, March 8, 2014, 76.

Furrer, Bernhard. 2008. Danger From the Alps. On the Value of Foresighted Organization. In: Meier, Petzet and Will 2008: 159-174.

Guccione, Biagio, ed. 2005. A Selection of Advanced River Cities in Europe … A Good Practice Guide. Firenze: Edifir-Edizioni.

Heyenbrock, W. 1987. Hochwasserschutz in Bayern. *Bau Intern, 7.*

Jongman, Brenden et. al. 2014. Increasing stress on disaster-risk finance due to large floods. *Nature Climate Change* 4, 264–268, http://www.nature.com/nclimate/journal/v4/n4/full/nclimate2124.html, accessed 08.03.2014.

Kongjian Yu, Zhang Lei and Li Dihua. 2008. Living with Water: Flood Adaptive Landscapes in the Yellow River Basin of China. *Journal of Landscape Architecture, autumn 2008,* 6-17.

Langenbach, Heike. 2007. Flood Management: Designing the Risks. *Topos, 60,* 77-82.

Lawrence, Roderick J. 2012. Rethinking People-Environment Relations with Interdisciplinary and Transdisciplinary Contributions. In: Vulnerability, Risk and Complexity: Impacts of Global Change on Human Habitats, Advances in People-Environment Studies Vol. 3, eds. Sigrun Kabisch, Annett Steinführer and Petra Schweizer-Ries: 39-49. Göttingen-Bern-Cambridge/Mass.-Toronto: Hogrefe.

Lieske, Heiko, Erika Schmidt and Thomas Will. 2012. Hochwasserschutz und Denkmalpflege. Fallbeispiele und Empfehlungen für die Praxis. Stuttgart: IRB Verlag.

Lieske, Heiko and Thomas Will. 2011. Grimma (Germany): A small-river flood in a small walled town, in: Drdácký et al. 2011, 97-102.

Lieske, Heiko. 2012. Flood Hazards, Urban Waterfronts, and Cultural Heritage. In: Vulnerability, Risk and Complexity: Impacts of Global Change on Human Habitats, Advances in People-Environment Studies Vol. 3, eds. Sigrun Kabisch, Annett Steinführer and Petra Schweizer-Ries: 89-100. Göttingen-Bern-Cambridge/Mass.-Toronto: Hogrefe.

McLane, James and Raphael Wüst. 2000. Flood Hazards and Protection Measures in the Valley of the Kings. *Cultural Resource Management, 6,* 35-38.

Meier, Hans-Rudolf, Michael Petzet and Thomas Will, eds. 2008. Cultural Heritage and Natural Disasters. Risk Preparedness and the Limits of Prevention. Heritage@ Risk Special Edition 2007, Deutsches Nationalkomitee von ICOMOS. Dresden: Thelem. Available from http://www.icomos.de/publications.php#heritage.

Mileti, Dennis S. 1999. Disasters by Design. In: The Changing Risk Landscape: Implications for Insurance Risk Management, ed. Neil R. Britton. Available from http://www.aonline-aon.com/public/intelligence/disasters_by_design.pdf.

Quarantelli, Enrico L. 2003. The Protection of Cultural Properties: The Neglected Social Science Perspective and Other Questions and Issues that Ought to Be Considered. Available from http://dspace.udel.edu/bitstream/handle/19716/734/PP325.pdf?sequence=1.

Schanze, Jochen et al. (eds.). 2008. Systematisation, evaluation and context conditions of structural and non-structural measures for flood risk reduction. London: Defra.

Spennemann, Dirk H.R. and David W. Look (eds.). 1998. Disaster Management Programs for Historic Sites. San Francisco, CA and Albury, Australia: U.S. National Park Service, Western Chapter of the Association for Preservation and Technology, and The Johnstone Centre, Charles Sturt University.

Stovel, Herb. 1998. Risk Preparedness: A Management Manual for World Cultural Heritage. Rome: ICCROM.

Taboroff, June. 2002. Natural Disasters and Urban Cultural Heritage: A Reassessment. In: The Future of Disaster Risk: Building Safer Cities, eds. Alcira Kreimer, Margaret Arnold and Anne Carlin: 263-271. Washington, D.C.: The World Bank.

Tourbier, J. T.; Schanze, J. (Eds.) : Urban River Rehabilitation. Proceedings. International Conference on Urban River Rehabilitation URRC 2005, 21st-24th Sept. 2005, Dresden (Germany). Dresden : IÖR, 2005.

Vereinigung der Landesdenkmalpfleger in der Bundesrepublik Deutschland: Denkmalpflegerische Belange in der Umweltverträglichkeitsprüfung (UVP), der Strategischen Umweltprüfung (SUP) und der Umweltprüfung (UP), *Arbeitsblatt 26* (2005).

Water: Design and Management. 2007. *Topos 59,* Special Issue.

WFD 2000: Directive 2000/60/EC of the European Parliament and of the Council of 23 Oct. 2000 establishing a framework for Community action in the field of water policy. Available from http://eur-lex.europa.eu/LexUriServ/LexUriServ.do?uri=CELEX:32000L0060:EN:NOT.

Wilson, M.D. and P.M. Atkinson. 2005. The Use of Elevation Data in Flood Inundation Modelling: A Comparison of ERS Interferometric SAR and Combined Contour and Differential GPS Data. *International Journal of River Basin Management, 3 (1):* 3-20. DOI: 10.1080/15715124.2005.9635241.

'Climate is what we expect, weather is what we get'

Managing the potential effects of oceanic climate change on underwater cultural heritage

Mark Dunkley

English Heritage, UK
mark.dunkley@english-heritage.org.uk

Introduction

English Heritage is the UK Government's statutory advisor on the historic environment of England and provides expert advice about all matters relating to the historic environment and its conservation as set out in the National Heritage Act 1983.[1]

Functions relating to underwater cultural heritage within the territorial waters of the United Kingdom derive from the National Heritage Act 2002 which extended English Heritage's general powers under Section 33 of the National Heritage Act 1983 to cover ancient monuments in, on, or under the seabed within the seaward limits of the UK territorial waters adjacent to England.[2] These powers include providing grant assistance in respect of protected wreck sites, and the provision of advice to any person in relation to any ancient monuments, in UK territorial waters adjacent to England.

In addition, the Secretary of State for Culture, Media and Sport issued Directions to English Heritage under Section 3 of the 2002 Act to exercise functions with respect to the Protection of Wrecks Act 1973 (in relation to historic wrecks situated in UK territorial waters adjacent to England) as well as 'wider responsibilities' for England's maritime archaeology. In fulfilling this latter responsibility, English Heritage advocates a seamless approach to conservation management which is not determined by where the sea is now – or where it will be in the future.

---

1   From March 2015, certain statutory and advisory functions of English Heritage will be transferred to a new body: Historic England.

2   'Underwater cultural heritage' is now the internationally accepted phrase used to refer to historical and archaeological material in the marine zone. In general usage, it has no specific temporal limit (Dromgoole 2013: 94).

Though not addressing the susceptibility of underwater cultural heritage to climate change, *Climate Change and the Historic Environment* (Cassar 2005) did note that resources need to be devoted to understanding how materials will respond to change in marine, coastal and terrestrial environments. The identification of major environmental threats to cultural heritage and the built environment has therefore been one of the core strands of England's National Heritage Protection Plan (measure 2 – threat assessment & response). Here, work has already begun to assess the potential effects of climate change by identifying natural and environmental threats to the historic environment in order to devise adaptive responses to those threats (see, for example, Croft 2013).

Nevertheless, the effects of natural and anthropogenic climate change on underwater cultural heritage have not been adequately considered or researched and are therefore not sufficiently understood to enable predictions of future change to be made at a local site scale.[3] We know that the oceans play an important role in mitigating climate change, taking up and storing about a quarter of anthropogenic carbon dioxide emissions through a combination of biological processes, solubility, and circulation patterns. Despite uncertainties in the chaotic climate system, this paper presents an innovative assessment of the potential *effects* of oceanic climate change on managing underwater cultural heritage in the UK, though the themes addressed will be of interest to all heritage managers and policy makers with responsibility for marine heritage assets beyond the UK.

There is abundant evidence for rises and falls of eustatic (global) sea level in accordance with climatic changes and thus many of the direct impacts of climate change are part of long-term processes that originated in the late glacial period around 12,000 years ago: they are not new. In fact, there is every reason to think that the current global 'warm' period is essentially similar to previous interglacials (Murphy 2009: 209). Whether or not there is universal acceptance of the *rates* of climate change impact described in this paper, the general observations presented here deserve careful consideration because they are based on evidence of a fragile, finite and non-renewable heritage which is vulnerable to much less than a catastrophic event.

Background

The main conclusions from the previous IPCC report (*Climate Change 2007;* IPCC (2013a)) have already been incorporated into government policy in the UK; most recently within the Department for Environment, Food & Rural Affairs (Defra) *UK Climate Change Risk Assessment* (HM Government 2012) which is being implemented through the *National Adaptation Programme* (HM Government 2013). English Heritage contributed to the programme (which sets out what government, businesses, and society are doing to become more climate

---

3   Initial considerations were, however, set-out by the UK's Institute for Archaeologists in autumn 2013. See Dunkley (2013a).

ready) with generic responses to climate change comprising two aspects: *mitigation* (actions to be taken to improve sustainability) and *adaptation* (undertaking early action by anticipating adverse effects of change).

For the historic environment in particular, English Heritage published a statement on *Climate Change and the Historic Environment* in 2008 (using data from the IPCC's Fourth Assessment Report) which was followed by advice in relation to *Flooding and Historic Buildings* in 2010. Unesco has already adopted a climate change strategy which is applicable to all World Heritage Sites (Unesco 2007). This strategy report considers that the principal climate change risks and impacts to cultural heritage comprise atmospheric moisture and temperature change, sea-level rises, wind and desertification plus the combined effects of climate and pollution / climate and biological change. However, the Unesco report is of limited value to curators of underwater cultural heritage as the focus of marine issues tends towards the identification of threats to ecosystems and biodiversity (as many marine World Heritage Sites are tropical coral reefs) while the threat to coastal archaeological sites is predominantly seen as being sea-level change driven.

Even at a European level, there is a paucity of references to underwater cultural heritage within studies of climate change impacts: most recently, the EU-funded *Climate for Culture* project addressed only the built heritage while the Noah's Ark project (Sabbione *et al* 2010) did not consider impacts on historic landscapes or maritime archaeology. Similarly, the European Environment Agency's (EEA) *Climate Change, Impacts and Vulnerability in Europe 2012* simply determined that impact patterns (identified as being largely a result of flood hazards alone) on tangible cultural assets (inclusive of museums) resembled those for infrastructure and settlements (European Environment Agency, 2012: 220).[4]

In September 2011, however, the UK Government published the *UK Marine Policy Statement* (HM Government 2011) which provides the framework for decision-making related to the UK marine environment. The Statement is intended to promote sustainable economic development, enable the UK to move towards a low-carbon economy and ensure a sustainable marine environment. The *Marine Policy Statement* acknowledges that the marine environment plays an important role in mitigating climate change and thus the collection of scientific evidence about the ocean underpins effective management and policy development. It is already accepted that for the UK's marine environment the impacts of climate change include relative sea level rise, increased seawater temperatures, ocean acidification and changes in ocean circulation which will all have some effect on underwater cultural heritage (HM Government 2011: 23).

The Intergovernmental Panel on Climate Change (IPCC) Fifth Assessment Report (*Climate Change 2013*: IPCC 2013a) provides a comprehensive assessment of the physical science basis of climate change, drawing on the scientific literature accepted for publication up to 15 March 2013. The report sets out the latest results from atmospheric physics, satellite and ground observation and computer

---

4   The European Environment Agency plans to publish a fully-updated version of the *Assessment of Climate Change Impacts in Europe* report in 2016.

modelling to bring our understanding of climate change up to date. It is the data from this report that underpin the assessments presented in this paper.

The broad effects of change on ocean processes

The oceanic hydrosphere comprises four basic zones: intertidal (the zone between high tide and low tide), pelagic (the open ocean), benthic (the bottom layer of the ocean) and abyssal (deep ocean) zones.

With the exception of addressing the abyssal zone, Defra's *Charting Progress 2: An assessment of the state of UK seas* (UKMMAS 2010) comprises a summary document which draws on the detailed evidence and conclusions on the use of the marine environment and identifies both the socio-economic value and resulting pressures of activities on the environment. It examines all the evidence together with a summary on the impact of climate change, and provides an assessment of the overall status of the UK's seas, with particular reference to the effects of climate change on ocean processes. The report concludes that the main changes in ocean processes over the past few decades are largely due to the effects of rising sea surface temperature, rising sea levels and ocean acidity. The changes are already affecting some sensitive ecosystems and could have significant long-term impacts.

Understanding and mitigating the effects of oceanic changes on underwater cultural heritage

UK policy has evolved to recognize that there are four broad effects of oceanic changes on the processes of the oceanic hydrosphere for the UK which have the potential to affect the future management of underwater cultural heritage: i) sea temperature, ii) sea level, iii) carbon dioxide and ocean acidification, and iv) circulation, suspended particulate matter, turbidity, salinity and waves (UKMMAS 2010: ix). Each effect is considered in turn below.

Sea temperature

The UK's annual mean air temperature has risen by about 1 °C since the beginning of the 20th century; in fact, 2006 was the warmest year in central England since records began in the seventeenth century. This upward trend in air temperature has generated an associated positive effect on sea temperatures. While temperatures in the oceans decrease with increasing depth, sea-surface temperatures around the UK have risen by between 0.5 and 1 °C from 1870 to 2007 with much of this change having occurred since the mid-1980s.

The global ocean will continue to warm during the 21st century, with heat penetrating from the surface to the deep ocean affecting ocean circulation (IPCC 2013b: 24). Consequently, UK climate projections indicate that UK shelf seas will be 1.5 to 4 °C warmer by the end of the 21st century (UKMMAS 2010).

The ocean takes up carbon dioxide (CO_2) from the atmosphere, but warmer water can hold less CO_2 than cooler water. Thus, as the climate warms, progressively less CO_2 can be taken up by the ocean and more is left in the atmosphere, which warms the climate further. Such a phenomenon is known as positive feedback. Warmer oceans are also indicative of more energetic oceans so that erosion in shallow contexts may be enhanced, controlled by the seabed topography around the UK.

One particular effect of ocean warming already noticeable in UK waters is the northward migration of invasive species; of particular relevance is the blacktip shipworm *Lyrodus pedicellatus*. *L. pedicellatus* is a species of shipworm that is active all year and appears to have invaded the UK from more southerly latitudes, possibly as a result of sea temperature increase. It has been recorded off Cornwall, in Langstone Harbour in Hampshire and on the *Mary Rose* protected wreck site in the Solent and in 2005 it was recorded on the coast at Sandwich, Kent (Llewellyn-Jones 2006). Despite being considered to be a major threat to wooden wrecks and other wooden structures, the GB Non-native Species Secretariat (NNSS) does not yet identify the cryptogenic *L. pedicellatus* as an invasive species to the UK.

English Heritage therefore commissioned a compilation and assessment of geographical baseline information on marine attritional threats to heritage assets in English waters, to include *L. pedicellatus* as well as the common shipworm, *Teredo navalis* (Figure 1).

Significantly, this baseline research, completed in June 2014, records that the reported northern limit of *L. pedicellatus* by 1980 was at 40° N but by 2007 had extended to 50° N (Palma 2014). Current records place *L. pedicellatus* around 51° N (Palma 2014). More work needs to be undertaken – such as identifying temperature thresholds of invasive species against projected water temperature changes - and we now plan to develop appropriate mitigation strategies with the NNSS and the European Science Foundation's marine woodborers network.

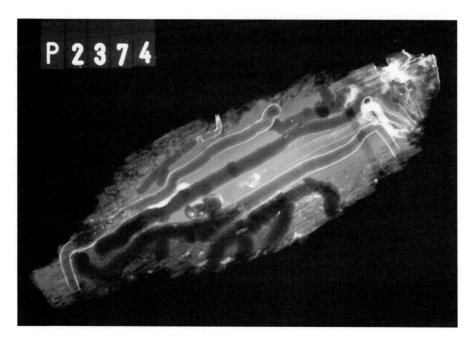

Figure 1. Evidence of marine attrition: the extensive infestation with Teredo navalis of this early eighteenth century barrel stave fragment becomes visible on the X-radiograph. In comparison, the fragment looked fairly intact on the surface (English Heritage).

Sea level

There are two principal causes of sea level rise: thermal expansion (for water expands as it warms) and the reduction of the cryosphere (melting). In the twentieth century, the average level of the UK seas rose by some 14 cm. UK climate projections of UK coastal sea level rise (not including land movement) for 2095 range from 12 to 76 cm, with an extreme scenario for sea level rise in the range of 93 cm to 1.9 m by 2100 (UKMMAS 2010). Global mean sea level will as well continue to rise during the 21st century (IPCC 2013b: 25).

While the effects of thermal expansion might be tempered by a more vigorous hydrological cycle with increased evaporation, the effect of sea level rise on archaeological diving projects will be to incrementally reduce the amount of time (and therefore productivity) an air-breathing diver can spend underwater safely. For example, a 20% increase in diving depth (between 25' and 30') results in a 32% decrease in a no-decompression dive time (source: US Navy Standard Air Decompression Table).

In addition, sea level rise increases the risk of accelerated erosion or increased flooding, while the infusion of land with salt may create difficulties related to *in situ* management methodologies at the coast edge. It also allows larger waves to approach the shore leading to damage and risk to coastal structures and monuments (for a fuller account of coastal impacts and coastal management, see Murphy 2014).

Rising sea level has also caused almost two-thirds of the intertidal profiles in England and Wales to steepen over the past 100 years. Continued sea level rise will thus affect the type and size of particles suspended in the coastal region. As more upper beach and terrestrial sediment is added to the marine environment, the stability of archaeological sites and monuments will be correspondingly affected. However, rising sea level alone should have little impact on archaeological remains underwater for material will be further removed from energetic wave zones.

Models suggest that seasonal mean and extreme wave heights will increase slightly to the south-west of the UK, reduce to the north, and experience little change in the North Sea (UKMMAS 2010). There will clearly be a moderate effect on the safe use, and productivity, of small workboats for fieldwork.

Carbon dioxide and ocean acidification

Carbon dioxide is present naturally and released from anthropogenic sources (e.g. combustion of fossil fuel). The oceans play an important role in mitigating climate change, taking up and storing about a quarter of anthropogenic CO_2 emissions through a combination of biological processes, solubility, and circulation patterns. Since pre-industrial times, the ocean has naturally absorbed about 30% of the emitted anthropogenic carbon dioxide, causing ocean acidification; between 1751 and 1994 average ocean surface pH is estimated to have decreased from approximately 8.25 to 8.14 (Jacobson 2005).[5]

---

5   pH is a measure of acidity using a logarithmic scale: a pH decrease of 1 unit corresponds to a 10-fold increase in hydrogen ion concentration, or acidity.

Despite a warmer ocean's lesser ability to take-up CO2, as noted above, further uptake of carbon by the ocean will increase ocean acidification, measured by recorded decreases in pH. Indeed, Earth System Models project a global increase in ocean acidification for all Representative Concentration Pathway scenarios.[6] The corresponding predicted decrease in surface ocean pH by the end of 21st century is in the range of 0.06 to 0.07 for RCP2.6, 0.14 to 0.15 for RCP4.5, 0.20 to 0.21 for RCP6.0, and 0.30 to 0.32 for RCP8.5 (IPCC 2013b: 27).

Dissolving excess atmospheric CO_2 in surface waters has already noticeably increased their acidity and this may in turn affect the ocean's ability to take up further CO_2. There is a high confidence in calculations which indicate that the pH of ocean surface water has decreased by 0.1 since the beginning of the industrial era (IPCC 2013b: 10).

A more acidic ocean will have a detrimental effect on metal structures and shipwreck sites, and the wider consequences for all underwater cultural heritage, including the corrosion potential of metal-hulled shipwreck sites, needs to be explored. The rates of potential decay are not well understood and so work is needed to further our understanding of the potential effects and impact of changes in ocean chemistry.

In order to begin understanding the effects of acidification, English Heritage commenced innovative research to understand the management requirements of metal-hulled vessels. A programme of ultrasonic investigation and analysis on the remains of two protected early submarines began off England's South Coast (Dunkley 2013b). This work was prompted by the necessity of understanding

Figure 2. The author undertaking ultrasonic thickness testing, Solent 2012, in order to begin understanding corrosion rates on metal-hulled historic wreck sites (Wessex Archaeology for English Heritage).

---

6   Representative Concentration Pathways (RCPs) are four greenhouse gas concentration (not emissions) trajectories adopted by the IPCC for its Fifth Assessment Report.

the stability of steel hulls of wreck sites without causing damaging and increased degradation (Figure 2). Similarly, the Western Australian Museum developed a methodology to measure the pH and corrosion potential of historic iron shipwrecks (Heldtberg *et al* 2004) while work in France is seeking to develop a corrosivity scale to help determine the rates of metal corrosion in seawater (J-B Memet, *pers. comm.*, 26 June 2014).

Recording pH levels on historic wreck sites in English waters is not a new concept: investigations in 2005 on the remains of HMS *Colossus* in south-west England, for example, recorded bed-level pH as part of a programme of environmental monitoring. Here, pH values of between 10.11 and 9.62 remotely collected via a sub-sea data logger (which also recorded dissolved oxygen, redox potential, temperature and depth) seem unreasonably alkali and are improbable for open seawater (Camidge 2005: 73). The same data logger was later used by Bournemouth University to collect more realistic data between July and November 2007 where an average pH value of 8.4 was recorded on the Swash Channel Wreck in Poole Bay, Dorset (P. Palma, *pers. comm.*, 8th September 2014).

Such work has hitherto been limited to individual (wooden) wreck sites, rather than part of a wider systematic programme of research associated with alloys of iron, aluminium or copper. English Heritage has since commenced such a programme to compile current bed-level pH values (coupled with temperature & depth measurements) levels, during planned diving fieldwork around England from 2014. Using a Hanna Instruments Piccolo® Plus pH meter, archaeological divers are, for the first time in British waters, able to collect pH data to an accuracy of ±0.01 (Figure 3). The instrument was used for the first time in the immediate vicinity of the German submarine UB 31, which lies off England's South-East coast, where a pH value of 8.31 was recorded. Such data will assist with change

Figure 3. Archaeologists commencing the first systematic programme of bed-level pH baseline recording in the UK. The use of such data will, in the long term, assist in the management of change (Wessex Archaeology for English Heritage).

management in the marine environment though a much wider programme of investigation is required for there is anecdotal evidence that pH values can, at depth, vary over a tidal cycle.

However, we recognise that such work will be a long-term project conducted over an extended period and it will be some time before we can make accurate judgements about the rate of acidification relative to natural annual and inter-annual cycles of pH. Greater links to current research (which is not driven by the need to understand impacts on underwater cultural heritage, such as the European free ocean carbon dioxide enrichment experiment) will be essential in order to determine wider variability.

Increased acidification will also have an effect on biogeochemistry by harming native marine fauna that build shells of calcium carbonate, such as the shipworm *Teredo navalis*. The indirect effects of this harm upon wooden archaeological remains and coastal structures are not yet known. In addition, the direct effects of acidification upon the stability and condition of exposed wooden structures and iron and steel shipwrecks are not well understood, though decreases in ocean pH have the potential to increase current rates of metal corrosion.

Owing to the wider risks posed by chemical attrition, English Heritage plans to work with the UK Ocean Acidification Research Programme in order to better understand the effects of chemical changes on underwater cultural heritage.

Circulation, suspended particulate matter, turbidity, salinity and waves

The general circulation of the oceans defines the average movement of seawater which follows a specific pattern. The ocean circulation pattern exchanges water with varying characteristics, such as temperature and salinity, within the interconnected network of oceans and is an important part of the heat and freshwater fluxes of the global climate (May 2008: 238).

It is believed that changes in ocean temperatures and wind patterns, resulting from the combined effects of overall climate change, will affect and alter oceanic currents. However, the large-scale circulation of the Atlantic Ocean, which helps to maintain the relatively temperate climate of Northern Europe, has shown high variability in recent years but no clear trend (UKMMAS 2010).

Other circulation patterns are likely to be as variable in the future as they are today, being mainly controlled by the complex topography of the seabed around the UK, as well as by highly variable tides, winds and density differences.

The upper ocean to the west and north of the UK has become saltier since a fresh period in the 1970s, but trends within the shelf seas are less clear. These processes vary on daily to inter-annual timescales but show no significant trend over the past decade, except for a slight salinity decrease in the southern North Sea area and a slight increase in salinity across the northern North Sea, Scottish continental shelf and Atlantic north-west approaches.

Nevertheless, changes to ocean circulation patterns will have major implications for climate and will include changes in rainfall affecting the run-off from rivers. Climate change could also affect wave heights by changing the intensity of storms, or their tracks, with the resultant change in the suspension of bottom material in shallow areas. While there is very low confidence in storm projections, bigger waves have the capacity to impact the seabed at greater depths resulting in increased re-working (though the effects may be tempered by local conditions).

For underwater cultural heritage, the immediate impact is likely to be twofold: Firstly, the effect of increased turbidity will be to decrease underwater visibility for diving archaeologists and secondly, changes to the nature of particles entering the marine environment may enable better *in situ* preservation by reducing biological decay (though this may be offset by shallow-water erosion). However, as yet there are no detailed projections of change for suspended particles and turbidity, let alone sufficient understanding to scale-down national and/or regional predictions to a particular locality.

Concluding remarks

The IPCC Fifth Assessment Report provides the most up to date assessment of the physical science basis of the effects of climate change. The European Environment Agency has correspondingly updated projections for the European regional seas but we are a long way from understanding the full impacts on oceanic systems and predictions of changes are still largely hypothetical.

Nevertheless, the thematic approach adopted above enables the potential impacts of the four broad effects of oceanic climate change on the management of underwater cultural heritage to be gauged, in order to determine where initial research should be prioritized:

Without checks and intervention, the negative effects of change are likely to cause increased attrition of archaeological sites and objects. Used here, attrition means the gradual deterioration that all archaeological sites and monuments undergo as a result of the environment in which they are set. It is a particularly crucial factor for underwater cultural heritage which faces physical, chemical and biological threats, including changes in ocean temperature, increasing ocean acidification, and the damaging effects of invasive marine species.

English Heritage's own science strategy (English Heritage 2013), which aims to direct the detailed planning of support for heritage science, identifies the essential role of marine science in tackling the broad challenges posed by marine attrition.

Effect	Impact
Sea temperature	High negative impact when coupled with temperature rise
Sea level	Low negative impact when coupled with sea level rise
CO_2 and ocean acidification	High negative impact when coupled with reduced pH
Circulation, salinity etc	Net low positive impact

Table 1. Assessment of the impacts of the effects of oceanic climate change on underwater cultural heritage.

The identification of such environmental threats to cultural heritage is, it should be remembered, one of the core strands of the National Heritage Protection Plan and we now aim to work with the UK Marine Climate Change Impacts Partnership to develop a Special Topic Report Card in relation to the socio-economic impacts described in this paper.[7]

The purpose of this paper has been to stimulate initial debate about how the broad effects oceanic climate change might affect the management and curation of underwater cultural heritage. We need to be mindful about balancing the scale of effects or possible effects and it is recognised that more work needs to be done to clarify this balance so that priorities can be determined to as to devise appropriate mitigation measures to the potential effects of climate change within the UK marine area. However, the themes identified above apply equally to heritage managers and curators of underwater cultural heritage beyond the UK and should also serve as the basis for future research following on from projects such as the European collaborative research project to develop tools and techniques to survey, assess, stabilise, monitor and preserve underwater archaeological sites (see sasmap. eu). Tools to enable such preservation were also researched under the recent EU WreckProtect project (see Björdal & Gregory 2011).

On the 10th July 2014, Unesco tweeted that 'The ocean must be at the centre of intl [sic] policies on climate change. It's aberrant that it occupies a marginal role.' This tweet was used as a platform to link to Unesco's news release of the launch of the Ocean and Climate Platform 2015 which will bring together research communities and civil society with the aim of placing the ocean at the heart of international climate change debate. The platform is being launched ahead of the next Conference of Parties to the United Nations Climate Change Convention (COP21), which will take place in Paris in November 2015.

This paper has shown that in advance of Unesco's Ocean and Climate Platform, English Heritage is already undertaking work that will enable us to begin to understand the physical, chemical and biological changes happening within our seas; threats that are not presently well understood and ones that will take time to fully comprehend. This research is also contributing to emerging strategies for marine science in the UK (see Dunkley 2014) which, when coupled with the *English Heritage Science Strategy* (2013), will help ensure that archaeological remains underwater can continue to be enjoyed by this and future generations.

References

C.G. Björdal & D. Gregory. 2011. *WreckProtect. Decay and protection of archaeological wooden shipwrecks*. London.

K. Camidge. 2005. *HMS* Colossus *Stabilisation Trial. Final Report*. Unpublished report for English Heritage.

M. Cassar (2005) *Climate Change and the Historic Environment*, Centre for Sustainable Heritage, University College London.

---

7   See http://www.mccip.org.uk/special-topic-report-cards.aspx

Centre for Maritime Archaeology. 2011. *The Impacts of Climate Change on the Built Heritage of Northern Ireland*, Northern Ireland Environment Agency.

A. Croft. 2013. *Assessment of Heritage at Risk from Environmental Threats: the What and Where of Major Threats*. Key Messages Report for English Heritage. Birmingham.

English Heritage. 2008. *Climate Change and the Historic Environment*. London.

English Heritage. 2010. *Flooding and Historic Buildings*. London.

English Heritage. 2013. *English Heritage Science Strategy*. London.

European Environment Agency. 2012. *Climate Change, Impacts and Vulnerability in Europe 2012*, report ref. No. 12/2012.

S. Dromgoole. 2013. *Underwater Cultural Heritage and International Law*, Cambridge University Press.

M. Dunkley. 2013a. The potential effects of oceanic climate change on the management and curation of underwater archaeology, *The Archaeologist*, No. 89, Autumn 2013, p.60-62.

M. Dunkley. 2013b. Ultrasonic Thickness Testing: devising new ways to manage marine heritage, *Research News*, 19, p.30-31.

M. Dunkley. 2014. Immersed in technology: a strategy for marine science, *Research* News 20, p.6-7.

M. Heldtberg, I.D. MacLeod & V.L. Richards. 2004. Corrosion and cathodic protection of iron in seawater: a case study of the *James Matthews* (1841), *Proceedings of Metal 2004*, National Museum of Australia, p.75-87.

J.E. Llewellyn-Jones. 2006. Another beachcomber's breakfast, *Mollusc World*, 12, p.10.

HM Government. 2011. *UK Marine Policy Statement*. London.

HM Government. 2012. *UK Climate Change Risk Assessment: Government Report*. London.

HM Government. 2013. *The National Adaptation Programme*. London.

IPCC. 2013a. *Climate Change 2013: The Physical Science Basis. Contribution of Working Group I to the Fifth Assessment Report of the Intergovernmental Panel on Climate Change* [Stocker, T.F., D. Qin, G.-K. Plattner, M. Tignor, S.K. Allen, J. Boschung, A. Nauels, Y. Xia, V. Bex and P.M. Midgley (eds.)]. Cambridge University Press, Cambridge, United Kingdom and New York, NY, USA, 1535 pp.

IPCC. 2013b. *Summary for Policymakers. In: Climate Change 2013: The Physical Science Basis. Contribution of Working Group I to the Fifth Assessment Report of the Intergovernmental Panel on Climate Change* [Stocker, T.F., D. Qin, G.-K. Plattner, M. Tignor, S.K. Allen, J. Boschung, A. Nauels, Y. Xia, V. Bex and P.M. Midgley (eds.)]. Cambridge University Press, Cambridge, United Kingdom and New York, NY, USA.

M.Z. Jacobson. 2005. Studying ocean acidification with conservative, stable numerical schemes for nonequilibrium air-ocean exchange and ocean equilibrium chemistry, *Journal of Geophysical Research – Atmospheres*, 110: D07302.

R.M. May. 2008. *The Britannica Guide to Climate Change*. London.

UK Marine Monitoring and Assessment Strategy (UKMMAS) community. 2010. *Charting Progress 2: An assessment of the state of UK seas*. London.

P. Murphy, C. Pater & M. Dunkley (2008) Out to sea: climate change and the maritime historic environment, *Conservation Bulletin*, Issue 57: Spring 2008, p.17-19.

P. Murphy. 2009. *The English Coast. A history and prospect*. London.

P. Murphy. 2014. *England's Coastal Heritage. A review of progress since 1997*. English Heritage, Swindon.

P. Palma. 2014. *A desk- based assessment to compile baseline information on recorded presence of the shipworms Teredo navalis and Lyrodus pedicellatus in English Waters*, Unpublished report for English Heritage, ref. 6804.

C. Sabbione, P. Brimblecombe & M. Cassar. 2010. *The Atlas of Climate Change Impact on European Cultural Heritage. Scientific Analysis and Mangement Strategies*. London/New York: Anthem Press.

Unesco. 2007. *Climate Change and World Heritage*, World Heritage Reports 22. Paris.

Water as an Agent of Creation and Destruction at Petra

Douglas C. Comer

dcomer@cultralsite.com

Water is inextricably linked to the history of Petra, the World Heritage Site in southern Jordan that is famed for the highly photogenic beauty of the hundreds of tombs there, which are cut into the colorful sandstone cliffs that surround the ancient city. Without the development of a sophisticated water management system by the Nabataeans, an Arab group that established a kingdom made enormously rich through trade of incense, spices, and other precious commodities, the urban settlement would not have been possible. With water for human and animal consumption, industry, monumental display, and hygiene, this urban center in the desert emerged more than two thousand years ago, with all the amenities expected of a major city in the Classical world. Damage to that system brought about by development, for which tourism has been the catalyst, has now placed the archaeological remains at Petra, including its famous tombs, in danger.

The word *Petra* is thought to have come from the Greek word for stone. The aesthetic contribution of the rose colored sandstone to the structures within Petra is striking; the relationship of the stone formations of the region to the practicalities of water management might be less so. The sandstone canyons in which the administrative and religious center of the ancient city is located are at an elevation of approximately 1,000 meters. Seismic activity formed fissures in this formation, and flowing water widened these to canyons. This water originated from limestone highland to the west, which reaches elevations of almost 1,700 meters.

One of the fissures in the sandstone formation was carved by the movement of water into a very narrow slot canyon more than a kilometer long. This leads to the core area of Petra, where the Nabataeans built temples, administrative buildings, nymphaeum, water garden, baths, and a Cardo Maximus lined with market structures. In the walls of this slot canyon, called the Siq, can be seen niches for offerings, bas relief carvings of deities and one of a camel caravan, the sort used to convey the spices, incense, silk, and other precious commodities traded by the Nabataeans. Walking through the Siq, just before it widens into the broad valley where major civic building and houses were constructed by the Nabatean, one encounters the most renowned of the many hundred tombs at Petra. This tomb, today called Al-Khazna, was probably prepared for King Aretas IV, who ruled

Figure 1. Al-Khazna glimpst through Siq, icon of Petra and the nation of Jordan, draw to millions of tourists.

Nabataea from 9 B.C. to 40 A.D. (although there is some dispute about this date, see Khairy, 2011: 172-174). The array of symbolism and the presence of Al-Khazna suggest that the Siq was a processional entryway into Petra. The construction of Petra's grandest tombs, including Al-Khazna, and the standing structures within the city seems to have begun in a flurry of activity sometime around the advent of the Common Era.

The visual appeal of Al-Khazna and the Siq (Figure 1) are enormous; together, with Al-Khazna glimpsed through a meander of the Siq, they often inspired feelings of awe. Numbers of tourists increased rapidly after Al-Khazna and the Siq appeared during the dramatic finale of the third movie in the *Indian Jones* series, released in 1989. This was just a few years after Petra was inscribed on the World Heritage List, in 1985. Al-Khazna is now a global icon, and one that has

Figure 2. Drape of IKONOS satellite photo over landscape surface model (DEM), showing Jabal Shara in the background, the administrative and religious center of Petra at the lower left, and the Siq leading past Al-Khazna and into the Petra Center from the lower right.

Figure 3. Geologic zones pertinent to Petra hydrology. Limestone highland formation to the right, sandstone formation in which Petra is located to the left, unconformity and spring zone in the center.

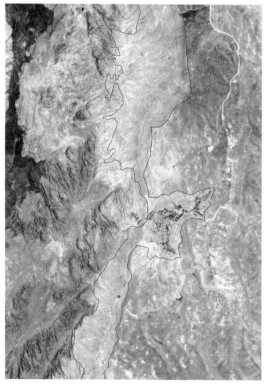

been embraced by the country of Jordan, where images of the tomb can be seen everywhere. Ironically, development of facilities and amenities for the tourists who flock to see this icon has altered the hydrology of Petra and the region around it in ways that threaten the fabric of Al-Khazna, the Siq itself, the hundreds of other tomb within Petra, what remains of the standing structures that one clustered in the core of the city, and the stratigraphic integrity of below-ground archaeological sites that have yet to be discovered.

Sources of Water

Springs

Just to the west of the sandstone formation with an elevation of approximately 1,000 meters in which Petra is to be found is a limestone one that soars to almost 1,700 meters (Figure 2). Where the two meet is an unconformity, a gap between the two on the slope that drops almost 700 meters from the highest point on Jebal Shara (Jebal meaning mountain, and Shara being the supreme deity of Nabataeans) to the urban core of Petra (Figure 3). Along this unconformity, water emerges from the limestone aquifers that are charged by winter rains, creating a line of springs (Figure 4). In Arabic, these are called *ain*, which can be translated as either "spring" or "eye." The most prominent today are Ain Mousa, Ain Umm Sar'ab, Ain Braq, Ain Dibdiba, Ain Ammon, al Beidha, and Ain Bebdbeh. The names of each suggest the importance of water sources to local communities; for example, Ain Mousa means the Spring of Moses. Local oral histories identify this spring as the one created, in the Biblical account, by Moses. In this story, the Edomites, the group that inhabited the valley of Petra as early as the 7th century BC, denied entry to the Israelites who being led from captivity in Egypt by Moses. Deprived of a place of refuge and replenishment, Moses in anger struck a rock outside of Petra with his staff, causing a stream of water to issue forth (Figure 5).

Ortloff (2005: 95), in his very valuable work on Petra hydrology, says of the springs, that

> "...these interdependent assets to provide a continuous, year-round water supply to the city is crucial to understanding Nabataean contributions to hydraulic science. While water storage was a partial key to the city's survival, a number of springs internal and external to the city ...provided water that was channeled and/or piped to the city. This constituted the main water supply of the urban centre."

Ortloff notes that Strabo (2000) mentions the Petra springs: "... *and the inside part of the city having springs in abundance, both for domestic purposes and for watering gardens ...*"

Figure 4 (next page). Locations of Petra springs are seen here as blue dots, some notable archaeological sites and features as red dots.

Spring Feature Key

29. Ein Bedebdeh
31. Ein Sader
32. Ein Musa
33. Ein Julwakh
34. Ein Elhajeem
35. Ein Brack
36. Am Botmah
37. Zoeetreh

Landscap Feature Key

1. Nymphaeum
2. "Great Temple"
3. Temenos Gate
4. Temple of Winged lions
5. Petra Church
6. Qasr al-Bint
7. Museum
8. Al-habis high place
9. Urn Tomb
10. Turkmaniyya Tomb
11. Ad-Deir (Monastery)
12. Theatre
13. Al-Khazneh (Treasury)
14. As-Siq
16. Dam

15. Al-Muthlim Tunnel
17. Visitors Center
18. Rest House
19. Obelisk Tomb
20. Crown Plaza Hotel
21. Zurabah Cistern
22. GTZ building
23. Umm Qussa Cistern
24. Al-Amti Canyon
25. Siq al- Barid
26. Neolithic Village
27. Bir al-Arayis
28. The "Elephant Rock"
30. Jabal al Kubtha

Figure 5. Moses striking rock, causing water to gush forth. Regional oral history identifies this spring with Ain Musa, in the village of Wadi Musa, and once a source of water for ancient Petra. 1563 Tintoretto Moses Striking the Rock, Wikimedia Commons.

The quote taken from Strabo is provocative: there are today no springs within what was the urban core of Petra (although springs occur at Wadi Sabra, a smaller Nabataean settlement located approximately eight kilometers from the Petra core). There are several reasons why springs might have once been found within the central area of Petra that are no longer there today. To begin with, intense tectonic activity is not unusual in the region. A major earth quake destroyed approximately half of the city in the 4th century AD, and another is generally regarded as the cause of total depopulation in the 8th century AD. Such events can open or close springs, and can cause reduced or increased flow for springs that survive them.

Precipitation

What is more important to the understanding of the overall hydrological system at Petra is that the volume of water that springs yield depends upon the degree to which aquifers that feed it are recharged. On the slopes between Jabal Shara and Petra can be seen agricultural terraces of the sort that have been documented at other Nabataean sites; in the Negev Desert, for example (Figure 6). The terraces, when they functioned as intended, provided water to crops, but at the same time, the crops stabilized soils. While plants can wick moisture from soils into the leaves of the plant, where moisture can evaporate, precipitation at Petra is typically in the winter months, when plants are largely dormant. Little water under these conditions is drawn into the body of the plant above ground, which is of greatly

Figure 6. This IKONOS satellite image shows one of the springs along the sloping unconformity between Jabal Shara and Petra, Ain Dibdiba as a darker area containing several very dark. Roughly rectangular, fields at the center top of the image. Note that water from Ain Dibdiba could be distributed to fields downslope from the watercourse that leads from the spring, but that the field terracing system would also harvest and channel water from precipitation.

reduced surface, and so evaporation is minimal. Plants roots continue to stabilize soils, however, and enough plant material remains above ground to slow water movement, minimal, in any case, because of terracing. Water unused by the plants would have provided recharge for springs downslope. Recharge rates have been found to increase as agriculture is introduced into semi-arid and arid ecosystems in many places in the world (Scanlon, et al., 2005:1591). As Seiler and Gat (2007 :64) have noted, "Many human activities result in groundwater recharge; from the very beginning of agricultural terracing of hills, later irrigation contributes to enhanced recharge….)" Irrigation of the fields between Jabal Shara and Petra was provided from both precipitation and from springs along the unconformity.

Precipitation also fed directly into a system of barrage dams, water channels, reservoirs, and cisterns that harvested and stored water, which also enhanced recharge as stored water seeped into soils below. This water was thereby made available for use by the inhabitants of Petra. Humans and animals consumed water, of course, but it was also needed for hygienic purposes, for industrial use, for the baths that served an important social function, and for display in fountains and in at least one paradesio, a water garden, that has been found at Petra. Theatrical displays of water in such structures bolstered the authority of those who administered Petra.

Water Management in the Context of Cultural Strategy

The development of the hydrological system at Petra represents a radical change in Nabataean culture. It is one not so much driven by technological or engineering innovation--the Nabataeans occupied a region in which the remnants of water management systems of the sort that eventually adopted dotted the landscape—as by economic forces that prompted them to embrace agriculture and to recognize apply engineering solutions that had been developed in the region for millennia.

Terraces were obviously constructed only after the Nabataeans began to engage in agriculture. Agriculture was not always practiced by the Nabataeans. Diodorus Siculus said in his *Universal History* (2.48-49; 19.94-100) that the Nabataeans in 312 B.C. had great wealth, which they accumulated only from trade. In this year, they were attacked by Antigonus Monopthalmus (Starky, 1955: 84–85). Those in the attacking army reported that all of the expected trappings of an agricultural society were absent at Petra. There were no houses, fields, and temples; in fact, that these were prohibited by Nabataean law, along with anthropomorphic images. They also reported that the punishment for violating these laws was death.

As this would indicate, the Nabateans were institutionalizing modes of behavior that enforced a nomadic lifestyle. Living without permanent settlements, the Empty Quarter of the Arabian Peninsula was their home. In a landscape without rivers, only they could travel with assurance across vast distances, and only they knew places where water could be found. The wealth that they accumulated they could transport. When the forces under command of Antigonus Monopthalmus invaded Petra, the inhabitants had gone into the desert where they could not be followed. All that the Greeks found were some bars of silver, left behind in haste.

When the Nabataeans embraced agriculture, examples of the technology that they needed for this were all around them. In what is now Jordan, landscapes designed to harvest and store water from precipitation predate Petra by many millennia. What is generally regarded as the earliest dam in the world can be found in northern Jordan, at the Tell Jawa site. It is a complex structure formed of two walls of stone (basalt), with fill between them of soil, clay, and ash that was compacted in a way reminiscent of rammed earth. It is 80m long and 5m high, and formed a reservoir in which 31,000 cubic meters of water were stored. Early excavations provided a mid- 4th millennium BC date of construction. More recently; others have argued that first construction of the dam is more likely to have been at the beginning of the 3rd millennium BC. (Fahlbusch, H, 2009: 14). Fahlbusch argues that this carefully designed and constructed dam was the product of incremental engineering sophistication that began 8,400 years ago, as witnessed by sites in southern Jordan. At Wadi Abu Tulaya, near a Pre-Pottery B Neolithic site, one finds barrage dams that collected seasonal precipitation at a field, and, below, directed water into a storage facility. A second barrage system is located at Wadi Ruweishid ash-Sharqi, where two of these dams diverted water as irrigation to fields. Fahlbusch bases his 8,400 BP date on three C14 dates samples associated with these barrage dams (Fahlbusch, 2009: 16).

Thus we have an indication that in southern Jordan, 3000 years before what has been regarded by archaeologists and historians of engineering as the earliest dam in the world, were the essential elements of the Nabataean water management system at Petra: barrage dams, distribution to agricultural fields, and reservoirs. To look at this in a slightly different way, the Nabataeans put together their complicated water harvesting system using components first employed at sites not far away 5,000 years before. They did this, however, only after making the transition from an economy based solely in trade of precious commodities to one that depended, increasingly, on agriculture.

Driving this transition was the steady advance of the Roman frontier. In 66 B.C., Pompeii waged a successful war on the pirates that had preyed upon commercial shipping in the Mediterranean, rendering the Mediterranean a Roman sea. In 31 B.C., with the Battle of Actium, Octavian, later Caesar Augustus, defeated Antony and Cleopatra, winning Egypt, and securing maritime trade routes on the Red Sea as well as the Mediterranean. By 25 B.C., Augustus was insisting that the Nabateans reveal their overland trade routes through the Empty Quarter. The Nabataeans bridled at this, and Augustus simply appropriated the trade in precious commodities, moving commodities from the southern shore of the Arabian Peninsula through the Red Sea and thence to Alexandria, and from there to Rome (Starky, 1955: 94). As Rome fortified its position in *Felix Arabia*, finally annexing Nabataea in 106 A.D. and building forts and other military installations, troops were stationed there, and these personnel required sustenance. They preferred the cuisine associated with Rome, and the Nabataeans began to practice agriculture in earnest, growing grains, olive trees, and grapes on hillside terraces.

Degradation of the Water Harvesting System and Resulting Damage to Archaeological Resources

Ortloff proposes that open channels were used to transport water from the upslope springs to the city before terracotta pipes were installed for this purpose. These same open channels were surely used to divert precipitation from heavy rain events into Wadi Siyaha and away from the Siq itself. A robust water diversion barrier was placed by the Nabataeans at just the location required for this, and it was restored after a 1963 flash flood in the Siq that took the lives of 27 French tourists in the Siq (Al-Qudah, 2011: 150). If the open channels were among the earliest structures built at Petra to manage water flow, as Ortloff suggests, then the diversion barrier at the junction of the Siq and Wadi Siyaha might have been required because the other components of the water management system, including the terracing, barrage dams, cisterns, and reservoirs, all of which acted to mitigate the volume and velocity of water moving into the sandstone canyons from the limestone highland above, might not have been in place at that time. Floods through the Siq were probably common during the winter rainy season before the water management system was fully developed, rain events then can deliver half of the average year's precipitation in a few days. The urbanization of Petra and accompanying agriculture economy both demanded a solution to the problem and suggested one, given the necessity of terracing for agricultural purposes.

Tourism visits to Petra have increased greatly since the inscription of the site on the World Heritage List in 1985, as seen in the chart below. Management capacity has not kept pace with this rapidly increasing visitation, as is clearly indicated by damage to tombs and archaeological sites that are well documented (see, for example, Paradise, 2012). Yet the greatest damage has been from unbridled

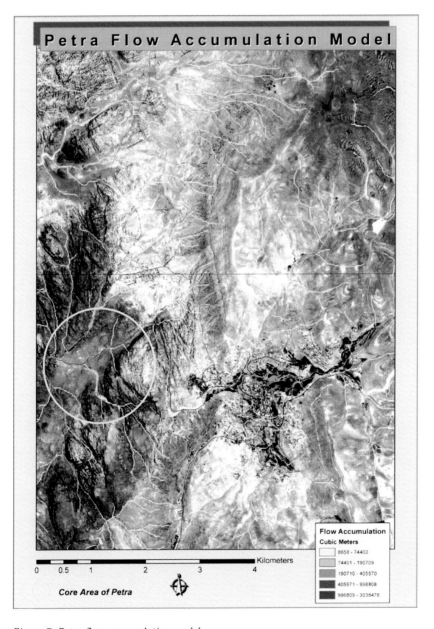

Figure 7. Petra flow accumulation model.

development upslope from the urban core of ancient Petra, in particular in Wadi Musa, the village that is adjacent to the World Heritage Site. An indication of the radical alteration of the landscape that this development has produced can be seen in Figure 7. The red oval in the black and white aerial photo on the left shows the location of the village of Wadi Musa in 1953, the one on the right the village in 1993. Both were taken in months that are typically without much rainfall. By the latter year, only eight years after the inscription of Petra on the World Heritage List, and just four years after Al-Khazna was featured in the *Last Crusade* episode of the Indiana Jones series, it can be seen by comparison of the photos that much has changed on the Wadi Musa landscape.

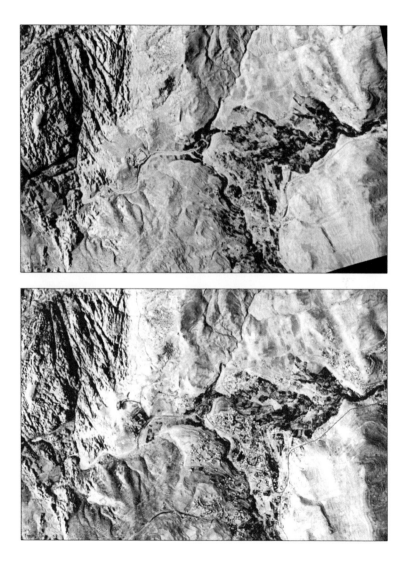

Figure 8. Comparison of Wadi Musi in 1967 and 1993. Both extensive field plots and upland areas have been developed into tourist accommodations, greatly increasing the area covered by impermeable surfaces.

The most deleterious of these changes was the introduction of impervious surfaces. Hotels, restaurants, roads, and parking lots do not absorb precipitation; instead, water from precipitation is shed by these surfaces. Under extreme conditions, this water has produced what have been recognized as flash floods. This was the case, for example, in the 1963 incident in which a tour group of 23 was drowned, and in 199?, when a flood within the boundaries of Wadi Musa swept two young men who were walking along the dry bed of the watercourse that gives the village its name (Wadi Musa) to their deaths, carrying their bodies many kilometers downstream, into the core area of Petra, near the nymphaeum there.

Such flood waters damage archaeological sites and features in a number of ways. The first is by simple water erosion of structures and features carved into rock walls or the remains of standing structures, and by percussion as materials carried with the flood strike what is left of standing structures or tombs and other carved features, including the remains of ancient water channels and pipes, bas reliefs, ritual niches, and inscriptions. Further damage to stone surfaces, including tomb facades, is produced when water finds its way into cracks that were created by percussion or simply through pores in the sandstone. Freezing temperature at night and thawing temperatures during the day are common in the winter at Petra. Water expands when it turns to ice, widens crevices and pores, the next freeze-thaw cycle widens them further until stone crumbles, sometimes taking large areas of façade away when this occurs . Floods also erode soil, which exposes, dislocates,

Figure 9. Note patterns of sandstone deterioration at Petra tombs: water acts to deteriorate sandstone in several ways. One way that this occurs is when salt laden water is absorbed by sandstone at the base of tombs, producing characteristic keyhole shape for ground level doors, also sandstone spalls away from facades, taking with it tomb embellishments. photo by Diego Delso, Wikimedia Commons, License CC-BY-SA 3.0

and sometime washes away subsurface archaeological materials. Finally, damage is produced by salts and other minerals that have been dissolved in water, which is then absorbed by the rock from which tombs have been cut, or the stone blocks used in standing structures. As the water that has been absorbed by dries, crystals are formed that force apart the very granules that make up the sandstone from which tombs and standing structures have been created (see, for example, Smith and McGreevy, 1988: 697–705; Gabler, et al., 2007: 428) (Figure 8).

Conclusion

The water harvesting system of barrage dams, channels, reservoirs, and cisterns found at Petra can be found at much older sites in the region, sites that might be as much as five millennia older. It is certainly likely that the extent and complexity of the Petra system is the greatest seen at archaeological sites in Jordan, and among the most remarkable in the ancient world, yet the system almost surely drew heavily upon examples provide by more ancient, nearby systems. The relationship of this system to the springs that also provided water to Petra was obviously intimate, although ascertaining exactly how the two complemented one another will require further study. Nonetheless, even now it is clear that the integrated system made possible the founding and continued occupation of a sophisticated urban environment for hundreds of years.

Degradation of the water harvesting system in the region around the ancient city has produced substantial deterioration of archaeological materials at Petra. Research into how water harvesting and spring productivity are related might be used to identify ways by which to arrest the deterioration of archaeological resources that will continue until water is diverted from them. It might also suggest programs and actions that might reverse desertification of the landscape in the region through re- vegetation and recharging aquifers.

Literature Cited

Al-Qudah, K.A. 2011. Floods as Water Resource and As a Hazard in Arid Regions: A Case Study in Southern Jordan. *Jordan Journal of Civil Engineering*. Vol. 5, No 1.

Butterfield, R. 1964. *Ancient Rome*. New York (NY): Odyssey Press.

Diodorus Siculus. Universal History (2.48-49; 19.94-100). English edition: Oldfather, C. H. Book in English, Greek, Ancient (to 1453). Library of history: Bibliotheca Historia. Cambridge, MA: Harvard University Press.

Fahlbusch, H. 2009. Early Dams. *Proceedings of the Institution of Civil Engineers, Engineering History and Heritage*. 162. February 2009 Issue EH1. Pages 13–18. doi: 10.1680/ehh2009.162.1.13

Gabler, R.E, J.F. Petersen, L.M. Trapasso. *Essentials of Physical Geography*. Belmont, CA: Thomson Higher Education.

Khairy, N. I. 2011. The Mada'in Saleh Monuments and the Function and Date of the Khazneh in Petra. *Palestine Exploration Quarterly*, 143, 3, 167-175.

Labus, M. and J. Bochen. 2012. Sandstone degradation: an experimental study of accelerated weathering. *Environmental Earth Science* 67:2027–2042 DOI 10.1007/s12665-012-1642-y

Ortloff, C.R. 2005. The Water Supply and Distribution System of the Nabataean City of Petra (Jordan), 300 BC- AD 106. *Cambridge Archaeological Journal*, 15, pp 93-109 doi:10.1017/S0959774305000053.

Paradise, T. 2012. Architecture and Deterioration in Petra: Issues, Trends, and Warnings. In, D. Comer, ed., *Tourism and Archaeological Heritage Management at Petra*, New York: Springer Press.

Scanlon, B.R., R.C. Reedy, D.A. Stonestrom, D.E. Prudic, and K.F. Dennehy, 20005, Impact od Land Use and Land Cover Change on Groundwater Recharge and Quality in the Southwestern US. *Global Change Biology*, 11, 1577-1593, doi: 10.1111/j.1365-2486.2005.01026.x.

Seiler, K.-P. and J.R. Gat. 2007. Groundwater Recharge form Run-Off, Infiltration and Percolation. Dordrecht, The Netherlands: Springer.

Smith B.J. and J.P. McGreevy. 1988. Contour scaling of a sandstone by salt weathering under simulated hot desert conditions. *Earth Surf Proc Land* 13:697–705.

Starky, J. 1955. The Nabataeans: A Historical Sketch. *The Biblical Archaeologist*, 18 (4), 84–106.

Strabo. 2000. *Geography*, vol. VII: Books 15–16. (The Loeb Classical Library.) Cambridge (MA): Harvard University Press.

Powell, J.H. 1989. Stratigraphy and sedimentation of the Phanerozoic rocks in central and south Jordan, part B. *Natural Resources Authority*, Bulletin 11.

Tsunami and heritage after the 2011 Great East Japan Earthquake

Katsuyuki Okamura

The Great East Japan Earthquake that struck Japan on the 11th of March 2011, one of the largest seismic events the world has seen for generations, affected a vast area covering parts of the Tohoku and Kanto regions, stretching for more than 500 km north to south. In Miyagi, Iwate and Fukushima prefectures the damage was particularly severe. The subsequent tsunami (tidal wave) reached more than 30 m in height in certain areas and inundated areas several kilometers inland, destroying virtually everybody and everything in its path (Fig. 1). Almost 20,000 people died or have been lost. It also caused a meltdown at the Tokyo Electric Power Company's Fukushima No. 1 nuclear power plant forcing the evacuation of people living in the proximity. Without doubt, the damage this disaster caused was the most serious since WW II.

Figure 1. The 2011 tsunami at 15:25 on the 11th of March, taken from the 5th floor of Miyako City Hall, Iwate Prefecture. Photo by Shin'ya Kumagaya (Iwate Nippou Press).

The damage inflicted upon cultural heritage was also very significant and wide-ranging. Speaking only of designated national cultural properties, more than 754 items are confirmed to have been damaged, including five national treasures, 160 important cultural properties, ninety historic sites and buildings as well as hundreds of paintings, carvings, craft goods, ancient documents, and ethnological and archaeological artefacts (Agency for Cultural Affairs 2012). The tsunami washed away a vast number of cultural properties in museums, public buildings, temples, shrines and private houses located in coastal areas. Multiple rescue operations have been undertaken by committed experts and volunteers from all over the country (Kaner, Habu & Matsui 2011, Matsui 2011, Okamura et al. 2013, Tateishi 2014, Hanazato, Kariya & Yano 2014). In addition, the reconstruction of the affected regions has necessitated a series of excavations carried out with the cooperation of a number of archaeologists from all over Japan (Negita 2012).

Although nearly 4 years have passed since the disaster, a number of problems have not yet been solved, and some have newly emerged. In response to the severity and enormity of the damage caused by the tsunami, national and regional governments are now constructing massive tide embankments along the coast. Moreover, the devastated settlements are being relocated and reconstructed on higher ground, free of the fear of future tsunami damage. However, this construction will sharply separate the sea from the land. For people living in the coast area, particularly fishermen, the sea is not only a rich repository of natural resources, but, dare I say, represents their very lives. Essentially, the construction of the embankment will damage the cultural landscape. It has also caused a 'bubble' economy leading to a boom in construction work and an increase in material costs in the region. This hinders the reconstruction of homes by the local people and consequently may cause a decrease in population. So we must ask: for whom is this embankment being constructed? This traditional 'hard' approach against 'nature' needs reconsidering.

Another issue concerning heritage involves the preservation of *shinsai ikou* (lit. disaster remains, memorial buildings or structures related to the disaster). Preserving certain damaged buildings and/or beached ships *in situ* could be considered an effective method of handing down not only the misery but also lessons regarding the great disaster to future generations. However, it may also arouse bitter memories and, in severe cases, PTSD with those who survived. So, which, if any, sites should be preserved?

The present paper will firstly review what has happened and is happening, particularly as to the cultural heritage in the devastated area, and how it was rescued and researched. Next it will additionally present a newly emerging issue: dilemmas concerning the heritage and communities during the subsequent reconstruction process. Finally, it will clarify the way in which these issues and challenges relate to the socio-political questions of Japan's contemporary society and the beyond.

Rescuing heritage

About a month after the Earthquake, rescue workers were very active in many areas across the devastated region. The immediate need was to evacuate the damaged cultural properties and relocate them to temporary storage facilities where they could be kept in appropriate conditions and where necessary treatment could be conducted.

The Agency for Cultural Affairs has organized an extraordinary committee for the rescue of damaged and endangered cultural properties, launching a rescue project in April 2011 (Agency for Cultural Affairs. 2011). In the Miyagi Prefecture, the headquarters were set up at the Sendai municipal museum. Staff members of the Agency and National Institutes for Cultural heritage were dispatched in order to undertake this project, unprecedented in nature and scale, in collaboration with staff members of the prefectural and municipal boards of education and local academic associations. In total 6,800 people joined the rescue works at ninety locations in Iwate, Miyagi, Fukushima and Ibaragi Prefectures for 2 years (Shimotsuma 2014.). Amongst the scholarly societies involved, the Network for the Conservation of Historical Documents spearheads the rescue project. For instance, as of 2013, the Miyagi Branch has rescued tens of thousands of items from ninety collections (Sato 2014). The network had initially been established by Historical Societies in the Kansai region in response to the Hanshin-Awaji Earthquake of 1995.

In the devastated areas, ancient documents, ethnological and archaeological artefacts, and the like are being rescued from damaged museums, archives, shrines and the homes of individuals (Fig. 2). These items are cleaned and given first-aid

Figure 2. Recovering historical documents from a warehouse on the 7th of April 2011 by the Miyagi Historical Documents Conservation Network in Ishinomaki City, Miyagi Prefecture. Photo by Mr. Hidekazu Saito.

conservation treatments, including high speed vacuum freeze-drying in the case of water-damaged Japanese paper documents (Matsui 2011, Tateishi 2014). One of more difficult tasks is to extract salt from the rescued objects. The reason for this is: a variety of materials, ranging from paper documents to stuffed animals, as to which the technology for each material has not been firmly established. Even now conservators are literally dealing with thousands of objects through trial and error. The Rikuzentakata City Museum has continuously been undertaking these stabilizing treatments on c.460.000 objects, while not only striving to develop stabilization techniques but also creating a new methodology with the cooperation of related organizations (Kumagai 2014).

Certain universities have applied the results of this work to education and training for students. For instance, Prof. Koji Kato, a folklorist from Tohoku-gakuin University, mentioned how this rescue work offered the students a good, practical opportunity to learn about and appreciate the meaning of heritage and its research. He worked with students rescuing objects to then display them at the University museum, identified them with the help of the owners and produced an oral history for each object. A number of reports on rescue works have been published, providing museum staff with useful and practical lessons with regard to disaster mitigation. They often point out the importance of maintaining regular exchanges of information and setting up solid networks as to mutual support.

In particular, the Cultural Heritage Management issues in Fukushima differ from those of other areas due to radiation contamination, which in addition to the effects of the earthquake and tsunami has displaced 120,000 people (i.e., 6% of the total population of Fukushima) from the affected areas or their homes. Many people still live in temporary housing. As to the cultural heritage, the majority of the major cultural properties have been rescued from the restricted area thanks to committed archaeologists and heritage managers in Fukushima. These objects are stored in safety, but where and how to exhibit them has not yet been decided and is under serious discussion (Schlanger, Nespoulous & Demoule 2015).

This year the Agency submitted a budget request for the establishment of a 'Disaster prevention and rescue centre for cultural properties'. Centralizing rescue operations and preservation for cultural heritage in disaster emergencies is greatly anticipated. The reason for is that the question has been unsettled since the 1995 Earthquake.

Saving underground heritage

Another serious issue consisted of the immovable underground heritage. Concerned archaeologists could predict what would happen to archaeological remains in the Tohoku affected area, as they faced the same situation after the 1995 Hanshin-Awaji earthquake (Okamura et al., 2013). The problem was becoming acute as the phase shifted from the initial clean-up to the reconstruction of the destroyed infrastructure and villages/towns, since there are c.6,000 archaeological sites in

Miyagi and 13,000 in Iwate Prefecture. Especially in the Sanriku Coast, more sites (often proposed for a new town) are located on the hills than coastal plains. Archaeologists also anticipated the existence of many undiscovered sites.

In April 2012 the Agency of Cultural Affairs issued a notice entitled 'Regarding Cultural Properties Management Related to the Restoration and Reconstruction Associated with the Great East Japan Earthquake', as they had done for the 1995 Hanshin-Awaji Earthquake. It consists of four articles, but the points emphasize the need for a speedy excavation so as to not delay reconstruction works, and the active dissemination of research results to local people and developers. As a means to undertake the necessary excavation, Iwate, Miyagi, Fukushima Prefectural Boards of Education and the Agency of Cultural Affairs requested other local governments for an archaeological labour force. Next, from April 2012 on, twenty archaeologists were sent to engage in excavation prior to the reconstruction of towns and other infrastructure (called *Fukko* (Reconstruction) excavations, Negita 2012). Their number jumped to sixty archaeologists from twenty prefectures from April 2013 on. In the case of the 1995 Earthquake, a total of 121 archaeologists were sent to the affected area from as many as fourty prefectures for a three-year period.

The Agency initially planned to continue this support system for 3 years, but extended the programme in order to meet the demands from local governments. For instance, Iwate Prefectural Centre for Archaeological Heritage excavated 172,272 square meters in total prior to reconstruction at thirty sites in fiscal 2013. Amongst them, 81,925 square meter at twenty-one sites were carried out

Figure 3. Excavating the Niidatate medieval fortified village site, Minami-sanriku town, the Miyagi Prefecture. The tsunami washed away the entire village at the foot of the hill.

prior to the construction of the Sanriku Coast motorway, and 83,423 square meters at six sites prior to the construction of new towns in elevated areas by the Relocation Project. Land readjustment projects accompanied other excavations. Various remains were discovered including (a) a Jomon period (the prehistoric era between *c.*12,000 BC and 300 BC) settlement, (b) an ancient or medieval *tatara* steel making kiln which used sand iron, a very popular feature in this region and (c) a fortified medieval settlement (Fig. 3). Despite the immediate issues faced by archaeologists, archaeological investigations were surprisingly carried out in almost the same way as they had before the earthquake: reconstruction work continued smoothly, thanks to the reinforced AHM and the effort of the stakeholders. Numerous discoveries had enough impact to alter the understanding of the local history. The public was often invited to open days.

As to archaeological heritage in Fukushima, a serious discussion is in progress (Schlanger, Nespoulous and Demoule 2015). A Government proposal to build an 'interim' storage facility for radioactivity-contaminated soil in Futaba and Okuma was accepted by a Fukushima Governor, Mr. Yuhei Sato, in September 2014. However, because it is so large, 19 square km, it will affect the historical landscape of a region containing at least sixty archaeological sites.

Even though there are still certain difficult issues including the publication of reports and utilization of archaeological finds due to the lack of heritage managers in coastal municipalities, towards the end of 2013, excavations associated with Town Relocation Project were almost finished and *Fukko* excavations were reaching their culmination. Projects scheduled for 2015 have requested a total of fifty-seven archaeologists from other prefectures and municipalities. This raises the question: how excavations have been possible even in such difficult conditions? This may be attributed to the robust nature of Japan's AHM and its engaged public archaeologists (Okamura 2013, cf. Demoule 2002, 'the "socialist" model' in: Kristiansen 2009).

Learning from the past

Japanese people have paid more attention to past natural disasters including earthquake and tsunamis since the Great East Japan Earthquake. Even as historians attempt to disseminate this information to the public through media, certain archaeologists have hypothesized that even from as early as the Jomon period, the fear for a tsunami has been handed down from generation to generation. Excavations have revealed that Jomon villages, like currently existing shrines, were positioned outside the tsunami's reach. Excavations also reveal past disasters. In 1988, the geologist, Dr. Akira Sangawa, established 'Earthquake archaeology'. In it he researched and reexamined traces in the ground as to past earthquakes, identifying them with earthquakes recorded in historical documents. He also utilized such information for public disaster prevention. 'Earthquake archaeology' was widely discussed amongst field archaeologists when 'ground liquefaction' was often cited after the 1995 Hanshin-Awaji earthquake. One year after the 1995 earthquake, we compiled 'Earthquake traces unearthed' with the cooperation of approximately 150 archaeologists from all over Japan. It covered all the traces of past earthquakes excavated at 378 sites (Maibun-kyuen renraku kaigi & Maizou-bunkazai kenkyu-kai (ed.) 1996). The report stirred a great public interest, and was widely covered by major national newspapers.

Similarly, after the 2011 Earthquake, Tohoku archaeologists started working hard on research and reexamination for traces of deposits from past earthquakes and tsunamis as to public disaster prevention. Behind the scenes, they agonized over whether they had properly disseminated information on past tsunamis. Mr. Hirohiko Saino from Sendai City Board of Education is one of the archaeologists who tackled this subject (Saino 2012). He first directed an excavation in 2006 at the Kutsukata Site near Sendai City prior to the construction of a motorway and found a layer of white sand covering 2000 BP (middle Yayoi Period) paddy fields. In order to clarify if the layer was a tsunami deposit, he and Prof. Hideaki Matsumoto, a physical geographer from Tohoku-gakuin University, carried out thirty-eight drillings in order to confirm the continuity of the tsunami deposits from the inland limit to the paleo-shoreline of 2000 years ago. By means of a thorough research of the deposits, including grain size analysis, they finally determined that the white sand was definitely a tsunami deposit, and discovered that the scale of the 2000BP tsunami was approximately same as the 2011 tsunami.

Mr. Saino and other Tohoku archaeologists have furthered the study along the Sanriku coast in order to identify the 869 Jogan and 1611 Keicho earthquakes and tsunamis. In addition, they have begun clarifying the movements and changes of the then population before and after the earthquakes by means of a settlement pattern study. Mr. Saino asks himself the question: how research on tsunami traces should be developed? He then mentions three directions: (a) developing geo-scientific interdisciplinary research, (b) identifying tsunamis, the damage they cause and the recovery from it in human history, and (c) offering research results as to disaster prevention divisions and building a cooperative relationship with them. His suggestions may lead Japanese archaeologists to extend from specific 'Tsunami' research to more general research, which would include earthquakes, landslides, flooding, volcanic activities, etc. in order to establish 'Disaster' archaeology.

The idea of 'Disaster' archaeology was raised after the 1995 Earthquake, but we could not establish a system to regularly collect and analyze data. However, in April 2014, it was decided that the Nara National Research Institute for Cultural Properties should start creating a database for all the traces of natural disaster across the country from excavation reports and set up a network of experts while developing research methods and technology over the next 5 years.

Changing landscape and struggling with a dilemma

The history of the Japanese Archipelago cannot be discussed without including its people's response to disasters. In particular, the history of Sanriku Coast can be called one of grappling with tsunamis. In a controversial move, the government has proposed a plan to build a 386 km stretch of tide embankments in three of the affected prefectures of which 46 km has already been completed. The total cost will be up to 800 billion yen (7 billion US dollars) albeit that the significance and effectiveness of certain walls is questionable and under discussion (Graham 2014). As for the planned height of walls, 16 m at a maximum and an average of 11 m in Iwate, and 14.7 m and 7-8 m in Miyagi, victims have raised a number of objections including: 'It is even more dangerous, for we cannot see the sea'; 'Destroying the landscape will have a negative influence on the local tourism industry'; and 'It will have an adverse effect on our lives and our fishing port' (McCurry 2014). The first lady, Ms. Akie Abe, also opposes the construction under the current conditions due to dangers to the local tourist industry and ecosystem. Without doubt, certain embankments are unnecessary and should be reconsidered, as all the local resident have already moved to higher ground and there is nothing left to protect. In Kesennuma City, the town planning committee and town council submitted a request to lower embankment to 5 m from the 9.9 m the prefecture government proposed and collected 405 signatures from 566 local residents.

Prof. Akemi Yamauchi mentions the ongoing discussion on the construction of the tide embankment (Yamauchi 2012): 'The notion to protect people with such a huge structure arises from the central government, not from the fishing villages'. The 'wisdom' and practical knowledge accumulated from a life lived next to the sea is needed in order to reduce the damage of natural disasters. However, the height of embankments has become a greater focus for the central government and a prerequisite for reconstruction than a consideration for the local people. The government tends to misunderstand wishes of the local residents in relation to the embankment, and due to a poor choice of language may fail to explain their intentions to the local people. Already fishermen have experienced a serious deterioration of their environment and are concerned about additional negative effects to fishing from embankment construction.

Prof. Akemi Yamauchi continues, 'Tohoku people suffer from a trauma. It is now a part of their mindset and it comes from a long history of being subordinate to the central government, and it affects their lives and landscape. This history created the foundation of dependency on the central government' and 'to construct the embankment forcibly would create serious issues which would weaken community ties, smash a young man's dream and put an end to the history of the community.'

Creating new 'heritage'

The Reconstruction Agency produced a document 'Concerning support for the preservation of memorial buildings or structures to commemorate the disaster in November 2013. The Agency decided to apply the Reconstruction Grant to the preservation of a maximum of one building or structure in each municipality, as long as the following conditions were met (a) the structure can be positioned within the total reconstruction planning, (b) the expenses for its maintenance must be paid by the municipality, and (c) it requires the consensus of the local residents. For example, in Miyagi Prefecture,a total of ten buildings or structures from seven municipalities, including schools, a police station and a platform for a railway station, were nominated and are under examination by the Panel of Experts.

Figure 4. The Disaster Mitigation Office of Minami-sanriku town, Miyagi Prefecture, on the 7th of September 2012.

Among them is Arahama Elementary School, which was struck by a 7.2 m high tidal wave. From it 300 people including children, teachers and local residents were rescued 27 hours after the Earthquake occurred. The Sendai City government plans to hold hearings with local residents in order to determine whether or not to preserve the school.

Basically, nominated structures are supposed to be accepted by local residents, but there are certain exceptions to this guideline, including Disaster Mitigation Office of Minami-sanriku town (Fig. 4). Here, a 15.5 m high rising tide swallowed forty-three evacuees in this three-story, 12 m high building. Minami-sanriku town council granted a petition by local residents to demolish it in September 2012. After the town mayor had initially scheduled its removal for September

2013, later in November 2013 he accepted a proposal from the Panel of Experts to reconsider its preservation.

Who can or should decide on the preservation of memorial structures after a great disaster? Does the decision lie with local residents, the local government or even the central government? The people concerned with managing heritage should observe how new 'heritage' is being created, as once we did for the Hiroshima Peace Memorial.

A future view: 'sustainability' in development and heritage

I have made an overview of heritage issues following the Great East Japan Earthquake, in particular those relating to the resulting tsunami. While we have seen certain efforts towards regional revitalization by means of rescuing local heritage, by not only exploring the past but also creating a new heritage for the future, we have also seen a high priority placed on conventional development in the construction of embankments and the restarting of nuclear power stations all over the country. They appear as a contrast as well as a conceptual conflict between the 'matured' and the 'development'.

The Earthquake exposed a feature of Japan's modernity, in which Tohoku region played an important role. The people of Tohoku have contributed to the growth of cities, especially the Tokyo metropolitan area in terms of labour forces, military power, food and energy. As mentioned above, they cannot help but hold a certain inferior complex and feeling of subordination to the Central Government. Nevertheless, the people of the Sanriku Coast have embraced a rich maritime culture. Not one fisherman I have met resents the sea. They spend time differently and sense to city dwellers. Their common community cooperative activities demonstrate to us the way to share and help each other. I appreciate that they value 'continuity' rather than 'persistent development', and in that sense, they are already 'mature'. Japanese people tend to believe in a monolithic culture forgetting we are live in a multi-cultural society. Mutual respect between cultures should be secured. The urban thought, or obsession, with persistent development, time-control, cost-effectiveness etc, increasingly assails inhabitants of globalized capitalist countries, including Japan.

Water and heritage are both important for life. However, we have learned that water now and again seriously threatens our lives, and that people occasionally forget their heritage and the lessons of past disaster. By means of the investigation of the true power and mechanism of the Earthquake, as well as the frequency of aftershocks, certain seismologists and geologists have begun to argue that the Japanese archipelago and the surrounding areas have entered a phase of increased seismic activity. In addition, the on-going disaster at the Fukushima No.1 nuclear power station sustains the sense of an impending crisis. We had hoped that the citizens of Japan would be more prepared than ever to sincerely listen to the messages from the past. However, as time passes, the attention and interest directed to the earthquake and tsunami have faded from the public consciousness.

Thus the message the concerned managed to bring by means of the mediation of our experiences and heritage has been forgotten.

As experts of the past and heritage caretakers, we must continue to present the long-term interaction between nature and human society and between history and heritage. At the same time, we should continue to ask ourselves: what is a sustainable development and how can we manage heritage in a more 'matured' society?

Acknowledgements

I would like to express my deep gratitude to Robert Condon for his advice and assistance with translation and proofreading.

References

Agency for Cultural Affairs. 2011. Call for your cooperation in saving and recovering cultural properties damaged by the Tohoku-Pacific Ocean Earthquake. Available at: http://www.bunka.go.jp/bunkazai/tohokujishin_kanren/chokan_message_e.htm (accessed 30 November 2014).

Agency for Cultural Affairs. 2012. Damages to cultural properties in the 'Great East Japan Earthquake'. Available at: http://www.bunka.go.jp/english/pdf/2011_Tohoku_ver14. pdf (accessed 18 July 2012). (accessed 30 November 2014).

Agency for Cultural Affairs. 2013. Actions for Recovery and Reconstruction from the Great East Japan Earthquake; Initiatives the Agency for Cultural Affairs Has Taken to Date. Available at: http://www.bunka.go.jp/bunkazai/tohokujishin_kanren/pdf/chokan_message_7.pdf (accessed 30 November 2014).

Demoule, J.-P. 2002. Rescue archaeology: the French way. *Public Archaeology*, 2: 170-7.

Graham, K. 2014. Japan's 'Great Wall' for tsunami protection questionable. Digital Journal, Jun 29, 2014. Available at: http://www.digitaljournal.com/news/environment/japan-s-great-wall-for-tsunami-protection-questionable/article/388119 (accessed 30 November 2014).

Hanazato, T., Y, Kariya & K, Yano (eds). 2014. Progress report of Great East Japan Earthquake recovery – present state of affected cultural heritage, Japan ICOMOS National Committee

Kaner, S., J. Habu & A. Matsui. 2011. Rescuing archaeology affected by the Japanese earthquake and tsunami. *Antiquity* 85. Available at: http://www.antiquity.ac.uk/projgall/kaner329/ (accessed 30 November 2014).

Kristiansen, K. 2009. Contract archaeology in Europe: an experiment in diversity, *World Archaeology* 41(4): 641-648.

Kumagai, K. 2014. Stabilizing treatment by Rikuzen Takata City Museum, Progress report of Great East Japan Earthquake recovery – present state of affected cultural heritage: 25, Japan ICOMOS National Committee.

Maibun-kyuen renraku kaigi & Maizou-bunkazai kenkyu-kai (eds). 1996. Hakkutsu saretajishin-konseki [Excavated traces of past earthquakes]. Osaka: Maibun-kyuen renraku kaigi & Maizou-bunkazai kenkyu-kai.

Matsui, A. 2011. Heritage rescue in the wake of the Great Eastern Japan Earthquake. *SAA Archaeological Record* 11.4: 11-15.

McCurry, J. 2014. Tsunami-proof 'Great Wall of Japan' divides villagers, The Guardian, 29 June 2014. Available at: http://www.theguardian.com/world/2014/jun/29/tsunami-wall-japan-divides-villagers (accessed 30 November 2014).

Negita, Y. 2012. Archaeological excavation for reconstruction on the building of new communities. Available at: http://archaeology.jp/sites/2012/rebuilding.htm, (accessed 30 November 2014).

Okamura, K., A. Fujisawa, Y. Kondo, Y. Fujimoto, T. Uozu, Y. Ogawa, S. Kaner & K. Mizoguchi. 2013. The Great East Japan Earthquake and cultural heritage: towards an archaeology of disaster, *Antiquity* 87 (2013): 258-269.

Okamura, K. 2013. Ethics of Commercial Archaeology, *Encyclopedia of Global Archaeology*: 2482-5, Springer.

Saino, H. 2012. Hakkutsu-tyosa de kensyutsusareta Sendai Heiya no tsunami konseki [Excavated evidence of tsunamis in Sendai plain], *Quarterly of Archaeological Studies* 232 (2012): 6-11.

Sato, D. 2014. Actions for recovery and protection of privately-owned historic documents damaged by the earthquake by Miyagi Shiryo net (Miyagi Historic Documents Conservation Network), Progress report of Great East Japan Earthquake recovery – present state of affected cultural heritage: 23-24, Japan ICOMOS National Committee

Schlanger, N., L. Nespoulous & J. Demoule. In press. Year 4 at Fukushima. A 'disaster-led' archaeology of the contemporary future, *Antiquity* (2015).

Shimotsuma, K. 2014. Recovering efforts in cooperation among private and public sectors, Progress report of Great East Japan Earthquake recovery – present state of affected cultural heritage: 2-3, Japan ICOMOS National Committee.

Tateishi, T. 2014. Overview of cultural properties affected by disaster in the Great East Japan Earthquake of March 2011, Microbial biodeterioration of cultural property, Proceedings of the International Symposium on the Conservation and Restoration of Cultural Property 2012, National Research Institute for Cultural Properties: 29-33, Tokyo. Also available at http://www.tobunken.go.jp/~ccr/pub/symp2012/symp2012_03.pdf#search='Cultural+properties+rescue+program%5D' (accessed 30 November 2014).

Yamauchi, A. 2012. Bouchotei ni yoru oka to hama no bundanga Sanriku wo derashineka suru [Separating the land from the seashore by embankments will make the Sanriku Coast a déraciné place], Available at: http://webplanners.net/2012/12/08/323/ (accessed 30 November 2014).

Reinforcing the link between Water and Heritage in order to build Disaster Resilient Societies

Rohit Jigyasu

President, ICOMOS-ICORP
Professor and UNESCO Chair holder on Cultural Heritage and Risk Management
Institute of Disaster Mitigation for Urban Cultural Heritage
Ritsumeikan University, Kyoto, Japan

Abstract

We tend to associate heritage with historic buildings and monuments overlooking the fact that water is one of the most critical life-sustaining resources around which civilizations have evolved. This relationship is manifested in the form of intricate water systems resulting in the development of various typologies of structures (e.g., tanks, wells, canals, baths, aqueducts etc.). These traditional knowledge systems for harvesting the water demonstrate a detailed understanding of local geographical and geological characteristics, which are not only tailored to tap optimum utilization of the underground and surface water but also to ensure their recharge for a long term sustainability. Undoubtedly, water is an inseparable part of our heritage.

The importance of water is also manifested in its spiritual relationship to people resulting in the evolution of many sacred cultural landscapes around natural sources of water (e.g. rivers, lakes) as in the case of the city of Varanasi (India). Last but not the least, water has served as the main source of transport of people and goods, resulting in the cross-fertilization and further enrichment of various cultures. In fact these multiple interrelationships between humans, water and other aspects of local environment have sustained cultures and civilizations over time.

This intricate relationship between water and heritage has also determined how people have managed disaster risks caused by floods to which they are frequently exposed. This is achieved not merely by resisting the forces of nature through technical interventions such as the construction of embankments along rivers but also by adapting the living pattern of communities around regularly occurring phenomena e.g., floods.

Traditional water systems not only demonstrate the wisdom of the past that has evolved through a series of trials and errors. These systems also have great potential for emergency responses following disasters. For example the traditional system of water tanks (*hitis*) located in the dense historic urban fabric of the Valley of Kathmandu (Nepal) or wells and underground tanks locally known as *tankas* in the historic Walled City of Ahmedabad (India) have great potential to serve as important sources of water supply during emergency situations. One can also find examples of indigenous warning systems among communities with regard to the prediction of hydrometeorological hazard events. Their usefulness should also be explored in the light of changing rainfall pattern due to various factors including climate change.

Unfortunately rapid urbanization and development has taken their toll on the 'heritage of water' especially in the light of their limited protection and conservation. This has not only resulted in the loss of these irreplaceable cultural resources but has also damaged local ecological systems and in the process increased the vulnerability of communities to natural disasters.

It is time for us to realize the enormous potential of the heritage of water and utilize it efficiently and creatively in order to create disaster resilient societies. The present chapter will highlight these challenges and the potential of water and heritage.within a global context especially referring to South Asia.

Keywords: *Tangible Intangible, Water, Cultural Landscape, Ecosystem, Natural Disasters, Resilience, Sustainability.*

Introduction

A cultural heritage encompasses all tangible and intangible aspects of human creative activity inherited from previous generations. It is considered by communities, groups or society at large to be of value, and therefore maintained in the present and transmitted to future generations for their benefit. A cultural heritage is important as a source of memory and inspiration,. Moreover, it contributes to the national and local community identity, which is fundamental for a sense of place and social cohesion (Communities and Local Government, 2009). Tangible cultural heritage includes monuments, groups of buildings, sites and cultural landscapes (UNESCO, 1972) whereas an intangible cultural heritage includes the practices, representations, expressions, knowledge, skills of communities and groups, and on occasion individuals as well as instruments, objects, artefacts and cultural spaces associated therewith (UNESCO 2003).

Within this broad scope, the heritage related to water is significant: water is one of the most critical life-sustaining resources around which civilizations have evolved. This relationship is manifested in the form of intricate water systems resulting in the development of various typologies of structures (e.g.,tanks, wells, canals, baths, and aqueducts etc.), which along with associated movable components are undoubtedly an important part of the cultural heritage. However, the importance of water is also manifested in its spiritual relationship to people resulting in many cultural practices and rituals that form part of the intangible heritage.

Undoubtedly, a water-related heritage is a source of traditional knowledge systems which demonstrate a detailed understanding of the local geographical and geological characteristics tailored for the optimum utilization of the underground and surface water as well as ensuring their recharge for a long-term sustainability. Moreover, knowledge embedded in water-related heritage contributes towards building resilience of communities against disasters. Therefore their significance calls for seeking their proactive role in a sustainable development and disaster risk reduction rather than in the mere preservation of physical fabric.

Typologies of water heritage

A well is perhaps the most common typology of a water heritage used for accessing water since pre-historic times. With the increasing need for water, especially when the location of a water source did not exist at the same location as the settlement, a system in order to transport water through a wider network was created. Let us now look at a few examples of significant water heritage structures, many of which are also on the World Heritage List.

The Cantayo Wells and Channels (Puquios) in Nazca Valley (Peru) is an old system of aqueducts with more than fifty channels. The Shushtar Historical Hydraulic System in Iran consists of two main diversion canals on the river Kârun of which the Gargar canal is still in use, providing water to the city of Shushtar via a series of tunnels that supply water to mills. Forming a spectacular cliff from which water cascades into a downstream basin, it then enters the plain situated south of the city. Here it has enabled the creation of orchards and farming over an area of 40,000 ha, known as Mianâb (Paradise) (UNESCO 2009).

Another well-known water system is formed by the *qanats* of Gonabad (Iran). It consists of series of wells enabling the inhabitants to live in a dry land with very scarce rainfall. Such system on occasion incorporated the principles and advantages of creating wells in order to locate aquifers and to create blowholes, releasing pressure as well as allowing people to descend in order to maintain the sub-surface parts such as aqueducts, thus ensuring the flow of water. As a part of this wider water distribution system, the well remained as a functional component and not as an element for design. (UNESCO, 2015)

During the early medieval era, the construction of stepped wells in order to tap ground water evolved into a distinct form of architecture in the northwestern frontiers of the Indian Subcontinent. Here traditional communities established in arid or semiarid zones found ground water and devised techniques in order to access and protect it. These stepped wells (locally known as *baolis* or *vavs*) helped in collecting and preserving underground water: the most critical natural and cultural resource in a region where water was precious and, at times, a rare commodity. The Rani ki Vav, a World Heritage Site, is the testimony of the development of this single component water management system, prevalent in this area since the Indus Valley Civilization (2500 BC). The pure functional design of water structure as seen with the Rani ki Vav also evolved as an outstanding piece of architectural design showing perfection in manipulating a built volume of unique proportions into smaller spaces, frames and corridors. They efficiently control the microclimate,

Figure 1. Rani-ki-Vav. This World Heritage Site in India is an outstanding example of a subterranean water structure well replete with religious, mythological and secular imagery represented by more than 500 principle sculptures and more than 1000 minor sculptures arranged within multiple levels and friezes.

Figure 2. Another typology of a stepped water tank serving multiple uses is found at the World Heritage Site of Champaner (India).

protect and store ground water and achieve an aesthetic quality unparalleled by any other water structure. Moreover, this unique stepped well is adorned with religious, mythological and secular imagery represented by more than five hundred principle sculptures and more than a thousand minor sculptures arranged within multiple levels and friezes (Livingstone 2002). (Figs. 1 and 2)

In many instances, the scope of water heritage extends way beyond single structures. It has contributed towards shaping entire settlements such as the town of Tongli (China) with networks of canals and more than fourty-nine bridges built during the Song and Qing dynasties. (Fig. 3)

Water is also an inherent part of settlements evolved along river banks or natural lakes and canals, which have been efficiently tapped for multiple uses. The importance of water manifested in its spiritual relationship with people has also resulted in the evolution of many sacred urban landscapes around natural sources of water (e.g., rivers, lakes) as with Varanasi, one of the most sacred cities of Hindus in India.

In fact the tangible components of historic urban landscapes built in relation to water sources (e.g., public buildings, housing, spaces) often play an irreplaceable role in the manifestation of intangible cultural heritage. The reason for this is that they serve to carry out collective social activities at city or neighbourhood levels For example, the stepped river fronts (ghats) in the sacred historic city of Varanasi (India) on which the devotees carry out various rituals and practices. (Fig. 4)

Often heritage values for the inhabitants are closely related to their collective memories associated with water sources or buildings and spaces of which water is an essential element. The continuity of these memories helps in maintaining the social networks or norms in traditional communities that are inherent part of their social capital.

The spaces with associated water heritage components can take the form of public squares or routes. They are tied to people by means of an intangible heritage defined by (a) religious or spiritual associations and belief systems or (b) memories linked to events shared at various levels ranging from a larger community to distinct social groups or families and clans, and even at an individual level. Moreover, water has also determined boundaries that have often consciously or subconsciously contributed towards protecting local ecosystems, thereby ensuring the sustainability of historic urban landscapes.

Water heritage has also shaped large cultural landscapes as in the case of the Subak System on Bali (Indonesia), which consists of five rice terraces and their water temples covering 19,500 ha. The description of this location on the website of UNESCO World Heritage Centre states:

> "The temples are the focus of a cooperative water management system of canals and weirs, known as subak, that dates back to the 9th century. Included in the landscape is the 18th-century Royal Water Temple of Pura Taman Ayun, the largest and most impressive architectural edifice of its type on the island. The subak reflects the philosophical concept of Tri Hita Karana, which brings together the realms of the spirit, the human world and nature. This philosophy was born of the cultural exchange between Bali and India over the past 2,000 years and has shaped the

Figure 3. The town of Tongli (China) is a world heritage city with a network of canals and bridges which has been in continuous use for more than 2 centuries.

Figure 4. Banaras, also known as Varanasi, is one of the most sacred cities for Hindus in India. It waterfront is lined with ghats on which various rituals and practices have been carried out for ages.

landscape of Bali. The subak system of democratic and egalitarian farming practices has enabled the Balinese to become the most prolific rice growers in the archipelago despite the challenge of supporting a dense population." (UNESCO, 2015).

Another good example comprises the irrigation systems of the Hampi World Heritage Site (India). In continuous use for more than 5 centuries ever since it was established in the erstwhile capital of Vijayanagara kingdom, these systems have since contributed towards sustainable livelihood source of local communities, who have been practicing agriculture for generations.

These relationships reinforced by intangible heritage values determine how communities view and apply natural and human resources (e.g., land, water, landscape, buildings) as assets reaching beyond mere economic values. As such these are considered not just for sale or consumption but for protection and maintenance while deriving multiple benefits from them. Most commonly this is achieved by gaining social acceptance through rituals, practices and belief systems serving as guidelines dissimilar as to their nature and scope when compared with currently practiced rigid urban controls that specify regulations frequently outlining what not to do rather than what to do (Bandarin and Oers eds. 2014).

Last but not least, water has served as the main source of transport of people and materials. This has resulted in the cross-fertilization and further enriching of various cultures. In fact these multiple interrelationships between humans, water and other aspects of local environment have sustained cultures and civilizations over time (ICOMOS 2013).

Impact of Disasters on Cultural Heritage

Recent disasters have caused immense damage to our cultural heritage. They include the October 2013 earthquake followed by the typhoon Haian that struck Philippines resulting in extensive damage to the renowned Bohol churches. In 2012, a fire caused by a short circuit almost completely destroyed the Wangdue Phodrang Dzong (Bhutan), an important site previously placed on the tentative World Heritage tentative list.

The climate change increases the number of disasters and their devastating impacts. Between 1988 and 2007, 76% of all disaster events were hydrological, meteorological or climatological in nature accounting for 45% of the deaths and 79% of the economic losses caused by natural hazards. (ISDR 2008).

Coupled with other factors, the climate change has resulted in an increase of flood incidents especially affecting historic urban areas and heritage sites located along rivers. For instance, the 2011 floods severely affected the World Heritage Site of Ayutthaya (Thailand). The 2010 floods affected many archaeological sites and vernacular settlements located along the Indus River (Pakistan). Flashfloods due to unprecedented heavy rains in Uttarakhand State (India) in 2013 caused the destruction of many historic temples. In 2010 storms in Western Europe flooded several historic town centres. Numerous World Heritage Cities built along the coast and rivers are therefore at greater risk from floods. Climate related disasters can also damage various physical or spatial attributes of cultural heritage existing

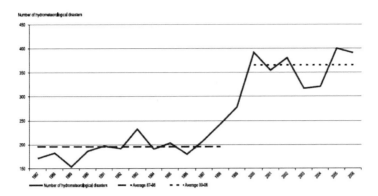

Figure 5. The occurrence of hydrometeorological hazards between 1987 and 2006.

as systems (e.g., traditional water systems, visual connections etc.) or individual components (e.g., buildings, trees etc.), which are now and again part of the larger systems.

In addition, climate change related phenomena (e.g., higher temperatures, higher temperature fluctuation, relative humidity) are often responsible for the aggravation of underlying risk factors, which increase the vulnerability of cultural heritage that can result in disasters. For example in 2008 the forest fires in eastern Europe which posed a high risk to the World Heritage Sites of Olympia in Greece.

The likelihood of increased weather extremes in future therefore gives cause to great concern: the number or scale of weather-related disasters will also increase thereby impacting cultural heritage.

The Contribution of Heritage to Resilience

However, water related heritage - both tangible and intangible - is not just a passive resource liable to be affected and damaged by disasters. Rather it has a proactive role to play in building the resilience of communities as well as saving lives and properties. Countless examples illustrate this. Traditional knowledge systems embedded in water heritage having evolved over time through successive trials and errors can play a significant role in disaster prevention and mitigation, thereby contributing to a more sustainable development. Such local knowledge often equips communities to better face natural hazards through lifestyles, customs and traditional livelihoods (ISDR et al. 2013)

This intricate relationship between water and heritage has also determined how people have managed disaster risks caused by floods to which they are frequently exposed. This is achieved not merely by resisting forces of nature through technical interventions such as construction of embankments along rivers but also by adapting living pattern of communities around these regularly occurring phenomena. For instance, Majuli in Assam (India) believed to be the largest river island in the World with a unique local ecology is prone to annual flooding due to the mighty Brahmaputra River that swells during the summer months.

The vernacular housing in the area applying bamboo constructed on stilts has evolved as a sensitive response to the local factors, notably floods inundating the island on a regular basis. The light bamboo structure enables easy dismantling and relocation, in the event that the area is affected by floods. Moreover, the nature of the material and joinery allows for the flexibility of structures, especially useful in the event of an earthquake to which this region is highly prone (Fig. 6). In addition, the traditional settlement pattern is such that the location of structures, roads and bridges are annually readjusted according to the flooding pattern (ICOMOS 2013). The case demonstrates a remarkable capacity of traditional technology to adapt to the nature of hazards and develop a harmonising living relationship with them, rather than merely resisting them. Such wisdom is also seen in many coastal communities who over the centuries have not only become capable of foreseeing natural hazards, but are also better equipped to deal with them by means of various measures. In fact, when traditional skills and practices are sustained, they can contribute to the rebuilding of resilient communities after disasters. Local crafts people can rebuild shelters applying local knowledge and resources, salvage and reuse materials from collapsed structures. This not only helps the community to reduce external dependencies but also provides livelihood sources crucial for sustainable recovery in the long term. In this sense, cultural heritages including those related with water make optimum use of locally available resources and fulfill the socio-cultural needs of communities (ISDR et al. 2013).

Traditional water systems not only demonstrate the wisdom of the past that has evolved through series of trials and errors, they also have great potential for emergency response following disaster. For example, the traditional system of water tanks (*hitis*) located in the dense historic urban fabric of the Valley of Kathmandu (Nepal) or wells and traditional water storage tanks *(tankas)* in the historic Walled

Figure 6. The vernacular housing in bamboo on the river island of Majuli (India) is built on stilts in order to protect it against regular floods.

Figure 7. The traditional water system comprising of hitis in the Valley of Kathmandu not only serves the daily needs of inhabitants but is also a source of an emergency water supply during disasters.

City of Ahmedabad (India) have great potential to serve as important sources of water supply during emergency situations especially when one cannot rely on municipal water system that often draws water through pumps operated by electricity (Fig. 7). One can also find examples of indigenous warning systems among communities in order to predict hydrometeorological hazardous events. Their usefulness should also be explored in the light of varying rainfall pattern due to factors including climate change.

Last but not least, the symbolism inherent in heritage is also a powerful means of communicating risks and help victims to recover from the psychological impact of disasters by providing a sense of belongingness at the time when victims go through trauma and loss. Traditional social networks (often centered around water heritage such as tanks) provide mutual support and access to collective assets, which are effective coping mechanisms for community members.

Urbanization process and impact on Water Heritage

Urbanization is one of the key factors to increasing the vulnerability and risks to people, properties and economy. The world is passing through a great urban upsurge. In 2007 the numbers of people living in cities has equaled those in villages. It is rising ever since. In fact it is projected that, between 2007 and 2025, 1.29 billion people will be added to cities and that forty-eight cities in the world will have reached a density level of more than 15000 inhabitants per square km. Interestingly, all of them will be in developing countries. Concentrating people, properties, infrastructure and capital stock, cities are increasingly vulnerable to natural and human induced disasters (Oers, R.V and Bandarin, F. (eds.), 2014).

As the 2011 Recommendation on the Historic Urban Landscape states:

> *"Rapid and uncontrolled urbanization may frequently result in social and spatial fragmentation and in a drastic deterioration of the quality of the historic urban environment and of surrounding rural areas. Notably, this may be due to excessive building density, standardized and monotonous buildings, loss of public space and amenities, inadequate infrastructure, debilitating poverty, social isolation, and an increasing risk of climate-related disasters."*

> *"Urban growth is transforming the very essence of many historic urban landscapes. On the one hand, urbanization provides economic, social and cultural opportunities that can enhance the quality of life and traditional character of urban areas; on the other hand, the unmanaged changes in urban density and growth can undermine the sense of place, the integrity of the urban fabric, and the identity of communities. As a consequence, historic urban landscapes are losing their functionality, traditional role and populations, thereby negatively impacting the intangible heritage that has characterized them for generations."* (UNESCO 2011)

Unfortunately rapid urbanization and development has taken their toll on the 'heritage of water' especially in the light of their limited protection and conservation that tends to focus on monuments. This has not only resulted in the loss of these irreplaceable cultural resources but has also damaged local ecological systems and, in the process, increased vulnerability of communities as to natural disasters.

New residential and commercial developments spring up even before the infrastructure is in place. This process undoubtedly has an adverse impact on the water heritage as many traditional urban systems and local ecological processes e.g., the water system of the *hitis*, the traditional step wells in the Valley of Kathmandu are being damaged beyond repair or have fallen into disuse (Jigyasu 2010).

In fact, the destruction of ecological systems and loss of traditional knowledge due to urbanization also increases the vulnerability of historic cities to disasters. Let us now consider the case of the historic city of Srinagar (India). It was struck by unprecedented floods in September 2014 after the region had received more

Lakes and wetlands of Srinagar and its suburbs

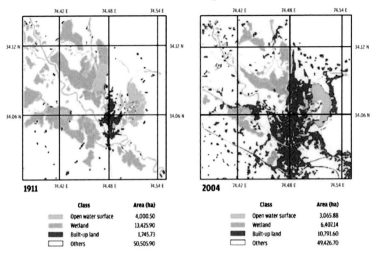

Class	Area (ha)
Open water surface	4,000.50
Wetland	13,425.90
Built-up land	1,745.73
Others	50,505.90

Class	Area (ha)
Open water surface	3,065.88
Wetland	6,407.14
Built-up land	10,791.60
Others	49,426.70

Figure 8. The quantification of the loss of the spatial extent of lakes and wetlands in the suburbs of Srinagar city during the 1900s, using a geo-spatial approach (Rashid and Naseem 2007).

Figure 9. At the World Heritage Site of Ayutthaya, many canals have fallen into disuse thereby restricting the water drainage capacity in the event of heavy rainfall.

than 550 mm of rain in 1 week. Although the amount of rainfall was very high, the crucial question is whether the city would have faced the same catastrophe if its wetlands and other water bodies that were inherent part of the historic urban landscape had been in good shape.

An investigation into historical data carried out by Rashid and Naseem (2007) revealed that between 1911 and 2004, Srinagar had lost more than 50% of its water bodies due to urbanisation.

"Dal Lake in Srinagar, one of the largest freshwater lakes in the world and a key landmark of the city, has been reduced to one-sixth of its original size. Srinagar city, a century earlier had a unique ecological set up with extensive areas under wetlands, lakes and water channels. Though siltation brought about in the lakes and wetlands especially during floods was but natural, yet subsequent encroachment, earth filling, planting and constructions by individuals and converting water channels into roads, presents a living example of how these valuable assets of natural landscape of Srinagar were destroyed." (Rashid and Naseem, 2007)

These factors were responsible for the massive floods that inundated Srinagar in September 2014. In fact, a similar situation has been observed at the World Heritage Site of Ayutthya (Thailand) that was inundated following devastating floods in 2011. The ancient city located on a river island had an extensive network of canals and water gates controlling the ingress and egress of water during heavy rains. However, many of these canals and water gates had been filled up or fallen into disuse thereby restricting the water drainage capacity in the event of heavy rainfall (Fig. 9). The disturbance of ecosystems due to urbanization also causes certain cities to be vulnerable to droughts as in the case of Bangalore (India).

Fortunately the open spaces of many historic cities (often anchored around water heritage structures) remain surprisingly intact whereas the built fabric undergoes a rapid transformation. One of the reasons for this is: these open spaces and associated water structures (e.g., wells) still serve the collective social and religious purposes of communities. For example, in the town of Patan (Valley of Kathmandu, Nepal), traditional settlements include well established networks consisting of rest places (patis/sattals), water sources, wells, stone water spouts (*hitis*), water tanks and ponds strategically located in open squares and at street junctions and village entrances. These serve as places for settlers and visitors to carry out daily activities. In the event of a disaster, these resting places can also serve to shelter the injured, whereas water sources used for drinking can double as a local fire hydrant (Oers, R.V and Bandarin. F. (eds.), 2014). These public places characteristically witness community gatherings, the playing of traditional music or just chatting. All can help to maintain a rapport among the local people when facing a catastrophe too. In this way the tangible attributes of water heritage carrying intangible/social values have the potential to enhance cooperation among residents during a crisis. Moreover, they may well serve as locations for disaster preparedness training.

Conclusion

There needs to be a larger recognition of water heritage, not merely as a relic from the past to be cherished and preserved for posterity but also as an asset that could play a more proactive role in the efficient utilization of precious water resources while ensuring (a) the continuity of traditional skills and knowledge in harnessing water and (b) the fulfillment of new needs and aspirations as well as a long term sustainability.

It is also important now to not only recognize and realize the enormous potential of the heritage of water but to utilize it efficiently and creatively in order to create disaster-resilient societies. Such an approach would address (a) the increasing vulnerability of communities and their living environments resulting from the loss and degradation of traditional knowledge and (b) the need to search for solutions creatively, through continuous trial and error. This evolutionary process defines the true essence of traditional knowledge embedded in water heritage that should be integrated into larger planning and management systems through measures aimed at regeneration of traditional livelihoods, ecological planning, sustainable development and disaster risk reduction.

In fact, water heritage is also determined by the way people perceive nature based on culturally defined value and belief systems that form an important, often intergenerational, source of information. Some of this valuable information, relating in particular to its spiritual dimensions, may not yet be considered in current ecosystem management. The reason for this may in part be: such knowledge is inaccessible and difficult to be understood by outsiders including conventional conservationists and ecosystem managers. Hence, accounting for the various world views and their corresponding cultural and spiritual values of water heritage in the practice of ecosystem management forms a challenge for managers, policy-makers and local people alike (Verschuuren 2007: 299). This certainly calls for a fundamental shift in conservation approach i.e., from a reactive to a more proactive approach aimed at addressing the change rather than mere static preservation in the 'original' state defined by a particular time period.

References

Communities and Local Government. 2009. *Draft Planning Policy Statement 15: Planning for the historic environment*, Communities and Local Government Publications, London, Available at http://webarchive.nationalarchives.gov.uk/20120919132719/http://www.communities.gov.uk/documents/planningandbuilding/pdf/consultationhistoricpps.pdf (accessed on 2 January 2015).

Centre for Research on the Epidemiology of Disasters (CRED) – Annual Disasters Statistical Review 2006, Brussels, May 2007.

ISDR. 2008. Hyogo Framework for Action-Pedia. Available at http://www.eird.org/wikien/index.php/Climate_change on 10 December 2014.

ISDR, ICOMOS-ICORP, ICCROM, UNESCO World Heritage Centre. 2013. Heritage and Resilience: Issues and Opportunities for Reducing Disaster Risks, for the 4th Session of the Global Platform for Disaster Risk Reduction, 19-23 May 2013 in Geneva, Switzerland Available at http://icorp.icomos.org/index.php/news/44-new-icorp-publication-heritage-and-resilience (accessed on 17 January 2015).

ICOMOS. 2013. ICOMOS Conference: Water and Heritage: Protecting Deltas Heritage Helps. Available at http://www.icomos.nl/media/Water_and_Heritage/ 57001_Conference_DEF_lowres-1_kopie.pdf (accessed on 17 January 2015).

Jigyasu, R. 2014. 'The Intangible Dimension of Urban Heritage'. In: Oers, R.V and Bandarin, F. Reconnecting the City: The Historic Urban Landscape Approach and the Future of Urban Heritage", Wiley Blackwell.

Jigyasu. 2010. Urban Cultural Heritage for Sustainable Resilience: Case of Patan in Kathmandu Valley, Nepal. In: 'Urban Risk Management in South Asia: Launch of Global Campaign on making Cities Resilient', SAARC Disaster Management Centre, New Delhi.

Livingstone, M. 2002. *Steps to Water: The Ancient Stepwells of India.* Princeton Architectural Press.

Rashid, H and Naseem, G. 2007. 'Quantification of loss in spatial extent of lakes and wetlands in the suburbs of Srinagar City during last century using geospatial approach'. In: Sengupta, M. and Dalwani, R. (eds.) 2008. Proceedings of Taal 2007: the 12th World Lake Conference, pp. 653-658.

UNESCO. 1972. *Convention Concerning the Protection of the World Cultural and Natural Heritage*, UNESCO, Paris, available at: http://whc.unesco.org/en/conventiontext (acccessed on 2 January 2015).

UNESCO. 2003. Convention for the Safeguarding of the Intangible Cultural Heritage, UNESCO, Paris, available at http://www.unesco.org/culture/ich/en/convention (accessed on 2 January 2015).

UNESCO World Heritage Centre. 2009. 'Sacred mountain in Kyrgyzstan enters List along with Iran's Shushtar water system and Royal tombs in Republic of Korea'. Paris, Available at http://whc.unesco.org/en/news/529/ (accessed on 17 January 2015).

UNESCO. 2011. UNESCO Recommendation on the Historic Urban Landscape, Available at http://whc.unesco.org/en/activities/638/ (accessed on 25 April 2013).

UNESCO World Heritage Centre. 2011. UNESCO Recommendation on the Historic Urban Landscape, Available at http://whc.unesco.org/en/activities/638 (accessed on 17 January 2015).

UNESCO World Heritage Centre. 2012. http://whc.unesco.org/en/tentativelists. Retrieved 2012, from www.whc.unesco.org/en/: http://whc.unesco.org/en/tentativelists/?pattern=wells&type=&state=&theme=&region=&criteria_restrication=&date_start=&date_end=&order=.

UNESCO World Heritage Centre. 2015. Cultural Landscape of Bali Province: the *Subak* System as a Manifestation of the *Tri Hita Karana* Philosophy. Available at http://whc.unesco.org/en/list/1194 (accessed on 17 January 2015).

UNESCO World Heritage Centre. 2015. Qanats of Gonabad, Tentative List. Available at http://whc.unesco.org/en/tentativelists/5207 (accessed on 17 January 2015).

Verschuuren, B. 2007. An overview of cultural and spiritual values in ecosystem management and conservation strategies. In: Haverkort, B. and Rist, S. (eds.) *Endogenous Development and Bio-cultural Diversity, The Interplay of Worldviews, Globalisation and Locality.* Compas/CDE, Series on Worldviews and Sciences, No. 6, Leusden, The Netherlands, pp. 299-325.

Between pragmatism and cultural context

Continuity and change in Ifugao wet-rice agriculture

Stephen Acabado[a] and Marlon Martin[b]

a. Department of Anthropology, University of California-Los Angeles
b. Save the Ifugao Terraces Movement, Inc.

Abstract

This paper looks at the processes that affect the conservation of the Ifugao rice terraces, a UNESCO World Heritage Site. We focus on the increasing dominance of non-local rice varieties, particularly, lowland, commercial rice varieties and investigate the role of farmers and Ifugao communities in the continued existence of the terraces. We also define the Ifugao rice fields as *habitus* and the nexus of Ifugao social relationships. We argue that conservation programs change the way they look at living cultural environments since farmers and communities make practical decisions whose ultimate intention is the continuity of their cultural norms. The paper's main goal is to understand why Ifugao farmers do what they do.

Keywords: *Ifugao, habitus, conservation, Philippines.*

Introduction

Recent trends have witnessed the increasing participation of local communities in heritage conservation (i.e. Anderson 2001; Brokington 2004; Reti 1999; Vernon et al. 2005;). Of particular interest are the conservation programs at UNESCO-listed cultural heritage sites, where top-down approaches have been utilized to protect the degradation of the sites. With the realization that sustainable conservation programs are mostly effective if stakeholders are actively involved, academics and heritage conservation workers have clamored for a larger participation of communities directly affected by site conservation programs (Clark 2001; Lennon 2003; Bandarin 2003; Edroma 2004; Hampton 2005).

In the UNESCO World Heritage Site of the Ifugao Rice Terraces (IRT), Philippines (Figure 1), Ifugao communities have been actively involved in the conservation of both the tangible and intangible heritage (SITMo 2008; Acabado et al. 2014). For the most part however, and due to funding and economic pressures, conservation programs in the region are top-down, with national government agencies (e.g. Department of Agriculture, Department of Environment and Natural

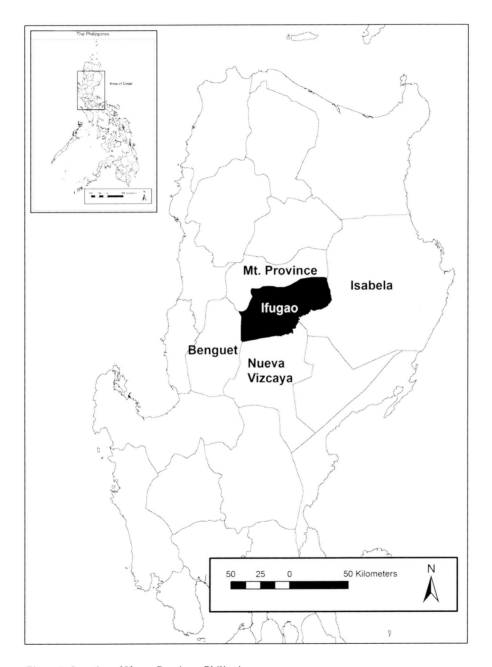

Figure 1. Location of Ifugao Province, Philippines.

Resources) spearheading the projects. Community narratives have emphasized the shortcomings of these projects since local beliefs have been ignored.

This paper aims to show the dynamic nature of heritage conservation in Ifugao where water management, the agricultural system, rituals, ecological knowledge and gender relationships are intertwined. They are part of a system that needs to be accounted for in conservation and development projects in the region. We argue that the Ifugao agricultural system can be thought of as a *habitus* (Bourdieu 1977) and the nexus of Ifugao social relationships where individuals situate themselves in the larger social environment. *Habitus* is defined as "… systems of durable, transposable dispositions, structured structures predisposed to function as structuring structures" (Bourdieu 1990: 53). The concept is useful in looking at production shift in Ifugao and how farmers make decisions. As the market economy exerts its influence on Ifugao communities, conservation programs have to take into account the ability of the Ifugao farmer to make practical decisions.

We further contend that practice theory (Bourdieu 1977, Giddens 1984) is a helpful tool in conservation programs in living cultural environments such as the Ifugao rice terraces. As Ortner puts it, practice theory helps to understand *why people do what they do* (1984).

Practice as a theoretical orientation (Ortner 1984: 127) that emerged as one of anthropology's guiding principles in the last 5 decades. It looks at how individuals react to challenges, particularly, power shifts. We maintain that continuity of the Ifugao rice terraces and the structure that allows the system to flourish is founded on the Ifugao's ability to situate themselves into differential power relationships. With the pressures exerted by the market economy, the intention to produce rice has changed from prestige to monetary gains. The ongoing negotiation between prestige and market production is redefining the Ifugao identity. A nuanced understanding of this negotiation will allow conservation planners and policy makers to develop a more meaningful conservation program in Ifugao.

Ifugao farmers' decisions in maintaining their customary lifestyle – and the agricultural system – have been widely affected by the increasing assimilation of the Ifugao in the larger Philippine society and the pressures brought by market forces. Their decisions however, have been deliberate. Even as we see the adoption of new agricultural practices (and with them, the disappearance of what have thought of as customary rituals) and introduction of commercial rice varieties, new social relationships emerge. Our paper looks at this phenomenon by focusing on the Ifugao farmers' adoption of lowland rice varieties and the impact of the agricultural shift in Ifugao ecology. We also look at customary Ifugao water management system. It is important to note that major disruptions in the Ifugao water management system dispel further degradation of the terraces.

Observations and narratives collected by Marlon Martin (an Ifugao and a heritage conservation worker) and Acabado's ethnography of Ifugao agriculture form part of the dataset used in this paper. We also utilized data obtained by the Save the Ifugao Terraces Movement, Inc. (SITMo) under Ms. Jacy Moore's supervision to look at seed selection and the number of non-local rice varieties in two Ifugao municipalities (Kiangan and Hungduan). As suggested by Moore's

Figure 2. Rice terrace systems in Banaue, Ifugao (Photo credit: A, Javellana and H. Conklin).

data, the rice fields continue to be the nexus of Ifugao social relationship, even with the pressures exerted by the market economy.

Our goal in writing this paper is to emphasize the dynamic nature of Ifugao social and agricultural systems. Changes are inevitable, especially with the increasing influence of political economy in Ifugao culture. Understanding Ifugao farmers' choices necessitates a consideration of the role of agency in peoples responses to shifts in political economy and ecology. The Ifugao are able to meet these challenges by utilizing community cohesiveness and continual negotiations among community members.

The Ifugao

The Ifugao are one of several minority ethno-linguistic groups in the northern Philippines. They are also known for their rice terraces that were enshrined in UNESCO's List of World Heritage in 1995 (Figure 1). This listing recognizes the "…absolute blending of the physical, socio-cultural, economic, religious, and political environments…indeed, it is a living cultural landscape of unparalleled beauty" (UNESCO N.D.). Not only are the rice terraces a testimony to the ingenuity and intelligence of the Ifugao in their transformation of this mountainous landscape, but they also represent an enduring balance of the environment and the cooperative ability of the entire Ifugao community to develop and sustain the terraces. The terraces are not just productive habitat for village sustenance, they are also the site for ritual practice that integrates and sustains the social fabric of the Ifugao. Moreover, they are also the anchor for a diverse and productive environment that involves communal forest lands, taro and other wetland crops, and a complex agro-ecosystem that includes multiple cropping of herbs, a finely tuned annual cycle, zoning and planning, and livestock production as part of a system regulated by religious rituals and cooperative social organization.

At the turn of the twentieth century two prominent figures in Philippine anthropology began an intensive investigation of the Ifugao (Roy Barton and Henry Otley Beyer). Both scholars proposed a 2000-3000 year old origin for the Ifugao rice terraces, using observations and qualitative speculations on how long it would have taken the Ifugao to modify the rugged topography of the area. This 'long history' has become a kind of received wisdom that finds its way into textbooks and national histories. On the other hand, several scholars have proposed a more recent origin of the Ifugao rice terraces (i.e. Keesing 1962, Lambrecht 1967, Acabado 2009, 2012a). Using evidence from lexical information, ethno-historic documents, and archaeological data, these studies suggest that the terraced landscapes of the Ifugao are the end-result of population expansion into the Cordillera highlands in response to Spanish colonization. Lowland-mountain contacts even before the Spanish arrival might have facilitated the movement of lowland peoples to the highlands when the Spanish established bases in their locales.

The Ifugao has been subjects of several studies that have become classic examples in ethnography and landscape studies. Their terraces and intangible heritage has also made it to the UNESCO's List of World Heritage. However, their complex water management is still poorly understood, especially when it comes to the managerial requirements of both the agricultural system and irrigation.

Traditionally, the Ifugao are agriculturalists who have cultivated their locale for at least 300 years. Their agricultural system is governed by integrated patterns of mixed farming that include the management of private forests (*muyong*), swidden cultivation of sweet potatoes, pond-field cultivation of rice, inter-cropping of many secondary domesticates (i.e. sweet potatoes, potatoes, cabbage, and other cash crops), and the raising of pigs, chickens, and other forms of livestock. The pattern of agricultural system of the Ifugao is complex. Ecological, social, and cultural factors, including indigenous knowledge of how these factors are linked to each other and efficient utility affects this pattern.

The Ifugao water management system parallels those of other systems in Southeast Asia (i.e. Bali), where communities that use the same water channel share irrigation management duties (Lansing 1991; Lansing and Kremer 1993). Lansing's (1991) work in Bali introduces a model where cooperation emerged due to a "need to balance multiple agro-ecological concerns in a crowded landscape of terraced rice fields that could feasibly have been responsible for the emergence of Bali's yield-enhancing autonomous 'complex adaptive system' of agriculture-managing water temple congregations" (Schoenfelder 2003: 35). We argue that this cooperative and reciprocal management is also advantageous for the ecology of the Ifugao agricultural system. Our archaeological and ethnographic study among the Ifugao offer new insights into the rules that structure pondfield management system which requires collective participation at the community level that resist hierarchical control.

The sociopolitical organization of the Ifugao informs discussion regarding the managerial requirements of complex agricultural and irrigation systems. As mentioned above, autonomous groups rapidly constructed the Ifugao rice terrace systems. As the systems expanded, however, these autonomous groups could have faced conflicts regarding access to water, availability of labor, and cross-contamination of fields. Ethnographic data regarding agricultural production-related rituals, suggest that the Ifugao avoided such conflicts utilizing rituals as a form of activity synchronization. This system, however, has degraded because of the assimilation of the Ifugao in the larger Philippine society.

The Ifugao social organization is considered as ranked, with the elite (called the *kadangyan*) owning most of the productive rice fields. Those who do not own rice fields, and thus, do not have access to rice throughout the year are called the *nawotot* (the poor). Other members of the community who owned rice lands but do not have enough prestige to be considered as *kadangyan* are called the *tagu*. The nature of Ifugao social organization has been described in previous ethnographic studies (Barton 1919, 1922, 1930, 1938, 1955; Lambrecht 1929, 1962; Conklin 1967, 1980; Dulawan 2001; Pagada 2006; Medina 2003; Kwiatkowski 1999). Dulawan (2001, 5) and Conklin (1980, 5) illustrate the Ifugao social world as being guided by a bilateral kinship system. The structure of the Ifugao culture underlies an abiding concern with the competitive development of land for terracing and rice production, elaborate traditional rituals that on all occasions involve interaction with deceased kinsmen, and a deep interest in status and rank as well as in the inherited wealth that the latter customarily requires (Conklin 1980, 5).

District	Land Area (m2)	Yield (bundle)	Yield (kg)	Population (1970)*	Rice Requirement (kg)
Amganad	451,891	75,650	109,693	530	193,450
Bannawol	1,920,254	321,466	466,125	3,255	1,288,075
Bayninan	281,382	47,106	68,303	390	142,350
Hengyon	931,944	156,015	226,222	689	251,485
Kababuyan	2,135,471	357,495	518,368	2,295	837,675
Kinnakin	800,262	133,970	194,257	575	209,875
Lugu	339,177	56,781	82,332	370	135,050
Nabyun	129,309	21,647	31,389	160	58,400
Nunggawa	400,726	67,085	97,273	222	81,030
Ogwag	406,548	68,059	98,686	401	146,365
Poitan	1,084,772	181,600	263,319	1,310	478,150
Pugu	497,748	83,327	120,824	270	98,550
Tam'an	248,395	41,583	60,296	60,296	109,500

Table 1. Estimates of rice production from 13 agricultural districts in Banaue, Ifugao, vis-à-vis rice requirements of the population. Estimates are based on a family of five, requiring at least 2.5 kg of rice per day. Rice production numbers are based on Conklin's (1980) estimate from Bayninan agricultural district between 1962 and 1970. Estimates for other agricultural districts were based on a one-to-one correlation between cultivated rice land area and production numbers from Bayninan (From Acabado, in press).

Customarily, the ranking in Ifugao society is important in their agricultural system. The *kadangyan* owns the rice fields and they control access and distribution of rice as food and ritual item. The *nawotwot* would need to work in the fields of the *kadangyan* for them to receive rice as a form of payment for their labor. The *nawotwot* are also associated with swidden cultivation, where they obtain most of their carbohydrate needs, particularly from sweet potato. Indeed, the term *nawotwot* literally means *root crop eater*. Acabado's (in press) previous work has suggested that rice produced in the rice fields of Ifugao is not enough to feed the whole population (Table 1).

Ifugao social structure is an essential component of rice cultivation and swidden farming. Cooperation among kin during terrace building, planting, harvesting, repair of walls and irrigation channels, and different rituals requires precise coordination. As an example, the existence of cooperative work-groups *uggbu* and *baddang*—which are regulated by kinship and territorial affiliation—is responsible for community-wide cooperation, a necessity in the Ifugao landscape and agricultural system.

The sustainability of the terraces in the modern world depends on this ritual community life just as much as it has for several hundred years. But the future of the terraces is endangered by challenges in the form of declining labor force, competition for wage labor, modernization, and the modern industrial agriculture that has transformed the Philippines in the last few decades into a major producer of commercial rice and other agricultural products. Ifugao province is one of the poorest in the Philippines with a poverty rate of 47.5% of the population, second highest in the Cordillera, and sixth highest in the Philippines generally. This rate of poverty, the outflow of Ifugao youth in search of opportunities in the general economy, and the degradation of the environment by the introduction of modern agricultural practices including high yielding rice varieties, chemical fertilizers and pesticides threaten the existence of the Ifugao culture and in turn the sustainability of the terraces as they are integrally connected with traditional community knowledge and practice. Furthermore, World Heritage recognition has introduced a tourist economy into the region that although has some benefit for employment and small business development, also contributes to undermine the fabric of cooperative community organization required for the maintenance of traditional rice farming.

The construction, use, and maintenance of Ifugao irrigation system is governed by cultural strategies that seek to minimize conflict. As a primary resource for rice production, effective water management is paramount to the conservation of the Ifugao rice terraces. Radical means are necessary to revive communities and cultural practice within which the rice terrace landscapes are embedded.

Ifugao agricultural system

The Ifugao subsistence strategy is based on the complementary systems of irrigated rice-terraced fields, swiddens, and agroforestry (Acabado 2012b). Currently, the Ifugao agricultural system is guided by integrated patterns of mixed farming that include the management of private forests (*muyong*), swidden cultivation of sweet potatoes, pond-field cultivation of rice, inter-cropping of many secondary domesticates (i.e. sweet potatoes, potatoes, cabbage, and other cash crops), and the raising of pigs, chickens, and other livestock (Conklin 1980: 36). Although rice terraces dominate the Ifugao landscape, their agricultural system is a complementary system (Rambo 1996) that includes swiddening, agroforestry, and irrigated rice pond fields.

A cross-section of a typical Ifugao agricultural system is presented in Figure 3, demonstrating some Ifugao agricultural strategies. Within a particular watershed, several types of land-use categories make up the agricultural system: two types of forest cover – '*inalahan* (upslope community-owned forests often composed of open-access communal areas) and *muyong* (privately owned woodlots managed with definite boundaries); *habal* (swidden; unirrigated slopeland, cultivated with root crops, usually, sweet potatoes); *labangan* (house terraces; residential sites); *na'ilid* (drained fields; levelled terraced areas for cultivation and drainage of dry crops such as sweet potatoes and legumes); and *payo* (irrigated rice fields; leveled, terraced farmland, bunded to retain water).

An important aspect of Ifugao agricultural terrace ecology and maintenance is the land-use category of *muyong/pinugo*, or privately owned woodlots. These woodlots serve as the watershed of a particular terrace system and are invaluable for terraces whose primary source of water are the springs located in these woodlots. Although hydrologic studies (Hamilton and King 1983; Bruijnzeel 1990; Saberwal 1998) in the last three decades suggest that heavy forest cover actually results in more groundwater usage, these woodlots protect low-lying fields from runoff and erosion, maintain the supply of surface and irrigation water (through cloud-intercept), stabilize relative humidity, and improve the soil's nutrients and physical

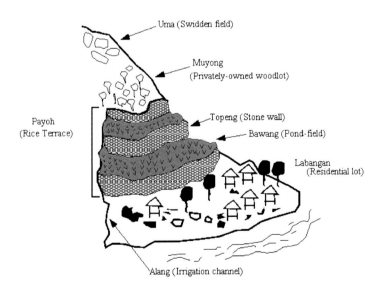

Figure 3. Profile of an Ifugao agricultural terrace (adapted from Conklin 1980).

and chemical properties (Conklin 1980: 8). Indeed, more logging in the vicinity of Banaue in the early 1980s accelerated runoff and evapotranspiration, exacerbating Ifugao's water shortages during the dry season (Eder 1982).

Muyongs also exemplify a sustainable agro-forestry and assisted natural regeneration system making them an indispensable component of Ifugao economy. Timber for construction and woodcarving; rattan, cane and bamboo for basketry, fruit crops and other forest products are sourced from the *muyong* through a highly regulated custom of selective harvesting.

Historical Roots of Ifugao Culture

The Ifugao rice terraces were thought to have been built over 2,000 years ago in very ancient Philippines culture (Beyer 1955) but are now known to have been a response to both the incursion of Spanish colonization in the Cagayan Valley lowlands to the northeast in the 17th century (Keesing 1962; Acabado 2009, 2010, 2012a) as well as an adaptive response to climate change and growing aridity in the Cagayan lowlands during the Little Ice Age in the 13th to the 19th centuries (Peterson and Acabado, in press). The rice terraces may have been developed in already pre-adapted pond fields originally developed for taro and other wetland farming (Acabado et al. 2012). Other components of this complex community farming system include the maintenance of communal forests in the highlands, common lands for other highly bio-diverse plantings of forbs, and integration of swine and water buffalo into the subsistence and ritual patterns of the community.

Radiocarbon dates from terrace studies indicate the antiquity of rice farming in the terraces no earlier than the late 16th century (Acabado 2009, 2010a, 2010b, 2012a, 2012b, 2012c) and that fields in the early settlement of Kiyyangan (Kiangan, Ifugao) were most likely wetland agricultural pondfields for the cultivation of taro. These pondfield systems nonetheless prepared terrain and waterways for the development of rice terraces at two critical junctures in the region: 1) Adaptation to the effects of the AD 1300 event that would have stressed western coastal terrain and eastern valleys from drought, while providing adequate rainfall in the rain shadow of the cordillera for highland farming; and, 2) Accommodation to Spanish control of the people and resources of the region by escaping into mountain refugia.

The Spanish colonial government was not able to establish a long-term presence in Ifugao (and the whole Cordillera region). The end of the Spanish regime however, saw the arrival of the Americans in the Philippines. William Henry Scott's portrayal of the relationship between these new colonialists and the "natives" was an amicable one (Scott 1974). These friendly relations could have been a product of a different administrative strategy that was employed by the Americans.

The arrival of the Americans also signaled the rapid assimilation of the Ifugao in a wider Philippine society. The 300+ years of Spanish presence in the Philippine lowlands seemed to have provided a false impression that the upland peoples (including the Ifugao) were different from lowlanders. This impression persists in present-day Philippines, where Cordillera peoples (including their agricultural strategies) are deemed inferior to lowlanders, when in fact, centuries of rice terracing show that they have been practicing sustainable forms of intensive and extensive agriculture.

The imposition of state policies, which are based on lowland realities, has unintended but dire consequences for Ifugao farming. For instance, non-formal cooperative farmer groups (based on reciprocal relationships) previously handled irrigation management, but since the Philippine state has policies on irrigation, this cooperative system has broken down and disrupted Ifugao customary practices. The introduction of commercial rice, in the guise of higher yielding varieties, has also negatively impacted Ifugao terrace ecology since commercial rice tends to require synthetic and harmful fertilizers and pesticides. Also, since rice seedlings for commercial rice are readily available from seedling banks, the role of the elder female farmer, who has knowledge of traditional heritage *tinawon* varieties, has been drastically diminished. More importantly, the cooperative nature of Ifugao farming is severely impacted by monetary needs.

Cooperative Nature of Terrace Farming and Water Management

Terrace farming emerged from a long history of community practice and belief that has been highly adaptive in the development and maintenance of farming landscapes in the Cordillera. The lifeblood of the terraces derives from the traditional knowledge of the local people honed through generations of trial and error. From this traditional knowledge, customary law, spirituality and community values evolved specifically to address local needs and sensibilities. It is this *localized development* that makes the terraces resilient to development changes that are coming from the outside but that also is fundamentally important to their sustainability. These external influences are the same that are now threatening the integrity of the Ifugao Rice Terraces as a world heritage site and a living testimony to the genius of Ifugao generations gone by. Without maintenance of these cultural and community practices the preservation of the landscapes is threatened.

Development and modernization of the terraces need to be copacetic with conservation principles and systemic approaches that have emerged from a long and resilient tradition. The maintenance of rice terraces is dependent upon cooperative groups called *baddang*. The *baddang* is a reciprocal work group where farmers tend to others' fields with the expectation that the other farmer will help in the labor requirement of the former. However, due to the market economy, and the premium that has been placed on monetary values, this cooperative work has degraded. Rituals associated with the agricultural cycle have also suffered immensely, to the point that only two, out of the hundreds of agricultural districts (*himpuntonaan*) in Ifugao apply the practice that is called *puntonaan* (ritual plot or parcel).

The concept of *puntonaan* and the existence of *tomona* (village ritual heads) in customary Ifugao society offer a perspective toward understanding Ifugao ecological knowledge. This practice synchronizes agricultural activities within an agricultural district (fields within a valley, usually sharing an irrigation source). *Puntonaan* is a plot or parcel in the "center" of an agricultural district (*himpuntonaan*) owned by the *tomona*. The *puntonaan* is traditionally the first to be cleaned, planted, transplanted, harvested, among other activities related to terrace agriculture.

These activities are signified by specific rituals sponsored by the *tomona*. Once a *tomona* has performed the ritual and initiated a particular agricultural activity, other members of the *himpuntonaan* can start to work on their fields. Otherwise, larger, fields owned by the elite, *kadangyan*, might be worked on first because of labor requirements.

This practice has largely disappeared in Ifugao agricultural rituals. Owing to the expense associated with a *tomona*-sponsored ritual (which includes pigs and chickens to feed the village and visitors, rice, and wine), only two agricultural districts have retained this practice. Maintenance of fields, rituals, and basic social relationships previously revolved around the rice agricultural cycle. The cultivation of *tinawon* varieties is central to this Ifugao social life. Heritage varieties are central to ritual practice as they are locally adapted to cordilleran conditions and annual farming cycles have co-evolved around their seasonality. Since commercial rice does not follow the same cycle as the *tinawon* varieties, its increasing use has disrupted both the social and environmental aspects of Ifugao society.

The practice of *puntunaan* and *tomona* applies to the ecology of Ifugao agricultural terraces. Mutual support among farmers within a terrace system is integral to the effectiveness of drying or flooding of fields as a method of pest control. A single farmer's attempt to reduce pests on a field without the coordination of other farmers would be futile because pests will simply migrate from field to another field. However, if all fields in the system are burned or flooded in coordination with the rest of the fields, pest populations can be reduced. Synchronization of activities related to pest control would make both kinds of fallow (burnt or flooded) effective for reducing population of rice pests. Just as individual farmers manage their paddies by controlling the flow of water, so do larger social groups control pest cycles by synchronizing irrigation activities.

Gender roles are also an important component of the Ifugao agricultural system and have been disrupted by economic and political changes in the region. In a time when gender issues have become a universal concern, the customarily gender-equal Ifugao society took a step backward as far as the sexes are concerned. Take for instance the role of women in the terraces. In earlier times, the planting of the *tinawon* was an accepted domain of women, a practice logically based on the compatibility of the sensitive *tinawon* seedlings and the gentler hands of women. The change to hardier, less pressure-sensitive lowland rice allowed the men to do the transplanting themselves. As men can do transplanting faster than the women, they are hired to do transplanting by rice field owners. The woman, if ever hired for transplanting work, earn a daily wage lower than the men (P200.00 for women, P250.00 for men in the central Kiangan area.) This discrepancy can be clearly observed in the Nagacadan World Heritage Site in the upper Kiangan district where both lowland rice and the traditional varieties are planted side-by-side. The seasonal maintenance work in the *muyong* is also disrupted as men spend longer time in the rice fields.

The customary fallow period that comes after the harvest season, a time for the soil to replenish itself, is no longer observed due to the shorter growing season of the higher-yielding varieties. The intensive use of terraced ponds after several years of planting the new rice has depleted soil nutrients resulting in low harvest yields. This has necessitated the use of synthetic fertilizers to augment naturally occurring soil nutrients. Furthermore, the new rice, being an introduced species, is highly susceptible to pests and has no natural resistance to viral or bacterial diseases. So the government has introduced chemical pesticides to combat these. The results are devastating. Edible mollusks, shellfish and fish that used to supplement the Ifugao diet have died off en masse in the terraces due to toxicity caused by industrial chemicals. The golden apple snail (*Pomacea canaliculata*) on the other hand, introduced by the government's Department of Agriculture supposedly to augment the protein source of farmers, has turned out to be a voracious omnivore devouring everything in its path including rice plants, smaller snails, fish and other amphibian eggs. Once again, pesticides have been introduced to control this pest.

Ifugao intangible culture has also suffered from introduction of modern farming practice. The role of ritual and the centrality of belief systems that involve *tinawon* varieties is disregarded. Since the introduced commercial varieties have no ritual value whatsoever, rice rituals have ceased to be practiced. One no longer hears the chanting of the *hudhud* epic during planting or harvesting of the *tinawon* rice. This UNESCO-declared Masterpiece of the Oral and Intangible Heritage of Humanity is currently being taught to children in primary schools as a last-ditch effort in intangible heritage conservation. Without the customary practices that necessitate their accompaniment, the rich and complex oral tradition of the Ifugao will cease to exist sooner than later. Non-contextual performance of cultural rituals for tourism only reflects the desperate state of conservation in the province. Communal practices that revolved around the traditional agricultural cycle have lost their meaning resulting in sudden changes in the socio-cultural makeup of terraces communities. Customary labor practices and gender roles changed as a result of the changing of rice varieties in the terraces, an effect never perceived by any of the development agencies involved in the shift to lowland rice.

The changing nature of Ifugao water management

The Ifugao water management system is a community-based irrigation system where farmers sharing a common irrigation source coordinate their activities and share in the maintenance of the irrigation infrastructure. The system also illustrates the complementary nature of swidden fields, forest cover, and irrigated terraces. Swidden fields and communal forests are considered common property, while irrigated terraces and forest cover on top of a terrace system is considered private property. Irrigation infrastructure is a commons property. The presence of both commons and private property in Ifugao explains the apparent stratification and access to land in Ifugao society, a concept termed Common-Pool Resource (CPR) by Ostrom (1990). A *CPR* is a resource system that is available for all members of a community to use (Ostrom 1990:30). These resources are usually limited, therefore, agreed upon rules are instituted that all joint users understand. Customary water management in Ifugao is predicated in this agreement.

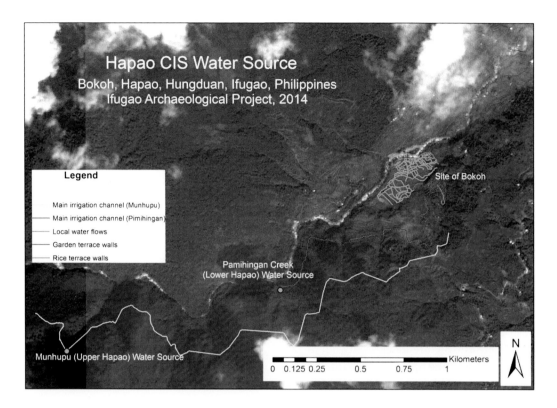

Figure 4. Main irrigation channels in Brgy. Hapao, Hungduan, Ifugao. These irrigation canals have been converted to concrete structures by the National Irrigation Administration.

The assimilation of the Ifugao in the state system and market economy, however, has degraded the Ifugao water management system. Previously, fields that share the same irrigation source conduct annual maintenance work based on cooperative work groups. They also engage in reciprocal labor exchange and contribute expenses associated with the maintenance work. If a farmer is unable to participate in the actual maintenance work, he (maintenance work is customarily a male-centered activity) is obligated to provide an agreed upon bundles of rice to feed the work group. In addition, a fine is meted to a farmer unable to participate or contribute to the endeavor.

In recent decades, the National Irrigation Administration, a state agency, has taken the lead in the maintenance of irrigation systems in Ifugao. This activity is associated with funds provided by the national government. Although it is still the farmers who carry out the repairs and maintenance of the system, they are paid monetarily by the project. This has immense implication in the sustainability of the Ifugao agricultural system as the basic socio-political dynamic that has regulated the social and ecological fabric of the Ifugao has eroded. As a case in point, the National Irrigation Administration sponsored a project to convert the Ifugao irrigation system into concrete structures in Hapao, Hungduan (Figure 4) in 2003. The principle behind the structural change was conceived by engineers who thought that concrete irrigation channels require less maintenance than earthen structures. Most of the workers who were hired to help with the constructions were local farmers. They were paid monetarily, based on the prevailing wage standards. However, a few weeks after the completion of the project, a typhoon caused several small landslides that buried segments of the system. The local farmers could not muster enough workers as farmers were waiting for the national government to pay them to repair the damaged portions of the system. In the summer of 2014, the system is still inoperable.

Water distribution has also become a source of conflict among Ifugao farmers. Previously, the customary Ifugao socio-political organization has controlled the synchronization of water distribution among fields sharing a common water source, but because of the erosion of the cooperative principle, it is now normal to see farmers guarding their irrigation channels with guns.

New Rice Varieties

The Ifugao, as a people, were not colonized by the Spanish and were only placed under state control during the American occupation in the early 1900s. Rapid economic and political transformations started during this era. Implementing development initiatives in IRT communities involves understanding of the terraces not simply as structures of antiquity but as a living system of people, environment and customary practices. Modern development conflicts with the sustainability of the rice terrace landscapes and community farming practice and contradict the preservation of these living relics of the fading past.

In the 1970's, the Philippine government launched its own Green Revolution Program to boost the agricultural sector and wean the country from its dependence on agricultural imports. Rice, as the staple food of Filipinos, was prioritized for maximum production. New varieties of commercial rice, products of intensive research by the International Rice Research Institute (IRRI) based in the Philippines, were distributed for cultivation all over the Philippines. The Ifugao Rice Terraces were not spared from this "revolutionary" development initiative. Heirloom Ifugao rice varieties, the *tinawon*, harvested only once a year, were substituted with the new high-yielding varieties promising double or even triple the usual harvest volume. The campaign by the government was so effective, most traditional farmers readily shifted to the high-yielding varieties. The initial years of HYV cultivation delivered as promised, but the negative results of HYV cultivation will be felt only after several years after the demise of the local culture within which *tinawon* varieties are embedded. The accruing effects of chemical fertilization, pesticides and disruptions of biodiversity are already apparent, and will contribute to a degrading environment in the rice terraces.

Currently, there is an urgent need to document the vanishing 7 rice (tinawon) varieties that are known to be cultivated in the Ifugao Rice Terraces. Several authors (e.g. Harold Conklin, Maria Stanyukovich, Roy Barton) have emphasized the centrality of rice in Ifugao social and political life. Indeed, rituals and social relationships have customarily been revolving around rice and rice production. As a case in point, there is a specific ritual associated with each step in rice production. This, however, have changed since the introduction of commercial

Commercial Varieties	Tinawon Varieties
52	Binogon
82	Botnol
222	Iggamay
C-12	Imbannig
C-2	Imbuukan
C-4	Madduli
C-4 red	Mayawyaw
Diamond	
Halaylay	
Ingaspar	
Ingaspi	
Korean	
Migapas	
Minmis	
Mukoz	
Mulmug	
Munoz	
NSCI-208	
Pakulsa	
Oakland	
Oklan	
Oklan Minaangan	
Pangasinan variety	
PJ-27	
PJ-7	
RC-218	
RI-152	
RI-238	
Romelia	
RP 224	
Super 60	
Taiwan	
Thunder	

Table 2. Known and named commercial and local rice varieties cultivated in Kiangan and Hungduan Municipalities.

rice (developed by the International Rice Research Institute) spearheaded by the national government through the National Food Authority (Table 1). As noted, more and more younger Ifugao would rather work in the lowlands rather than learn the farming techniques that their ancestors have practiced, and the commercialization of Ifugao rice has changed customary gender roles whereby elder Ifugao women were once the sole bearers of seed selection information, but men and wage laborers are increasingly handling these traditional cultural roles. The changes to farming practice to support the new commercial rice varieties have already had a significant impact on customary culture, and arguably will hasten the decline of community systems that are integral to preservation and sustainability of the terrace landscapes.

The increase in the number of commercial rice varieties in Ifugao has swamped the terraced rice fields of Ifugao, particularly, those of the rice terraces in Kiangan (Figure 5). Moore (2014) has gathered data that indicate the dominance of non-local rice varieties in at least two agricultural districts that she investigated. We surmise that this is partly influenced by the proximity and elevations of Kiangan compared to Hungduan —higher elevation sites are still too cold for most commercial rice varieties.

It has been more than 40 years since green revolution (commercial) rice varieties have been introduced in Ifugao as part of the Philippine government's Rice Sufficiency Program (Salas 1985). Although they have negatively impacted Ifugao culture and terrace ecology, it has also brought economic stability to Ifugao farmers. Since *tinawon* varieties are not commonly traded because they are prestige food, the shift to commercial rice varieties have provided a source of income to Ifugao farmers. The challenge now is to include this shifting agricultural system to the conservation programs of the Ifugao rice terraces.

Water management and heritage conservation

The conservation of the Ifugao rice terraces is tied in with the conservation of tangible and intangible Ifugao heritage. The context where rice terracing is embedded revolves around the centrality of rice in Ifugao culture. From gender dynamics, to cosmology, to identity formation, rice and its production and consumption shapes the Ifugao worldview. Water plays an important part in this

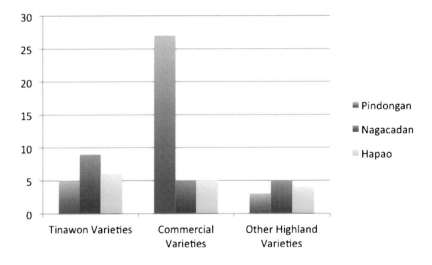

Figure 5. Rice varieties cultivated in three villages investigated by J. Moore. Note: Other highland varieties are rice varieties developed by other Cordilleran groups (i.e. Bontoc, Kalinga).

process as water is also entrenched in the ecological and social aspects of the Ifugao agricultural system. Indeed, water is considered as both a destructive force and as a source of life. Barton (1919) recorded the *great flood* myth among the Tuwali-Ifugao of Kiangan. Barton surmises that the flood myth is a form punishment for wrongdoing and shame as well as rebirth (p. 111).

Water management is also paramount to conserving the Ifugao rice terraces: without water, rice and the terraces will disappear, and the Ifugao culture as we know it. There is a need to involve the communities responsible for the conservation of the terraces in all aspects of conservation programs. For the most part, top-down approaches bring adverse effects in the ecological and social aspects of rice production in the region. As mentioned above, the intention to produce rice in Ifugao in the past was not for trading and the intensification of production was based on social factors, rather than economic pressures (Acabado 2012b). A nuanced understanding of Ifugao production system and social dynamics need to be addressed by policy makers if they intend to develop a more sustainable conservation program.

We further suggest that in the conservation of the IRT, long-term plans have to be in place to ensure continuity not just of the physical but equally of the intangible aspect of this cultural heritage. Implementing development initiatives in IRT communities involves understanding of the terraces not simply as structures of antiquity but as a living system of people, environment and customary practices. The indigenous knowledge of the Ifugao on terraced agriculture, an all-encompassing system that includes rice fields, forests and people, is a major consideration in all development initiatives in terraces communities. UNESCO in its official description of the IRT states thus, "The maintenance of the living rice terraces reflects a primarily cooperative approach of the whole community which is based on detailed knowledge of the rich biodiversity of biological resources existing in the Ifugao agro-ecosystem, a finely tuned annual system respecting lunar cycles, zoning and planning, extensive soil and water conservation, mastery of a most complex pest control regime based on the processing of a variety of herbs, accompanied by religious rituals (UNESCO, ND)."

Central to all this is the Ifugao method of rice cultivation. It dictates the synchronized movement of labor, production and community rituals. It is the fulcrum that holds the system in place so much so that removing this from the equation causes a major disruption in its continuity. In Figure 5 above, Ifugao communities that maintain local varieties have remarkably more of the customary practices that meet UNESCO's criteria for a world heritage site. Other than the World Heritage Site criteria, communities that maintain indigenous rice production have retained more of the customary practices reminiscent of old Ifugao culture including the practice of the old religion and the prevalence of communal labor relations in the maintenance of the IRT. All other applications of traditional knowledge including forest conservation, organic food production, and traditional stone-walling and vernacular architecture are also ubiquitous in traditional rice areas.

The importance of traditional knowledge in the maintenance of the IRT has been recognized by local conservation organizations in Ifugao but lack the necessary support from the national government to make it an institutionalized program in the formal education sector. The passing down of indigenous knowledge to younger generations of Ifugaos is of extreme importance to the continuity of the rice terraces. In 2006, the Save the Ifugao Terraces Movement (SITMo) in partnership with the local Ifugao State University embarked on an ambitious project to institutionalize indigenous knowledge education in the formal education sector as an adjunct to the establishment of community learning centers in terraces communities. This strategy of transferring local knowledge in both formal and informal education level is a work in progress and seeks to save the terraces in particular and Ifugao culture in general, for generations to come.

Another conservation approach applicable in the IRT is to address the economic inadequacies prevalent in Ifugao communities that lead to terraces abandonment, land-use conversion or out-migration of farmers from farming villages. Traditional subsistence economies in Ifugao are becoming things of the past and communities will have to join the mainstream economic flow or get lost in the currents of the global village. The booming tourism industry, albeit an anathema to indigenous cultures, somehow holds promise if managed properly following the tenets of sound eco-tourism guidelines. The involvement of terraces communities in tourism activities will tap on the Ifugao's natural craftsmanship, off-farm activities based on traditional enterprise activities such as weaving and carving. Major assistance in marketing will be necessary. The value chain development of terraces community products such as woven textiles and wood carvings, made during the fallow period of the terraces, will greatly supplement farmers' income. Putting a premium on the Ifugao traditional rice can also make a breakthrough in the organic food market notwithstanding its marketability as a product of a World Heritage Site.

A community-led eco-tourism model pioneered by the Save the Ifugao Terraces Movement (SITMo) demonstrates the sustainability of culture-sensitive tourism through community involvement. The tours centered on the traditional rice cycle of the Ifugaos from land preparation, planting to harvesting. The different stages of the cycle are packaged as tourism attractions and visitors are invited to participate in them "hands-on". The Rice Cycle Tours, as it came to be known, necessarily involved the farmers whose participation made them direct beneficiaries of tourism revenue, a reversal of their roles in the usual tourism setup where they stand to benefit the least from tourist arrivals in the province. The tours showcased rice rituals whenever present and visitors participate with the community in the work being done in the terraces. In 2013 alone, SITMo registered a total of US$50,000 in eco-tourism revenues for the heritage municipality of Kiangan, a relatively great improvement compared to zero income in tourism by the same community before the tours started. Payments are made directly to farmers, farmers' organizations and other community groups that are involved in the tourism activities including tour guiding, homestay accommodations, local transport services, cultural shows and sales from terraces products.

The rice cycle tours however did not limit itself as an enterprise initiative but expanded to become a catalyst for cultural "revival". Rice rituals that were nearly forgotten were again performed in their proper context, albeit undoubtedly, tourist entertainment became a value added purpose. It also encouraged farmers to go back to planting traditional varieties as the tours can only include fields planted to the native varieties. Tourism and cultural conservation sounded oxymoronic at first but making the enterprise community-led and guided by the sound principles of eco-tourism made it promising as far as conservation and community benefits were concerned.

Why farmers do what they do

Conservation programs in Ifugao are heavily focused on infrastructure repair (irrigation canals, collapsed terrace walls, and road improvement) and recently, developing markets for *tinawon* varieties. Indeed, the national government, through the Department of Public Works and Highways has allotted US$19 million for infrastructure development in the Municipality of Kiangan alone (US$72 million for the whole province). The cultural foundation of agricultural production has been largely ignored, and the unintended consequences to Ifugao customary culture have been magnified.

As *habitus*, the Ifugao agricultural fields become the arenas where status and power are played out. Since the Ifugao base their status on the amount of rice land holdings that they own, the shift to market production empowers the non-elite to gain economic power and prestige through monetary wealth. The non-elites also now have control over labor since the cooperative labor groups have been replaced by wageworkers.

The increasing dominance of commercial rice varieties in Ifugao indicates that the primary concern to produce rice is to gain monetarily, even in areas that are included in the UNESCO World Heritage List. The terraces have become a source of income, thus conservation programs should focus less on the infrastructure, but more on Traditional Ecological Knowledge that will be lost because of the changing nature of production.

Acknowledgments

This paper is part of a larger research program, the Ifugao Archaeological Project (IAP). The IAP is a collaborative research program between the National Museum of the Philippines, Archaeological Studies Program-University of the Philippines, UCLA, and the Save the Ifugao Terraces Movement, Inc. Previous field seasons of the IAP were supported by generous grants from the National Geographic Society, the National Museum of the Philippines, the University of Guam, and the UCLA. The authors are indebted to the efforts of Jacy Moore, Vanessa Morado, and Jacqueline Equinio in collecting seed data from Ifugao farmers through Glenn Stone's project, "GM Crops and Indigenous Management," supported by the John Templeton Foundation. We also wish to acknowledge the constructive comments provided by two anonymous reviewers, their reviews were very helpful in the final form of this paper. We alone are responsible for the final product and take responsibility for any errors of fact or interpretation.

References

Acabado, S.B. 2009. A Bayesian approach to dating agricultural terraces: A case from the Philippines. *Antiquity* 83: 801-814.

Acabado, S.B. 2010. *The archaeology of the Ifugao rice terraces: Antiquity and social organization*. PhD Dissertation, Department of Anthropology, University of Hawaii.

Acabado, S.B. 2012a. Taro before rice terraces: Implications of radiocarbon determinations, ethnohistoric reconstructions, and ethnography in dating the Ifugao terraces. In M. Spriggs, D. Addison, And P.J. Matthews (Eds), *Irrigated Taro* (Colocassia Esculenta) *in the Indo-Pacific: Biological And Historical Perspectives. Senri Ethnological Studies.* Vol (78). National Museum of Ethnology: Osaka.

Acabado, S.B. 2012b. The Ifugao agricultural landscapes: Complementary systems and the intensification debate. *Journal Of Southeast Asian Studies* 43(3): 500-522.

Acabado, S.B. 2013. Defining Ifugao social organization: "House", field, and self-organizing principles in the Northern Philippines. *Asian Perspectives* 52(2): 161-189.

Acabado, S.B. (in press). *Antiquity, archaeological processes, and highland adaptation: The Ifugao rice terraces*. Manila, Philippines: Ateneo de Manila University Press.

Acabado, S.B., J. Peterson, G. Barretto-Tesoro, and M. Horrocks. 2012. *The 2012 field season of the Ifugao archaeological project: The old Kiyyangan village*. Unpublished Report to the National Museum of the Philippines.

Acabado, S.B., M. Martin, and A. Lauer. 2014. Rethinking History, Conserving Heritage: Archaeology and Community Engagement in Ifugao, Philippines. The SAA Archaeological Record 14(5): 12-17.

Anderson, P. 2001. Community-based conservation and social changes amongst South Indian honey-hunter: An anthropological perspective. *Oryx* 35(1): 81-83.

Bandarin, F. World heritage partners for conservation. In *World Heritage 2002: Shared Legacy, Common Responsibility*, pp. 12-13. Paris: World Heritage Centre, UNESCO.

Barton, R. F. 1919. Ifugao law. *University of California Publications in American Archaeology and Ethnology* 15:1–186.

Barton, R. F. 1922. Ifugao economics. *University of California Publications in American Archaeology and Ethnology* 15(5): 385–446.

Barton, R. F. 1930. *The half-way sun: Life among the headhunters of the Philippines*. New York: Brewer and Warren.

Barton, R. F. 1938. *Philippine pagans: The autobiographies of three Ifugaos*. London: George Routledge & Sons, Ltd.

Barton, R. F.1949. *The Kalingas: Their institutions & custom law.* Chicago: Chicago University Press.

Barton, R. F.1955. *Mythology of the Ifugaos.* Philadelphia: American Folklore Society.

Beyer, H.O. 1955. The origins and history of the Philippine rice terraces. In *Proceedings of the Eighth Pacific Science Congress, 1953.* Quezon City: National Research Council of the Philippines.

Bourdieu, P. 1977. *Outline of a Theory of Practice.* Cambridge: Cambridge University Press.

Bourdieu, P. 1990. *The Logic of Practice* (Translated by Richard Nice). Stanford: Stanford University Press.

Brokington, D. 2004. Community conservation, inequality and injustice: Myths of power in protected area management. *Conservation and Society* 2(2): 411- 432.

Bruijnzeel, L. 1990. *Hydrology of moist tropical forests and effects of conversion: A state of knowledge review.* Paris: UNESCO International Hydrological Programme.

Clark, K. 2001. Preserving what matters: Value-led planning for cultural heritage sites. *Conservation: The Getty Conservation Institute Newsletter* 16(3) 5-12.

Conklin, H.C. 1967. Some aspects of ethnographic research in Ifugao. *Transactions of the New York Academy of Sciences* 30: 99-121.

Conklin, H.C. 1980. *Ethnographic atlas of Ifugao.* London: New Haven.

Dulawan, L. 2001. *Ifugao: Culture and history.* Manila: National Commission for Culture and the Arts.

Eder, J. F. 1982. No water in the terraces: Agricultural stagnation and social change at Banaue, Ifugao. *Philippine Quarterly of Culture and Society* 10: 101-16.

Edroma, E. 2004. Linking universal and local values for the sustainable management of world heritage sites. In *Linking Universal and Local Values: Managing a Sustainable Future for World Heritage,* pp. 36-42. World Heritage Papers 13. Paris: UNESCO WHC.

Giddens, A. 1984. A. Giddens. *The constitution of society.* Berkeley: University of California Press.

Hamilton, L., and P. King. 1983. *Tropical forested watersheds: Hydrologic and soils response to major uses or conversions.* Boulder, Colorado: Westview.

Hampton, M. 2005. Heritage, local communities and economic development. *Annals of Tourism Research* 32(3): 735-759.

Keesing, F. 1962. *The ethnohistory of Northern Luzon.* Stanford: Stanford University Press.

Kwiatkowski, L. 1999. *Struggling with development: The politics of hunger and gender in the Philippines.* Boulder, Colorado: West View Press.

Lambrecht, F. 1929. Ifugaw villages and houses. *Publications of the Catholic Anthropological Conference* 1:3:117-141.

Lambrecht, F. 1962. Religion of the Ifugao. *The Philippine Sociological Review.*

Lambrecht, F. 1967. The hudhud of Dinulawan and Bugan at Gonhadan. *Saint Louis Quarterly* 5: 527-71.

Lansing, J.S. 1991 *Priests and programmers: Technologies of power in the engineered landscape of Bali*. Princeton, N.J.: Princeton University Publishers.

Lansing, J.S. and J.N. Kremer. 1993. Emergent properties of Balinese water temple networks: Coadaptation on a rugged fitness landscape of Bali. *American Anthropologist* 95: 97-114.

Lennon, J. 2003. Values as the basis for management of world heritage cultural landscapes. In *World Heritage 2002: Shared Legacy, Common Responsibility*, pp. 120-126. World Paris: Heritage Centre, UNESCO.

Medina, C. 2003. *Understanding the Ifugao rice terraces*. Baguio City, Philippines: Saint Louis University, Cordillera Research and Development Foundation.

Moore, J. 2014. Consequences of the introduction of commercial cultivars on the Ifugao rice terraces world heritage site. MA Thesis: Leiden University.

Ortner, S. 1984. Theory in anthropology since the Sixties. *Comparative Studies in Society and History*, 26(1): 126-166.

Ostrom, E. 1990. *Governing the commons: The evolution of institutions for collective action*. Cambridge: Cambridge University Press.

Pagada, E. 2006. *Ifugao folkways and folklores: A compilation of articles on Ifugao customs and folklores*. Self published.

Peterson, J. and S. Acabado. (in press). Did the Little Ice Age contribute to the emergence of rice terrace farming in Ifugao, Philippines? *National Museum Cultural Heritage Journal*, 1:1.

Rambo, A.T. 1996. The composite swiddening agroecosystem of the Tay ethnic minority of the Northwestern Mountains of Vietnam. In *Montagne Mainland Southeast Asia in Transition*, ed. Rerkasem, B., pp. 43-64. Chiang Mai: Chiang Mai University Consortium.

Reti, I. 1999. Community management of conservation areas in countries of the South Pacific region. In *World Natural Heritage and the Local Community: Case Studies from Asia-Pacific, Australia and New Zealand*, pp. 141-154. Paris: UNESCO.

Saberwal, V. 1997. Science and dessicationist discourse of the 20th Century. *Environment and History* 3(1997): 309–43.

Salas, R.M. 1985. *More than the grains: Participatory management in the Philippine Rice Sufficiency Program 1967-1969*. Tokyo, Japan: Simul Press Inc.

Schoenfelder, J. 2000. The co-evolution of agricultural and sociopolitical systems in Bali, *The Indo Pacific Prehistory Association Bulletin* 20 (Melaka Papers, Volume 4).

Scott, W.H. 1974. *The discovery of the Igorots*. Quezon City: New Day Publishers.

SITMo. 2008. *Impact: The Effects of Tourism On Culture and Environment in Asia and the Pacific: Sustainable Tourism and the Preservation of the World Heritage Site of the Ifugao Rice Terraces Philippines*. Thailand: UNESCO Bangkok.

UNESCO. N.D. Rice Terraces of the Philippine Cordilleras. http://whc.unesco.org/en/list/722 (accessed, August 23, 2014).

Vernon, J., S. Essex, D. Pinder, and K. Curry. 2005. Collaborative policy making: Local sustainable projects. *Annals of Tourism Research* 32(2): 325-345).

Water Services Heritage and Institutional Diversity

T.S. Katko[a], P.S. Juuti[b], P.E. Pietilä[c] and R.P. Rajala[d]

a. UNESCO Chair in Sustainable Water Services, Adjunct Professor, DSc. (Tech.),
Tampere University of Technology, tapio.katko@tut.fi
b. Adjunct Professor, PhD, University of Tampere petri.juuti@uta.fi
c. D.Sc. (Tech.), Tampere University of Technology pekka.e.pietila@tut.fi
d. D.Sc. (Tech.), University of Technology riikka.rajala@uta.fi

Abstract

The chapter explores the role of heritage especially in water services. It is based on research of the long-term development of water services in several countries by the team since the mid-1990s and covers technological development in the context of management, institutional, policy and governance issues. We argue that development of sustainable and resilient water and wastewater systems requires understanding the institutional framework of a country, as well as its administrative and legal traditions.

A differentiation between water services and water resources needs to be made. Europe alone has a huge diversity of relationships between citizens/customers, water and wastewater utilities, local governments and the private sector. The approach of larger urban systems is generally more top-down, while rural systems – such as water cooperatives – often apply a bottom-up approach based on citizens' initiatives.

Water utilities can also promote the recognition of heritage and safeguard institutional memory by publishing research-based books on their long-term development. Such recorded information has proved valuable for decision-makers on water services when the time frame is exceptionally long.

Keywords: *water supply, sanitation, stormwater, administration, legislation, organisations.*

1. Introduction: Tradition of Administrative and Legal Cultures

"History never looks like history when you are living through it."
   John W. Gardner

From a historical perspective, the current global situation with water is a product of social, economic, and ideological developments that started some two hundred years ago. According to Hassan (2001), the current predicament is a result of the fragmentation of management and a marketing ethos that regards everything as a commodity, and profit as the ultimate objective. Myllyntaus (2004, 11) points out that

> *"technology has no autonomous power; thus, it is dependent on human decisions and actions. On the other hand, science, technology, and political decisions can assist in solving environmental problems. In the case of water-related problems, technology is not only a culprit, but also a helping hand in fixing those problems".*

The beginning of the industrial revolution and the related urban growth gradually created the need for centralised water and sanitation services. In many respects, England was the forerunner of modern water supply and sanitation, and related innovations soon spread from that country to Germany, other parts of Europe, and the US. As European cities expanded, sanitary and environmental problems challenged city governments, which often saw modern technology as the solution (Hällström, 2002: 17; Juuti, 2001). Melosi (2000) showed how European water technology was transferred to, and eventually developed, in America.

Hassan (cited by Brown 1988) argues that the demands of industries, such as cloth finishing and dye works, persuaded cities to take an active role in water provision, rather than a concern for public health. On the other hand, Gaspari and Woolf (1985) show that in 122 cities in the US, sewage systems reduced mortality significantly, while water-filtration systems had no impact on it. More recent impact studies on developing countries show certain variation depending on conditions. Yet, the overall trend is that improved water supply results in somewhat lower mortality, and the impacts are even bigger when sanitation is included. However, the best results are achieved by also providing health education.

In Finland, the first water supply and sewerage systems of urban centres in the 1870s to 1890s were in most cases constructed simultaneously, although often under separate organisations. Demand for water was created particularly by the needs of fire-fighting (Juuti, 1993; 2001), while drinking-water supply and sanitation, and in some cases industrial needs, also played important roles.

1.1 Diversity in Institutional Cultures in Selected Countries in Europe

The current differences in water-resources and services management and related cultures have historical roots. Barraqué (2003) formulated a rough typology of water-resources management and institutional cultures in Europe based on

Germanic vs. Roman legal origins, as well as centralised vs. subsidiary traditions. The only three states where management has been based on river-basin institutions – Spain, England/Wales, and France – are centralised monarchies. Yet, each of them has evolved along its own path. Besides, in some countries, river-basin authorities like those of the Nordic countries, have been formed on a voluntary basis.

In England and Wales, water-resources policy has been centralised in the post-war period, particularly after the establishment of the River Basin Authorities in 1963. Water supply and sewerage systems became centralised in 1974 with the establishment of Regional Water Authorities. Consequently, the more recent extreme example of water privatisation during Prime Minister Thatcher's Government (1979–1990) set England and Wales clearly apart from other European countries, and even world-wide (Hukka and Katko, 2003).

Spain, Portugal, and Italy have systems built on Roman law, whereas the systems of England and Germany are based on Germanic law. In Spain, Portugal, and Italy, the political history of the 20th century also largely explains the ways and emphases of water-resources management. Germany has a long tradition of local drainage associations, while river basin management has not been institutionalised, except for the famous Ruhrgenossenschaft. Due to the strong subsidiarity in Germany, water policy is in the hands of 16 states (Länder), rather than the federation (Bund). In the Netherlands, development started with water boards that later became involved also in wastewater treatment and water quality control (Uijterlinde et al. 2003). Particularly in water-supply centralisation has been very strong (Blokland and Schwartz, 2012). The Nordic countries have a very strong tradition of subsidiarity and thus fall in the same category as the Netherlands and Germany.

According to Barraqué (2003), it is difficult to place France in any of the above categories. On one hand, France is clearly a follower of Roman law and the centralised tradition. Yet, the six water-basin authorities have become largely subsidiary institutions. As for water services, the role of municipalities has declined over time. After WWII, several Central European as well as the Baltic countries were subjected to the highly centralised Soviet tradition of state water management but after the collapse of the Soviet Union they reintroduced municipal ownership with different types of private sector involvement. Although the typology presented by Barraqué (2003) applies mainly to water resources, it also explains the differences in subsidiarity traditions, and thus the role of local governments. This difference is crucial when examining the evolution of water and sewerage services in various countries.

1.2 European Traditions in Legal Systems

Newman and Thornley (1996) presented an interesting comparison of the European countries and five 'families' in terms of their legal and administrative traditions. According to them, there is general agreement in the literature that European countries fall into five key categories: British, Napoleonic, Germanic, Scandinavian, and East European. Newman and Thornley (1996: 30) noted that the British legal style is largely isolated from the others. However, the Scottish legal system maintained its identity since Scotland remained an independent kingdom until the early 1700s. Thus, it is no wonder that water services in Scotland have developed differently than those in England and Wales.

The Napoleonic legal family, originating in France, is the largest in Europe by the number of countries belonging to it. This legal style has the tendency to use abstract legal norms and enjoy greater theoretical debate than the British style. The enduring nature of the commune as a basic building block of local administration still has considerable importance in France, Belgium, and Switzerland. The commune originally derived from the administrative structures of the Catholic Church. The historical roots and various paths to democracy led in any case to different administrative structures (Benney, cited by Newman and Thornley 1996: 32).

The Germanic legal family, covering Germany, Austria and Switzerland, is regarded by Newman and Thornley (1996: 33–34) as a distinctive branch of the Napoleonic one. In Germany, there was no central power to impose a unified legal system like in England and France. Thus, the existing law in Germany became increasingly obsolete, and there was no authority to rationalise the various existing laws. Most continental countries had already developed their codes by the time the German one was formulated. However, the German code influenced considerably those of Eastern Europe. The German Constitution is a federal one, where the central government shares power with the regions.

The Nordic legal family (Nordic is a more accurate term than 'Scandinavian' as used by Newman and Thornley: authors' note) includes Denmark, Finland, Iceland, Norway, and Sweden. This family is clearly different from the British one, and closer to the other two. The historic dealings between Nordic countries were largely based on conquests by the Danish and Swedish empires. In medieval times, Nordic laws were based on Germanic law, but were later also influenced by the French Revolution. The administrative structure of the Nordic family is regarded as a hybrid: the central government normally has its own agency operating at the regional level. Although local authorities have gradually been reorganised into larger units over the years, local self-governance has a long history and is seen as one of the cornerstones of the Scandinavian constitutions (Newman and Thornley, 1996: 34–35). According to Nygård (2004), Finnish health legislation was largely based on the English and other Scandinavian countries' tradition until 1927, whereas municipal legislation mainly followed the German (Prussian) tradition.

In Eastern Europe, from the end of WWII to the early 1990s, administrative systems were highly centralised where the state did not delegate authority to local governments. Although each country seems to proceed along its own path, Newman and Thornley (1996: 35–36) noted that a common past is likely to have caused similarities. As for water services, at least the East European countries seem to have selected several different paths in the 1990s after the collapse of the Soviet Union.

When comparing the development of local governments in Europe, Batley (1991: 216) recognised three main types of reforms in terms of service delivery. Firstly, the trend to expand the role of local government, and to free it from restrictions exemplified by the shift to general grants in the Netherlands and Norway, and the more dramatic adoption of deregulation and free commune experiments in Scandinavia. Secondly, the improvement of public service practices including setting of performance standards, staff training for greater responsiveness, strengthening of user influence, and neighbourhood decentralisation. Thirdly, the introduction of business methods and competitive practices in the public sector, such as devolution of budget responsibilities, contracting out, and charging fees for services. According to Batley (1991), a clear distinction was made in the early 1990s between services that could be contracted out or franchised and those that should remain under direct municipal control or be provided by the voluntary sector.

Around the same time, Stoker (1991) pointed out that the establishment of local governments in Eastern Europe was considered central for establishing and maintaining a democratic process. Stoker also reminded how post-war growth in public spending, especially in relation to the welfare state, increased service provision and local government services. Yet, the more difficult economic situation after the mid-1970s has led to concerns about public spending. However, as Stoker (1991) mentions, the challenge of local government is broader than the 'fiscal crisis' due to the wider economic and social change affecting the operational environment of local governments.

In the early 1990s, most of Europe was moving down the path of greater decentralisation. The establishment of viable local democracy was seen as vital in Spain and Italy, while France and Italy had also undertaken decentralisation measures. The Nordic countries have traditionally had a local government focus. Stoker (1991) argues that Britain, in contrast, was moving in the opposite direction – towards a more centralised system in which local government would have more of an agency status. Such power relations between central and local governments, and the clear differences in their traditions and present status, should also be kept in mind when thinking of the key long-term changes in water services. Globalisation, European integration, and the developments in Eastern Europe in the 1990s, have also influenced these patterns.

All in all, it is obvious that the different legal and administrative traditions, 'families', related to urban planning, as well as the trends and changes in the roles of local governments in different regions and countries, certainly have implications for the development of water and sewerage services and thus sustainable decision-making in the long-term. Historical traditions have also obviously influenced how services, including water and sewerage, have developed and are managed even today.

After this introduction, we will first discuss, based on literature and examples, the difference between water resources and water services and then provide examples of the institutional diversity of water services in six European countries. Thereafter, the heritages of Dutch water boards, water cooperatives and user associations, as well as the levels of integration of water and wastewater services, will be discussed mainly based on Finnish experiences. Finally, we will share our experiences from recording and analysing the heritage of water utilities based on books depicting their histories.

2. Dimensions of Water Services Heritage

During the last decade, integrated water resources management (IWRM) has become one of the basic water service-related paradigms. IWRM calls for the planning of water resources use on a larger geographical scale than the typical water services areas (Fig. 1). While water resources' planning requires a wide geographic perspective, the subsidiarity principle calls for *water services management at the lowest appropriate level*. One current challenge in terms of publicity and decision-making is the *'invisible city'* of which water and wastewater systems are important parts. How can they be made more visible to people and decision-makers? After all, studies indicate that *citizens* do value water services and rank them high, immediately after education and health services (Aarnio and Määttä, 1994).

In connection with water services organisations, it is good to remember the definition of institutions by D.C. North, a Nobel Laureate in Economics (North, 1990). He used the soccer analogy and defined institutions as the 'rules of the game', while organisations were the 'players'. The related New Institutional Economics (NIE) calls into question many ideas of the more classical schools of thought. Grigg (2010), on the other hand, considers institutions to consist of three major elements: Policy, Empowerment, and Control.

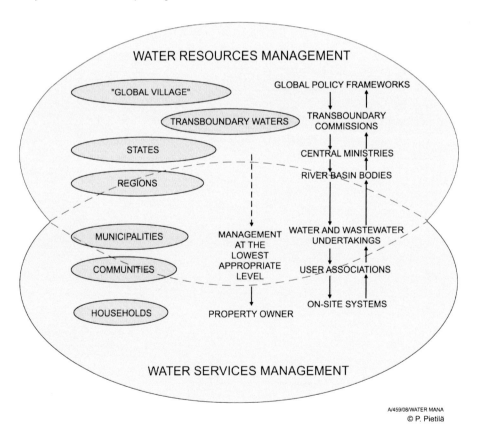

Figure 1. Water resources vs. water services management: levels of systems and major related bodies.

From the water services' point of view, the fundamental issue globally is that in spite of the 'fad of privatisation', especially during the 'international privatisation decade from 1995–2003' (Franceys, 2008), some 90% of the world's water works, some 95% of its wastewater works, and probably close to 100% of its stormwater systems are still owned by local governments or respective public bodies. Privatisation experiments were not only carried out in Latin America, but also in Africa and the transition economies. That policy proved less than successful as shown by international evaluations (Annez, 2006; PPIAF, 2009), and researchers like Bakker (2010), Castro (2008) and Hall and Lobina (2013).

2.2 Institutional Diversity of Water Services in Europe

The development of centralised water and wastewater services has been closely linked with urbanisation. When cities grew and population concentrated in urban areas, water sources within the cities become polluted, causing epidemics such as cholera outbreaks. Early developed major cities, such as London, have had piped water-distribution systems since the late 16th century. During the 19th century, centralised water supply and sewerage systems were built in major cities throughout Central and Northern Europe.

The first water distribution systems were typically built by private companies, but by the beginning of the 20th century cities had taken over the responsibility for water supply from private enterprises except in France. A century later, the idea of private concessions and long-term contracts was reintroduced as a 'new innovation' and promoted by international financing institutions ignoring historical lessons. Soon it was discovered that such arrangements require extensive regulation which is beyond the capacity of developing countries. Furthermore, as the experiences from England and Wales show, a proper regulatory system is very expensive. More recently, remunicipalisation of former privatised utilities has taken place, for instance, in Paris and Berlin (Water Remunicipalisation Tracker, 2014).

When piped water distribution became more widespread, the volume of wastewater that had to be discharged increased significantly, which made the need to develop sewerage systems acute. It was difficult to establish and run sewerage systems on a commercial basis which forced municipalities to shoulder the responsibility. Even though municipalities are typically responsible for sewerage and wastewater treatment, states have also financially supported particularly the construction of wastewater treatment plants in several countries. Central governments and their environmental authorities have also promoted water pollution control by requiring municipalities as well as industries to build wastewater treatment plants.

Even though municipalities play a central role in the provision of water services, there are major differences between the organisational set-ups (Fig. 2). The variation is caused by differences in administrative traditions and patterns of different countries, as well geographical, climatic, and environmental conditions. In the Nordic countries, administration has been largely decentralised and local authorities have been vested with large responsibilities. Accordingly, water and wastewater systems have been built and are operated by municipally owned entities. However, outsourcing is used widely, meaning that municipal utilities use many services of private companies. A special feature in Finland and Denmark is that in smaller population centres and rural areas people themselves have often established cooperatives for organising their water services. Interestingly, such water cooperatives are practically non-existent in neighbouring Sweden and Norway (Pietilä, 2013).

In Germany, water and gas have often been supplied by a single municipal company, while sewerage and wastewater treatment have been provided by a municipal department. In the Netherlands, water supply and distribution, sewerage and wastewater treatment are also managed and operated on a decentralised basis. Water supply and distribution are the responsibility of publicly owned water companies. Municipalities provide sewerage, while drainage and wastewater treatment are the responsibility of regional water boards. A special feature in the Netherlands is the role of the water boards, in existence since the 1200s, originally established for purposes of flood protection and land drainage of low-lying areas.

In the Soviet Union, the central government through its regional companies was responsible for water and wastewater services. When Lithuania regained independence in 1990, it inherited the former Soviet structure, where water

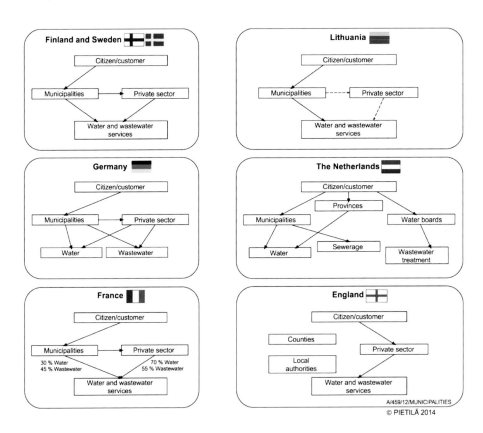

Figure 2. Simplified institutional arrangements and heritage of water services in six European countries: the relationships between citizens/customers, local and regional bodies, municipalities, private sector, water and wastewater utilities, and cooperatives (Pietilä, 2013: 102, modified).

| WATER & HERITAGE

companies were fully equipped and manned to manage and operate the services in-house. In Lithuania, as well as in other Baltic countries, private sector service providers have gradually emerged, and municipal water companies no longer carry out all their activities with their own staff, but use also services of private companies.

France has its own way of managing water and wastewater services. It has a long tradition of small municipalities entering into an agreement with a private company to manage and operate their water and wastewater systems based on long-term concessions or lease contracts. The evolution of this practice can be explained to a large extent by the large number of municipalities. Many French municipalities have a population of only a couple of hundred people, and it would be difficult for such small entities to organise water and wastewater services independently.

England and Wales are clear exceptions to the common practice of municipally owned and managed systems. There water and wastewater services were reorganised into regional water authorities in 1974. In 1989, these public water authorities were totally privatised, and the shares of these companies became tradable in the stock market. Currently, Thames Water, which is responsible for London's water services, is owned by a consortium of investors led by an Australian banking group.

2.3 Heritage of Dutch Water Boards

One quarter of the Netherlands lies below sea level, but over the centuries a large share of it has been reclaimed. Local water boards have played a major role in the work since the threat of floods resulted in their establishment or polder cooperation.

Initially, villagers drained peatlands as a communal effort to make them suitable for human settlement. Drainage caused the soil levels to drop and thereby forced local communities to build dikes for flood protection. The construction and maintenance of dikes, drainage canals, and locks were carried out by local communities with materials and labour contributed by the villagers. Between 1250 and 1600 the management of drainage systems in most of lowland Netherlands was transferred from the self-governing village communities to regional water boards (van de Ven 1996, cited by Ankersmit 2007).

Although the local communities were initially well represented in the regional water boards, the influence of the smallholder farmers declined gradually due to commercialisation of the rural economy. The boards became mainly governed by members of the aristocratic elite, and they developed into highly respected governing bodies since they could cope with floods and improve drainage. The Delfland Water Board from that period is shown as an example in Fig. 3.[1] In 1798 a national authority for water management was established (Ankersmit, 2007).

Before 1800, the water boards were predominantly rural, but along with urbanisation in the 19th century they became more and more involved in urban water management and later also water pollution. In 1970 the water boards

---

1   https://www.rijksmuseum.nl/nl/search/objecten?q=CRUQUIUS&p=1&ps=12&ii=2#/RP-P-1918-413,2 (accessed 1-1-2015).

Figure 3. A painting of the district governed by the Delfland Water Board, the Netherlands by Cornelis Koster, Jacob Cruquius and Nicolaas Cruquius from 1750.

were put in charge of water quality management, issuing of licenses, as well as constructing and operating wastewater treatment plants. More than half of the revenues of the water boards now come from pollution charges. The Dutch water boards have survived for almost a thousand years and are thus an interesting example of decentralised water management. Yet, over time their number has also decreased due to efficiency requirements (Ankersmit, 2007).

2.4 Heritage of Water Cooperatives and User Associations

In addition to municipal water utilities, Finland and Denmark have a large number of water cooperatives established by people who wanted better water services. Finland is a sparsely populated country with a large proportion of its population living in rural areas. After World War II, Finland faced economically hard times, and municipalities were not able to establish or extend their water and sewerage systems to the extent residents wished. As Finland has a long tradition of cooperatives in different fields, it was not a strange idea for people to establish a cooperative to solve their water supply problem already around 1900 (Table 1). Even though Finland as a whole is blessed with abundant water resources, there are areas where groundwater resources are scarce, and the quality of surface water is not good due to run-off and soil conditions. This is true particularly in

I 1900–1950	II 1950–1970	III 1975–1990	IV 1990s to present	V
- Built without financial support - Willingness to continue as independent co-operatives is strong	- Stronger role of munici-palities and state → loans and grants for organising rural water services	- Mostly in rural areas - Actively encouraged and supported by municipalities - Less independent than earlier co-operatives → weaker ownership, passive members	- Mostly in rural areas - Sanitation - External pressure significant in setting up - Often planned as temporary solutions	- Larger water co-operatives - Operate in mid-size towns, very similar to municipal utilities; how-ever, non-profit basis - Employees → skilled labour

Table 1. Development phases of water cooperatives in Finland (Takala, et al., 2011).

Western Finland, where several rural townships established water cooperatives in the 1940s and 1950s. Since then, these cooperatives have expanded so that many of them now cover the entire municipality and provide water services to up to 99% of the population. Table 1 describes the five major development phases of water cooperatives in Finland. The first four involve rural areas in chronological order whereas the fifth involves larger water cooperatives that have grown over time and now provide water services to townships of up to 15 000 people.

Another group of water cooperatives in Finland consists of ones in rural areas outside population centres. In many cases, municipal water utilities have found it too expensive to extend their water and sewer networks to sparsely populated rural areas. Thus, it has been up to the residents to try and find out ways to improve their water and wastewater services. Since cooperatives were familiar structures to the people, they were suitable for providing these needs. In the 1960s through the 1980s, many such cooperatives were established to supply good quality water in sufficient volumes to dairy farms with most of the construction work done by the users themselves. During the last twenty years, many more cooperatives have been established in rural areas. As the requirements for wastewater treatment were made radically stricter in 2004, practically all the water cooperatives established during the last ten years also provide wastewater services. Currently, there are about 300 municipal water utilities and over 1 500 water cooperatives or user associations in Finland. Water cooperatives supply water to some 10% of the population in Finland.

Denmark also has a strong tradition of water cooperatives. Unlike in Finland, Danish cooperatives are not involved in wastewater services, as the legislation states that management of wastewaters is the task of municipalities. But in water supply the cooperatives play a strong role. There are about 2 500 cooperatives which supply water to more than 40% of the Danish population (GEUS, 2010). Water supply in Denmark is almost entirely based on groundwater, and cooperatives typically have their own groundwater intake system. Cooperatives or similar organisations exist also in other countries like Bolivia (Nickson, 2009), Kenya (based on-going studies), but this tradition has hardly been mentioned in the global water discussion. More well-known are the water user associations involved in irrigation and similar uses as examined, i.e., by Ostrom (1990).

The unique values of cooperative water management, at least in the Finnish case, derive from the idea of using local resources and willingness for cooperative action in a country with large rural areas and quite low population density. It is obvious that only they have made it possible to produce services also for rural and urban fringe areas.

2.5 Levels of Integration of Water and Wastewater Services

The first urban water and wastewater, as well as solid waste, systems were established in Finland in the late 1800s. Early on, they used to be highly interconnected, but became gradually separated in terms of organisation (Katko and Nygård, 2000). Interestingly enough, in the 1970s, after the Wastewater Fee Act of 1973 and the Act on Water and Wastewater Works of 1977 came into force, the earlier separate urban water and wastewater entities started merging. The combining of water and wastewater services under a single entity, at least in the case of urban water supply utilities, undoubtedly has several merits since the same water goes through both systems. A survey of the share of merged utilities in 2009 showed that at that time, 16 (80%) of the 20 largest utilities had become merged – two of them were regional water and wastewater companies – while the rest had made other arrangements. Yet, in the case of supra-municipal systems, separate utilities may be more justified if local geographical conditions so require (Katko et al., 2010).

2.6 Recognising the Value of Water Heritage

It is obvious that we need some understanding of the pasts, to be able to assess the presents and the futures – the plural form is used intentionally to introduce alternative interpretations. This is especially important in the case of water services infrastructure which must be assessed over an exceptionally long time horizon (Kaivo-oja et al., 2004). As George Santayana (1863–1952) reminded: "*Those who cannot remember the past are condemned to repeat it.*"

Over the years, the authors have had the privilege to conduct studies and publish books on the history of water utilities (Fig. 4). Under proper arrangements and agreements between the parties such multidisciplinary studies have proved useful and been positively received. Books can preserve cultural heritage, promote reputation management, record vanishing knowledge, and reveal new facts. They can even be used as fundamental evidence in decision-making.

3. Discussion

In the water sector, especially in water services management, we have to understand institutional, policy and governance issues and traditions. Thus, water heritage plays a very important role. These issues should also be taken more into account in educational programmes for water professionals, where they have so far been largely ignored. That also requires multi- and interdisciplinary understanding and collaboration.

Figure 4. Books on long-term development of water services ordered by utilities and produced by the CADWES[2] and IEHG[3] teams.

Discussions on the reorganisation of water and wastewater services to improve the efficiency and possibly increase the role of the private sector in service production have been held across the world. Liberalisation of water services has also been discussed in the EU. The leading principle since the establishment of the EU has been free trade between the member states. Yet, water services differ substantially from consumer goods, and it has been widely understood that the same commercial principles do not apply to a natural monopoly service such as water. Thus, the EU will probably not require opening up the water sector to private service producers.

Water services are commonly regarded as services of necessity which should not be left for private actors to exploit. When municipalities play their typical central role in the provision and production of water and wastewater services, and most people are satisfied with the level of the service they receive, there is no political pressure for privatisation. Rather, the opposite is true: there has been political pressure in a number of countries and localities to ensure through remunicipalisation that water services remain in public hands. History also proves that the private sector has often played an important role by producing construction, consultancy and other services.

2   Capacity Development of Water and Environmental Services www.cadwes.com.
3   International Environmental History Group http://www.uta.fi/yky/tutkimus/historia/projektit/iehg/index.html.

Water services management systems vary depending on administrative and legal traditions and other natural and social conditions. Their relationship to cultural heritage is partly indirect. Preserved historical materials and artefacts such as buildings, water towers, etc. often remind us of their importance.

4. Conclusions

The following conclusions can be drawn as regards water services institutions and heritage:

1. Local governments play a fundamental role in water services provision and production;

2. Smaller systems, such as water cooperatives and the earlier water boards of the Netherlands, have demand-based bottom-up organisations;

3. By having studies made on their long-term experiences as a basis for the futures, several water utilities have recognised the need to promote water heritage, and to use it as a basis for their current activities and for their futures;

4. Better understanding of water heritage requires stronger appreciation of inter- and multidisciplinary collaboration.

On the whole, the development of sustainable and resilient water and wastewater systems for the futures requires recognising and understanding the institutional framework of a country, the local community as well as its administrative and legal traditions, and the overall socio-economic development and history.

5 References

Aarnio, R., and T. Määttä. 1994. (Original in Finnish) *Julkiset palvelut ja kuluttajat.* Suomen kuluttajaliitto. Selvityksiä 1/1994.

Ankersmit, W. 2007. *Dry Feet, Clean Water. 800 Years of Regional Water Management by Water Boards in the Netherlands.* 5th IWHA 2007 Conference, 13-17 June, 2007. Tampere.

Annez, P.C. 2006. *Urban infrastructure finance from private operators: what have we learnt from recent experience?* World Bank Policy Research Working Paper 4045.

Bakker, K. 2010. *Privatizing water. Governance failure and the world's urban water crisis.* Cornell Univ. Press.

Barraqué, B. 2003. Past and future sustainability of public water policies in Europe. *Natural Resources Forum* 27(2): 200-211.

Batley, R. 1991. Comparisons and lessons. In *Local Government in Europe. Trends and Developments*, R. Batley and G. Stoker (eds), 210-229. Mac Millan.

Blokland, M. and K. Schwartz. 2012. Upscaling and internationalization of the Dutch water supply sector. In *Water Services Management and Governance: Past Lessons for a Sustainable Future*, eds. Tapio Katko, Petri Juuti and Klaas Schwartz, and ass. ed. R. Rajala, 149-156. London: IWA Publishers.

Brown, J.C. 1988. Coping with crisis? The diffusion of waterworks in late nineteenth-century German towns. *The Journal of Economic History* 48(2): 307-318.

Castro, J.E. 2008. Neoliberal water and sanitation policies as a failed development strategy: lessons from developing countries. In *Progress in Development Studies*, ed. Ed Brown. Special Issue on 'GATS and development: the case of the water sector'. 8(1): 63-83.

Franceys, R. 2008. GATS, 'Privatization' and institutional development for urban water provision: Future postponed? *Progress in development Studies* 8(1):45-58.

Gaspari, K.C., and A.G. Woolf. 1985. Income, Public Works, and Mortality in Early Twentieth-Century American Cities. *The Journal of Economic History* 45(2): 355-361.

GEUS, 2010. Water supply in Denmark. Danish Ministry of Environment, Geological Survey of Denmark and Greenland (GEUS), 18 p.

Grigg, N.S. 2010. *Governance and Management for Sustainable Water Systems*. London: IWA Publishing.

Hall, D., and E. Lobina. 2013. The birth, growth and decline of multinational water companies. In *Management and Governance: Past Lessons for a Sustainable Future*, eds. P. Juuti, T. Katko, and K. Schwartz and ass. ed. R. Rajala, 123-132. London: Water Services IWA Publishers.

Hassan, F.A. 2001. *Water: the mainstream of civilization*. 2nd IWHA Congress. 8-13 Aug, 2001. Bergen, Norway.

Hukka, J.J., and T.S. Katko. 2003. Water privatisation revisited – panacea or pancake? *IRC Occasional Paper Series* 33. Delft, the Netherlands. Available: http://www.irc.nl/page/6003.

Hällström, J. 2002. *Constructing a pipe-bound city. A history of water supply, sewerage and excreta removal in Norrkoping and Linköping, Sweden, 1860-1910*. Doctoral dissertation. Linköping University.

Juuti, P. 1993. (Original in Finnish) *Suomen palotoimen historia*. (History of Finnish Fire Fighting) Helsinki.

Juuti, P. 2001. (Original in Finnish) *Kaupunki ja vesi. Tampereen vesihuollon ympäristöhistoria 1835-1921*. [Water and City] Acta Electronica Universitatis Tamperensis 141. Available: http://urn.fi/urn:isbn:951-44-5232-1. Accessed 28 Nov 2014.

Kaivo-oja, J.Y., T.S. Katko, and O.T. Seppälä. 2004. Seeking for Convergence between History and Futures Research. *Futures, Journal of policy, planning & futures studies* 36: 527-547. doi:10.1016/j.futures.2003.10.017.

Katko, T., and H. Nygård. 2000. Views of research on the Evolution of Water, Wastewater and Solid Waste Services. *Tekniikan Waiheita* 18(4): 14-19.

Katko, T.S., V.O. Kurki, P.S. Juuti, R.P. Rajala, and O.T. Seppälä. 2010. Integration of water and wastewater utilities: A case from Finland. *J AWWA* 102(9): 62-70.

Melosi, M.V. 2000. *The Sanitary City. Urban Infrastructure in America from Colonial Times to the Present*. Baltimore: Johns Hopkins University Press.

Myllyntaus, T. 2004. Writing on water. In *From a Few to All: Long-term development of water and environmental services in Finland*, eds. P. Juuti and T. Katko, 7-14 (Foreword). KehräMedia Inc.

Newman, P., and A. Thornley. 1996. *Urban planning in Europe. International competition, national systems and planning projects*. Routledge.

Nickson, A. 2009. *Organisational Structure and Performance in Urban Water Supply: The Case of The Saguapac Co-Operative in Santa Cruz, Bolivia.*

North, D.C. 1990. *Institutions, Institutional Change, and Economic Performance*. Cambridge University Press.

Nygård, H. 2004. (Original in Swedish) *Bara ett ringa obehag? Avfall och renhållning i de finländska städernas profylaktiska strategier, ca 1830-1930* (Only a bit of nuisance? A prophylactic perspective on sanitary services in Finland, 1830-1930). Doctoral dissertation. Åbo Akademi University Press. 402 p.

Ostrom, E. 1990. *Governing the Commons. The evolution of institutions for collective action.* Cambridge University Press.

Pietilä, P. 2013. Diversity of the water supply and sanitation sector: roles of municipalities in Europe. In *Water Services Management and Governance: Past Lessons for a Sustainable Future*, eds. P. Juuti, T. Katko,and K. Schwartz and ass. ed. R. Rajala, 99-111. IWA Publishers. 196 p.

PPIAF (Public-Private Infrastructure Advisory Facility) 2009. *Annual Report*. Available: http://www.ppiaf.org/sites/ppiaf.org/files/publication/PPIAF-AR2009.pdf

Stoker, G. 1991. Introduction: Trends in European Local Government. In *Local Government in Europe. Trends and Developments*, eds. R. Batley and G. Stoker, 1-120. Mac Millan.

Takala, A., V. Arvonen, T. Katko, P. Pietilä, and M. Åkerman. 2011. Evolving role of water co-operatives in Finland – Lesson learnt? *International Journal of Co-operative Management* 5(2): 11-19.

Uijterlinde, R.W., A.P.A. Janssen, and C.M. Figueres, eds. 2003. *Success factors in self-financing local water management. A contribution to the Third World Water Forum in Japan* 2003. 81 p.

Ven, G.P. van de. 1996. *Manmade lowlands. History of water management and land reclamation in the Netherlands*. Utrecht.

Water Remunicipalisation Tracker. 2014. Corporate Europe Observatory and Transnational Institute.

The framework of skills and knowledge shared in long-enduring organizations in the improvement of irrigation efficiency in Japan

Mikiko Sugiura[a], Yohei Sato[b] and Shinsuke Ota[c]

a. Faculty of Foreign Languages (Global Education Center),
Sophia University, Tokyo, Japan
Room 616 of Bldg.10, 7-1 Kioicho, Chiyoda-ku Tokyo, 102-0094, Japan
sugiura_mikiko@sophia.ac.jp.

b. Professor Emeritus, the University of Tokyo, Japan
744-1, Kurakake, Tsukuba, Ibaraki, 305-0024, Japan
sato-yoh@mail2.accsnet.ne.jp

c. The Japan Association of Rural Solutions for Environmental Conservation and
Resource Recycling, Japan
5F Nougyoudoboku Kaikan, 5-34-4 Shinbashi, Minato-ku, Tokyo, 105-0004, Japan
shinsuke-ota@r5.dion.ne.jp

Abstract

Improving the efficiency of water use is one of the critical tasks in the irrigation sector on a global scale. On a regional scale, the skills and knowledge that build sustainable water management have been determined by many long-enduring organizations. The cultivated rice irrigation system (irrigation commons) consists of both physical irrigation structures and institutions. The system, which was disseminated from the continent to the Japanese archipelago more than 2500 years ago, show peculiarities in each of them. Though the system has experienced technological development, legal reforms and modernization in order to improve irrigation efficiency, the inherited skills and knowledge and the stratified structures resulting from rural villages can still be observed in modern farmers' irrigation groups worth highlighting and protecting, such as the Land Improvement Districts (LIDs) in Japan.

Keywords: *cultivated rice irrigation, the commons, irrigation facilities and institutions, mura, stratified structures, LIDs.*

1. Introduction

Improving the efficiency of water use is one of the critical issues faced on a global scale. The irrigation sector, which absorbs a fair portion of the total quantity of water used, faces the impact of such criticism. However, on a regional scale, the skills and knowledge necessary for a sustainable water use in the agriculture industry (henceforth referred to as OMM, meaning Operation, Maintenance and Management) have been handed down by long-enduring organizations working in Japan as a valuable heritage.

The purpose of this paper is to present a realistic picture of the cultivated-rice irrigation management to the policy as well as the scholarly communities by focusing on the institutional framework of knowledge and skills. Based on the archaeological knowledge of recent decades (Ikehashi, 2005), Japan possesses a management system as to the irrigation of cultivated rice spanning at least 25 centuries of history. The institutional and technical skills as well as the knowledge gained from these centuries of experience have been passed down and developed through much trial and error for more than 2500 years in the Japanese archipelago, helping to the improve irrigation efficiency and reasonable water use.

An essential point of the present paper is the fact that the irrigation efficiency mentioned here is from the viewpoint of sustainable water use that would be obtained through the interaction of human and nature (i.e., with biodiversity serving as an index). Irrigation efficiency can be improved by means of technology and institution management. Both methods have been explored historically in many regions.

This point of view of sustainable water use appears in numerous forms reflecting the setting of the respective states. The Netherlands, a nation known as a man-made land (van de Ven 1993) has accumulated a large quantity of skills and knowledge concerning the harmonization between the natural environment and the human society against the rise in sea levels resulting from global warming, as a considerable amount of the land is indeed below sea level.

For more than 25 centuries skills and knowledge concerning irrigation management have been accumulated in the Japanese archipelago through the experience of withdrawing and dividing water. The irrigation commons, which is one of the common-pool resources (CPRs) discussed by Ostrom, has improved the irrigation facilities (e.g., reservoirs, tanks, headworks, barrages, canal networks). Not only a technological development in the design, construction and materials applied in the facilities, but also the institutional factors (i.e., skills and knowledge), were also required in order to increase the efficiency of an irrigation system. Considering the trial-and-error history of the cultivated rice irrigation system, an institutional framework is as important as the facilities themselves. Of significance is that the basic institutional framework for irrigation management has been passed on from generation to generation in Japan (Iwata & Okamoto, 2000). Such a conserved framework can also be found in the case of the Philippines to which Coward refers, (Coward,1979; Ostrom, 1995).

2. Past scholarly achievements as the basis of this article

This article is subject to the following scholarly achievements. In addition to Ostrom's comprehensive comparative studies regarding the irrigation commons as one of the long-enduring institutions and management for CPRs, systematic research on the conflict between the irrigation commons and also between water sectors were carried out by Shinzawa. Okamoto also studied the social relationship of the irrigation commons during a drought period and proposed a model of the WUOs based on rural villages (*mura*) (Shinzawa and Okamoto, 1978). In terms of the OMM by the LIDs in Japan, Ishii's study on the block rotational irrigation contributes much to the content of the present article (Tajima, Ishii and Miwa, 2009). More directly, in addition to the results of reallocation of water resources between appropriators in commons published by Sugiura (Sugiura, 2005), this article is also based on the conference paper presented at the International Association for the Study of the Commons held in 2013 (Sugiura, Ishii & Tajima, 2013).

3. The setting of cultivated rice irrigation in the Japanese archipelago

Distinguishing features of cultivated rice irrigation

Cultivated rice irrigation (i.e., not rain-fed rice or wild rice) in the Japanese archipelago has been taking place for more than 2500 years (Ikehashi, 2005). In terms of its origin, an influx of people from the continent arrived in Japan via the Korean Peninsula with a complete system of specific techniques for the irrigation of cultivated rice, which had been perfected along the Yangtze River. The original inhabitants of Japan followed this way of cultivation. The systematic techniques applied in order to grow cultivated rice by means of irrigation are expressed as a series of the following processes: nursery, paddling and transplanting. Since then, Japanese cultivators have preferred growing rice above other grain crops (i.e., wheat, barley, buckwheat), maize and potatoes. This is partly because cultivated rice paddies can reach higher productivity in terms of yield, calories per gram and profitability than other food crops.

Such a preference for rice paddies has resulted in the expansion of irrigation. The Japanese archipelago is located in the temperate zone and belongs to the monsoon region, where a high precipitation is expected on average. However, during a rainy season, it is necessary to provide a supplemental irrigation corresponding to the cultivation term. It was required to reclaim the rice paddies as a unique apparatus, surrounded on all four sides with bunds (i.e., pools of water with a depth of *c.*10 to 15 cm), and evened on the interior for cultivation use accompanied not only by means of irrigation but also by a surface and/or subsurface drainage at the same time.

As a result of reclamation, there existed 3.400.000 ha of irrigated rice paddies in 1965, whereas the fields for other use (i.e., orchards, tea fields, mulberry orchards, meadows etc.) covered 2.700.000 ha in total. Modernization and industrialization has decreased both of these areas leaving 2.500.000 ha of irrigated rice paddies and 2.000.00 ha of fields for other use in 2005. The latter fields were not irrigated at all prior to WW II, but were all rain fed. However, 20% hereof is now equipped with an irrigation system, whereas rice paddies have all been irrigated throughout history.

Elements of the irrigation system: facilities and institutions

A cultivated rice irrigation system called an irrigation commons consists of two elements: facilities and institutions. As the latter functionalize the former substantially, irrigation facilities can be regarded as a heritage if both get together and continue to exist. Although these elements are regarded as a resource system within the framework of CPRs (Ostrom, 1995 pp. 30–33), the specific case of the irrigation commons has not yet been examined in sufficient detail.

There are many physical facilities in an irrigation system, as mentioned above. In addition to rice paddies as an apparatus, a reservoir or a tank is located upstream of the river. Weirs withdraw the water. Pumps facilitate irrigation and drainage. Canals are also indispensable for irrigation commons. On the other hand, as to institutions, the following elements are core to the system: (a) the members of an organization who are eligible to utilize the irrigation water (b) farmers' irrigation organizations that distribute the water to each paddy plot, (c) the shared rules among an organization and (d) a mechanism bringing members into compliance. The term institutions refer to software including not only the shared rules but also the members and organizations. In this sense, the term is applied in a broader sense than with Ostrom, who regards institutions as "the sets of working rules that are used to determine who is eligible to make decisions in some arena" (Ostrom, 1995, p. 51).

Irrigation efficiency

Irrigation efficiency is a concept concerned with sustainable water use achieved through positive interaction between human and nature. In this context, irrigation efficiency can be improved in two main ways: technology and institution management, both of which have been explored historically. Technology can not only be improved but also changed as time goes by whereas institution management remains basically unaltered in terms of social, economic, political and administrative principles.

Water distribution, which is an example of institution management, reflects irrigation efficiency. If we say that the profit obtained by means of cultivation is a function of three variables (i.e., the potential cultivated area, the cost of physical facilities including construction and maintenance and the inflow volume at each diverting point), farmers (i.e., cultivators) have achieved an optimal solution by choosing the correct balance between these three applying a process of trial and error over years.

Each of these processes has been repeated until a clear consensus was finally formed concerning the location the facilities should be built, what type of material should be adopted (i.e., pebbles, rocks, sand etc.) and how the facilities were to be designed. Once a consensus was reached concerning the facilities and next the available volume of water was decided accordingly, the consensus became a rule shared even during a drought. This consensus is based on the premise: they keep their agreement not to infringe upon a prior-appropriation rule. Consequently, the best efficiency as to water use has been attained. Moreover, a maximized profitability is secured by means of their practices and knowledge.

4. Irrigation associations in Japan today: Land Improvement Districts (LIDs)

The Land Improvement Act

Having improved the technology of cultivated rice irrigation for more than 2500 years, the core of this system are the farmers. In other words, the skills and knowledge obtained are passed down by co-operative farmers and WUOs as governability. Such skills and knowledge involve withdrawing water from a river course in accordance with the fixed rules and delivering irrigation water to paddy plots on a fair basis.

In terms of the current situation, and with these basic principles unchanged, the skills and knowledge concerning irrigation management have been retained within the modernized legal framework. The land reform introduced just after WW II, ahead of the Participatory Irrigational Management (PIM), by international organizations resulted in absentee land owners being unseated by many peasants. Water distribution among the sectors (i.e., agriculture water, domestic water, industrial water, water for hydrologic power generation) is implemented in the administrative process based on the River Act. Water rights are available by means of an administrative approval after voluntarily applying to the Minister of Land, Infrastructure and Transportation. The Land Improvement Act also administrates the establishment and management of farmers' irrigation organizations. Farmers sharing in the management of the irrigation facilities voluntarily apply to the Minister of Agriculture, Forestry and Fisheries in order to become established and will obtain approval for the establishment of Land Improvement Districts (LIDs) from the same ministry.

The present irrigation projects and the LIDs

The current Irrigation projects consist of two parts: the construction of irrigation facilities and the facilities management. The LIDs will work to ensure fair water delivery to each rice paddy plot. The point here is that although present irrigation organizations and irrigation projects are maintained within the modernized legal framework, the LIDs are based on skills and knowledge in terms of institutional management.

5. The institutional structure and the OMM of the LIDs

Membership

The basic framework of a cultivated rice irrigation system has remained unchanged. Essentially, water is diverted from a river, distributed through a network of canals expanding like tree branches and delivered to each rice paddy plot at the end of these branches. Traditional farmers' irrigation associations have been modernized by means of several legal reforms. However, they retained their framework based on the rural villages (*mura*). The point here is: how to identify a membership of the farmers' irrigation associations and how clear the pathway is. In the case of the LIDs, it is clearly identified by the Beneficiary Pay Principle (BPP): those who receive benefits must pay for it in the form of an OMM fee.

Rights and duties

From a legal perspective, the Ministry of Agriculture, Forestry and Fisheries or a prefectural governor has commissioned a LID in order to manage the associated irrigation facilities. Practically speaking, the LID staff implements the specific details of OMM on the main facilities (including the main and secondary canals) under the supervision of the LID. The farmers' irrigation groups manage the minor facilities such as the tertiary and quaternary canals. The members of farmers' irrigation groups render their services to irrigation management. This implies that their water rights correspond to duties such as the working out of the OMM and cost sharing (i.e., the payment of membership fees).

In addition to the rights and duties, the Land Improvement Act allows all the farmers utilising irrigation water provided by the LID to compulsorily participate in their LID by a 67% majority vote of the identified members, even if a member disagrees with a membership issue. In practice, more than a 95% majority vote of members is desired as a means of securing cooperation among members. In addition, it is legally possible to collect an amount from each individual in order to cover the LID's administrative costs and construction projects.

Organizational structure and its management

For the benefit of explaining its organizational structure and management: a LID with 5000 ha of irrigated paddies and 7000 members is assumed to be a characteristic LID in Japan. These features reflect a democratic system. In terms of election, LIDs have a bottom up approach based in rural villages. Here an elected board of directors will compel members to follow their decisions due to a transfer of all rights of decision to such a board.

- All LID members are eligible to vote in the election of their representatives. In general approximately we see 120 people in a typical case with one vote per person regardless of their farming area, family background, gender, income and other factors.

- The representatives gather at the General Assembly more than twice each year in order to work through various points on the agenda concerning management similarly to the Japanese Diet.

- The General Assembly elects ten directors who comprise a board of directors. Four auditors join the board in order to ensure fairness and accountability.

- The board of directors appoints a Director General who is called the President.

- The LIDs can employ engineers, office workers and other staffs within its budget regardless if they are members of the LID or not.

- Generally speaking, remunerations are forwarded to the Director General (except in the case of per diem work) and to LID employees whereas other directors, auditors and representatives receive their payment on a per diem basis.

- The term limit as to representatives, the Director General, and auditors is 4 years whereas employees retire aged 60 or 65 years old.

A stratified structure as the irrigation commons

The irrigation system for cultivated rice paddies adheres to a stratified structure of irrigation organizations. The water is distributed through the network of irrigation canals until it reaches each paddy plot cultivated by beneficiaries. In other words, each canal needs a farmers' irrigation organization assigned to it, which makes water available to all the end-users through the arborized irrigation canals.

The physical setting determines the stratified structure of the irrigation canals and the farmers' irrigation organizations as a whole. These organizations are formed along main, secondary, tertiary and quaternary canals. Therefore, the traditional cultivated rice irrigation systems, as a so-called the commons, are formed at each weir along a river (Sugiura, Ishii and Tajima, 2013). The stratified structure appears in terms of the specific knowledge of irrigation management (i.e., the work as to operation and maintenance), institution management (i.e., representative election etc.), distribution of scarce irrigation water (i.e., decision and implementation of water rotation) and others. The minimum unit of the stratified structure is a rural village or rural village institutions (*mura*). Many similar cases can be observed abroad.

6. The comparative illustrations of water distribution

As described above, water distribution has an effect on irrigation efficiency and is one of the examples of institution management. Irrigation efficiency in this context is achieved through a process of trial and error repeated until consensus concerning the facilities (i.e., location, design, materials, operation, minor repairs etc.) was finally reached (Japan International Cooperation Agency, 2011).

Here we have four cases on two levels of water distribution: river-to-canal and plot-to-plot. As a matter of principle, water that is withdrawn is distributed to more than two irrigational groups in accordance with water rights decided on a

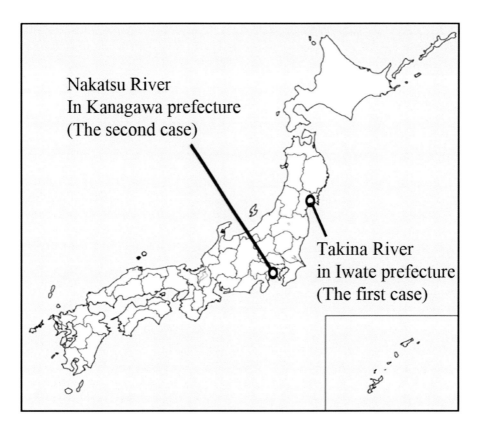

Figure 1. The location of the Takina and Nakatsu Rivers.

first-come-first-served basis (i.e., first in time, first in right). In these examples dated to between the 17th and 19th centuries, we can observe how the consensus concerning irrigation facilities has had an impact on water distribution and the content of water rights.

Cases of river-to-canal

The first and second cases examined concern the location of diversion weirs along a river, indicating a relationship located at the most upper irrigation canal.

The first case is located on the Takina River (Fig. 1), an affluent of the Kitakami River in the 17th century (i.e., *c*.400 years ago). It represents the location of diversion weirs for ten irrigation groups (Fig. 2) and the rough sketch of each weir (Fig. 3). The second case is located on the Nakatsu River (Fig. 1), an affluent of the Sagami River. These facilities have been modernized within the past century and include the location of diversion weirs (Fig. 4), a rough sketch of two of them (Fig. 5), and the current situation of one diversion point (No. 5) in Fig. 4 (Fig. 6).

In terms of the Takina River, each weir was maintained as it was originally designed. Combining various materials (e.g., pebbles, stones, rocks) in their original state, the available water volume was distributed into each irrigation group

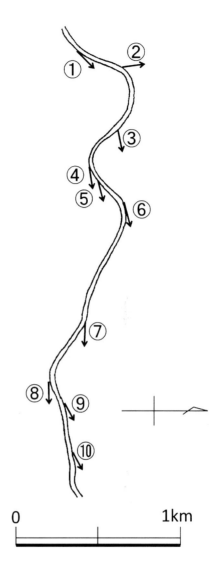

Figure 2. The Takina River and the diversion weirs. Original drawing by Miwa, H.

0   1km

through its own weir. Consequently, the water rights have been settled without permitting any arguments along this river.

The region along the Takina River has suffered from less water than demanded. The catchment basin was relatively narrow in comparison with all the rice paddy fields, most of which were developed during the pre-Edo period (17th to 18th century). Thus any irrigation water conflict often occurred in this area between water users groups depending upon the Takina River. This water conflict is widely known as the 'Water Fight in Shiwa' (Shiwa-no-mizugenka). The conflict was so severe that more than a few peasants were killed or injured. Twenty-seven division weirs were built along the Takina River over a distance of 10 km, delivering irrigation water for rice paddy fields of c.822 ha in 1672. Due to the advantageous position of up-stream diverters, all surface stream water was divided among the up-stream irrigation groups. The down-stream irrigation groups depended upon

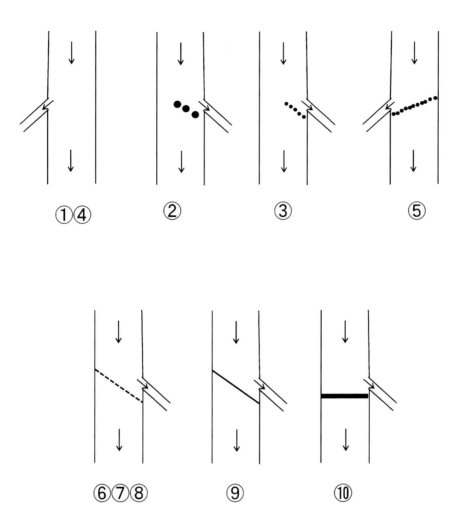

Figure 3. A sketch of the structure of each diversion weir.Original drawing by Sato, M. (1978).

underflow water from the alluvial fan seeping into canals. Although irrigation water conflicts often occurred until 1952 when the Sannōkai Dam was constructed upstream of the Takina River, the consensus concerning the diversion weirs had been maintained among them, working as the distribution mechanism along the Takina River.

These peculiarities are common in the case of the Nakatsu River during the 19th century. Due to the fluctuation, water conflicts among up-stream and down-stream irrigation groups often became intense. Although the material applied changed from stones, gravels, clay and others to modernized materials such as a wooden frame and concrete, the observance of agreements among irrigation groups concerning the location of each weir and the customary practices among water users groups contributed to the sustainable use of irrigation water.

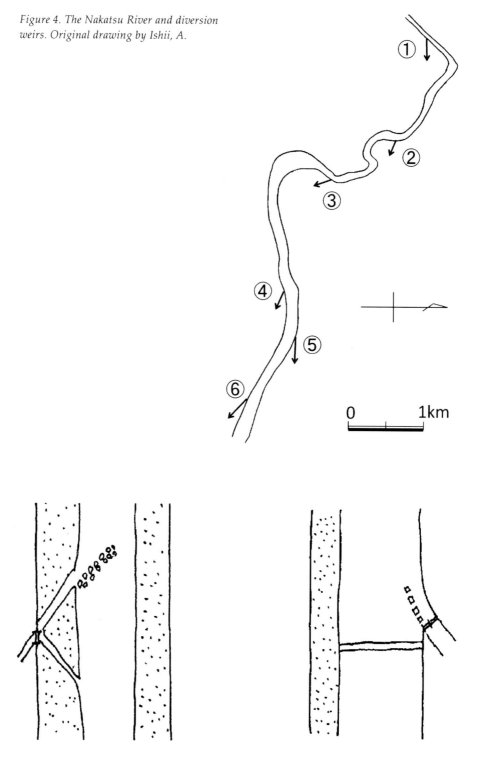

Figure 4. The Nakatsu River and diversion
weirs. Original drawing by Ishii, A.

0   1km

Figure 5. A sketch of the structure of diversion weir No. 1 and No. 3 in Fig.4. Original
drawing by Shinzawa, K. & Okamoto, M. (1978) Processed and modified by Ishii, A.

Figure 6. The current state of the diversion weir No. 5 in Fig. 4. Photograph by Ishii, A., August 2014.

Cases of plot-to-plot

Ostrom describes the typical layout of the fields of the Zanjera Irrigation communities in the Philippines (Fig. 7) as an example of a CPR (Ostrom, 1995; Coward, 1978). This case shows the irrigation facilities and water management of plot-to-plot irrigation, but does not offer any details concerning the delivery of water at the quaternary level.

Shiroyone-no-Senmaida (meaning: the thousands of paddy plots in the Shiroyone area) in Wajima City is renowned for its rice terraces and water management techniques that have existed for more than several hundred years. This area was officially designated as a precious site of Globally Important Agricultural Heritage Systems (GIAHS) in 2011.

More than 1000 plots, each on a small-scale ranging from 10 m² to a few dozen m² (totalling only *c*.3 ha), are provided with irrigation water through 5 km of canals. The outstanding point here is that the water is distributed quite fairly by means of an elaborate and precise distribution practice.

Fig. 8 shows a portion of this practice by describing one cultivator by one circle (henceforth called a block). The system is complicated so that the water from one block flows into several blocks and the irrigation water is repeatedly reused. The complexity of this system requires an adjustment through trial and error until all cultivators reach a final agreement, which had been retained without alterations.

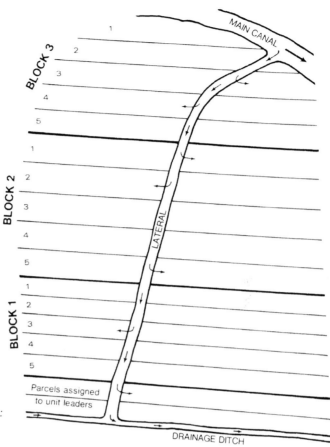

Figure 7. The Zanjera irrigation system (Ostorm: 1990).

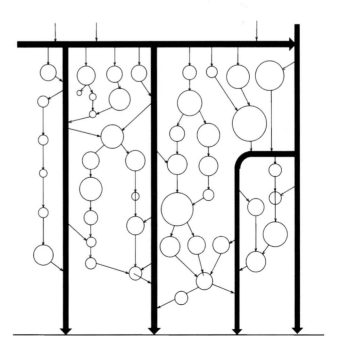

Figure 8. The water distribution in a rice terrace. Original drawing by Tamura, Z. (2003). Processed and modified by Ishii, A.

Figure 9. The paddy plot and inlet/outlet. Original photograph by Tamura, Z. (2003). Processed and modified by Ishii, A.

Within each block, as shown in Fig. 9, a plot-to-plot irrigation has been implemented. For example, plot B intakes water via A. Plots C and D can receive water through q and r.

7. The Participatory Irrigation Management

The Participatory Irrigation Management (PIM) is one of development polities and states the necessity of forming an irrigational organization. It is notable that prior to this policy LIDs were organized in Japan, presenting the significance of indigenous skills and knowledge in the OMM of facilities and water distribution. In this context, the institutional framework of LIDs proposes a good reference for the PIM in the following perspectives:

- Institutionalization of farmers' irrigational organizations

- Cost/labour-sharing in institutional management

Furthermore, when compared to LIDs, the PIM has several points to be reconsidered in terms of sustainability of resource management and institution:

- The perspective of the Public Private Partnership (PPP)

This was originally included in the LID management scheme. In the legal framework of LIDs, as previously explained in the context of present irrigation projects, the authority (under the name of the Minister of Agriculture, Forestry and Fisheries) is in charge of the construction of irrigation facilities in response to farmers' voluntary requests. Management, on the other hand, is under the control of the farmers' irrigation groups in commission. Indigenous skills and knowledge are utilized in management. In this sense, LIDs propose the possibility of a PIM concept for the future.

- Majority of voting and other democratic procedures
  LIDs demonstrate the necessity of elaboration as to the institutional management in foreign projects.

- The problem of identifying membership
  This is the main cause of poor collection of irrigation fees and thus one of the tasks for international organizations to overcome. Based on local villages (*mura*) in the stratified structure of the irrigation commons, membership could be identified without any difficulty.

- The combination of duties (i.e., OMM, cost-sharing etc.) and rights (i.e., the withdrawal of water, voting etc.)
  This should be included in the fundamental principles of the PIM: beneficiaries should pay for benefits. The lack of ownership initiative in unsuccessful foreign projects is largely caused by a lack of understanding of the corresponding relationship between them.

Considering these points, the skills and knowledge (which appear in a management framework of a LID) are implicative for the PIM, rather retain essential properties as the intrinsic PIM.

8. Conclusions

The cultivated rice irrigation system consists of irrigation facilities as well as irrigation management, which are indispensable to each other in terms of efficient water use and sustainability through the proper interaction of humanity and nature. Therefore, the perspective of institutions, which substantially allows facilities to function, is important when considering the value of heritage.

The skills and knowledge as to irrigation management have been regarded as the irrigation commons, CPRs, managed by long-enduring organizations. LIDs, examples of these organizations, have not only matured the governance of the irrigation groups but have also come with governability among farmers.

As irrigation technology has developed, irrigation facilities as well as the supportive skills and knowledge were modernized changing their appearances. In certain cases, the rules applied to water distribution were reviewed and modified accordingly. Here, the fundamental framework of irrigation management itself remains based on rural villages (*mura*) within the stratified structure of the irrigation commons and played the principal role in readjustment of the rules. Thus, institutional skills and knowledge regarded as heritable are necessary for a sustainable OMM of the irrigation commons, supporting cultivated rice irrigation system for more than 2500 years ever since it was disseminated from the continent to the Japanese archipelago.

The framework of common-pool resources could also be a principle for tackling the recent changes of rural society. With the increasing burden of proper management of terminal irrigation facilities by a decreasing number of farmers, it was recognized that a new government-led program should be implemented (to be introduced in 2007) by mobilizing non-farmers with the understanding that the framework of CPRs within rural villages (e.g., skills and knowledge) was core to institutional management (the Ministry of Agriculture, Forestry and Fisheries of Japan, 2010).

The invariance of following factors is notable: the physical properties of water (i.e., gravity-fed and fluctuation) and the social characteristics of irrigation associations, which have been in charge of irrigation management institutions. The cultivated rice irrigation system, which embraces facilities and institutions, has proven to be sustainable regardless of time and space. It can be sustainably passed down as heritable to future generations by properly adapting to technical and social changes.

Acknowledgement

We would like to acknowledge the dedicated support of Prof. A. Ishii who presented the generous opportunity to pursue this topic and encouragement based on a corroborative study.

References

Coward, E. Walter Jr. 1979. Principles of Social Organization in an Indigenous Irrigation System, *Human Organization* 38: 28-36.

Ikehashi, Hiroshi. 2005. *The origin of cultivated rice paddy* [*Inasaku-no-kigen* originally in Japanese]. Kodansha Press: Tokyo.

Iwata, Toshiharu. and Okamoto, Masami. 2000. The stratified construction of the Japanese farmer water users community and its function [Nihon-no-jusouteki-nouminsuirisosiki-no-kouzou-to-kinou originally in Japanese], *Transaction of rural planning* 2: 181-186. Japan International Cooperation Agency (JICA). 2011. *Participatory Irrigation Management Organizations in Japan.* JICA: Tokyo.

Ministry of Agriculture, Forestry and Fisheries of Japan. 2010. *Interim Report of Farmland-water-environment preservation and enhancement program* [*Nouchi-mizu-kankyo-hozenkoujyo-taisaku-no-chukanhyoka*: originally in Japanese].

Ostrom, Eliner. 1990. *Governing the Commons; The Evolution of Institutions for Collective Action.* Cambridge University Press: Cambridge.

Sato, Masao. 1978. *People living with Takina River* [*Takinagawa-ni-ikiru-hitobito*: originally in Japanese]. Michinoku-nousan-mondai-kenkyujo.

Shinzawa, Kagatou. and Okamoto, Masami. 1978. *Development and coordination among water users and sectors* [*Suiri-no-Kaihatsu-to-chosei*: originally in Japanese]. Jicho-sha: Tokyo.

Sugiura, Mikiko. 2005. Factors of Water Trade in Japanese History: Case Study of Kamiyokoyama village in Niigata Prefecture, *Journal of Water and Environmental Issues*, 18: 1-14.

Sugiura, Mikiko., Ishii, Atsushi., and Tajima, Masahiro. 2013. Collisions of traditional Commons with the modernized institution of rice-paddy irrigation systems in Japan, Conference paper at the 14th Conference of International Association for the study of the Commons http://dlc.dlib.indiana.edu/dlc/bitstream/handle/10535/8972/SUGIURA_0133.pdf?sequence=1.

Tamura, Zenjiro. 2003. *The Enigma of terraced rice field* [*Tanada-no-nazo*: originally in Japanese]. TEM Kenkyujo: Nousan-gyoson-bunka-kyokai.

Tajima, Masahiro., Ishii, Atsushi., and Miwa, Hajime. 2009. Practice and mechanism of rotational irrigation in the rice-paddy, *Journal of the Japanese Society of Irrigation, Drainage and Rural Engineering.* 77(7): 559-562.

Van de Ven, Gerard. 2004. *Man-made lowlands: History of water management and land reclamation in the Netherlands.* Uitgeverij Matrijs: Utrecht.

The Deltaworks: heritage and new space for a changing world

Marinke Steenhuis

The Deltaworks as national project of technique and culture

The construction of the Deltaworks in the period 1956-1986 has been defining for the economic, environmental and social development of southwest Netherlands. With the Afsluitdijk, the Zuiderzee polders, the port of Rotterdam and the (prematurely foundered) Ecological Masterplan (Ecologische Hoofdstructuur), the Deltaworks belong to the 'big five' of the 20th century engineering projects that have shaped our watery land. Our delta and the way in which the Dutch live in this dynamic landscape, elicits international admiration. The accumulation of environmental and cultural activities in this area is huge. The delta forms the cradle of our culture, an area that is home to millions of people, it is where two

Figure 1. Photo of inundated Zeeland (ML).

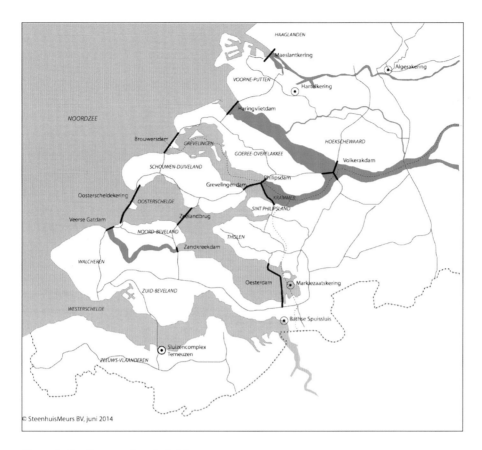

Figure 2. Outline map Steenhuis/Meurs.

major European ports are located, where farmers cultivate their crops, and where many people go on holiday for the historical towns and the recreational facilities and natural beauty. After the 1953 Floods, when 2000 people drowned and large parts of Zeeland and South Holland were inundated for months, fourteen dams and barriers were constructed within 25 years protecting the vulnerable Dutch delta against storm surges.

With the Delta programme, the Delta Act of 2012 and the Delta Decisions of 2014, the issue of the cultural assessment and future of the dams and barriers has become more urgent. So far cultural history was regarded as subordinate to measures to improve structurally the water safety in the Netherlands. However, in this research the new face of the heritage sector is shown; here the preservation of objects is not the sole objective but rather the building of new environmental qualities on top of existing qualities. The two parties laid down in a covenant that the cultural-historical values of public works should be considered in transformational projects, so that a more area-oriented way of working is created in which the interests of the economy, environment and heritage are evaluated and integrated. And thus the Netherlands takes leave of the sectorial approach which originated in the Environmental Planning Act (Wet op de Ruimtelijke Ordening)

(1965), and conversely specific solutions are sought which will emphasise and strengthen the recognisability, history and identity of our land.

The research team took this as its starting point and carried out intensive research of sources and fieldwork, wrote a cultural-historical analysis and evaluation of sixteen works in the Delta in their environmental context.[1] In this study, entitled *50 years of Deltaworks – the Deltaworks viewed from a cultural-historical perspective*, (50 jaar Deltawerken – de Delta werken bekeken vanuit cultuurhistorisch perspectief) the barriers and dams were investigated in a wider landscape context. The team distinguishes in this study the historical value (the story behind it), the planning framework (how are the values now guaranteed/protected) and formulated essential characteristics (how can the values be used in the future). With the integrated approach of the Deltaworks the course put into action before the war of integral design became the standard for our national environmental planning culture - until roughly the year 2000. Now that the present liberal cabinet abandons the central government steering with the 'Structure Outlook Infrastructure and Environment' (Structuurvisie Infrastructuur en Ruimte), large institutional parties, like Rijkswaterstaat (an agency of the Department of Infrastructure and the Environment and responsible for waterways and coastal defence), the National Railways and large real estate owners, take the lead. This pilot study sets out the

Figure 3. Overview in photos of 14 Deltaworks and two bridge and sluice complexes in the Delta. (Beeldbank Rijkswaterstaat)

---

1   The author is owner/director of SteenhuisMeurs bv, an office Schiedam/Paterswolde, SteenhuisMeurs, a bureau for cultural-historical research and environmental analysis.

conditions for an integral approach of technique, landscape and planning of the Deltaworks, as was definitely the case when the works were conceived.

The pilot study has been made on the basis of four main sources: the three-monthly Delta Reports (Deltaberichten) and annual reports of the Dutch Forestry Commission (Staatsbosbeheer), the National Archive and Zeeuws Archive (Deltadienst), existing literature, conversations and site visits with former employees of the Deltadienst, landscape architects and civil engineers. Without them the system and the beauty of the Deltaworks would not have come to life so strongly.

The 1953 Floods and the establishment of the Delta Service in 1956

"We are confronted, in my opinion, and expressed in plain words, by the choice to either raise more than a thousand kilometres of dikes by one metre or more – in some areas a task technically very difficult to execute – or to close a few tidal inlets in such a way that the coastline, which is threatened by the storm surges, is shortened considerably." (Minister J. Algera said on 21st February 1953, right after the Flood disaster).

The Deltaworks are famous as a defensive system; the whole world came and still comes to see the hydrological engineering wonder that after the 1953 Floods was executed at an accelerated pace. After all, the Storm Surge Committee had been working since 1939 on a plan to close off the great estuaries, so that the plans for a gigantic coastline shortening were in fact ready. The disaster of 1st February 1953 resulted in the political will and provision of the financial resources to execute this ambitious plan, as becomes clear from the above quote. But the meaning of the Deltaworks goes much beyond protection against the dangerous sea. In this national, cultural project politics and science came together in a splendid way, as did mathematics and hydrological engineering, environmental planning, landscape architecture and organisational acumen. The Delta Service, a project organisation founded in 1956, was the service that came under Rijkswaterstaat and that designed and coordinated the works. It was a highly effective service with extremely short lines to politics and science. The culture there was characterised, wholly against the spirit of the time, by horizontal knowledge structures and working with scenarios. In the 24 years that the Service existed, the organisation continually reinvented itself, thus new methods of food risk assessment, new social claims like ecology and nature values, but also new ways of thinking (scenario planning) were introduced. The objective of the co-ordinating Delta Service, abolished in 1980, was to make the Deltaworks not only flood defence but also to create landscape and recreational excess value and to halt the salination of agricultural soil. New agricultural lands, recreation beaches, islands, woods and recreation harbours were created in the wake of the Deltaworks. Zeeland escaped from its infrastructural isolation and became a leisure destination of the post-war welfare state. Now, about sixty years after the start of the Deltaworks, it is a surprise for many that really every detail of technique and the surrounding landscape has been designed accomodating a variety of environmental claims. Not only did the Deltaworks protect the southwest Netherlands, this Sleeping Beauty also woke up for the holiday makers and meant a structural change in the trade infrastructure, agriculture and fishing. New nature was created in the 1950s and evolved into new habitats.

Engineering art in the landscape

The State Service of Rijkswaterstaat (Ministry of Infrastructure and the Environment), as 'corporate designer of the Dutch landscape', has already close to a century a tradition of integrating engineering work with architectural and landscape care. This central government steering forms the secret of the Dutch environmental and landscape quality and creates a favourable climate for business development. In all large 20th century government projects for motorways, waterways, land consolidation and even power pylons technical specifications were accompanied by a landscape design. New infrastructure works represented the progress of the country, and deserved a careful fitting in, just as the large land reclamations of the 17th century had contributed to the landscape identity of this land created by people. For instance in the 1930s Ir G.A. Overdijkink addressed the landscaping around the national road scheme and the vegetation bordering the Twente canals. Also engaging top architects like Dudok and Roosenburg for the Afsluitdijk, also in the 1930s, indicated the pride Rijkswaterstaat took in technical process and beauty.

After 1945 the involvement of (landscape) architects in engineering works of Rijkswaterstaat was continued, culminating in the integral technical and esthetical design of the Deltaworks. With the execution of the Deltaworks the foundation was laid for the policy of integrating all aspects of environmental planning: waterways, agriculture, traffic, nature, recreation and social-cultural development. This interdisciplinary approach, started with the pre-war construction of the Zuiderzee polders and the reconstruction of Walcheren[2], had evolved into a 'win-win situation' in which the interests of the waterways (the dams and barriers), agriculture (land consolidation and protecting against the influx of seawater), traffic (social and economic opening up), nature, recreation (Grevelingen, Veerse Meer) joined up to determine the appearance of the southwest Netherlands and this approach applied to the Deltaworks became the standard for post-war regional planning and design.

Flood risk assessment

The collective brain of a new generation of mathematicians and hydrological engineers brought about a reassessment of the calculation of flood risks: instead of absolute flood calculations, the flood models were from then on evaluated based on probability calculations, while for the Oosterscheldt barrier the risk of failure was taken into account. A proponent of the new models was the secretary of the

---

2   M. Steenhuis, Stedenbouw in de landschap. Pieter Verhagen (1882-1950), Rotterdam 2007.

Storm Surge committee, Dr Ir Johan van Veen (1893-1959). From the evaluation report of the Deltacommissie Rapport Deltacommissie) which appeared in 1960 in six parts[3]:

> *"The Storm Surge committee departed from the earlier procedure in which the crown height of the dikes was determined on the basis of the water levels that were observed at different storm surges. The committee has investigated separately each factor that affects storm surges and further determined the maximums of each of these factors. Furthermore, a number of storm surges that had occurred were studied, while probability calculations showed the expected heights and frequencies of the high storm surges."[4]*

The Deltaworks led to research in new laboratories, like the scale models that were tested in the Waterloopkundig (hydrodynamic) laboratory 'de Voorst' in the then recently reclaimed Noordoostpolder and the Deltar computer (Delta Getij Analogon Rekenmachine) from 1960, the methodology of which is based on the analogy of the phenomena of water and electricity.

Sociology and planning

The insights of the social and planning sciences were introduced into the thought patterns of Rijkswaterstaat via the National Planning Office (Rijksdienst voor het Nationale Plan – RNP); engineers were thus assisted by social and planning researchers. Extensive research was undertaken into the opportunities for recreation, nature development, traffic flows, industry, agriculture and salination, and employment. The characteristic 'social engineering' of the post-war welfare state also put in an appearance; old peoples' homes were deemed necessary to 'put an end to the traditional living together in farming societies.'

Agriculture

For a long time Zeeland had to contend with agricultural soils turning brackish as a result of the seawater intrusion far into the land. Blocking the estuaries solved that problem and provided at the same time an opportunity to increase the productivity of agriculture through large-scale consolidations of highly fragmented holdings. Also landscape architects were intensively involved with the layout of the new agricultural parcels of land so that not only the coastal zone of the inundated areas changed shape but virtually the whole of Zeeland – under a central technical and esthetical direction.

Nature and recreation

Noticeable is also the ambition to develop, already in the 1950s, new green areas for the recreational purposes where the public would also get access to more public-friendly terrains. On the maps made by the RNP are nature and leisure areas

---

3   Rapport Deltacommissie, Eindverslag en interimadviezen (6 delen) Den Haag (1960).
4   Rapport Deltacommissie, Eindverslag en interimadviezen (6 delen) Den Haag (1960), deel 1, p. 16.

Figure 4. Landscape design land consolidation Schouwen-Duiveland, before and after.

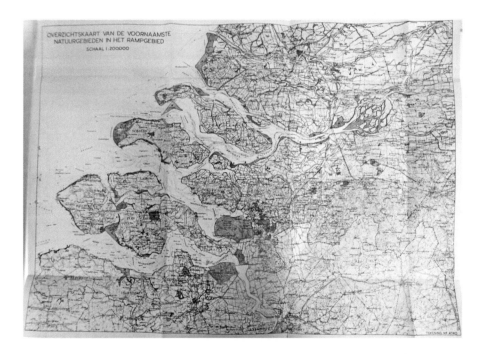

Figure 5. Nature map, National Archive.

indicated on sand flats in the closed-off estuaries, as well as along the new inland waterways. The maps indicated huge opportunities for the leisure demand of the Randstad Holland (conurbation of western Holland). So the Deltaworks were directly connected with the planning developments of the large cities in Holland. On the right of the map the Friesian lakes, the area of small lakes in Holland and the Veluwe are also referenced.

Infrastructure

The accessibility of Zeeland after the Deltaworks was mainly seen from the perspective of public recreation. After all, the horticultural possibilities for Zeeland were limited as were the possibilities for industry. Apart from transportation of agricultural produce, the road network should be able to absorb the tourists. In 195x the famous planner Ir Th.K. van Lohuizen in a speech for the Delta committee said:

> "When in the long run an uninterrupted line of dunes with a beach would form in front of the dams, great possibilities will be created for leisure activities. A 'beach road' behind those dunes would become very attractive, also for traffic to and from the Belgian coast."

That coastal road was built (the so-called 'Dam route'), but also a Zoomweg (fringe road) providing a convenient route for heavy traffic from Rotterdam in the direction of Bergen op Zoom and onwards.

The integration of all the above aspects will be clear in a closer consideration of the Brouwers dam, constructed between 1963 and 1972, and Volkeraks complex, constructed between 1957 and 1977.

Figure 6. Map with the coastal route and transport route, National Archive.

Brouwers dam: a landscape at sea

The Delta Service realised the 6.5 kilometre long Brouwers dam in the period 1963-1972. For the first time this service aimed at water safety involved the landscape designers of the State Forest Service (Staatsbosbeheer) in the design of this 'landscape at sea'. Together with the Grevelingen dam, the Brouwers dam closed off the Brouwershavense Gat, thus creating the salt and still Grevelingen Lake.

The Brouwers dam is, apart from the Oosterscheldt barrier, the largest work in the Delta plan. It was one of the four so-called 'principal works': primary dams that closed off an estuary from the influences of the North Sea. The scale of the work and the civil engineering methods were imposing, but the actual innovation of the Brouwers dam lay in the interdisciplinary approach of the design. Alongside the engineers of Rijkswaterstaat also landscape architects were given a prominent role. For the first time the form of the Deltaworks was not only determined by civil engineering requirements but also by 'soft' values like the proper fit into the landscape, good views and providing possibilities for recreational activities. Landscape architect professor Ir Adriaan Geuze:

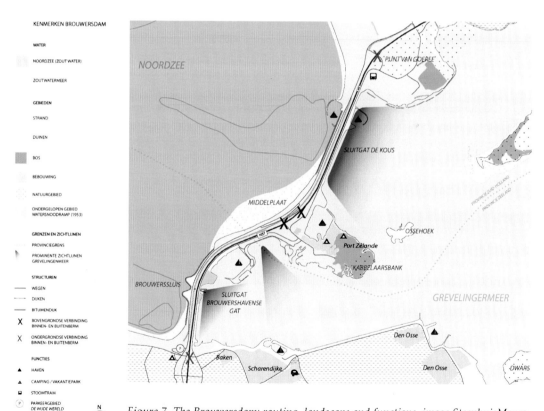

Figure 7. The Brouwersdam: routing, landscape and functions, image SteenhuisMeurs.

"The Brouwers dam has been designed so generously: you can go over the dam, under the dam and along the inside. She wears a beautiful crown, which over time nature has made! Drifting sand is now being swept away because of traffic. Don't sweep I would say. The Brouwers dam is the most beautiful spot of the Netherlands."

The Brouwers dam had to close off the 6.5 kilometre wide Brouwershavense Gat, a sea arm with a multitude of sand flats, salt marshes and mudflats. The start of the work had to wait until the Grevelingen dam had been completed. Without this secondary dam, which was located more inland, the rates of flow that would have been created in the Zijpe, the water connecting the Brouwershavense Gat with the Oosterscheldt, would have been too great.[5] When determining the location the Deltaworks took several factors into account. Firstly, the dam had to be as short and as cheap as possible, in addition the road on the dam had to link up in a logical manner with the new road pattern of the land consolidation on Schouwen-Duiveland, and lastly it was important to get as many sand flats and as much water area within the enclosure, which would be advantageous for the water balance and the planned recreation around the Grevelingen Lake created by the closure.[6]

The construction of the Brouwers dam took nearly ten years and was executed section by section. The construction methods and operating procedures with caissons and cable lifts, which were used with earlier dams, were tested and after further development adopted for the Brouwers dam. The idea was that in its turn the Brouwers dam would provide a testing ground before starting the final part of the Deltaworks, the complex Oosterscheldt barrier. The construction started out in the sea on the sandy Middelplaat and Kabbelaarsplaat. On each sand flat a dam section and a supply port was built. The sand that became available when excavating the port was used directly to raise the dam section. After building the dam sections and the relatively easy closing off of the narrow Kabbelaars canal between them, the last gaps De Kous (north, c. 14 metres deep) and the Brouwershavense Gat (south, c. 27 metres deep) were closed off. De Kous could be closed with permeable caissons (the construction method that had proved so successful in the Veerse Gat), but the great depth of the Brouwershavense Gat forced the engineers to use a different technique, namely the dumping of concrete blocks on the dam with the help of cable lifts, as earlier used with the Grevelingen dam.[7] It was absolutely essential that the two gaps were closed simultaneously as closing only one would create unmanageable currents in the other.

According to Ir M.J. Loschacoff, former director of the Delta Service, the Brouwers dam was the first dam for which the landscape aspects were explicitly considered in an integral, interdisciplinary approach.[8] The idea was to develop the whole area between the Brouwers dam and the Grevelingen dam, a total of 15,000

---

5   Driemaandelijks bericht Deltawerken no. 4 (1957-1959), p. 40 (Quarterly report).
6   Driemaandelijks bericht Deltawerken, no. 24 (1963-1964), p. 185.
7   Driemaandelijks bericht Deltawerken, no. 43 (1967-1969), p. 129.
8   M.J. Loschacoff, Forum 37 (1993) 1, p. 27.

hectares of water and land, as a scenic and recreation area with national appeal.[9] In 1967 Staatsbosbeheer designers Ellen Brandes and Nico de Jonge became responsible for the landscape plan – which encompassed the entire Grevelingen basin. The high ambitions resulted for the Brouwers dam in a nearly 6.5 km long 'landscape at sea', in which the dam, contrary to the Haringvliet sluices and locks or the Oosterscheldt barrier, as a technical tour de force was masked by a wide and gentle profile. On the outside of the dam towards the sea, the slope was covered with tarmac, a clear reference to its function as water barrier, with at the foot a vast beach, in fact a continuation of the sea coast. On the inside of the dam, the slope was greener and gentler, befitting the shore of a lake. Like a Dutch Copacabana – which by the way was designed at the same time – the dam features multiple spaces, with separate traffic flows for every user, whether passing through or recreational. The roads on the inside shoulder were constructed at different levels, thus providing everybody with an unobstructed view of the Grevelingen Lake. Good cycle and pedestrian routes linked (amongst others by tunnels) both sides of the dam. A continuation of the dune landscape was opted for where the dam reached Goeree-Overflakee. The latter had by the way also a pragmatic reason. Loschacoff: "*tarmac was expensive and environmental people loved sand and dunes. Making a dune in very deep water is expensive but at the Goeree dam head it would be cheaper as it was less deep, and at the same time more beautiful.*"[10]

Special attention was also given to the landscape design of the access roads to the dam, in particular the road between the Haringvliet dam and the Brouwers dam.[11]

An important point of departure for the further design was the recreational role that the dam would have to play. The Delta Service wrote in 1978: "*The areas closed in by the primary dams can be assigned a high recreational potential. The outside can develop into a new North Sea beach; on the inside the supply ports and construction docks can play a role in the development of water sports; while the adjoining flats and temporary islands will provide spaces for shore recreation.*"[12]

As recreational attraction the Brouwers dam was indeed successful from the outset. A large holiday camp has been established and events are organised there such as the World championships kite surfing and Concert at Sea.

The areas in the vicinity of the dam were going to be developed also for recreation according to the plan of 1967, but this proved to be too expensive. In 1977 a New Development Draft (Nieuw Inrichtingsschets) was determined for the Grevelingen basin in which the emphasis was moved from recreation to the development of nature and the use of the natural potential in the development of the now dry land areas. The Rijksdienst IJsselmeerpolders (State Service for the IJsselmeer polders) (RIJP) took over the baton from Staatsbosbeheer and became responsible for this design. This meant for the Brouwers dam that the Kabbelaars bank was further developed as a nature area and that the Punt van Goeree (Goeree

---

9   Marinke Steenhuis (red.), Maakbaar Landschap, p. 311.
10   Interview with M.J. Loschacoff, 3rd November 2013.
11   Annual report Staasbosbeheer1964, p. 13
12   Driemaandelijks bericht Deltawerken no. 85 (1978), p. 252.

Figure 8. Landscape design isles and shores of the closed estuary Grevelingen, State Forest Service, around 1966.

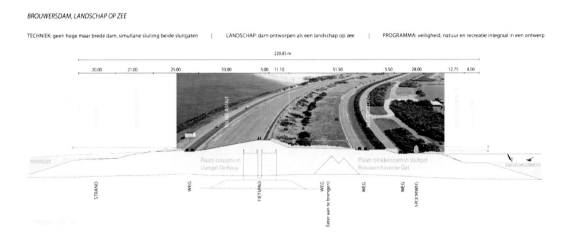

BROUWERSDAM, LANDSCHAP OP ZEE

TECHNIEK: geen hoge maar brede dam, simultane sluiting beide sluitgaten | LANDSCHAP: dam ontworpen als een landschap op zee | PROGRAMMA: veiligheid, natuur en recreatie integraal in een ontwerp

Figure 9. Profile of the Brouwersdam, image SteenhuisMeurs.

Point) was planted with shrubs and brushwood.[13] This emphasis on nature development committed to in the 1970s was expressed in another measure. In the original plans the Grevelingen Lake would become completely fresh water in order to serve as fresh water basin for amongst others agriculture. The disappearance of the tidal movement and the water slowly turning to fresh water would damage the existing ecosystem which could not be reconciled with the new ecological aims. It was therefore decided to try to retain the Grevelingen Lake as a salt water basin by building a draining sluice in the southernmost dam section.[14] Thus Europe's

13   Both these designs are from the hand of the landscape architect Eddy Hendriks.
14   Driemaandelijks bericht Deltawerken no. 79 (February1977), p. 508.

largest saltwater lake was created. Although a number of areas have become valuable breeding and nature areas, it has in the meantime been found that the water in the Grevelingen Lake gets too little oxygen.[15] The draining sluice near the Brouwershavensegat is not sufficient, there are therefore plans for a tidal plant near the closed off sea arm de Kous. At present the construction of a tidal power station on the Brouwers dam is widely discussed. On 10 October 2014 the Cabinet endorsed a Government White Paper on Grevelingen and Volkerak-Zoommeer (Rijksstructuurvisie Grevelingen en Volkerak-Zoommeer), in which the tidal power station is incorporated as project. A return of tides has its proponents and opponents: it will mean major ecological changes to the Natura-2000 designated area, which may involve raising of dikes and increasing heights of bridges over the Scheldt-Rhine canal.

The Volkerak complex

Not only protection against storm surges but also the strict separation of salt-fresh water was a major factor in the hydrological design. Between Goeree-Overflakee and Noord-Brabant, near the junctions where Haringvliet, Hollands Diep and Volkerak come together, is the 4.5 km long Volkerak dam and locks complex forming a traffic junction on water. Together with other works, the Volkerak dam forms a system that makes it possible to distribute the surface water of the rivers Rhine and Meuse.

If you would have to explain the complexity and meaning of the Deltaworks to a tourist, a visit to the Volkerak complex would be essential because of the successful combination of hydrological, traffic technical and landscape engineering. The works played as many as four roles in the Delta plan, which will explain immediately the complexity of this work. Apart from the function as secondary dam – to ease the construction of the Brouwers dam, the Oosterscheldt barrier and the Haringvliet dam there has been a desire since 1937 to connect the coastal areas of Zuid-Holland, Noord-Brabant and Zeeland.

Hydrologically the Volkerak works were given the task to transport the surface and ice water of the Rhine and Meuse via the Haringvliet to the sea. The Volkerak dam would keep separate the salt water that entered via the Haringvliet sluices into the Haringvliet and the fresh water of the Volkerak. Apart from a sluice for fresh water from the Hollands Diep, locks were also to be included for the important shipping route Antwerp-Rhine. In short: the Volkerak complex is a dam, a fresh-salt water barrier, a traffic roundabout, a bridge, a sluice and a lock in one. The final location of the works was the Hellegat (Hell Hole), the junction of the three waters Haringvliet, Volkerak and Hollands Diep. By giving the work the shape of a three-pointed star a hydrological division was created between the Haringvliet, the Volkerak and the Hollands Diep, as well as the desired connection between the three provinces. But above all there was here enough space to have enough distance between the sluices and locks to avoid problems with water flows.

---

15 http://www.zwdelta.nl/opgaven/rijksstructuurvisie-grevelingen-volkerak-zoommeer.htm, consulted on 14th October 2013.

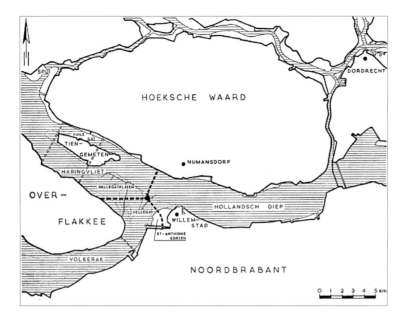

*Figure 10. Different delineations used in preparation of the
Volkerakwaterworks.*

After the construction of a supply port just west of Willemstad and the very
long land-reclamation and current-conducting dams – still visible in the landscape
– which made the construction easier, work on the western arm could start: a
dam over the Hellegats sandflats. With these existing sandflats as basis a 4.5 km
long dam was raised. A width of about 40 metres was sufficient for a dual-carriage
motorway, a cycling track and a road for slow traffic. As long as the Haringvliet
was not closed off, the surge of the waves was very strong on the northern side
of the dam. This side of the dam was given a gentle slope and a wave break dike
that could be removed once the Haringvliet had been closed. And lastly the deep
Ventjagersgaatje was closed off with cheap and currant-resistant Silex. At the same
time work was progressing on the Hellegats road junction at the centre of the
island. The island was raised with 800,000 m³ of sand to three metres above NAP
(Dutch Ordnance Datum). The government drew up the specifications for the
Haringvliet bridge and supervised the construction but as the bridge was not an
official water barrier it was financed by the company N.V. Brugverbinding Goeree-
Overflakee and Hoekse Waard. The total length of the bridge was 1200 metres.
One section of the bridge could be opened for shipping.

The construction of the eastern arm of the Volkerak dam with the sluices and
locks was more complex. The last gap was closed in 1969 with twelve permeable
caissons which were floated against the current to location. The complex of locks
with entry and exit ponds ended up partly in the former polder between the summer
and winter dikes of Maltha, an area of 'reed marshes' west of Willemstad. Here was
enough space for the construction of the locks. The locks including the ponds had
a total length of four km. As the Volkerak was one of the busiest shipping lanes of
the Netherlands, two locks were projected, with every lock chamber 320 metres

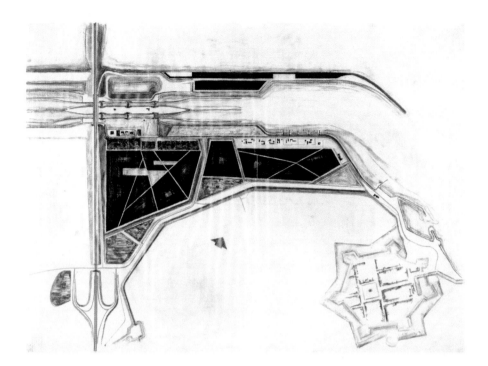

Figure 11. Landscape design around the sluices of the Volkerak, State Forest Service, around 1968.

long and 24 metres wide. The locks were equipped with a partition (intermediate head) halfway the lock chamber thus enabling several ships in close succession to be locked. In addition to a central control room, engine room and depot annex workshop, a small office was built on every lock island. Every head has a separate control panel allowing fully mechanised operation from the office.

The three legs of the Volkerak complex each have their very own character and not only because of differences in function or building method. The different landscape designs for each part of the Volkerak complex created an impressive series of planned landscapes. South of the sluice complex landscape architects Nico de Jonge and Ellen Brandes of Staatsbosbeheer designed a monumental wooded area to bridge the difference in scale between the huge sluice complex and the small-scale Brabant landscape. Diagonal paths cut through the wood ended up in open areas with shapes that were inspired by the searchlights. Ornamental shrubbery was planted around the office buildings. On either side of the ponds were windscreens of tightly planted lines of trees. A specially designed observation tower provided an excellent overview of the locks.

For the access road from the Hoekse Waard to the Haringvliet, Rijkswaterstaat investigated where this could be best sited. A determined effort was made to achieve a pleasing design in which the most important requirements were the perception of the landscape on the route towards the bridge and the view onto the river landscape. In contrast to the way the sluices and the bridge could be fitted into the landscape, the Volkerak dam and the Hellegats junction design allowed more

Figure 12. Volkerak Works in 1983. On top the Haringvliet bridge, at the bottom the Volkerak Works. Beeldbank Rijkswaterstaat.

room for nature. Landscape architect Bram Elffers of Staatsbosbeheer developed the vegetation plan for the dunes of the Hellegats juntion.

For the reclaimed lands south of the dam, Staatsbosbeheer made a proposal for woods, planting of trees and a beach. Later nature was given a free rein. At present it looks as if the vegetation developed spontaneously.

The road over the Haringvliet bridge and the Volkerak dam soon became a popular route considerably reducing the travel time between Zuid-Holland and Zeeland. In the 1980s the fly-over connection over the N59 was made for traffic from Willemstad to Zierikzee. The Hellegats juntion is still a busy traffic junction. The use of the locks complex also turned out to be heavier than expected. Particularly recreational shipping experienced a huge increase. Between 1970 and 1975 the complex was therefore expanded with a third lock for commercial shipping and a separate one for leisure craft. A sluice was also added to counteract the salt problem in the northern Delta basin. The Volkerak sluices and locks are nowadays seen as the busiest and biggest inland-navigation lock complex of Europe. As shipping is still expanding there are plans to enlarge the complex with a fourth lock in the future. A new operations building was recently built on the south side of the locks and the development of the grounds around it has been adjusted. In the wooded area perpendicular to the locks nature has gained the upper hand. The straight paths in the wood are overgrown with weeds and new winding footpaths have been built.

Self improving system

The culture at the Delta Service, determined by horizontal knowledge structures, thinking in models, and continual evaluation, was so strong that technical innovations and new social claims (for instance ecology) could be incorporated and the Deltaworks can be typified as the result of a self-improving system. In a so-called innovation matrix (see next page) we have described for each Deltawork the decisive technical, landscape and programmatic innovations.

The Deltaworks: building on existing qualities

The construction of roads across the dams opened up Zeeland, the isolated group of islands where customs, traditions, religion were frozen in time, to the rest of the Netherlands and vice versa. Zeeland had to enter the 20th century whether it wanted or not. The plans for large-scale land reclamation and the massive port developments gradually gave way to an emphasis on new nature areas (already mentioned in 1957!) and large areas for mass recreation, designed by top landscape architects. The construction of the Deltaworks was complemented by the creation of a first class landscape which made the southwest of the Netherlands a favourite destination for the Dutchmen with increasingly more spare time. Now, 55 years after the construction of the first Deltawork, some changes to the structures are unavoidable as the safety of our delta must always come first. The guiding design vision behind the landscape of the Deltaworks has lost none of its power or poetry and can be found in the alliance of geomorphology and vegetation and, just as essential, the feeling and experiencing of the transitions between sea and land, polder and dam. Notions like scale, unity, readability and an emphasis on transitions are crucial. The strength of the Deltaworks is the converging of the 'hard' and 'soft' worlds to a systematic structure of unparalleled cohesion. Technical innovations went hand in hand with landscape-, social and programmatic improvements. The views of social and planning sciences were introduced into the world of waterways and coastal defence via the National Planning Office (RNP). At present the roles seem to have reversed; the main focus is now to study and mitigate or compensate the economic, ecological and social consequences of the Delta decisions. Many parties are studying as many plans for different aspects. It is conceivable that that way we may miss the right moment to realise actual technical, programmatic and landscape innovations and to thus help the Deltaworks into the 21st century.

The superb quality of all the Deltaworks deserves that they are one by one investigated as a coherent system of barrier, dam, architecture, landscape, recreation, nature and agriculture. This is not meant to be a history lesson but

INNOVATION MATRIX: THE PROGRESSIVE SYSTEM OF THE DELTA WORKS

PERIOD	CONSTRUCTION	WORK	CHARACTERISTIC	TECHNIQUE	LANDSCAPE	PROGRAM
1932 Construction Afsluit dyke 1953 Flood						
1953 Foundation Delta committee	1954 - 1958	Algera storm barrier	Holland's safety lock	first storm surge barrier	lifting towers as a gateway to Delta, involvement aesthetic consultant	combination barrier, lock and road
1956 Foundation Delta service	1957 - 1960	Zandkreek dam	The basics	application of caissons on a large scale	limited attention to landscaping	combination of dam, lock and road, no recreation
	1957 - 1977	Volkerak works	Junction on the water	complex combination of various water management functions	design appropriate to each water management function	roundabout on the water
	1958 - 1961	Veerse Gat dam	Testing ground of the Delta Works	primary dam, using large caissons	attempt scenic embedding, formation artificial brackish lake	first experiment with additional recreational functions on dam
1965 Spatial Planning Act	1958 - 1965	Grevelingen dam	Broadening the horizon	first closure with cableway, experimenting with bulk materials	dam designed as part of the leisure and nature area	emphasis on recreational aspect, important for reachability Zeeland
	1958 - 1970	Haringvliet dam	Engineering art on display	primary dam, first drainage sluices complex, reuse of cableway	designed as civil engineering work, clear view from road	dam as a crowd puller with its own exhibits and parking lots
	1963 - 1965	Zeeland bridge	Monument at open sea	first bridge in open water	bridge designed as a landmark in the Oosterschelde	fast connection between the islands of Zeeland
1970 Foundation Club of Rome	1963 - 1972	Brouwers dam	Landscape at sea	not a high but a wide dam, simultaneous closing both gaps	dam designed as a landscape at sea	safety, nature and recreation in an integral design
1973 Opening Oosterschelde	1967 - 1986	Oosterschelde storm surge barrier	Crowning glory of the Delta Works	innovative techniques, strict dimensioning and tolerancing	barrier as inverse of the trenches, engineering guidance on design	dual objective in design: safety and nature
	1976 - 1987	Philips dam	Two face dam	sweet - salt separation system with buffer basins	function dam guidance on design; sweet-salty contrast landscape	viewpoint over the dam, segregation on the water
1978 Protest A27 Amelisweerd	1979 - 1989	Oester dam	Subdued allrounder	first sand closure of deep stream channel	by crisis retrenched design	limited recreational additional position on Speelmansplaten
1983 Economic crisis	1980 - 1983	Marquisate quay	Dam with two lifes	temporarily porous plug quay	formation wetland Markiezaats lake	temporary and permanent feature, linking nature, recreation, housing
	1980 - 1987	Channel and lock of Bath	Siphon of the Zoom lake	control of a large-scale water	integral landscape analysis prior to the design	combined with modest recreational facilities
1987 Decision flood barrier Nieuwe Waterweg	1991 - 1997	Hartel barrier	Lock on the back door	flexible protection of a busy shipping lane	.	
	1991 - 1997	Maeslant barrier	Barrier for an open port	flexible protection of a busy shipping lane	.	turning of barrier on the open port concept, construction consortium

Figure 13. Innovation matrix.

we have to keep thinking about the environmental quality. Landscape architect professor Ir Adriaan Geuze:

> *"The landscape of the Deltaworks is about the relation of man to the sea; they form one splendid ambiance, one of the few places where you as a person can feel an adventurer and at the same time drive your car over the tarmac roads. It is therefore not a world of signposts and entertainment, not a landscape for easy consumption."*

By identifying and appreciating this aspect, the 'intangible' heritage, and at the same time the particulars of every work, including an analysis of prevailing policy and future developments, insight will be created into opportunities and threats. A master plan, in which the course is set for every work in its integral context, is important in order to make (large-scale) changes pass well, technically, programmatically and socially (public support). If you know where you come from, then you can discuss more effectively choices for the future. It is definitely not desirable to freeze the Deltaworks in their context – programmatically it is necessary to differentiate and adapt to future hydrological and social wishes. The question is: how do the essential qualities of each work resonate in the new design stage, so that the Deltaworks gain yet more superb qualities? Professor Ir Bas Jonkman, Technical University Delft: *"The matrix can be a point of departure for this and can be used as checklist in the design."*[16]

16   We should like to thank:
- Drs Jacqueline von Santen (senior consultant Architectuurhistorie), Drs Ellen Vreenegoor (senior consultant Erfgoed en Ruimte), commissioners Rijksdienst Cultureel Erfgoed
- Drs Eli Gehasse (senior advisor cultuurhistorie en Gebiedsgericht werken) and Ir Maarten van der Vlist, (specialist Adaptief Watermanagement), Rijkswaterstaat
- Ir M.J. Loschacoff, Prof. Ir Tjalle de Haan, Deltadienst/Technical University Delft
- Prof. Ir Bas Jonkman, Technical University Delft
- Prof. Ir Adriaan Geuze, Wageningen University
- Ir Eddy Hendriks, Ir Matthieu Pinkers, Ir Evert Vermeer (Formerly Rijksdienst IJsselmeerpolders)
- Projectteam SteenhuisMeurs: Dr Marinke Steenhuis, Ir Johanna van Doorn, Drs Lara Voerman, Ir Joost Emmerik, Drs Minke Walda, Luc Timmermans, BA, Prof. Dr Ir Paul Meurs
- SteenhuisMeurs has considerable experience conducting a balanced discussion on cultural heritage and environmental quality. Cultural-historical investigations are not primarily aimed at formulating recommendations for conservation but rather at investigating scope for changes that do justice to the existing character. In the Q-team Afsluitdijk, Marinke Steenhuis was therefore asked to review all aspects of cultural history, while the office also works for Rijkswaterstaat on the design history and environmental quality of the national waterways. At the office every cultural-historical exploration is carried out by a team with architecture historians and engineers.

Beyond site protection

Embedding natural heritage into sustainable landscapes

Kenneth Irvine

Keywords: *natural heritage, cultural heritance, sustainable development, ecosystem services, scale, wider-countryside.*

Introduction

Water, heritage and development

> *Deterioration or disappearance of any item of the cultural or natural heritage constitutes a harmful impoverishment of the heritage of all the nations of the world.* (The UNESCO 1972 Convention concerning the Protection of the World Cultural and Natural Heritage)

Heritage recognises important social traditions, man-made structures and the natural environment that pass from one generation to another. The components of heritage are often inextricably linked. The British canals, ousted from prominence by the development of the 19th century rail network, are both a rich haven for wildlife and a treasured cultural heritage. The artificial lakes of the Netherlands, Denmark and the East of England created by the digging of medieval pits to extract peat for fuel, are regarded for both their cultural and biodiversity significance. Yet, our view of heritage can be distorted by the desire to create manageable categories, as well as changing perceptions.

The 1972 Convention concerning the Protection of the World Cultural and Natural Heritage (UNESCO, 1972; hereafter the Heritage Convention) distinguished *cultural heritage* (Article 1) from *natural heritage* (Article 2) and set in motion a process of designation of those sites that parties to the Heritage Convention considered to be of *outstanding universal value.* The Heritage Convention came about in response to threats to heritage from "not only [by the] traditional causes of decay, but also by changing social and economic conditions ..." (UNESCO, 1972). The attributes for sites designated under the Heritage Convention as natural heritage sites (Box 1) clearly indicate an elite status and fixed location, such that only the high-end quality sites of nature would merit protection. In marked contrast to the text of the UN Heritage Convention,

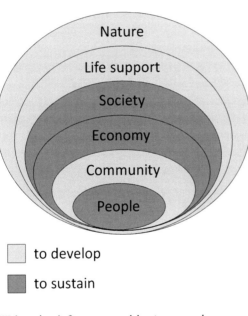

Nature
Life support
Society
Economy
Community
People

☐ to develop
■ to sustain

*Figure 1. Components of human
development nested in hierarchal
society and environmental
boundaries. Figure image
reproduced from United Nations
(2014). Prototype Global
Sustainable Development Report.
Online unedited edition. New
York: United Nations Department
of Economic and Social Affairs,
Division for Sustainable
Development, 1 July 2014. http://
sustainabledevelopment.un.org/
globalsdreport/.*

Wikipedia defines natural heritage as the sum total of the elements of biodiversity
and associated geological structures and formations, reflecting a much broader,
informal, view of what constitutes natural heritage.

The Heritage Convention was making a case for the protection of the
extraordinary *special places* at a time when statutory protection of species-rich or
particularly representative ecosystems was extremely limited. Since then, a broader
view of what comprises natural heritage has evolved. Nevertheless, the philosophy
of *ring-fencing* sites of highest value remains a central idea to protecting natural
heritage. In practice, this manifests as tiered systems of designation along a gradient
of *international, regional, national* and *local* importance. A focus on site-based
protection and management, however, misses a crucial element of sustainable
development. Disassociating *protected* sites from their place in the wider context of

the landscape reflects what might be termed an *illusion of control*, and somewhat at odds with a *wider countryside* view where natural heritage in the broader sense is a fundamental pillar of human development. The concept of human well being nested within tiers of socio-economic development and social and environmental sustainability is illustrated well in the Prototype Global Sustainable Development Report of the United Nations (2014) (Figure 1).

The taming of nature

> *Why did the stream dry up? I put a dam across it to have it for my use, that is why the stream dried up.* (Rabindranath Tagore 1913, The Gardener LII)

Managing water for beneficial use has shaped human development dating back over 5000 years (e.g. Bienert and Häser, 2004; Kummu, 2009; Tvedt and Coopey, 2010). Innovation solved technical challenges, and social norms emerged promoting cooperative management. In water scare regions, early well-organised societies placed restrictions through laws and customs on water use. The Code of Hammurabi of ancient Mesopotamia, dating back to about 1750 BC, included provisions for use of water, and punishments for failing to use scarce arable land productively (http://legacy.fordham.edu). The ancient Egyptians, Romans and Khmer empires all excelled at water management. Supply systems were developed that could transport water over large distances.

In recent centuries, technical discovery and innovation capitalised on water for power, irrigation, flood control, water transfers and shipping lanes, driving social transformation, wealth and trade. The taming of mighty rivers, harnessing power and water supply, was a sight of awe in the transformation of wilderness for human development. In 1935 on seeing the Hoover (originally named Boulder) Dam on the Colorado River, the American President Franklin D. Roosevelt commented "I came, I saw, and I was conquered, as everyone would be who sees for the first time this great feat of mankind" (www.presidency.ucsb.edu). In this vision of development, protecting natural heritage either for its own sake, or as provider of other services, hardly featured in the policies of the time. Control of water brought economic wealth and, at least at the macro-economic scale, possibilities for better social conditions.

In the same period that Roosevelt was commissioning the mighty dam, agricultural development in the arid American Mid-west was revealing a destructive side to human industriousness with land and water. The settlement of the Mid-west had been encouraged under the widely held belief that "rain followed the plow", based on the coincidence of some good years of rainfall with early settlements. The move for greater land development was spurred on by the 1902 Reclamation Act and an irrigated promised land (Reisner, 1986). In the 1930s, vast tracts of the American Mid-west turned into the infamous dust bowl, a consequence of natural grassland conversion to grain production, and overgrazing by the cattle that had replaced the indigenous, and well-adapted, buffalo herds of the open plains. Meanwhile, the Hoover Dam added to the regulation of the Colorado River and increased diversion of water for irrigation (Reisner, 1986).

Intensified management of the mighty river eventually reduced its flow to a trickle by the time it reached the Gulf of California (Cohen et al., 2001). No doubt that was considered successful management by the upstream riparian users, but not so good for downstream river function, or coastal food webs and human livelihoods dependent on the natural cycle of river flow.

When development exceeds the capacity of the ecosystems to provide sufficient materials and food, or when local infrastructure or societal coherence are unable to cope with external natural shocks, such as floods or droughts, whole civilisations can collapse (Diamond, 1997; Evans et al., 2013). Lacking the resistance to absorb environmental pressures or the resilience to recover from them comes with a heavy price (Scheffer, 2009).

Even celebrated ancient water management regimes could not cope with changes in the forces of nature. In South-East Asia, the decline of the Khmer empire coincided with three decades of drought followed by a very wet period that overwhelmed the water supply system based on long-distance canals and sophisticated water exchange between neighbouring catchments. The straight canal network now provided a conduit for rapid flow devastating the infrastructure at Angkor Wat, the centre of the civilisation (Buckley et al., 2010)

Development and natural limits

But man is a part of nature, and his war against nature is inevitably a war against himself. (Rachel Carson, Silent Spring, 1962)

In 1969 oily debris from industrial pollution floating on the Cuyahoga River in Cleveland (U.S) caught fire, an episodic occurrence dating back to 1868 (Ohio History Central, 2015). However, this time it was headline news, providing a symbol for the U.S. to take action over industrial pollution, and paving the way to the U.S. Clean Water Act of 1972. In Europe, increasing public disquiet over water pollution similarly led to a series of national laws and European Environmental Directives from the 1970s and increasingly stringent licensing and development regulations. While a similar realisation is now evident in many developing parts of the world, it is a tragedy of development that water pollution also continues as if it doesn't, in the end, matter.

Ultimately, societal water use has been a process of exploiting the natural capital of water resources for human benefits and to provide economic and social capital. This usually comes at the expense of natural capital. In its most basic manifestation water may be abstracted from its source and effectively converted to economic capital, as in intensive irrigation schemes. Industrial emissions from economic development may directly reduce natural capital through pollution of water bodies. When the environment has a large capacity to provide water for human economies and development, and sufficient resistance to dissipate impacts, or the resilience to recover from them, the costs of development on natural heritage may be limited or accepted as one worth paying. However, if the debt to natural capital becomes too high, or leads to pronounced inequality, it requires a reassessment of the relative tradeoffs.

Striking the balance between development for human material benefit and protection of natural habitats and the species they support lies at the heart of the relationship between development and natural heritage. The concept of *sustainable development* was popularised by the well-known report *Our Common Future* by Brundtland (1987), but its origins in modern times can be traced back to the seventeenth century work of Baruch Spinoza's *Ethica,* published in 1677, which advocated the necessity of man to live in harmony and work with, rather than subjugate, nature (Grober, 2012). Taken together with his thoughts on democracy and equity, it appears that his presence would not have been out of place among those who drafted the 1992 Dublin principles (http://www.un-documents.net/h2o-dub.htm) that shaped modern thinking on integrated water resource management.

Sustainable development and the need to balance natural, economic and social capital are predicated on two basic concepts. First, the capitals are interdependent. Second, there are inherent limits to how much natural capital can be reduced. The inherent limits to the use of natural capital was analysed by Meadows et al. (1972) in their report *The Limits to Growth.* Using new developments in systems analysis they simulated the consequences of increasing exploitation of natural resources, and the ultimate finite capacity of the Earth to cope with unrestrained development, resource exploitation and population increase. While some of the assumptions used in the models attracted some contemporary criticism (e.g. Jahoda et al., 1973), the validity of the models and predictions have been supported by more recent work (Turner, 2014). Technological innovation and measures such as limiting pollution through regulation cannot fundamentally change the limits within which ecosystems and the Earth's climate support human societies (Rockström et al., 2009).

Wisdom and Choice

> *Are not poverty and need the greatest polluters?* (Indira Ghandi, at the UN Conference on the Human Environment, Sockholm, 1972).

In the same year as the 1972 Heritage Convention, the UN Conference on the Human Environment at Stockholm recognised the need for global action if the people of the world were to live within the boundaries of natural resources. The speech of Indira Ghandi, the Indian Prime Minister, at the Conference on the Human Environment set the scene for a debate that continues to this day, even if the original remark quoted at the beginning of this section has at times been taken out of context (see http://lasulawsenvironmental.blogspot.nl/2012/07/indira-gandhis-speech-at-stockholm.html for full text) as an excuse to limit environmental protection under the cloak of development (Grober, 2012).

The wisdom of sustainability can be appreciated in well-chosen examples from traditional societies. In the rivers of British Columbia, complex traditions of exchanging gifts based on the abundance of fish harvest, and duty to reciprocate, are documented by Moss (2012). Richerson et al. (2002) describe the *Plan of Pitic,* codifying governance of water management in Northern Mexico in 1789, based on principles imported from water scarce regions of Spain. In Timor-Leste, traditional

Tara Bandu rooted in ancient ceremony, provides checks and balances limiting exploitation of fisheries, as well as for water and forests. In 16th-century Scotland, fishermen of the River Forth responded to a threat from increased shipping by moving from a reliance on fixed artificial weirs to boat-based techniques to catch migrating salmon (Hoffmann, 2012). Dependence on nature is not, however, necessarily synonymous with protecting it, and small-scale sustainability can be difficult in the face of increasing populations.

Hardin's (1968) *The Tragedy of the Commons* explains the drive for individual gain at the expense of the common good, a manifestation of the evolutionary *hardwiring* for the selfish gene (Dawkins, 1976). However, the pessimism of Hardin's analysis is not always born out, and Dawkins evolutionary perspective does not exclude the evolution of a genetic basis for cooperative behaviour operating at the level of the individual. Cooperative management can occur through respected social norms evolved from tribal customs of cooperation (Richerson and Boyd, 2000), clear and verifiable negotiated strategies, or enforced regulation. All three options require forms of social censor or punishment, but effective cooperative management appears best served by effective collective action and acceptance of its legitimacy. Heavy-handed, or imposed, top-down structures can be counterproductive, separating resource management from the necessary social order (Ostrom, 2000). This can even be a consequence of local participation, when external demands on local stakeholders enable local elites to capture the process (Lane and Corbett, 2005).

The 1972 UN Conference on the Human Environment for the first time laid out the global challenges and choices that would be required to accommodate human development without wrecking-havoc with the life support systems on which we all depend. The link with the World Heritage Convention may not have been explicit at the time, but both meetings and the processes they instigated provided an agenda for greater empathy for safeguarding natural heritage even if the focus varied between on the one hand setting up committees for the designation and protection of sites of *outstanding value* and, on the other, a less well defined, more general, approach to protection.

If the 1972 Conference on the Human Environment was an ensemble calling for wiser use of the planet's resources, the Rio Earth Summit of 1992 was the full blown orchestra that brought the ideas and discussion of sustainable development to widespread political and public attention. In between the two meetings, the concepts of sustainable development had been spelled out in the Brundtland (1987) report. The Johannesburg Declaration on Sustainable Development (UN, 2002), coming out of a following Summit in 2002, reasserted the interdependence of the three pillars of sustainable development (natural, economic and social). It included, in paragraph 13, an emphatic documentary of the loss of natural heritage:

"The global environment continues to suffer. Loss of biodiversity continues, fish stocks continue to be depleted, desertification claims more and more fertile land, the adverse effects of climate change are already evident, natural disasters are more frequent and more devastating, and developing countries more vulnerable, and air, water and marine pollution continue to rob millions of a decent life."

Unfortunately, international targets on halting biodiversity decline (European Commission, 2011; CBD, 2014) have been mostly unsuccessful. The highest loss occurs in inland waters, with approximately 20% of the world's 10,000 described freshwater fish species listed as threatened, endangered, or extinct in the last few decades (Darwall et al., 2011). An almost monotonic decline of wetlands has been ongoing since the 1700s (Davidson, 2014). The pressures on, and loss of, wetlands is particularly poignant given that the *Ramsar Convention on Wetlands,* that came into force in 1975, is the oldest intergovernmental environmental agreement, currently with 168 signatories. Any assessment of natural heritage and water can only conclude that international policies for global protection of natural heritage are not succeeding, even if in some countries protection of designated sites has been effective. It is clear that a different approach is needed.

Natural heritage: scales and perspectives

Water is not a commercial product like any other but, rather, a heritage which must be protected, defended and treated as such. (Preamble to the EU Water Framework Directive; Council of the European Communities, 2000)

It is difficult to argue against the prescience of Ferdinand V. Hayden, an early and enthusiastic advocate of Yellowstone National Park, set up in 1872. Hayden canvassed for "setting aside the area as a pleasure ground for the benefit and enjoyment of people" warning that "the vandals who are now waiting to enter into this wonder-land will in a single season despoil, beyond recovery, these remarkable curiosities, which have required all the cunning skill of nature thousands of years to prepare" (Merrill, 2003).

Hayden viewed Yellowstone as a place where people could enjoy and respect nature, but the protection and appreciation of natural heritage occurs at a range of scales, and social contexts. While places identified or perceived as rich in biodiversity, culture or landscape beauty merit protection for multiple reasons, the gradual erosion of the wider natural landscape diminishes natural heritage, as well as linked social capital and cultural capital.

The isolation of designated sites from the wider environment makes little ecological sense in general; and especially so for water-related natural heritage, where connectivity in the catchment is of fundamental importance. Examples of a landscape-based approach exist. The U.K. National Parks are nurtured as working landscapes of outstanding natural beauty, where citizens live proudly within the setting of a rich natural heritage. The UNESCO Biosphere Reserves, designated under the Man and the Biosphere programme, have an area of high nature conservation value at their core, but adopt a strategy for the need to balance

a

b

c

d

Plate 1. Images of the impact of water on natural heritag. a: Intact papyrus swamp, Kenya; b. Mississippi coastal wetland with dead cypress trees, U.S.; c: valley wetland converted to rice crops, Rwanda; d: calcareous wetland, Croatia.

development with natural heritage in surrounding areas. The European Landscape Convention, the French Regional Natural Parks (Parcs Naturels Régionaux; PNR), the Catalan Landscape Observatory, and the Canadian Heritage Rivers System have similar aims, promoting importance of local heritage and recreation, and fostering local citizen cooperation and pride. The U.S. Clean Water Act provides a tiered system of protection, with tier 3 maintaining and protecting the highest quality waters, designated as 'Outstanding National Resource Waters' (ONRW); that could be an entire landscape area. While all these examples encompass large areas, they are still essentially site-specific. At the other end of the scale are areas of natural heritage which permeate the landscape, and outside the boundaries of any specific designation. These include small pockets of, often diverse, habitat within urban landscapes that provide refuge for wildlife and citizens, and solace from metropolitan bustle. In rural landscapes, patches and corridors of nature act not only as wildlife corridors and visual disruption of agricultural or deforested monotony, but can serve as buffers to sediment and nutrient emissions from land to water (Newson, 2010). Naturally, the wider network of habitats lie across a scale of quality of natural heritage (Plate 1), but e.g. a drained marsh or intensified grasslands clearly does not have the same natural heritage worth as natural or *semi-natural* habitat.

Protecting natural heritage across all landscapes is being attempted by the European Water Framework Directive (WFD) with policies of meeting minimum quality of waterbodies and "no deterioration" of the water environment of the better quality waters. In principle this could provide a wider countryside approach to the protection of natural heritage, including recognising the importance of maintaining connectivity of water in the landscape. It is a policy instrument that could safeguard water resources and refugia of biodiversity in smaller sites in conjunction with a wider network of waterbodies. The overall and embracing philosophy of the WFD suggests increased policy awareness of the broader picture, even if integration with other policies is an ongoing challenge (Hering et al., 2010; Irvine, 2009). Such policy integration is, however, fundamental to connect natural heritage with sustainable development.

A framework using ecosystem services for safeguarding heritage

Free water is wasted water. World Commission on Water (2000)

The Millennium Ecosystem Assessment (2005) presents the case that human development and well-being is dependent on a sufficient extent of natural ecosystems and the services they provide. That the ecosystem centered approach is often advocated but insufficiently realised most probably reflects that 1) many of the important economic values of wetlands are underestimated or un-recognised, and 2) the loss of natural heritage occurs at local scales far removed from the finesse of air-conditioned conference halls. Identification of ecosystem services (Fig. 2) connects policy with economics and natural heritage (Carpenter et al., 2009; De Groot et al., 2010; Russi et al., 2013; Kremen and Ostfeld, 2005). However, the ecosystem services concept is often interpreted simply as *provisioning* service, neglecting the *supporting* services provided by habitat structure and the biogeochemical and physical *regulating* services. The rich cultural heritage epitomised in historic or religious traditions, or modern recreation, is often

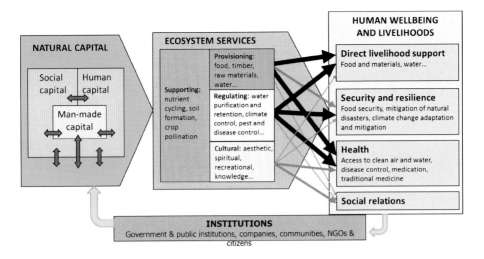

Figure 2. Contribution of natural capital to human well-being and livelihood. Reproduced from Patrick ten Brink, adapted from Laure Ledoux in ten Brink et al 2012, building on MEA (2005) and TEEB (2011).

subsumed under the non-specifics of *cultural services* that are so far not well integrated into the ecosystem services frame (Hernández-Morcillo et al., 2013; Soini and Berkeland, 2014). The emphasis on *provisioning* service is understandable given the global focus on economic development and basic human needs for food, water and energy. Enhancing provisioning services without disproportionately affecting the natural heritage of habitat integrity is undoubtedly a key challenge. Better spatial planning opens up opportunities for landuse that maximises use of water resources while protecting natural habitat. Greater recognition of the financial benefits of ecosystem services provides a business case for integrated heritage protection (OECD, 2010).

Costanza *et al.* (1997) valued the world's ecosystems at U$33 trillion/yr in 1995. A subsequent analysis estimates annual losses of trillions of dollars since then (Costanza et al., 2014). While the tendency to "impact now, restore later" may be justified to effect short-term economic growth, safeguarding existing natural heritage is likely a more cost-effective and reliable strategy than later, often unsuccessful, restoration (Hilderbrand et al., 2005; Feld et al., 2011; Palmer et al.,2010; Scheffer, 2009). Reclamation of China's coastal wetlands is estimated at an annual loss of U.S. $31 billion of ecosystem services, representing about 6% of the country's gross marine products, not to mention the dramatic decline of coastal wetland birds (CCICED, 2010; Ma et al., 2014). Reversing that impact is an uncertain and costly proposition.

Recognising the link among the different services, and reflecting their true value for sustainable development, rather than as a comodified "price for services", is gathering pace (Russi et al., 2013). For the natural heritage of water, considering wetlands as multipurpose *green infrastructure* (Mitsch and Gosselink, 2007) provides an approach where all wetland habits are seen as natural heritage, and incorporated as such in spatial planning. Neglecting the importance of natural infrastructure has many tragic examples. Removal of mangroves along the coasts of Sri Lanka and Thailand deprived the coast natural protection that could have reduced loss of life and property following the 2004 tsunami. The deprivation of sediment replenishment to the delta of the Mississippi has led to dramatic loss of coastal wetlands over the last century. Together with the loss of wetland cypress trees after opening the Mississippi River – Gulf Outlet (MRGO) played its role in the flooding of New Orleans during Hurricane Katrina in 2005. These well-known examples merely emphasize the necessity for intact natural heritage within the landscape, and their incorporation into the everyday thinking of development.

Into the future

> *Water holds the key to sustainable development. We need it for health, food security and economic progress.* (Ban Ki-Moon, Secretary-General of the United Nations, October 2013).

The so-called food, energy and water nexus identifies the drivers for development over the next 50 years, and presumably beyond. With projections for 9 billion people by 2050, the Food and Agriculture Organisation (FAO) have indicated the need for a doubling of food production by then (FAO, 2006). Current estimates of >70% of freshwater surface waters abstracted for agriculture is also likely to increase (U.S. National Intelligence Council, 2012). As the world, and especially Africa, seeks to increase agricultural yields in the coming decades (Chauvin et al., 2012, Hachigonta et al., 2013), improved farming, water harvesting and land stewardship techniques are needed to increase yields while reducing overall pressures (Critchley and Gowring, 2012). While it is tempting to tackle food insecurity through greater use and conversion of wetlands, this is a high risk strategy that can also erode further the less visible *regulating* ecosystem services provided by wetlands, such as water and carbon retention (Falkenmark et al., 2007; Falkenmark et al., 2009). All impacts on nature's infrastructure requires careful analysis of the drivers and trade-offs for longer-term sustainable use (Asselen et al., 2013; Simonit and Perrings, 2011; Falkenmark et al., 2007; Falkenmark et al., 2009; Wood et al., 2013).

The incorporation of natural heritage in development involves multiple scales, challenges conventional wisdom, requires reconciliation of strong views and vested interests. Concerns for energy security have spawned a new generation of major dam building (Zarfl et al., 2014). Dams have major effects on habitat, species and people, and can impact on millions of people who depend on migratory fish for food and livelihoods, and the environmental flows that support downstream biological production (Poff et al., 1997). Often driven by overly optimistic projections of economic benefits and underestimates of costs (Ansar et al., 2014), dams can have far reaching political ramifications. Governance structures conducive to sound management in many parts of the world may be seriously limited, but capacity building networks continue to develop and fiscal and technical measures are available that can sustain, rather than degrade, water-based natural heritage.

Policy instruments and protocols are available to help Environmental Impact Assessment (EIA) in relation to development projects and Strategic Environmental Assessment (SEA) for Plans, Policies and Programmes. While EIA has been an increasing requirement in many parts of the world over the last four decades, both through national legislation and as a condition of international loans (Bekhechi and Mecier, 2002; Withanage, 2006; Bond and Pope, 2012), its effective implementation is still often lacking, especially within national planning procedures (Morgan, 2012). SEA, often a much more challenging concept to implement is, nevertheless, applied as a mechanism for development and capacity building (Partidário et al., 2011), and could be used to better link with ecosystem services and their response to disturbance (OECD, 2006; Slootweg and Jones, 2011).

In 2000, the United Nations Millennium Declaration considered Respect for Nature as a fundamental value, resolving *in all [our] environmental actions a new ethic of conservation and stewardship,* and *to stop the unsustainable exploitation of water resources.* The 3rd African Environmental Outlook (Opio-Odongo, 2013) specified the importance of natural heritage and noted its rapid loss largely due to rapid population growth and agricultural expansion. The 11th meeting of the Conference of the Parties (COP) of the Convention on Biological Diversity (CBD, 2012) declared "Investment in *natural capital* will deliver significant co-benefits for sustainable development" and that "benefits are likely to significantly outweigh costs". Substantial economic benefits can, for example, be gained from protecting intact ecosystems for supply of high quality drinking water (Gras and Benoît, 1998; TEEB, 2009).

Conclusions

The global messages of the importance of natural heritage of water for development and human well-being could not be clearer. However, policies seemingly designed to safeguard natural heritage might have unintended negative effects if protection of specific sites is seen as permission for wider reductions of natural heritage in the wider landscape. Protecting sites of *outstanding value* is a cornerstone of the 1972 Heritage Convention. Protection of designated sites certainly provides a repository of biodiversity, but not alone sufficient in addressing the challenges of development, and dependence of human well-being on ecosystems. Translating that message into global and local institutional frameworks, governance and associated capacity building provides powerful opportunities in aligning the goals of the natural heritage of water and global development. The connected history of natural and cultural heritage blurs the boundaries of definition, but an eclectic view of water and its related heritage is more necessary now than at any time in human history. Indeed, a greater general recognition of the links between natural and cultural heritage, and better incorporation into ecosystem assessment and valuation is an emerging need.

At local scales, awareness of the link between local action and global response is often limited and, even if present, overshadowed by an understandable focus on short-term economic improvement. In general terms, subsidies, agricultural policies, and associated extension services that drive the loss of natural heritage are still more common than those that promote its protection and wise use, with wetlands a particular case in point. Nevertheless, understanding the connection between development and natural heritage has come a long way since 1972.

Not least of the challenges for the future is that poverty remains a fundamental constraint to sustainable development, and links between poverty and ecosystem integrity and biodiversity variable (e.g. Lucas et al., 2014, Roe et al., 2013). However, the global poor are often more intimately connected to their landscape than those on the rise to relative riches (Mombo et al., 2013). Heritage protection can provide motivation for ecosystem protection, and ecosystems can help make the case as a counterbalance to a more narrowly focused approach to development. Individuals and communities value landscapes when they feel connected to them, and enhancing understanding of hidden economic worth can play an important role in their sustainable use.

Water has always been connected to human development, and will continue to be so. In the need to set global targets, the U.N. Millennium Development Goals (http://www.un.org/millenniumgoals) with a focus on water supply and sanitation largely neglected the inclusion of water's natural heritage, which both provides the habitat for source waters and is impacted by discharges. The forthcoming Sustainable Development Goals provide a promise to redress that. Promoting wider networks of intact habitats provides a natural heritage resource to help meet, rather than restrict, development goals. It is a message that can contribute to the next chapter in the intriguing history of water, culture and development.

Acknowledgements

I am grateful to the two anonymous reviewers and Ellen Pfeiffer for their time and critical comments that greatly improved a previous version of the manuscript, and the numerous conversations that I have had with friends and colleagues in trying to grapple with the complexities of sustainable development and its link with ecosystem integrity.

References

Ansar, Atif, Bent Flyvbjerg, Alexander Budzier, and Daniel Lunn. 2014. Should we build more large dams? The actual costs of hydropower megaproject development. *Energy Policy* 69: 43–56. doi:10.1016/j.enpol.2013.10.069.

Bekhechi, Mohammad A., and Jean-Roger Mercier. 2002. *The Legal and Regulatory Framework for Environmental Impact Assessments*. The World Bank. doi:10.1596/0-8213-5115-X.

Bienert, H.-D., and J. Häser. 2004. *Men of Dikes and Canals: The Archaeology of Water in the Middle East*. Rahden: Marie Leidorf.

Bond, Alan, and Jenny Pope. 2012. The state of the art of impact assessment in 2012. *Impact Assessment and Project Appraisal* 30: 1–4. doi:10.1080/14615517.2012.669140.

Brundtland, G. H. et al. 1987. *Report of the World Commission on Environment and Development: Our Common Future.* doi:10.1080/07488008808408783.

Buckley, Brendan M., Kevin J. Anchukaitis, Daniel Penny, Roland J. Fletcher, Edward R. Cook, Masaki Sano, Le Canh Nam, Aroonrut Wichienkeeo, Ton That Minh, and Truong Mai Hong. 2010. Climate as a contributing factor in the demise of Angkor, Cambodia. *Proceedings of the National Academy of Sciences of the United States of America* 107: 6748–52. doi:10.1073/pnas.0910827107.

Carpenter, Stephen R., Harold A. Mooney, John Agard, Doris Capistrano, Ruth S. Defries, Sandra Díaz, Thomas Dietz, et al. 2009. Science for managing ecosystem services: Beyond the Millennium Ecosystem Assessment. *Proceedings of the National Academy of Sciences of the United States of America* 106: 1305–12. doi:10.1073/pnas.0808772106.

Carson, Rachel. 1962. *Silent Spring.* Harcourt: Houghton Mifflin.

CBD. 2012. *Resourcing the Aichi Biodiversity Targets: A First Assessment of of the Resources Required for Implementing the Strategic Plan for Biodiversity 2011-2020.* UNEP/CBD/COP.

CBD. 2014. *Global Biodiversity Outlook 4.* Montreal: Secretariat of the Convention on Biological Diversity.

CCICED. 2010. *Annual Policy Report: Ecosystem Management and Green Development.* Beijing: Secretariat of the China Council for International Cooperation on Environment and Development.

Chauvin, N. D., F. Mulangu, and G. Porto. 2012. *Food Production and Consumption Trends in Sub-Saharan Africa: Prospects for the Transformation of the Agricultural Sector. WP 2012-011.* Addis Abeba: UNDP Regional Bureau for Africa.

Cohen, Michael J., Christine Henges-Jeck, and Gerardo Castillo-Moreno. 2001. A preliminary water balance for the Colorado River delta, 1992 - 1998. *Journal of Arid Environments*, 49: 35–48.

Costanza, Robert, Ralph D'Arge, Rudolf de Groot, Stephen Farber, Monica Grasso, Bruce Hannon, Karin Limburg, et al. 1997. The value of the world's ecosystem services and natural capital. *Nature* 387: 253–60.

Costanza, Robert, Rudolf de Groot, Paul Sutton, Sander van der Ploeg, Sharolyn J. Anderson, Ida Kubiszewski, Stephen Farber, and R. Kerry Turner. 2014. Changes in the global value of ecosystem services. *Global Environmental Change* 26: 152–58. doi:10.1016/j.gloenvcha.2014.04.002.

Council of the European Communities. 2000. Directive 2000/60/EC of the European Parliament and of the Council – Establishing a framework for Community action in the field of water policy. *Official Journal of the European Communities* L327, 1-73. Brussels.

Critchley, W., and J. Gowring. 2012. *Water Harvesting in Sub-Saharan Africa.* London and New York: Earthscan, Routledge.

Darwell, William, Kevin Smith, David Allen, Robert Holland, Ian Harrison, and Emma Brooks. 2011. *The Diversity of Life in African Freshwaters: Under Water, Under Threat. An Analysis of the Status and Distribution of Freshwater Species throughout Mainland Africa.* Cambridge and Gland: IUCN.

Davidson, Nick C. 2014. How much wetland has the world lost? Long-term and recent trends in global wetland area. *Marine and Freshwater Research* 65. doi:10.1071/MF14173.

Dawkins, R. 1976. *The Selfish Gene.* Oxford: Oxford University Press.

de Groot, Rudolf, Rob Alkemade, L. Braat, L. Hein, and L. Willemen. 2010. Challenges in integrating the concept of ecosystem services and values in landscape planning, management and decision making. *Ecological Complexity* 7: 260–72. doi:10.1016/j.ecocom.2009.10.006.

Diamond, Jared. 1997. *Guns Germs and Steel. The Fates of Human Societies.* New York, London: W. W. Norton.

European Commission. 2011. Our life insurance, our natural capital: An EU biodiversity strategz to 2020. Communication from the Commission to the European Parliament, The Council, The Economic and Social Committee and The Committee of the Regions COM(2011) 244. Brussels.

Evans, Damian H., Roland J. Fletcher, Christophe Pottier, Jean-Baptiste Chevance, Dominique Soutif, Boun Suy Tan, Sokrithy Im, et al. 2013. Uncovering archaeological landscapes at Angkor using lidar. *Proceedings of the National Academy of Sciences of the United States of America* 110: 12595–600. doi:10.1073/pnas.1306539110.

Falkenmark, Malin, C.M. Finlayson, and L. Gordon. 2007. Agriculture, water, and ecosystems: avoiding the costs of going too far. In *Water for food, water for life: a comprehensive assessment of water management in agriculture*, ed. D. Molden, 234–77. London: Earthscan.

Falkenmark, Malin, Johan Rockström, and Louise Karlberg. 2009. Present and future water requirements for feeding humanity. *Food Security* 1: 59–69. doi:10.1007/s12571-008-0003-x.

FAO. 2006. *World Agriculture: Towards 2030/2050: Prospects for Food, Nutrition, Agriculture and Major Commodity Groups. Interim Report.* Rome.

Feld, Christian K., Sebastian Birk, David C. Bradley, Daniel Hering, Jochem Kail, Anahita Marzin, Andreas Melcher, et al. 2011. From natural to degraded rivers and back again : A test of restoration ecology theory and practice. In *Advances in Ecological Research, Vol .44*, ed. Guy Woodward, 1st ed., 44:119–209. doi:10.1016/B978-0-12-374794-5.00003-1.

Gandhi, Indira. 1972. Address to the plenary session of the United Nations Conference on Human Environment, Stockholm 14th June, 1972. http://lasulawsenvironmental.blogspot.co.uk/2012/07/indira-gandhis-speech-at-stockholm.html. Accessed 28 Mar 2015.

Gras, M., and F. Benoît. 1998. Influence des systèmes de culture et des pratiques agricoles sur la qualité de l'eau minérale de Vittel. *Le programme de recherches AGREV. Comptes Rendus de l'Académie d'Agriculture de France*, no. 5: 166–68.

Grober, Ulrich. 2012. *Sustainability. A Cultural History*. Totnes: Green Books.

Hachigonta, Sepo, Gerald C. Nelson, Timothy S. Thomas, and Lindiwe Majele Sibanda. 2013. *Southern African Agriculture and Climate Change: A Comprehensive Analysis*. Washington D.C.: IFPRI. doi:10.2499/9780896292086.

Hardin, Garrett. 1968. The tragedy of the commons. *Science* 162: 1243–48.

Hering, Daniel, Angel Borja, Jacob Carstensen, Laurence Carvalho, Mike Elliott, Christian K. Feld, Anna-Stiina Heiskanen, et al. 2010. The European Water Framework Directive at the age of 10: A critical review of the achievements with recommendations for the future. *The Science of the Total Environment* 408: 4007–19. doi:10.1016/j.scitotenv.2010.05.031.

Hernández-Morcillo, Mónica, Tobias Plieninger, and Claudia Bieling. 2013. An empirical review of cultural ecosystem service indicators. *Ecological Indicators* 29: 434–44. doi:10.1016/j.ecolind.2013.01.013.

Hilderbrand, R.H., A.C. Watts, and A.M. Randle. 2005. The myths of restoration ecology. *Ecology and Society* 10: 19. http://www.ecologyandsociety.org/vol10/iss1/art19/.

Hoffman, R. 2012. Rioting townsmen destroy abbey's salmon weir in medieval Scotland. *Arcadia* 12.

Irvine, Kenneth. 2009. Harmonizing assessment of conservation with that of ecological quality: Fitting a square peg into a round hole? *Aquatic Conservation: Marine and Freshwater Ecosystems* 19: 365–69. doi:10.1002/aqc.1050.

Jahoda, M., K.L.R. Pavitt, H.S.D. Cole, and C. Freeman. 1973. *Models of Doom, A Critique of the Limits to Growth*. London: Universe Pub.

Ki-Moon, Ban. 2013. Secretary-General's opening remarks at Budapest Water Summit, Budapest, Hungary, 8 October 2013. United Nations. http://www.un.org/sg/statements/index.asp?nid=7184. Accessed 28 Mar 2015.

Kremen, C., and R. Ostfeld. 2005. A call to ecologists: measuring, analyzing, and managing ecosystem services. *Frontiers in Ecology and Environment* 3: 540–48.

Kummu, M. 2009. Water management in Angkor: Human impacts on hydrology and sediment transportation. *Journal of Environmental Management* 90: 1413–21.

Lane, Marcus B., and Tony Corbett. 2005. The Tyranny of localism: Indigenous participation in community-based environmental management. *Journal of Environmental Policy & Planning* 7: 141–59. doi:10.1080/15239080500338671.

Lucas, Paul, Marcel Kok, Måns Nilsson, and Rob Alkemade. 2013. Integrating biodiversity and ecosystem services in the post-2015 development agenda: Goal structure, target areas and means of implementation. *Sustainability* 6: 193–216. doi:10.3390/su6010193.

Ma, Zhijun, David S. Melville, Jianguo Liu, Ying Chen, Hongyan Yang, Wenwei Ren, Zhengwang Zhang, Theunis Piersma, and Bo Li. 2014. Rethinking China's new Great Wall. *Science* 346: 912–14. doi:10.1126/science.1257258.

Meadows, D.H., D. Meadows, J. Randers, and W.W. Behrens. 1972. *The Limits to Growth*. London: Universe Books. doi:10.1111/j.1752-1688.1972.tb05230.x.

Merrill, Marlene Deahl, ed. 2003. *Yellowstone and the Great West: Journals, Letters, and Images from the 1871 Hayden Expedition.* Lincoln: University of Nebraska Press.

Millennium Ecosystem Assessment. 2005. *Ecosystems and Human Well-Being: Synthesis.* Washington D.C.: Island Press.

Mitsch, W.J., and J.G. Gosselink. 2007. The value of wetlands: Importance of scale and landscape setting. *Ecological Economics* 35: 25–33.

Mombo, Felister, Stijn Speelman, Joseph Hella, and Guido Van Huylenbroeck. 2013. How characteristics of wetlands resource users and associated institutions influence the sustainable management of wetlands in Tanzania. *Land Use Policy* 35: 8–15. doi:10.1016/j.landusepol.2013.04.010.

Morgan, Richard K. 2012. Environmental impact assessment: The state of the art. *Impact Assessment and Project Appraisal* 30: 5–14. doi:10.1080/14615517.2012.661557.

Moss, B. 2012. *Liberation Ecology: The Reconciliation of Natural and Human Cultures.* Excellence in Ecology. Oldendorf/Luhe: International Ecology Institute.

Newson, M. 2010. Understanding 'hot-spot' problems in catchments: the need for scale-sensitive mechanisms to secure effective solutions for river management and conservation. *Aquatic Conservation: Marine and Freshwater Ecosystems* 20: S62–72.

OECD. 2006. *Applying Strategic Environmental Assessment –good Practice Guidance for Development Co-Operation. DAC. Guidelines and Reference Series.* New York: OECD.

OECD. 2010. *Paying for Biodiversity. Enhancing the Cost-Effectiveness of Payments for Ecosystem Services.* Paris: OECD.

Ohio History Central. 2015. Cuyahoga River Fire. http://www.ohiohistoryhttp// www.ohiohistorycentral.org/index.php?title=Cuyahoga_River_Fire&oldid=33991. Accessed 28 Mar 2015.

Opio-Odongo, J. 2013. *Africa Environment Outlook 3: Summary for Policy Makers.* Nairobi: UNEP.

Ostrom, Elinor. 2000. Collective action and the evolution of social norms. *Journal of Economic Perspectives* 14: 137–58. doi:10.1257/jep.14.3.137.

Palmer, M.A., H. Menninger, and E.S. Bernhardt. 2010. River restoration, habitat heterogeneity and biodiversity: A failure of theory or practice? *Freshwater Biology* 55: 205–22.

Partidario, MR. 2011. SEA process development and capacity-building–A thematic overview. In *Handbook of Strategic Environmental Assessment*, eds. R. Aschemann, T. Jahn, and M.R. Partidario, 437–44. London: Earthscan.

Poff, N.R, J.D. Allan, M.B. Bain, J.R. Karr, K.L. Prestegaard, B.D. Richter, R.E. Sparks, and J.C. Stromberg. 1997. The natural flow regime. A paradigm for river conservation and restoration. *BioScience* 47: 769–84.

Reisner, M. 1986. *Cadillac Desert. The American West and Its Disappearing Water.* New York: Viking.

Richerson, P.J., and R. Boyd. 2000. Built for speed. Pleistocene climate variation and the origin of human culture. *Perspectives in Ethology* 13: 1–45.

Richerson, P.J., R. Boyd, and J. Paciotti. 2002. An evolutionary theory of commons management. In *The Drama of the Commons*, eds. E. Ostrom, T. Dietz, N. Dolšak, P.C. Stern, S. Stovich, and E.E. Weber, 402–43. Washington D.C.: National Academy Press.

Rockström, Johan, Will Steffen, Kevin Noone, Åsa Persson, F. Stuart Chapin, Eric Lambin, Timothy M. Lenton, et al. 2009. Planetary boundaries: Exploring the safe operating space for humanity. *Ecology and Society* 14: 32. http://www.ecologyandsociety.org/vol14/iss2/art32/.

Roe, D., J. Elliott, C. Sandbrook, and M. Walpole, eds. 2013. *Biodiversity Conservation and Poverty Alleviation. Exploring the Evidence for a Link*. Chichester: Wiley-Blackwell.

Russi, D., P. ten Brink, A. Farmer, T. Badura, D. Coates, J. Förster, R. Kumar, and N. C. Davidson. 2013. *The Economics of Ecosystems and Biodiversity for Water and Wetlands*. London, Brussels: IIEP.

Scheffer, Marten. 2009. *Critical Transitions in Nature and Society*. Princeton: Princeton University Press.

Simonit, S., and C. Perrings. 2011. Sustainability and the value of the 'regulating' services: Wetlands and water quality in Lake Victoria. *Ecological Economics* 70: 1189–99.

Slootweg, R., and M. Jones. 2011. Resilience thinking improves SEA: a discussion paper. *Impact Assessment and Project Appraisal* 29: 263–76.

Soini, Katriina, and Inger Birkeland. 2014. Exploring the scientific discourse on cultural sustainability. *Geoforum* 51: 213–23. doi:10.1016/j.geoforum.2013.12.001.

Tagore, R. 1913. The Gardener LII. In *Collected Poems and Plays of Rabindranath Tagore*. New Delhi: Rupa Paperback, 2002.

TEEB. 2009. *The Economics of Ecosystems and Biodiversity for National and International Policy Makers. Summary: Responding to the Value of Nature*. UNEP/TEEB.

TEEB. 2011. *The Economics of Ecosystems and Biodiversity in Local and Regional Policy and Management*. London: Earthscan.

ten Brink, P, L Mazza, T. Badura, M. Kettunen, and S. Withana. 2012. *Nature and Its Role in the Transition to a Green Economy*. Brussels, London: IEEP.

Turner, Graham. 2014. *Is Global Collapse Imminent? An Updated Comparison of The Limits to Growth with Historical Data*. Melbourne. MSSI Research Paper Series 4.

Tvedt, T., and R. Coopey. 2010. *A History of Water: Rivers and Society: From Early Civilizations to Modern Times. Volume 2, Series 2*. London: I.B.Tauris & Co Ltd.

U.S. National Intelligence Council. 2012. *Global Trends 2013. Alternative Worlds*. Washington D.C.: National Intelligence Council.

UNESCO. 1972. *Convention Concerning the Protection of the World Cultural and Natural Heritage*. Paris: UNESCO.

United Nations. 2002. *Johannesburg Declaration on Sustainable Development. World Summit on Sustainable Development. A/CONF/199%20*. New York. United Nations.

United Nations. 2014. *Prototype Global Sustainable Development Report.* New York. United Nations.

Van Asselen, Sanneke, Peter H. Verburg, Jan E. Vermaat, and Jan H. Janse. 2013. Drivers of wetland conversion: A global meta-analysis. *PloS one* 8: e81292. doi:10.1371/journal.pone.0081292.

Withanage, H. 2006. *Advocacy Guide to ADB EIA Requirement.* Manila: Asian Development Bank.

Wood, A., A. Dixon, and M. McCartney. 2013. Conclusions, Transforming wetland livelihoods. In *Wetland Management and Sustainable Livelihoods in Africa*, eds. M. Wood, A. Dixon, and M. McCartney, 258-270. London: Earthscan, Routledge.

World Commission on Water. 2000. *A Water Secure Future: Vision for Water, Life and the Environment.* Marseille: World Water Council.

Zarfl, Christiane, Alexander E. Lumsdon, Jürgen Berlekamp, Laura Tydecks, and Klement Tockner. 2014. A global boom in hydropower dam construction. *Aquatic Sciences.* doi:10.1007/s00027-014-0377-0.

The Santa Cruz River

Four Millennia of Water Heritage and Security in the U.S.-Mexico Border Region

Rafael de Grenade[a] and Robert G. Varady[b]

a. Postdoctoral Research Associate
Udall Center for Studies in Public Policy
University of Arizona

b. Deputy Director and Research Professor, Udall Center
(corresponding author; rvarady@email.arizona.edu)

Context and Introduction

An inquiry into the historical role of water in assuring societal security—via a river's contribution to regional identity and to traditional food-production systems—may yield insights into desert cultures of the past. Perhaps more importantly, such a probe can offer critical clues to the future of water in desert cities. Tucson, Arizona, a city of nearly a million inhabitants in the Sonoran Desert, may seem an unlikely place for such a query. We believe, however, historical water management techniques and practices development in this region, when combined with new technologies, may offer approaches to increase water sustainability in cities around the globe. We consider the term 'water heritage' to be the collective traditions, beliefs, practices, and developments of place-based water use and management in the region through time, passed from generation to generation. Understood in this way, water heritage can be seen as a source of wisdom and inspiration for the future.

Tucson lies just 100 km north of the border with Mexico, in a semiarid stretch of the U.S.–Mexico border region (Fig. 1). The city—which sits astride the now-perennially dry Santa Cruz River—and its hinterlands have been occupied by humans for at least 10 000 years and by farming cultures for at least the last 5 000 years (Fish and Fish 1994; Logan 1999). The city draws its name from 'S-cuk Son,' meaning 'at the base of the black hill' in the local O'odham language. This referred to a series of springs that emerged in the river channel near the volcanic complex of Sentinel Peak and Tumamoc Hill, just west of downtown Tucson. The extension of a volcanic ridge under the channel forced deeper water to the surface, and created

Figure 1. Tucson, Arizona, and the Santa Cruz River valley. Photo credit: © PLKresan, kresanphotograph.com.

a stretch of year-round river flow. For several thousand years, this historic site of a 'perched aquifer' and the longer, riverine oasis complex of the Santa Cruz River have served as a source and center of life in the central Sonoran Desert region, a desert which extends across large areas of the southwestern United States in Arizona and California, and northwestern Mexico. The Santa Cruz River has a rich and enduring water heritage, which we define as the inherited legacy of the river and its use and management through time. This story begins in ancient times and follows the Santa Cruz through the demise of its flowing water, mesquite (*Prosopis spp.*) *bosques* and flood-irrigated agriculture, to the emergence of a water-conscious city. This experience may serve as a lesson from our desert city to other arid, urban environments around the world.

In an arid environment, a riverine oasis may be thought of as a place where groundwater reaches the Earth's surface and creates a permanent or ephemeral riparian habitat along a river channel. An 'oasis' is also a cultural construct where humans engage with scarce resources to create a positive and self-sustainable environmental niche in arid surroundings (Laureano 2001). This cultural concept characterizes traditional water management in the riverine oases of the Sonoran Desert, where non-industrialized farming communities persisted, and even thrived along river courses for at least the last four millennia. The Santa Cruz River supported settled farming communities and provided a corridor of travel, trade, exploration, and migration through the region that has shaped the landscape and cultures of the U.S.-Mexico borderlands.

Natural History of the River

The headwaters of the Santa Cruz River originate in the San Rafael Basin, a semiarid grassland in southeastern Arizona. The Santa Cruz flows south across the U.S.-Mexico border, and then takes a sweeping turn to double back into the United States, near the twin cities of Nogales, Arizona, and Nogales, Sonora. The

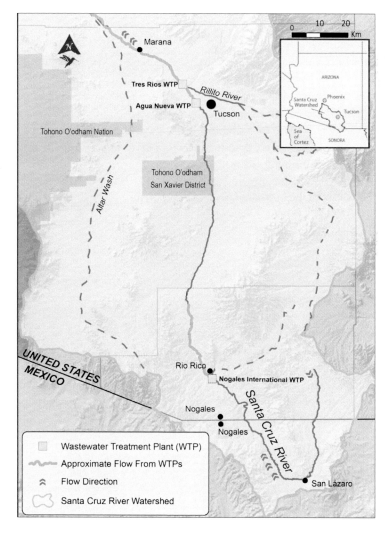

Figure 2. Map of the binational Santa Cruz River and its watershed. Base map courtesy of the Sonoran Institute.

river flows in a northwesterly direction, through the Tucson basin, and beyond (Fig. 2). The river drains an area of around 22 225 sq km before it meets the Gila, which traverses Arizona westward to join the Colorado River, and eventually the Gulf of California (Webb et al. 2014). On most maps, one cannot trace this journey, since the river virtually disappears into the desert sand except during extreme flooding events in winter, or after summer monsoon rains.

The Santa Cruz River has traced a path through the Tucson Basin for about a million years, and more precise geologic records have documented the path and depth of the channel for the last 9 000 years (Webb et al. 2014). The river followed a process of down-cutting and filling—with alternating braided streams, high water tables, and down cutting—and until the late 1800s, supported continuous riparian vegetation of cottonwoods, willows and mesquite *bosques* (forests), extensive wetlands, and intermittent stretches of flowing surface water along its course (Gregory and Nials 2005).

Almost 150 km of streams within the Santa Cruz watershed still flow year-round, though most of the river and its tributaries are 'xeroriparian' areas, dry most of the year but characterized by water-loving flora and fauna along the river corridors. A few natural *cienega*s, or riparian marshlands, can still be found near the headwaters and upper drainages, and several human-developed wetlands provide wildlife habitat and recreational opportunities. In the Sonoran Desert, most of the biotic activity can be found along these waterways, including 60% to 70% of wildlife and up to 90% of the bird species. The river corridors of southeastern Arizona host over 400 songbird species and provide critical north-south migratory flyways for over 200 subtropical songbirds as well as wintering and migrating waterfowl (SCVHA and Center for Desert Archaeology 2005).

Indigenous History

For at least ten millennia, the region has been home to numerous indigenous peoples, beginning with prehistoric Paleoindian groups like the Clovis culture to the present tribes of southwestern United States and northern Mexico; and including Uto-Aztecan peoples (e.g., Tohono O'odham, Yaqui, and Tarahumara), settled nomadic (mostly Athabascan) tribes, plains Indians (e.g., Comanche), Algonquians (e.g., Kickapoo), and other ethnic groups (e.g., Seri) and their descendants (Fish and Fish 1994; Logan 1999)[1]. These communities relied on the region's sparse resources, and archaeologists have shown that they devised modes of crop domestication and agriculture by means of intensive and extensive rainwater harvesting and floodwater diversion and use of canals. Channels uncovered in Arizona and in neighboring New Mexico demonstrate that crops were regularly irrigated during prehistoric times (Fish et al. 1986; Logan 1999; Mabry 2005a).

Indigenous cultures managed the intermittent flow of the Santa Cruz River to support agrarian societies in the greater Tucson basin for almost the last four millennia. Pre-historic peoples planted Mesoamerican crops—including corn,

---

1   There are over 30 American Indian tribes on the U.S. side of the border (21 of them officially recognized), and about 15—though lacking official status—on the Mexican side.

squash, beans and cotton—and locally harvested, domesticated, and cultivated native tobacco and small herb and grass species (Fish et al. 1986; Mabry 2005b; Doolittle and Mabry 2006). They lived in pit houses situated near elaborate canal and field systems on the river flood plains. Excavations at the site of Las Capas, northwest of Tucson near the confluence of the Santa Cruz and Rillito Rivers, revealed 3,200-year old irrigation canals, with main diversion and transport ditches delivering water into a network of smaller channels and gridded gardens (Mabry 2008). These canals are now considered to be the oldest and most enduring hydrological and agricultural systems known in the United States.

Archaeologists believe that the field and canal systems emerged in place, a local evolution of a hydraulic society. The complex irrigation systems necessitated community collaboration to build and maintain diversion and delivery canals, and allocate water flow to the fields throughout the growing season. Excavations at the Las Capas site revealed layer upon layer of farming plots, irrigation canals and pit houses. Radiocarbon dates from samples of maize at the site indicate a continuous habitation of settled farming communities for about five hundred years, 1250–750 BC (Mabry 2008). Canal sequences show an increase in length, use, labor requirements, efficiency, water control, and irrigated area, corresponding with more concentrated populations. These agricultural systems, examples of small-scale water management, represent the earliest beginnings of hierarchical agricultural societies in the region. The duration and continuity of the occupation, thickness of midden (refuse) deposits, number of artifacts, and high degrees of wear, maintenance, and recycling of stone tools make Las Capas a highly unique Early Agricultural Period (1200 BC–AD 150) site in the U.S. and Mexico borderlands. Prehistoric farming communities along the Santa Cruz River maintained close social contact and developed extensive trade routes that reached from Mexico to California to acquire metals such as copper, silver and gold, shell jewelry, obsidian, textiles, salt, and seeds as well as exchange agricultural and water-management knowledge and technologies (Mabry 2003).

The Hohokam culture arrived around AD 450, and constructed carefully engineered irrigation systems. The Hohokam introduced new varieties of crops and domesticated the native tepary bean (*Phaseolus acutifolius*), agave (*Agave* spp.*)*, little barley (*Hordeum pusillum*), panic grass (*Panicum* spp.) and devil's claw (*Proboscidea parviflora*) (Fish and Nabhan 1991). They eventually extended their irrigation complexes to the Phoenix Basin farther north, creating over 500 km of main ditches using skills honed in the Santa Cruz River watershed (Fish 2000). The environmental variability of the region led to an employment of several types of farming and water-management technologies. In addition to diverting water into canal networks from perennial flows, the Hohokam practiced floodwater farming of *bajada*, or lower mountain slopes and lower arroyos, capturing and spreading ephemeral flows laden with nutrient-rich organic debris onto agricultural fields. They also utilized broader overland sheet flow with simple rock constructions designed to intercept, direct and concentrate stormwater.

These low-tech landscape manipulation strategies included shallow contour terraces created by lines of single stone, diversion walls, grids, and rockpile mounds. In the Tucson area, the Hohokam used these rockpile mounds to cultivate agave extensively across hundreds of hectares of the lower mountain bajadas (Fish et al. 1992; Mabry 2005b), in a review of the literature documented six distinct agricultural practices in the U.S. Southwest region of the Sonoran Desert: dry farming, rainfed farming, water-table farming, runoff farming, flood farming and irrigated farming. These strategies, often utilized in combination by the same farming communities, evolved to optimize harvest and minimize risk in a highly variable climate and local environment.

Related O'odham tribes, presumed descendants of the Hohokam, later inhabited the greater Southwest, from Jalisco, Mexico, to Phoenix, Arizona, and from the San Pedro River to the Gulf of California. The Sobaípuri O'odham lived in permanent farming villages along the Santa Cruz and neighboring San Pedro Rivers. The Tohono O'odham were traditionally two-village people, living in the foothills during the winter, and farming along temporary desert washes in the summer using *ak-chin*, or flood irrigation farming (Dobyns 1974; Nabhan 1983; Rea 1997). The term *ak-chin* means, 'At the mouth of the wash,' or 'Where the wash disappears into the sand,' and it refers to the diversion of ephemeral floodwaters during summer monsoon storms. The Tohono O'odham people planted cottonwoods and willows in living fencerows to slow, direct, and spread the stormwater over a broad area and trap suspended silt and organic matter. When the waters receded, they planted seeds of many different traditional crops such as varieties of corn, beans and squash in the fertile, moist ground. O'odham peoples still grow several landraces of the 'three sisters,' which they call *huñ* (maize), *bawi* (tepary beans), and *ha:l* (squash). These desert peoples, as did many others around the world, built upon a long legacy of diverse farming and irrigation technologies and developed innovative strategies to make the most of their very limited soil and water resources.

Spanish Control of the Santa Cruz

O'odham peoples were farming along the Santa Cruz River, known in the O'odham language as *Hikdán*, when the prominent Jesuit missionary Father Eusebio Francisco Kino first arrived to the area in the late 1600s (Seymour 2012). Padre Kino, as he was known, first traveled north, down the Santa Cruz valley in 1691, and named it the *Rio del Santa Maria*. The term *Santa Cruz* (Holy Cross in Spanish) first appeared on the neighboring San Pedro River, as the name Kino gave to settlements of Sobaipuri-O'odham. A later Spanish presidio, also on the San Pedro took the name of Santa Cruz. In 1787, the garrison moved to the Santa Maria River, and ultimately, the river took the Santa Cruz name.

The region had become the northern frontier of the Spanish empire and the edge of European civilization in western North America. Padre Kino established the Tumacacori and San Xavier del Bac missions along flowing stretches of the Santa Cruz River, south, or upstream of Tucson. In 1692, Kino wrote of encountering

Figure 3. Tucson in 1810, illustration © Paul Mirocha. Thanks to Doug Gann, and the Arizona State Museum for the historical research.

around 400 Sobaípuri O'odham farmers irrigating crops at the base of Sentinel Peak. Here, at *S-cuk Son*, Kino established a small *visita* as a religious outpost of the San Xavier mission. This site later became the *Misión San Agustín*.

The Spanish developed their own canal systems, called *acequias*. These irrigation ditches reflect water management technologies from the Roman and Islamic influences on the Iberian Peninsula long before the New World conquests. The word *acequia* derives from the Arabic *as-saquiya*, or irrigation canal. Early Spanish missionaries constructed irrigation systems as an integral part of their evangelizing and colonizing strategy. The missions were centers of *reducción*, to concentrate indigenous tribes and convert them to Christianity. The farming and foodways practices of the early missionaries were a key component of this process.

The Spaniards utilized indigenous neophytes to dig an *acequia madre*, or 'mother' ditch that intercepted the flowing river. This canal delivered water to lateral ditches that watered the floodplain fields and orchards. They lined some of these canals with rock or lime mortar, and in places created holding ponds to regulate the flow of water to the fields. Jesuit missionaries introduced many Old World crops and livestock species to the region—fruit trees such as fig, date palm, sour orange and sweet lime, pomegranate, quince, peach, apricot, apple, pear and olive, grape vines, grains such as barley and winter wheat, culinary herbs and vegetable crops from across Europe and Africa as well as horse, burro, sheep, goat, and cattle breeds (Dunmire 2004) (Fig. 3).

Spanish missionaries, soldiers and settlers, as well as crypto-Moors and crypto-Jews introduced other desert-adapted crops from arid regions around the world, and added to the complex irrigation systems along the Santa Cruz (Sheridan 2004). Spanish water law and customs remain part of the Southwest water jurisdiction as a legacy of this historical period. Throughout the settled history of the basin, different peoples have adopted existing agricultural practices and crops and blended them with new methods and species, creating a four-millennia agricultural continuum.

Early American Agriculture on the River

After the Gadsden Purchase in 1854, Hispanic, Anglo, and non-Anglo farmers of many nationalities arrived to the region and practiced irrigated agriculture on the floodplains above the Santa Cruz River. By the late 1800s, Tucson became a thriving, diverse center of soldiers, entrepreneurs, farmers, and merchants. Though now a part of the United States, its strong Hispanic elite and Mexican heritage closely bound the city to its cultural past—the majority of the town's inhabitants were Mexican, and agriculture and ranching provided the economic mainstay of the region (Sheridan 1986). An 1879 newspaper reported almost 16 200 ha of cultivated land along the Santa Cruz River (Hadley 2003).

The growing population put increasing demands on the Santa Cruz River for irrigation, drinking water, recreation, and mill power (Varady and Ward 2009; Webb et al. 2014) (Fig. 4). In 1863 and again in 1883, the river was dammed to

Figure 4. The still-flowing Santa Cruz, circa 1900, taken from the flank of the volcanic Sentinel Peak. Note the growing city of Tucson in the background. Courtesy of the Arizona Historical Society.

power flourmills, and the resulting lakes provided recreation opportunities, such as duck hunting, to the town's residents. A few years later, local entrepreneurs with an eye toward expanding regional agricultural production diverted river water upstream of the Mexican-American community's traditional acequia systems. These immense canals, designed to intercept the subsurface flow of the Santa Cruz, eventually led to massive arroyo cutting and erosion of the river floodplain (Cooke and Reeves 1976; Mabry 2006). The advent of groundwater pumping in the 1890s, initially fueled by woodburning pumps was the beginning of the end of Tucson's riverine oasis.

A final exotic and vivid example of downtown Tucson's oasis in the early 1900s was Carillo's Gardens. Sourced from natural springs, the gardens featured three man-made lakes, three hectares of fruit trees and roses, including 2 000 grape vines, 500 peach trees, 200 quinces, 60 pomegranates and nine apricot trees (Sheridan 1986). The entertainment oasis also boasted high-end modernity with a saloon, shooting gallery, restaurant, dance pavilion, private rooms, and 12 bathhouses with hot baths, a zoo, and a circus. Upstanding Tucson citizens held formal dance parties with orchestra music, enjoyed picnics, and spent weekend afternoons boating, eating ice cream, and listening to music. The garden's founder, Leopoldo Carillo, was a wealthy Tucson rancher and businessman born in Sonora, Mexico, in 1836. He had traveled widely for his business, and wanted to bring the beauty of gardens he had seen in California to the early frontier town. His gardens symbolized the end of the frontier days of Tucson and its rise into a regal and lush desert city. The gardens have long disappeared, along with most of the floodplain fields irrigated from the flowing Santa Cruz.

Demise of the Santa Cruz

A series of natural and human events precipitated the demise of the riverine oasis and interrupted the continuous four-millennia practice of irrigation and agriculture. Overgrazing, woodcutting, and other resource extraction activities transformed the desert landscape (Bahre and Hutchinson 1985; Bahre 1991). Aquifer levels dropped, and farming became a costly and more difficult endeavor in the region as canal headgates were stranded high above the river flow in the incised channels. Groundwater pumping and deeper canal structures kept the valley's agriculture alive until catastrophic floods in 1940 irreparably damaged most of the irrigation systems in the Tucson area (Sheridan 1986; Webb et al. 2014). Modern technologies for water extraction exacerbated the sinking aquifer. Over the last century, the once superficial and flowing water table has plummeted over 76 m, causing ground subsidence and forcing residents and municipal water companies to dig ever deeper wells (Hadley 2003). Down-cutting has dropped the river channel 9 m as it enters Tucson, and severe erosion has also channelized several of the river's tributaries. Across Tucson, sections of the river and its tributaries have since been stabilized with soil cement to prevent further damage. Urban development has now filled in the once fertile agricultural valley, and the flowing and wetland oases of the Santa Cruz River have all but disappeared, reviving only after intense rainstorms.

Water Scarcity and Food Security

Until the early 1990s Tucson was the largest city in the United States entirely dependent on groundwater (Martin et al. 1984). The city and surrounding suburbs have expanded to include more than a million people, tripling in size since the 1960s. To satiate Tucson's increasing thirst, the Central Arizona Project (CAP), a trans-Arizona canal now brings water diverted from the Colorado River to much of southeastern Arizona for municipal and agricultural water needs. A system of aqueducts, tunnels, pumping plants, and pipelines delivers water 541 km from the Colorado River to the border of the San Xavier Indian Reservation, 22 km southwest of Tucson (CAP n.d.). Completed in 1993, the canal provides the largest single source of renewable water in the state, and is also the single largest energy user and carbon emitter because of the pumping stations needed to lift the water some 730 meters across a rising landscape. The water arrives too highly mineralized and salinized from evaporation to supply the city directly; instead the water shares of the Tucson metropolitan area are pumped into the aquifer to be blended with groundwater and cycled back into the municipal water systems. The Tohono O'odham have expanded their farming of forage and food crops using CAP water, a legal and political success for the tribe that, though conflict-laden, may provide sources of poverty alleviation and regional water negotiating power in the future (Brown and Ingram 1987; Nuñez and Wallace 1993).

Many farmers in the greater Tucson region still produce annual and perennial food and forage crops using groundwater and Colorado River water provided through the Central Arizona Project. The region is an important producer of cotton, wheat, alfalfa, and pecans, and in some locations, fruit orchards and vineyards. Pecan production is highest in Green Valley, south of Tucson, where over 1 800 ha of pecan trees make it one of the largest irrigated pecan orchards in the United States. Farms in the area northwest of Tucson produce cotton and wheat—a Durham wheat produced in the area is exported to Italy to make flour for pasta. The San Xavier Co-op Farm on the Tohono O'odham Nation cultivates traditional crops of tepary beans, squashes, and melons, as well as alfalfa. The region also supports several local farmers' markets, 'pick-your-own' farms, wineries, research and conservation farms, agriculture and food related nonprofit organizations, and annual planting and harvest festivals, making it a vital source of food production despite its limited water resources (SCVHA n.d.).

Innovations in a Desert City

In recent years, Tucson has taken critical steps to restore some of the environment lost to development. In the process, the city has sought to become a national and international leader in developing innovative urban water programs for arid regions.

As an example, city codes instituted in 2008 mandate that new commercial buildings supply at least 50% of their landscaping water needs with harvested rainwater, the first city in the nation to adopt such stringent requirements. Many local businesses have turned to permaculture and landscape design ideas specific to arid regions—techniques that also existed in the prehistoric cultures of Tucson. These include harvesting rainwater off roof tops and surrounding spaces such as sidewalks, parking lots, plazas, and parks; selection of native tree, shrub and forb species; shading and mulch to prevent water loss; and the creation of terraces, basins, and swales to capture runoff. The City of Tucson also features educational sites such as Sweetwater Wetlands, a water treatment facility that is also an urban wildlife habitat with hundreds of migratory and resident bird species, making the site a valuable outdoor classroom. In fact, virtually every example of permaculture and landscape design across Tucson serves as a direct or indirect illustration for residents and visitors of how to reduce water demands and facilitate greater water security in an urban setting.

Local nonprofit organizations, such as the community-based Watershed Management Group, support private businesses and residences in harvesting rainwater for domestic and landscaping purposes. The nonprofits' programs also include community-improvement projects and infrastructure improvements, hands-on educational programs for schools, live demonstration sites, and water management certification and technical training. They hold community work days where volunteers assist, and are later assisted by, other volunteers in projects such as installing cisterns, curb cuts, and catchment basins; planting drought-tolerant native and agricultural species; creating sunken gardens; and designing filter systems to utilize runoff and wastewater in landscaping. The Watershed Management Group offers free classes that count toward city-sponsored rebates on cisterns and water harvesting systems. Specific lessons address how to consider the local landscape and weather patterns when designing for urban water sustainability and how to design and create water-sustainable outside private and public spaces.

Other lessons focus on using the mutualistic relationships of native desert plants, such as by planting native trees to attract pollinators, support local wildlife, and provide edible fruits, berries, seeds and nuts as well as to conserve water and build the soil. While many of these strategies may be found in the archaeologies of desert cultures around the world, working with the specific climate of the Sonoran Desert, selecting plant species and guilds from the extreme altitudinal gradients of the region's Sky Islands, understanding the unique relationships among native plant and animal species, and drawing from the long prehistoric and historic agricultural practices build on and extend the region's water heritage and adaptations.

Across the city, several neighborhoods have diverted street runoff for tree plantings on city right-of-ways. The Watershed Management Group, in partnership with the Arizona Department of Environmental Quality have offered specific grants to develop 'green' streets and neighborhoods in the city, and many individuals, communities, and nonprofits have also taken the initiative. Leaders such as Brad Lancaster's 'Harvesting Rainwater' intiative and the Sonoran Permaculture Guild have reconfigured urban spaces to be informative and inviting public spaces (Fig. 5). These groups offer information on the watersheds of Tucson, greywater and rainwater harvest and treatment, water harvesting events, local plant-species and landscape design strategies, public workshops, private classes, videos, websites,

Figure 5. Before and after photographs of a Tucson street right-of-way with native trees. Water drains from the street through curb cuts to fill sunken basins when it rains. Photograph: Brad Lancaster, harvestingrainwater.com.

blogs and books describing regionally-adapted water management practices to increase the 'green' spaces of Tucson.

Native Seeds/SEARCH is a local nonprofit that has worked since 1983 to conserve, document and distribute traditional crop varieties to prevent the loss of agricultural diversity. They maintain a seed bank of 2 000 varieties of arid-lands adapted crops and operate a 25-ha conservation farm in Patagonia. These varieties are given freely to local Indigenous groups and available to Tucson residents to create local drought-adapted food systems. Another agricultural site, The Mission Garden near downtown Tucson, managed by the Friends of Tucson's Birthplace, features a reconstruction of the original adobe wall of a Spanish *visita* surrounding 1.7 ha of educational and food producing gardens with over 50 kinds of traditionally harvested native plants, rare heirloom varieties of fruit trees and grape vines, and other Tohono O'odham, Spanish, Mexican, and American food crops that were historically grown in Tucson. This living museum interprets Tucson's 4 100-year agricultural and water management history.

The University of Arizona (UA) College of Architecture, Planning and Landscape Architecture offers green-building and water-harvesting programs and showcases innovative techniques across the university campus. A specific onsite demonstration and education program called The Underwood Family Sonoran Landscape Laboratory features a desert oasis that integrates both the built and natural environment, and the guiding principles of sustainable landscape architecture: water conservation, reduction of urban flooding, reduction of urban heat-island effect. The UA Water Resources Research Center, a research and extension unit and federally designated research center, promotes research, education, and policy development. A few key programs include water harvesting, groundwater governance and management, transboundary aquifer assessments, and water sustainability. Researchers at the UA Southwest Center, School of Anthropology, and Arizona State Museum conduct research, teach courses, and have published extensively on historical and modern water and food-security practices in the region, including Sonoran Desert-adapted agriculture and water management and agricultural strategies for climate change. UA researchers specialize in all aspects of water research and policy, including breakthrough studies on water quality and water reuse, water law, and surface and groundwater management. Tucson hydrologists excel in water-quality research and are actively investigating and testing the potential for supplying the city's water needs through harvested and reclaimed water. The region's heritage and collective innovation provide a wealth of knowledge, ideas, and techniques to create drought-resistant urban landscapes and increase Tucson's food and water security.

As in desert cities around the world, reclaimed water, wastewater, and stormwater are critical resources that are expected to be an ever more important part of the city's future. In the upper Santa Cruz River just north of Nogales on the U.S.-Mexico border, the release of treated effluent into the river has revived several miles of streamflow. Similarly, effluent recharge north of Tucson has also regenerated a section of the Santa Cruz on its path to the Gila.

At a more regional scale, Pima County, which includes Tucson, has developed large-scale rainwater and wastewater projects such as Sweetwater Wetlands and the Kino Environmental Restoration Project. The project, known as KERP, is a large-scale stormwater detention basin, flood-control facility, and riparian ecosystem in Tucson (KERP n.d.; Chavez 2006). The 50-ha site features an almost 3-ha lake that collects water from a 46 sq km watershed and is surrounded by native vegetation of marshlands, grasslands, and mesquite bosques. Stormwater harvested in the basin is used to irrigate the site and the grounds of a large nearby hospital, as well as a public ballpark and practice fields. The ponds and native terrestrial habitats support resident and migratory waterfowl, as well as shorebirds, songbirds, raptors, and a wide array of other wildlife. The site attracts birdwatchers year-round and also features a 3-km pedestrian and bicycle trail. The Tucson Audubon Society and scientists from the University of Arizona conduct research and bird surveys in the basin. The Kino Environmental Restoration Project is a pioneering site that provides flood control, stormwater detention, irrigation, enhanced water quality, wildlife habitat, and recreational opportunities for Tucson residents and visitors. The site serves as a model of what is likely to be Tucson's oasis future. Other riparian restoration/rehabilitation projects include the Wa:k hikdañ on the nearby San Xavier District of the Tohono O'odham Nation and the Tucson Audubon's Santa Cruz River Habitat Project northwest of Tucson near the town of Marana.

Though the perennially flowing Santa Cruz has vanished forever, these efforts offer hope for the region's water future and provide a vivid example of how people and the river are intimately braided through the region's history.

Water Heritage and Water Security

Tucson's water heritage can be a key to the city's future sustainability. According to the City of Tucson and Pima County, water pricing and other water-use conservation and efficiency measures such as public education, assistance and training programs, and water-conservation ordinances have slowed the rate of water use dramatically in the city (City of Tucson and Pima County 2009). This trend may allow for the city to continue its population and economic growth trajectories in the coming decades under the current social and environmental context. However, it raises questions as to its vulnerability to climate change, large population increases, and reallocation of the Colorado River.

Food security, or people's 'physical and economic access to sufficient, safe and nutritious food to meet their dietary needs and food preferences for an active and healthy life' (FAO 1996), has also become a critical challenge. The nearby borderlands see thousands of tons of food moving through from Mexico to distribution centers in California. But little of this food makes it to area residents, where poverty and food insecurity affect people of all ages and ethnicities.

Now, as the major food-producing areas of Mexico, California, Arizona, and much of the dry U.S. Southwest face unprecedented droughts and water shortages, the question of water security—i.e., sufficient supplies of good-quality water for human use and environmental sustainability (Scott, et al. 2013)—has become critically urgent. To confront this situation, it is valuable to rely on the diversity of strategies employed throughout the region's history. If an 'oasis' is a space where humans creatively engage with scarce resources to create a positive and self-sustainable environmental niche in arid surroundings, then Tucson continues to be such as oasis, even if the supply and nature of its relationship to water has changed substantially over the past four millennia. In the case of Tucson and the Santa Cruz River, a highly diverse and creative approach to optimizing a scarce resource can increase the long-term resilience of the city, the river, and local human and nonhuman residents.

The water heritage of the Santa Cruz River offers numerous lessons that may be adaptable in other cities in arid and semiarid environments:

- Regional water-security strategies should include appropriate use of rainwater and wastewater, as well as of the current available sources, wise landscape design, use of native plants and principles of arid-lands agroecology, public water-use education, and should promote private and public water conservation strategies.

- Water should be considered, treated, and economically valued as a scarce, non-renewable resource, especially in arid environments.

- Restoration of riparian habitats—even for small stretches—revitalizes wildlife, promotes recreation, enhances property value, and contributes to a city's sense of place and of itself.

- Benefiting from knowledge of effective, traditional water-management and food-growing practices—especially indigenous practices, when available—can contribute to innovative strategies for modern urban management.

- Drought-adapted species, as well as creation and creative use of microclimates can facilitate greater food production in arid conditions.

- Although an export agricultural economy has supported the region in the past, it has never done so sustainably, and regional consumers should be the first in line.

- Desert living should look like what it is, with cultures adapting to a diverse and highly variable local environment.

The Santa Cruz River literally and metaphorically crosses many divides: The U.S.-Mexico international boundary, and city, county, state, tribal, and private jurisdictions. Accordingly, the solution to its future as a geographic and cultural feature of the landscape will be a transboundary collaboration at many levels.

Acknowledgments

The authors gratefully acknowledge partial support from Lloyd's Register Foundation, a charitable foundation helping to protect life and property by supporting engineering-related education, public engagement and the application of research; and from the Morris K. Udall and Stewart L. Udall Foundation in Tucson, Arizona. The paper benefited greatly from expert editing provided by Robert Merideth of the Udall Center for Studies in Public Policy at the University of Arizona.

References

Bahre, C. J. 1991. *A Legacy of Change: Historic Human Impact on Vegetation in the Arizona Borderlands*. Tucson: University of Arizona Press.

Bahre, C. J. and C. F. Hutchinson. 1985. The impact of historic fuelwood cutting on the semidesert woodlands of southeastern Arizona. *Journal of Forest History* 29(4): 175-186.

Brown, F. L. and H. M. Ingram. 1987. *Water and Poverty in the Southwest*. Tucson: The University of Arizona Press.

CAP (Central Arizona Project). http://www.cap-az.com. Accessed 10 August 2014.

Chavez, Kathleen, M. 2006. *Ed Pastor Kino Environmental Restoration Project (KERP)*. Tucson: Pima County Regional Flood Control District.

City of Tucson and Pima County. 2009. *Water Conservation Technical Paper. Water/ Wastewater Infrastructure, Supply and Planning Study: Phase II*. Tucson: City of Tucson and Pima County.

Cooke, R. U. and R. W. Reeves. 1976. *Arroyos and Environmental Change in the American South-West*. Oxford Research Studies in Geography. London and New York: Clarendon Press, Oxford University Press.

Dobyns, Henry F. 1974. The Kohatk: Oasis and Akchin Horticulturalists. *Ethnohistory* 21 (4): 317-327.

Doolittle, William E. and Jonathan B. Mabry. 2006. Environmental mosaics, agricultural diversity and the Evolutionary adoption of maize in the American Southwest. In *Histories of Maize: Multidisciplinary Approaches to the Prehistory, Linguistics, Biogeography, Domestication, and Evolution of Maize*, ed. John E. Staller, Robert H. Tykot, Bruce F. Benz, 109-121. Amsterdam: Academic Press.

Dunmire, William W. 2004. *Gardens of New Spain: How Mediterranean Plants and Foods Changed America*. Austin: University of Texas Press.

Fish, Paul. R., Suzanne. K. Fish, Austin Long and Charles Miksicek. 1986. Early corn remains from Tumamoc Hill, Southern Arizona. *American Antiquity* 51(3): 563-572.

Fish, Suzanne. K. 2000. Hohokam impacts on Sonoran Desert Environment. In *Imperfect Balance: Early Landscape Transformations in the Precolumbian Americas*, ed. David L. Lentz, 251-280. New York: Columbia University Press.

Fish, Suzanne K., Paul R. Fish, and John H. Madsen. 1992. Evidence for large scale agave cultivation in the Marana Community. In *The Marana Community in the Hohokam World*, ed. Suzanne K., Fish, Paul R. Fish, and John H. Madsen. Anthropological Papers of the University of Arizona 56. Tucson: The University of Arizona Press.

Fish, Suzanne K. and Paul R. Fish. 1994. Prehistoric Desert Farmers of the Southwest. *Annual Review of Anthropology* 23: 83-108.

Fish, Suzanne K., and Gary P. Nabhan. 1991. Desert as context: The Hohokam environment. In *Exploring the Hohokam: Prehistoric Desert Peoples of the American Southwest*, ed. George J. Gumerman, 35-54. Albuquerque: University of New Mexico Press.

FAO (Food and Agriculture Organization of the United Nations). 1996. Rome Declaration on World Food Security. http://www.fao.org/docrep/003/w3613e/w3613e00.htm. Accessed 28 August 2014.

Gregory, David A. and Fred L. Nials. 2005. The environmental context of early agricultural period occupations in the Tucson basin. In *Subsistence and Resource Use Strategies of Early Agricultural Communities in Southern Arizona*, ed. Michael W. Diehl, 19-71. Anthropological Papers No. 34. Tucson: Center for Desert Archaeology.

Hadley, Diana. 2003. The changing Santa Cruz: 1680-1912. *Sonorensis* 23(1): 10-17.

KERP (Kino Environmental Restoration Project). http://rfcd.pima.gov/projects/kerp/. Accessed 10 July 2014.

Laureano, Pietro. 2001. *The Water Atlas: Traditional Knowledge to Combat Desertification*. Turin: Bollati Boringhieri Editore.

Logan, Michael F. 1999. Head-Cuts and Check-Dams: Changing Patterns of Environmental Manipulation by the Hohokam and Spanish in the Santa Cruz River Valley, 200-1820. *Environmental History* 4(3): 405-430.

Mabry, Jonathan B. (Ed.). 2008. *Las Capas: Early Irrigation and Sedentism in a Southwestern Floodplain*. Anthropological Papers 28. Tucson: Archaeology Southwest.

Mabry, Jonathan B. 2006. Geomorphology and stratigraphy. In *Rio Nuevo Archaeology, 2000-2003: Investigations at the San Agustín Mission and Mission Gardens, Tucson Presidio, Tucson Pressed Brick Company and Clearwater Site*, ed. Homer Thiel and Jonathan B. Mabry. Technical Report No. 2004-11. Tucson: Center for Desert Archaeology.

Mabry, Jonathan B. 2005a. Changing knowledge and ideas about the first farmers in southeastern Arizona. In *The Late Archaic Across the Borderlands: From Foraging to Farming*, ed., Bradley J. Vierra, 41-83. Texas Archaeology and Ethnobotany Series, Series Editor Thomas R. Hester. Austin: University of Texas.

Mabry, Jonathan B. 2005b. Diversity in early Southwestern farming and optimization models of transitions to agriculture. In *Subsistence and Resource Use Strategies of Early Agricultural Communities in Southern Arizona*, ed. Michael W. Diehl, 113-152. Anthropological Papers No. 34. Tucson: Center for Desert Archaeology.

Mabry, Jonathan. B. 2003. Oasis cultures: Prehistoric lifeways along a desert river. *Sonorensis* 23(1): 4-9.

Martin, W. E., H.M. Ingram, N. K. Laney, and A. H. Griffin. 1984. *Saving Water in a Desert City*. Baltimore: Resources for the Future Press.

Nabhan, G. P. 1983. Papago Fields: Arid lands ethnobotany and agricultural ecology. Doctoral dissertation. Tucson: University of Arizona.

Nuñez, A. and M. G. Wallace. 1993. Solutions or symbols? An Indian perspective on water settlements. In *Indian Water in the New West*, ed. T. R. McGuire, W. B. Lord, M. G. Wallace, 35-53. Tucson: The University of Arizona Press.

Rea, Amadeo M. 1997. *At the Desert's Green Edge: An Ethnobotany of the Gila River Pima*. Tucson: University of Arizona Press.

SCVHA (Santa Cruz Valley Heritage Alliance). n.d. http://www.santacruzheritage.org. Accessed 10 July 2014.

SCVHA (Santa Cruz Valley Heritage Alliance) and Center For Desert Archaeology. 2005. *Feasibility Study for the Santa Cruz Valley Heritage Area*. http://www.santacruzheritage.org/heritageareas/study.

Scott, C. A., F. J. Meza, R. G. Varady, H. Tiessen, J. McEvoy, G. M. Garfin, L. M. Farfán, M. Wilder, N. Pineda Pablos. 2013. Water security and adaptive management in the arid Americas. *Annals of the Assoc. of Amer. Geographers* 103 (2): 280-289.

Seymour, Deni J. 2012. Santa Cruz River: The origin of a place name. *Journal of Arizona History* 53(1): 81-88.

Sheridan, Thomas E. 2004. *Tumacacori Historic Resources Study*. National Park Service. http://www.nps.gov/history/history/online_books/tuma/hrs/

Sheridan, Thomas E. 1986. *Los Tucsonenses: The Mexican Community of Tucson, 1854-1941*. Tucson: University of Arizona Press.

Varady, R. G., and E. Ward. 2009. Transboundary conservation in context: What drives environmental change? In *Conservation of Shared Environments: Learning from the United States and Mexico*, ed. L. López-Hoffman, E. D. McGovern, R. G. Varady, and K. W. Flessa, 9-22. Tucson: University of Arizona Press.

Webb, R. H., J. L. Betancourt, R. R. Johnson, and R. M. Turner. 2014. *Requiem for the Santa Cruz: An Environmental History of an Arizona River*. University of Arizona Press, Tucson.

Cultural and touristic strategies for preservation and enhancement of Venice and its lagoon

Francesco Calzolaio[1]

f.calzolaio@culturnet.net

This paper focuses on the complex relationship between the waters of the Venice lagoon and the community of people who share its amphibious space, residents and visitors. Starting from a systemic analysis of the current situation of this World Heritage site, it proposes a structured response to three main issues, all of which stem from the delicate and fragile interface between land and water, from the gross imbalance between residents and visitors, and from the uncertain relationship between the community and its cultural heritage, at the level of the lagoon as a whole.

Crisis of identity

The first issue is a crisis of community identity. The lagoon community has identified itself intimately with the water since the time of the Serenissima Republic. Today, however, the lagoon has lost much of its functionality as an interconnected urban archipelago. It has also lost its unified management through the oldest public administration of the modern world: the water board (*Magistrato delle Acque*) founded in the 16th century and closed in 2014, because it had long ago ceased to play its role in actively managing the lagoon waters. In modern times its role had been mainly concentrated on implementing works of hydraulic engineering: the famous mobile barriers at the inlets to protect the lagoon from the exceptional high tides (*acque alte*). Territorial management of the lagoon has been split into many administrative bodies.

The polycentric network of communities facing the lagoon has become disintegrated, because the lagoon cities and villages look to their vis-à-vis on the mainland, easily accessible by car, rather than to their neighbours across the lagoon. The lagoon has become a barrier, whereas historically it united all the settlements.

---

1 President of the association Venti di Cultura; founder of the association Faro Venezia; member of Icomos Italy, Committee for the Industrial and Engineering Heritage of Europa Nostra; coordinator of the Committee for the Ecomuseum of the Venice lagoon; consultant to Unesco's 'Venezia e la sua laguna' site office, Comune di Venezia.

Figure 1. Cormorans at Cavallino. Photograph by Riccardo Matassi.

We must work to restore the lagoon's role as a mediator, a concentrator of social relationships. To this end, two bodies – the Committee for the ecomuseum of the lagoon, and the Steering Committee for the Unesco World Heritage Site 'Venice and its lagoon', strive to strengthen the links among institutions, associations and citizens around the lagoon. The association 'Venti di Cultura', together with these two committees, contributes to forging these stronger ties by means of organising a festival across the lagoon, one of the network of major festivals along urban waterfronts supported by the European Commission through the 'River of Opportunities' programme.

Crisis of access

The second handicap is the inadequate network of mooring points allowing effective interchange along the shores of the lagoon. The territorial and urban system around the lagoon has grown since WWII with infrastructure oriented to the rationalisation of land transport, to the detriment of the overall water transport and distribution network. The processes have continued to the point where many communities have only partial access to the network of the lagoon canals; in particular, they are handicapped due to the lack of quays, landing stages and mooring places in the lagoon network. It is essential to consolidate the places of land/water interchange, distributed around the perimeter of the lagoon, such as a sequence of interpretive centres of the local cultural resources. This is the objective of the Unesco office for Venice and its lagoon, based in the city of Venice, which is harmonising the municipal urban plans, and has drawn up an outline plan for the enhancement of the lagoon's landscape and culture. For the Unesco Venice office, the author is engaged in coordinating a team of professionals, including representatives from all the municipalities committed to opening or reopening their doors to the lagoon waterway network.

Crisis of tourism offer

The tourism offer of the lagoon is excessively concentrated in the central area of Venice. The outstanding cultural heritage concentrated here is visited by an impressive global audience, but is threatened by the loss of identification by the local community, as mentioned above. This antinomy could be envisioned as an opportunity for the 'heritage community' to become an interpreter of its material and immaterial heritage. Fernand Braudel reminds us: 'the foreigner has been fascinated, monopolised by the city, and he too easily disdains the inland sea which belongs to it as a plant belongs to its flower'.[2] Consequently, a sense of deprivation causes the tourists to be less motivated to return to Venice today. As stated in the National Geographic`s study on the most important Unesco World Heritage Sites, Venice is overwhelmed by tourists' monoculture, and visitors feel guilty of 'complicity in the degradation of the city'.[3]

Observing this saturation of the main routes in the city, one cannot help but regret the absence of any offer of cultural tourism based on a stay of several days in the lagoon, hence the Lagunalonga itineraries presented below.

Heritage-based development models

The pioneering work on the interplay between cultural landscapes and communities ensouls the approach presented in the present paper. The processes of participation in cultural heritage are inspired by the Council of Europe's 'Framework Convention on the Value of Cultural Heritage for Society', signed in Faro on 27 October 2005. The importance of participation is also underlined by the deterioration of the Italian landscape since WW II. This landscape has practically lost its fundamental role as the direct expression of the resident communities. The notion of 'participation' applied to the landscape suggests enhancement of the heritage community, formed by 'people who value specific aspects of cultural heritage which they wish, within the framework of public action, to sustain and transmit to future generations' (art. 2). The Faro Convention also promotes the reinforcement of social cohesion 'by fostering a sense of shared responsibility towards the places in which people live' (art. 8).

Participation in cultural heritage has seen radical changes in recent years. On one hand, inclusive processes have been put in place, giving citizens the chance to participate in transformation of their territory, to share choices consciously

---

2   Braudel Fernand, 1987, 'Il Mediterraneo', Bompiani, Rome. p. 51.
3   National Geographic, 'Best, Worst World Heritage Sites Ranked', November/December 2005 issue of National Geographic Traveller Magazine.

proposed by public authorities and/or by professionals. A precursor in Italy (and Europe) was the architect and town planner Giancarlo de Carlo, who as early as the late 1960s started teaching and implementing models of active and responsible participation of users in the design process.

Figure 2. A historical Caorlina in Treporti. Photograph by Davide Trapani.

Figure 3. The Nuovo Trionfo historical Trabaccolo at Pelestrina. Photograph by Davide Trapani.

On the other hand, participation in museums is designed to provoke a dynamic interaction between the visitor and the objects, no longer just static and (possibly) ecstatic, but involving a participatory experience of the user, searching for the meaning of the exposed material. It is no coincidence that local museums in the USA are called interpretive centres. The key is no longer an 'academic' description of the values of an aseptic area, but a multi-sensory experience offered to the visitor allowing each person to form his or her own interpretation. Similarly, science museums have for several decades sought to enrich the visitor's experience by going beyond the tactile, so-called 'hands on'[4], experience, in order to engage the visitor emotionally ('heart on') and intellectually ('mind on'). This means in a sense redefining the scientific narrative in the context of the visitor's experience and the wider 'landscape' to which the heritage refers. The network of science museums in Catalonia was a pioneer in this respect, the visitor experience being rooted in the sense of identity of the region. Facing the complexity and unpredictability of globalisation 'economic and social institutions have changed their dynamics and organisational methods (...), to face these challenges there has been a tendency to promote new, much more flexible organisations that can adapt to the new situations and which tend towards joining together and sharing authority, rather than transferring it to a higher level'.[5]

The Venice lagoon is clearly positioned on the border of these two paradigms of participation, where interactive exhibits and displays in numerous museums tell the story of transformations of the Venice lagoon over the centuries. It is essential today to take inspiration from the long 'cultural path' represented by the ecomuseum of the Venice lagoon, effectively distilling the countless traditions, artefacts, archaeology and activities as the 'DNA' of a homogeneous territorial system.

Venice and its lagoon, beyond their stereotypical image – as if immortal – have debated their contradictions for several decades. The contradictions are characteristic of modern society, between the local and the global, between environment and industry, between citizens and tourists, and of course between the centre and the periphery. Depending on how these contradictions are managed, Venice and its lagoon may attain a new equilibrium, a structured sustainability in the future; if not, the risk is asphyxiation, and the unsustainable lightness of an empty shell. Culture in general, involving the active participation of the 'heritage communities', has a crucial role in restoring the balance, so that the citizens continue to feel a sense of identity with their material and immaterial heritage, through museums and through environmental as well as productive resources.

One of the main issues is: to reorient the flow of tourists towards the lagoon and its polycentric community. The 'heritage community' is increasing day by day. It may be the lever for an authentic (re)interpretation of the heritage of Venice and

4   Wagensberg Jorge, 1998. 'Ideas para la imagination impura'. Tusquets, Barcelona.
5   Casanelles in Rahola Eusebi and Matamala Jaume, 'System of the Museum of Science and Technology of Catalogna'. In: Calzolaio Francesco, 2009. Rooms of the Ecomuseum of the lagoon of Venice, Granviale Editore, Venice, p. 175.

Figure 4. Rowing in the north lagoon. Photograph by Francesco Calzolaio.

its lagoon, where land and sea, nature and man, have become inextricably linked through centuries of constant reciprocal adaptation.

The Serenissima Republic successfully managed this precious and fragile equilibrium, just as the Italian Government and the Municipality are attempting to do today. However, where the public effort is currently focused on purely hydraulic parameters, we need to devote an equal amount of attention to the community living around the complex border between land and sea.

For most visitors and many citizens, the lagoon is merely a space to cross as quickly as possible; it is no longer perceived as the cradle of the polycentric history of Venice, nor as an environmental protected area of European importance, nor as a literal 'melting pot' of local products. Alongside the current institutional patchwork, there is clearly a need for a sustainable cultural development agency to foster these cultural resources. They are already partially available to citizens and tourists, but need to be consolidated by 'opening the doors' to countless and diverse features: natural 'oases' in the dunes, rivers and fish farms, museums of material culture, environment and production, interpretive centres of eno-gastronomic activities, handcrafts. These can brought together as the 'Ecomuseum of lagoon', as we shall see. However, we first need to deal with the potential demand, represented by the tourist, albeit introduced above as a threat, but who clearly also represents potential.

As already stated, the core objective is to strengthen the sense of identity of the citizen with the territory. This is under threat, and we cannot overlook the huge impact millions of visitors have on the landscape and on the daily lives of citizens.

Tourists asphyxiate the city, but are more and more discerning, and open to 'conscious' and responsible tourism. The Eurobarometer Survey on the attitudes of Europeans towards tourism[6] indicates growth in the percentage of those in search of destinations qualified as 'alternative' or 'emerging', allowing them to explore different cultures, traditions and local ways of life. The major motivations for the main holidays of European citizens are rest (54% ticked 'rest, recreation, sun and beach'), and discovery (23% ticked 'city, culture, nature and religion'). The favourite destinations are 'traditional' and 'well-known' (58%) but more than half of these (28%) aspire instead to go 'off the beaten track' in order to explore 'less obvious places'. Those who visit new destinations increasingly rely on internet and reports of acquaintances. In choosing a destination most Europeans are attracted to its environmental attraction (32%), and cultural value (27%).

One can also observe a clear trend in European tourism demand towards the appreciation of combinations of nature and culture, gastronomy and local products, tangible and intangible heritage.

Despite being underused, the Italian inland waters indeed offer a unique insight into an incomparable cultural and environmental heritage, including Unesco sites, parks and historical cities. In 2009, attempting to meet this demand, the association *Venti di Cultura* started an experimental annual rally or *cabotage* through the entire Venice lagoon (www.lagunalonga.it). The annual event originated from writing a guide on the diffuse museum network: 'Rooms of the ecomuseum of the lagoon of Venice', published by the Province of Venice (see Notes and sources 5). The thread weaving the cultural lagoon was first experienced in open boats by a small group of specialists and citizens. Then Lagunalonga was presented in national and international contexts e.g., European Tourism Day 2011, the Icomos 2013 conference on 'Protecting deltas: heritage helps' in Amsterdam, the World Canal Conferences in Toulouse (2013) and Milan (2014).

At each step in development of the project, the Lagunalonga promoters have resolutely searched for practicality and sustainability. The event and the underlying concept are now recognised as a driving force as to the community of those residing around the lagoon, a factor of identification. This is confirmed by the Committee for the Ecomuseum, which promoted the sequence of above-mentioned visits and events, and contributed to the production in 2014 of a documentary on the cultural resources, in collaboration with local institutions and associations.

At the same time, the Lagunalonga promoters have worked not only on the design but also on the implementation of tourist packages utilizing historical and innovative boats, hereby minimizing the impact on the fragile ecosystem.

Towards a more authentic relationship?

Discovering the precious and fragile heritage of the lagoon could be combined with the most advanced experiences of 'heritage communities'. Here citizens express and communicate to visitors their sense of identity and their own experience of vibrant

---

6   European Commission, Flash Eurobarometer 328 – The Gallup Organization, 2011. 'Survey on the attitudes of Europeans towards tourism', p. 22.

Figure 5. Bacan in Sant Erasmo island, the beach of the Venetians. Photograph by Francesco Calzolaio.

and authentic places. These nodes of the lagoon network are today pieces of a puzzle, which present us with only a hint of the overall picture. The entire picture has to be assembled, revealed and made accessible to a much wider audience by means of innovative models of interpretation and promotion.

This is one of the objectives of the Unesco World Heritage Site Management Plan for 'Venice and its lagoon' as coordinated by the City[7] and supported by activities carried out by the Committee for the Ecomuseum of the Venice Lagoon. The target of these processes is twofold: on one hand, the citizens of the municipalities inside the lagoon and the surrounding areas, and on the other hand the tourists 'animating' the coastline and the cities of the Veneto, the main Italian tourist region.

The Committee for the Ecomuseum of the lagoon, established in 2013 in application of a new regional law, includes all the associations that offer links between the cultural resources of the lagoon, the citizens residing around it and tourists. In response to the Unesco Site Management committee, the Ecomuseum group is engaged in enhancing the existing network of places and people connected by the inland waters of the lagoon, as a palimpsest full of extraordinary cultural resources, both tangible and intangible. This is a participatory process. The Ecomuseum's mission is to promote an integrated territorial cultural system,

---

7   Basili Katia, De Vettor Giorgio, 2014. Venice and its Lagoon UNESCO World Heritage Site. The Management Plan 2012-2018, 3b press, Venice.

bringing together existing environmental, productive and cultural resources, material and immaterial, through the identification of their main points of interest, connected by 'slow' paths, by water and bicycle. The Ecomuseum is therefore not just any museum; it is a network of citizens, institutions and activities striving to enhance the cultural resources in which the resident community recognizes itself and its history. These resources form the web, convey its *genius loci*, the most authentic figure of the plural and polycentric territory.

Restoring and consolidating an authentic relationship between citizens and the lagoon, reviving historic and compatible activities, promoting responsible tourism off the beaten track, enhancing the broad museum network: all these objectives make up a hugely ambitious programme with many challenges to be faced. Success can only be achieved through the combined efforts of the citizens – as users and witnesses – and the institutions, both local and international, and certainly not by means of a single gesture, decided by a single committee or a single plan. The development will be the result of a long multicultural process, which must in essence be both inclusive and participatory.

Tourism packages

All the above considerations have led to definition of the strategy now pursued by the Venti di Cultura partners: the 'Lagunalonga' cultural tourism packages. The Lagunalonga *cabotage* means spending a week in the Venice lagoon and along its tributaries, on a boat that proceeds slowly along the channels, in order to better to appreciate the delicate balance between nature and culture, as layered over the centuries, thanks to the countless and often extraordinary interactions between the lagoon and the people inhabiting it. Lagunalonga offers a unique access to the treasures of the lagoon, the priceless archaeological heritage, pristine nature reserves, rare artisans' products, and of course the food and wine. Lagunalonga will accommodate small groups of tourists in standards of luxury for a week, enabling them to discover the lagoon's *genius loci*. Passing by or through charming oases of calm and nature considered among the most valuable in Europe, the route winds through those countless features hallmarking Venetian civilisation: sandbanks, museums, islands, monasteries, oases, basilicas, dunes, vineyards and walled archaeological sites.

Lagunalonga[8] plans to offer four typologies of itineraries in order to interpret not only the large number of cultural and tourist resources spread throughout the lagoon, but also to invite visitors to make individual discoveries and appropriations, according to their personal aspirations.

The **Cultural Itinerary** is dedicated to the museums around the lagoon, and to the heritage of classical and industrial archaeology. The cultural programme includes various museums – the archeological museum of Altino, the Torcello Museum, the Burano Lace Museum, the Murano Glass Museum, the Museum of the Lagoon in Pellestrina and the Fishing Museum in Chioggia. The itinerary also opens the doors to an extraordinary industrial and military heritage: the Arsenale

---

8   www.lagunalonga.it.

in Venice, Porto Marghera, Forte Vecchio in Treporti and the network of Octagons in the south lagoon, Forte Marghera and Forte S. Andrea.

The **Enogastronomy Itinerary** is dedicated to local food products, fishing and crafts. It comprises a route for a gourmet to discover and taste the most characteristic products. It winds its way from the walled vineyards to the soft-shell crabs (*moeche*) introducing tourists to the violet artichoke of S. Erasmo, white beans, a broth from Chioggia (*broeto Ciosoto*) and many other dishes originating from the lagoon. One can experience various fishing techniques typical of the lagoon, fish farms, touristic fishing, from the lagoon to scuba-diving. At the end this route one can become acquainted with traditional handmade crafts, Murano glass, the original fishermen pipes of Chioggia, the crafts of seamen, smiths and local artisans.

The **Nature Itinerary** is dedicated to environmental resources of the lagoon, immersed in the silence of contemplation of the extraordinary natural and spiritual areas. One can encounter the lagoon's original and pristine natural resources, ranging from coastal dunes to salt marshes, mud flats, the WWF oasis and river parks as well as The spiritual resources (e.g., the convent islands, sites of meditation, churches). This transversal route serves to focus on the landscape and on ourselves.

The **Beauty Itinerary** provides us with a cross experience through nature, enogastronomy and culture.

These itineraries are more than a cruise on the lagoon: they are a door to magic, authentic and little-known places, combining adventure or relaxation, culture or sporting events, natural or gourmet cuisine. Lagunalonga will reconnect Venice with the 'amniotic fluid' of her lagoon.

The Tennessee Valley Authority

How the Development of the Tennessee River Influenced Archaeology in the Southeastern United States

Erin Pritchard, Michaelyn Harle and Pat Bernard Ezzell

Abstract

Created by an Act of the United States Congress in 1933 as a part of President Franklin D. Roosevelt's New Deal Program, the Tennessee Valley Authority (TVA) was tasked with improving the economic conditions of the Tennessee River Valley following the Great Depression. Toward this goal, the new agency initiated a series of dam constructions along the Tennessee River and its tributaries for the multiple purposes of flood control, navigation, and hydro-electric power. During the inception of these projects, it became apparent to archaeologists that thousands of archaeological resources were going to be destroyed as a result of the proposed construction and inundation of the reservoirs.

William S. Webb and David L. DeJarnette approached TVA with a proposal to conduct archaeological surveys and excavations prior to the completion of the dams. TVA fully supported this proposal and helped fund numerous excavations across the valley with labor support provided through the Works Progress Administration (WPA), the Civil Works Administration (CWA), and the Federal Emergency Relief Administration. These programs, also a part of Roosevelt's New Deal, utilized unemployed workers, providing additional help to the struggling economy in the southern United States. The results of these endeavors had a great influence on the development of professional archaeology in the Southeastern United States, including the establishment of culture history in the southeast and providing the professional training opportunities for many of the Nation's most influential early archaeologists.

TVA went on to construct, or acquire, 49 dams (29 hydroelectric projects) across the Tennessee Valley and expanded its responsibilities to include recreation, water quality and supply and environmental stewardship of its natural and cultural resources. While its power supply derives primarily from coal and nuclear plants today, managing the river system and balancing the competing uses along the waterways remains at the heart of this former grassroots agency.

The legacy of the TVA-WPA archaeological excavations continues today as the agency manages over 11,500 archaeological sites in the Tennessee Valley while remaining a responsible steward of the river system and balancing the competing interests of energy generation and transmission, economic development, recreation, and other environmental concerns that sometimes conflict with the management and protection of archaeological resources.

TVA and Regional Development

On March 4, 1936, the gates of Norris Dam closed with great fanfare. It was reported the next day in the *Birmingham (Alabama) Age-Herald* that an estimated three thousand people turned out for this momentous occasion. After all, Norris was the first construction project completed by TVA. United States President Franklin D. Roosevelt (FDR) at home at the White House, pressed a telegraph key to sound a siren on top of the dam, signaling the closing of the water gates, and numerous officials spoke eloquently about the importance of both the dam and of TVA. Dr. Arthur E. Morgan, serving as Chairman of the TVA board, stated that *"it is not as a structure by itself that it has greatest value, but as part of a unified system of control for the entire Tennessee River system."* It was this planned, unified system of dams that would provide the flood control, improve the navigation of the Tennessee, and as Morgan stated, *"contribute the prime power of every present and future dam from here to the Ohio River."* (Morgan, Address, March 4, 1936).

Figure 1. TVA Chairman Arthur E. Morgan admires a model of Norris Dam, the first hydroelectric project constructed by TVA, May 1937.

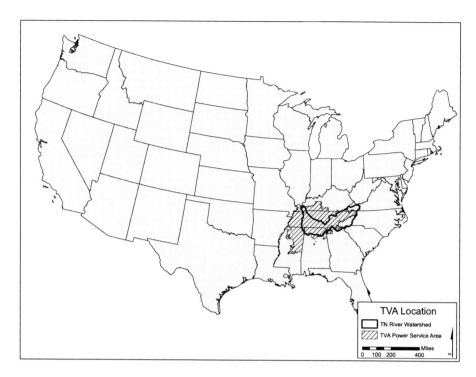

Figure 2. Location of Tennessee River Watershed and TVA Power Service Area in the United States.

In the 1930s as part of FDR's New Deal, Congress approved a number of unprecedented programs to help bring the nation out of the Great Depression. One of the most ambitious and most successful was TVA, one of the first comprehensive development programs for an entire river basin. Covering approximately 41,000 square miles, the Tennessee River Watershed includes 125 counties within much of Tennessee and parts of six other states: Alabama, Georgia, Kentucky, Mississippi, North Carolina, and Virginia. TVA also serves a larger area, the TVA Power Service Area, which covers 80,000 square miles and includes 170 counties in the same seven states. Two hundred one counties comprise both the Watershed and the Power Service area.

TVA was a departure from the traditional organization of the federal government. For the first time, a single agency was given responsibility for a unified approach to the development and wise use of natural resources in a specific region. The uniqueness of TVA lay in the range of functions combined for administration in one agency in one area--a single river valley. Congress and the President established TVA outside of the regular departments and made it accountable to the President and Congress for results. The law directed that TVA's headquarters be established outside of Washington, D.C., and placed among the people with whom it was to serve. TVA officials were directed to develop and administer their programs in cooperation with the various states and their departments, with the city and county governments, with organizations of citizens, with farmers and businessmen, and with other federal agencies. It was a decentralized national administration, bringing the national government closer to the people and making it more responsive to their wishes and needs.

And in 1933, the Tennessee Valley needed TVA. Dr. Arthur E. Morgan testified that in the fall of that year there were counties in the Southern Highlands with more than fifty percent of the families requiring some type of governmental assistance. Morgan pointed out that there were many *"prosperous communities"* in the Valley region, but that *"a considerable part of the population is on the verge of starvation."* Morgan characterized the problem as *"a very desperate economic situation."* (Duffus, 1946).

Starvation was not the only problem for the people of the Tennessee Valley. Many suffered from *"debilitating diseases such as malaria and hookworm."* Primitive farming practices resulted in depleted soil as well as soil erosion. It was common for half of the Valley population to be on relief; the per capita income of those in the Tennessee Valley region was half of that of the country as a whole. The birthrate was one-third above the national average. Levels of literacy were low, and the labor force was largely unskilled. Only three farms in one-hundred had electricity. Unchecked fires burned ten percent of the region's woodlands every year, and poor logging practices had nearly denuded forests that once offered endless miles of virgin timber (TVA, 1983b; cf. Clapp, 1956; Huxley, 1945; Whitman, 1939).

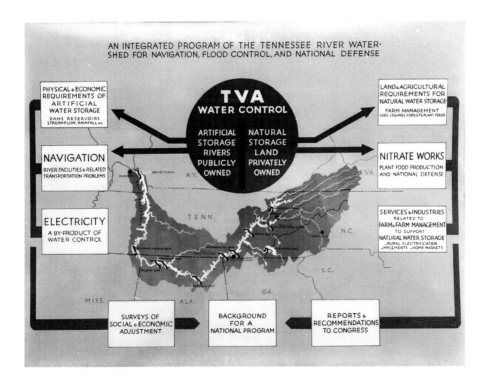

Figure 3. Integrated Resource Management Diagram, September 1939.

Annual flooding was another of the many problems facing the Tennessee Valley. Year after year, the Tennessee would overflow its banks, ruining crops, disrupting businesses, and in some cases, taking homes and lives. For example on March 7, 1917, *The Chattanooga Times* reported on one of the city's great floods: "*With the flooding of seven blocks of Main Street early yesterday afternoon South Chattanooga went under after a valiant fight lasting since Sunday. In other sections, inundated for three days, the water continues to rise and spread until it is estimated . . . 6,000 residents are homeless.*"

The situation was dire, but TVA went to work. Using the concept of integrated resource management, tackling resource problems together as opposed to isolating each problem, and by partnering with the states and local governments, TVA helped to transform a region.

As early as March 1936, TVA's board submitted its development plan to Congress. Known as *The Unified Development of the Tennessee River System,* this report recommended the construction of a series of locks and dams to form an integrated system for the control of the 652-mile Tennessee River from Knoxville to the Ohio River. This plan would prioritize the improvement of navigation in the Tennessee River and its tributaries and the control of flood waters in the Tennessee and Mississippi drainage basins. Provisions were also made for the generation, transmission, and sale of power created by the dams necessary for the primary purposes (TVA, Unified Development Plan, 1936).

This unified development plan was TVA's blueprint for serving this region. Almost everything the agency would do regarding navigation and flood control was discussed in this document. For example, an entire river system has been controlled and put to work. A stairway of nine dams and reservoirs provide a continuous nine-foot navigation channel permitting the movement of millions of tons of commercial freight traffic annually. TVA's multiple-use reservoir system has also provided eleven million acre-feet of water storage, making serious floods a thing of the past. Vast amounts of power have been developed and channeled into homes, farms, business, industry, and national defense. Today, TVA serves over 9 million residents and has just completed its fourteenth year in a row of 99.999 percent reliability. The development of new and better fertilizers improved Valley agricultural lands resulting in better farm income and rural life. Much eroded and abandoned land has been reforested. Recreation areas have been developed, and economic growth has occurred.

In 1933 personal income in the 201 counties region averaged $168 per capita, only 45 percent of the national level. By 2011, it was $34,442, some 201 times as much, while the national average multiplied about 110 times in the same period. In 1933 some 62 percent of the region's workers depended on agriculture for a living; this dropped to 0.4 percent of payroll workers by 2011. In 1933 only 6.5 percent of the region's employment was in manufacturing, but since that time the number of manufacturing employees has doubled. Most of this industrial growth is related in some degree to the improvements in water transportation, water supply, flood control, agricultural and forest raw materials availability, or power supply made possible by resource development—and to the growing markets for industry created by the region's economic progress. (TVA, 2013).

Archaeological Heritage Sites in the Tennessee River Valley

As plans for TVA's first reservoir project (Norris Dam) moved forward in 1933, archaeologists from the region realized that TVA's proposed mission would lead to the destruction of an untold number of important archaeological sites that were concentrated along the Tennessee River and its tributaries. These archaeologists petitioned TVA's chairman for an opportunity to conduct salvage excavations prior to inundation. No doubt their petition was bolstered by the fact that the development of TVA coincided with the FDR's New Deal initiative to put individuals affected by the Great Depression back to work through programs such as the WPA, CWA, and the Civilian Conservation Corps (CCC). Archaeology was seen as a useful vehicle for this initiative because it was highly labor intensive while requiring little additional capital investment (Lyon, 1996). Archaeological excavations started in January 1934 in the Norris Basin under the direction of William S. Webb. Webb would go on to serve as the central administrator of the TVA archaeological program. The Norris Basin project was followed by large scale archaeological excavations associated with the Wheeler, Pickwick, and Guntersville Reservoir projects in Alabama and the Chickamauga, Watts Bar, and Kentucky Reservoir projects in Tennessee.

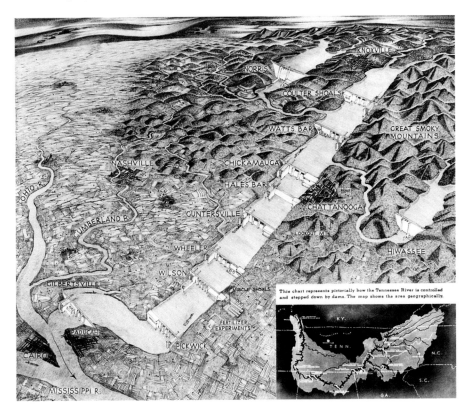

Figure 4. Map of TVA Water Control System Showing Dams, 1939.

Although New Deal archaeological projects occurred throughout the United States, the Tennessee Valley was especially attractive because of its year round temperate climate and location in a region that was already suffering when the Great Depression hit. Also attractive was that many of these archaeological sites, located along alluvial floodplains, were characterized by deeply stratified deposits and thus excavation required a vast amount of man power. So too were these stratified archaeological sites, some with considerable time-depth, attractive to archaeologists who were increasingly interested in the taxonomic method of cultural classification, championed by McKern (McKern, 1939; cf O'Brian and Lyman, 2001). The TVA excavations attracted a number of alumni of the University of Chicago field school under the direction of the influential anthropologist Faye-Cooper Cole. The field supervisors (e.g.,Thomas M Lewis, Madeline Kneberg, Jesse Jennings, Charles Nash, James Ford, William Haag, Stuart Neitzel, George Neumann, and Charles Fairbanks) gained invaluable experience working on these large scale TVA projects and would go on to become some of the most influential archaeologists working and would train many of the modern archaeologists working today(Haag, 1985; Jennings, 1994; Taylor, 2008).

The new techniques developed under the tutelage of Cooper Cole were brought by these young field supervisors and applied to TVA excavations. The techniques were refined to fit the archaeological sites of the Tennessee Valley. Prior to the 1930s, excavations in the South were opportunistic and focused on monumental architecture, such as earthen platform and burial mounds, with little regard to vertical control. With the New Deal TVA excavations, mound profiles and site stratigraphy were mapped in detail and photographed. The ' peeling' technique to mound excavation, which exposed entire horizontal surfaces, was first applied to the Hiwassee Island site in the Chickamauga Reservoir (Willey and Sabloff, 1974:30). Entire villages were excavated, uncovering millions of post molds, storage pits, and other features that contributed to a greater understanding of intra-site community organization. While attention still focused on the large earthen mound sites, some attempt was made for further exploration of cave sites, lithic extraction sites, and shell middens.

Perhaps the most important contribution by these TVA projects is their advancement of standardized recording and excavation techniques as evidenced by the *Manual of Field and Laboratory Techniques* developed by the director of the TVA Tennessee excavations Thomas M N Lewis and his partner Madeline Kneberg (Lewis et al,. 1995). Grid systems with square units were utilized for the surveying, mapping, and excavation of sites. Uniform unit, feature, and burial forms were created to standardize data collection along with detailed maps and photographs.

The resulting monographs from the excavations of the Norris (Webb, 1938), Pickwick (Webb and DeJarnette, 1942), Wheeler (Webb, 1939), and Guntersville (Webb and Wilder, 1951) Reservoirs were little more than site descriptions with trait lists. Although the Chickamauga Basin report was not published until it was edited and compiled by Lynne Sullivan in the 1990s (Lewis et al., 1995) and the Kentucky Reservoir and Watts Bar Reservoir reports were never published, perhaps two of the most influential reports to come out of the New Deal TVA excavations were the *Hiwassee Island: An Archaeological Account of Four Tennessee Indian Peoples* (Lewis and Kneberg 1946) and *Eva: An Archaic Site* (Lewis and Kneberg, 1961). Unlike the other reservoir monographs these two works shifted from purely descriptive to more interpretive and remain the foundation for the cultural histories established for the region (Kimball and Baden, 1985; Schroedl, 1998; and Sullivan, 2007).

The excavations produced vast collections of artifacts and accompanying photographs, maps, and records which continue to be curated by several university museums, whose genesis itself is directly, or at least indirectly, tied to these TVA excavations. Such is the case for the McClung Museum of Natural History and Culture at the University of Tennessee, the Alabama Museum of Natural History at the University of Alabama and the William S. Webb Museum of Anthropology at the University of Kentucky. Even during the height of these excavations, the subjects of analysis and curation were a source of contention between Webb and the director of the Tennessee TVA archaeological program, Thomas M Lewis. Whereas, Webb preferred to spend the money on fieldwork and labor, Lewis, realizing the scale of the information that was being produced by these projects, preferred to allocate more money to lab work (Lyon, 1996; Sullivan, 1999).

Following the United States entry into War World II, money for the TVA excavations and their subsequent analysis was reallocated towards the war effort. For instance, only two sites were excavated prior to inundation by the Douglas Dam which was constructed in less than thirteen months and completed in 1943. Already seen as a concern prior to entry into the war, archaeologists were immediately aware of the implications that this loss of funding would have on the analysis of these important collections. As money from the WPA and other New

Figure 5. William S. Webb and Thomas N. Lewis analyzing artifacts from Norris Reservoir, 1934.

Deal agencies diminished, many of the archaeological collections were stored with minimal or no analysis or proper curation.

These New Deal era TVA excavations led to the collection of millions of artifacts and the excavation of over 8,000 burials. Associated with these excavations are thousands of pages of field records, excavation maps, and photographs as well as drawers full of correspondence associated with these excavations. To illustrate, Sullivan (1995 xvii) reports that the Chickamauga Reservoir alone generated almost a half a million artifacts, including some 360,000 pottery sherds, and over 2,000 burials.

While undeniable that these artifacts and associated records continue to offer invaluable information in our understanding of the prehistory of this region, the legacy of these collections remains a daunting task for the museums who have been stewards of these collections (cf., Sullivan et al.,2010) and for TVA and other agencies who are responsible for them under federal regulations such as 36 CFR 79 and federal legislation such as the Native American Graves Protection and Repatriation Act (NAGPRA).

Throughout the 1950's and 60's TVA's commitment to archaeological projects wavered. The Tennessee Valley experienced post-World War II economic growth, and TVA's focus turned toward the construction of fossil fuel plants to meet the demand for affordable electricity. Only a reconnaissance level survey was conducted prior to inundation of Watauga Reservoir in 1948 and the archaeological excavations at Boone, Fort Patrick Henry, and Melton Hill Reservoirs were salvage operations consisting of the volunteer labor (Olinger and Howard, 2009).

With the passage of environmental legislation, such as the Reservoir Salvage Act in 1960, the National Historic Preservation Act in 1966 (NHPA), and the National Environmental Policy Act of 1969 there was a resurgence in archaeological data recovery for TVA projects. One of TVA's last dam constructions, the Tellico Reservoir Project, began in 1967, which included some 14,400 acres of land. The potential impact to a significant amount of archaeological resources was just part of the broader political, social and environmental controversies that plagued the project. Construction of the Tellico Dam became controversial when an endangered fish, the snail darter, was discovered in the Little Tennessee River. Environmentalist and opponents of the project brought a suit against TVA under the Endangered Species Act (ESA) and the project was in litigation for years (Wheeler and McDonald, 1986). One consolation for this delay was that archaeologists were able to do more extensive excavation to mitigate the large number of archaeological sites that were to be inundated. In addition to the snail darter, construction of Tellico would result in the loss of numerous 18th century Cherokee towns causing tension with the Cherokee Nation and Eastern Band of Cherokee Indians (Wheeler and McDonald, 1986; Schroedl 2009). The affected parties now had the legal backing to stand up for their interests.

While subject to more stringent regulations than the New Deal archaeological excavations, federal agencies, including TVA, were only just beginning to grapple with the impact of these new environmental laws on their day to day operations. So too was the field of North American archaeology in a state of flux with the

Figure 6. Archaeological Investigations at the Icehouse Bottom Site (Monroe County, Tennessee) that was Inundated by Tellico Reservoir.

introduction of ' New Archaeology' or processual archaeology and its greater emphasis on more scientifically grounded research and processes of cultural change (e.g., Wiley and Phillips, 1958). Thus, much of the archaeological research conducted during the Tellico Project was governed by processual archaeology as witnessed by a greater emphasis on *"research design, regional and intrasite sampling, focus on the reconstruction of subsistence and settlement patterns, attempts to decipher activity areas and site function, and the interpretation of human adaptation"* (Schroedl, 2009:68). The resulting archaeological work uncovered upwards of three hundred archaeological sites and led to the refinement of the cultural chronology of the region, especially the earliest occupations in the Tennessee Valley. This work also refined our understanding of protohistoric/historic Cherokee occupations and pioneered many techniques now common place in North American cultural resource management such as flotation, the use of heavy machinery, and waterscreening (Schroedl, 2009). In the end Tellico would put to test both new environmental legislation and new theoretical advancements in American archaeology to an unprecedented scale.

After the Tellico project was initiated similar large-scale archaeological surveys were undertaken in association with the construction of the Normandy Dam in 1972 and Columbia Dam in 1973 (for further discussion see Faulkner 2009). However, the emerging issues resulting from the new environmental regulations ultimately had a major impact on American attitudes toward dam construction. The case for the snail darter was ultimately heard by the Supreme Court which upheld a lower court ruling against TVA; however, Congress exempted the agency from the ESA at Tellico, and a bill was signed by President Jimmy Carter allowing the agency to move forward with the project (TVA, 1983a). Columbia Dam never was completed after significant environmental delays related to the presence of an endangered mussel. While some limited excavation occurred, full-scale archaeological investigations at Columbia were never completed (Dickson, 1976). The days of large scale reservoir projects in the Tennessee Valley had come to an end.

Many of the archaeological sites that were excavated during these early reservoir projects are now permanently inundated or only accessible during deep drawdowns of the reservoirs. Thousands of additional sites have now been located along TVA reservoirs as a result of more systematic surveys conducted in the last several decades. The archaeological record in the Tennessee Valley continues to expand as a result of annual surveys completed under its current management strategies that correspond with the agency's continued operation of the river system.

River and Heritage Management Today

Harkening back to the spirit in which the agency was initially established, TVA continues to place the quality of life for the residents of the Tennessee Valley as a priority in its daily operations. Its mission of service to the region through its work in the areas of energy, environment, and economic development is unique among federal agencies and utilities. Stewardship of the valley's natural and cultural resources, including archaeological resources located throughout the valley are part of TVA's commitment to the environment under its mission.

Today TVA manages approximately 293,000 acres of land surrounding its 49 reservoir projects with 460,000 acres of inundated land. Over 11,500 archaeological sites have been recorded on these lands and TVA protects and manages these resources pursuant to the American laws and regulations that protect them, such as NHPA, the Archaeological Resources Protection Act (ARPA), and NAGPRA. Most recently, the agency established a Natural Resource Plan (NRP) to integrate natural and cultural resource management with agency land planning, water resource management, and public engagement (TVA, 2014a). This plan has provided a foundation for integrated resource management that benefits water and land resources, including cultural heritage sites. TVA has also committed to develop a more specific cultural resource management plan to ensure long term, efficient, and consistent management of the archaeological sites, historic sites and historic structures under its stewardship. This effort will expand on the integration established in the NRP.

TVA continues to operate the Tennessee River system today much as it did in the beginning and hydropower continues to be the most reliable, efficient, and economical form of energy produced by the agency. Large-scale dam construction projects ceased as TVA focused on maintenance of its dams and reservoirs to meet its original mission of navigation, flood control and the production of affordable electricity in the Tennessee Valley as well as improvement of water quality, insuring adequate water supply, and providing recreational opportunities to the public. Hydroelectric power now provides only 10% of the agency's energy portfolio with a majority produced through coal, nuclear power generation and other energy sources (TVA, 2014b). Operation of the river system is evaluated on a regular basis to ensure the maximum benefit for all of these purposes, many of which can compete with one another. For example, maximizing recreational opportunities often comes at a price to natural and cultural resources, so the agency must balance these resources accordingly. The most recent update to the operation of TVA's river system occurred in 2004 when the agency undertook a valley-wide study to determine if such changes would *"produce greater overall public value for the people of the United States."* (TVA, 2014d).

Flood control remains a critical component in the management of the Tennessee River. Rainfall in the valley averages over 51 inches per year and TVA prevents an average of $240 million in flood damage in the valley and along the Ohio and Mississippi Rivers downstream (TVA, 2014a). In order to prevent major flood events, TVA must maintain appropriate flood storage during the period of December through May. To do so, reservoir elevation levels, particularly those in the tributary reservoirs above critical flood potential areas, are lowered to more than double the capacity for storage during these peak months. Reservoir levels increase again in the spring to prepare for the peak recreation period in the summer.

One consequence to this critical component of river operations is that when reservoir levels are lowered, sensitive archaeological resources that are normally covered by water throughout the summer months become exposed. These reservoir drawdowns can be advantageous as TVA's cultural resource management staff often use these opportunities of increased accessibility and visibility to identify and monitor archaeological sites on TVA land across the valley. Sites subject to repeated fluctuation of reservoir levels are monitored for erosional effects which in many areas have resulted in a significant loss of archaeological integrity. This is particularly evident on reservoirs with increased flood storage (such as those upstream of critical flood areas) (Boyd, 1985; Laird et al, 2008; Watkins, 2014).

Erosional effects from reservoir fluctuation are unfortunate side effects to the operation and management of the river system. These effects are further augmented by wave action resulting from boat traffic, loss of adequate shoreline vegetation buffers, and unauthorized excavation of archaeological sites exposed along the eroding shorelines (Lenihan et al, 1981). Erosion increases exposure of sensitive archaeological features, making them vulnerable to opportunistic looting. Looting, in turn, undercuts the bank, decreasing stability of overlying vegetation which results in an even greater increase in erosion and loss of shoreline buffer. Erosion not only effects archaeological resources, but can impact water quality as well as loss of property for both the federal government and private landowners.

The illegal excavation and removal of archaeological artifacts from public lands and black market sale of antiquities have been worldwide problems for centuries. Lands now owned and managed by TVA have been subject to vandalism and looting long before the agency's presence in the valley. Because a majority of the archaeological resources managed by TVA are located along or adjacent to the water, access is open to the public often in remote locations, making the sites difficult to monitor. As a result, archaeological sites are extremely vulnerable

Figure 7. Signage Used by TVA to notify the public on the
protection of archaeological sites located along the River.

to illegal excavation and vandalism. Looting activity on TVA land ranges from artifact surface collection during low reservoir pool levels to full destruction from unpermitted excavation. The most common documented offense has been the excavation of exposed features along eroded shorelines adjacent to TVA reservoirs.

TVA has taken a number of different approaches to combat this problem over the last several decades that include: increased enforcement of the ARPA regulations that make it illegal to remove or excavated artifacts from federally owned lands; protection of archaeological sites through various barrier measures; and increased educational outreach. The most effective method for permanent protection of sites located along the water is the placement of hard armor riprap along eroding shorelines. This type of barrier not only closes access to those interested in plundering features for personal or commercial gain, it reduces the erosion effects from the river and navigation traffic and also has a positive effect on water quality. TVA cultural resources staff works closely with the agency's water quality team to maximize the effectiveness of its shoreline protection program.

Unfortunately, it is not possible to protect all resources with hard armor as TVA manages over 11,000 miles of shoreline and stabilization can be very costly. The most effective method for reducing the looting problem in the United States is through public outreach and education. The very fact that outreach is a requirement under federal legislation demonstrates the importance of such efforts. Unfortunately, most school systems in the United States focus on post-contact history, lacking appropriate curriculum in the prehistory of our nation (Little, 2002), and many students never learn about archaeology until college. Providing outreach opportunities to local communities is imperative to the long term preservation of our national heritage. TVA maintains an active archaeological outreach program to communicate archaeological site protection needs to communities across the valley.

For example, in fiscal year 2014, TVA's archaeological outreach efforts reached an estimated 1,500 elementary and middle-school students in the Tennessee Valley.

The Future of Heritage Management in the Tennessee Valley

Cultural history in the Tennessee Valley and the southeastern United States has been greatly influenced by the development of its river systems. Without the early efforts of TVA, WPA, and other New Deal projects, a significant amount of archaeological data would have been permanently lost. Large, region-wide excavation projects are no longer common and archaeological investigations are often limited to small scale projects resulting from private construction or development. Federal agencies in the United States have now turned their efforts toward long term preservation and public education, protecting the remaining resources under their management.

Toward this effort, TVA continues to survey, identify, and monitor archaeological sites annually. In recent years, TVA has revisited a number of sites previously thought to have been destroyed and/or excavated as a result of TVA-WPA excavations in the 1930s and 40s, only to find that these sites maintain significant integrity, warranting not only additional research, but further protection. Modern investigative methods such as Light Detection and Ranging (LiDAR), ground penetrating radar, magnetic gradiometry, and other non-invasive techniques have allowed the agency to explore archaeological resources without the need for excavation. These techniques not only maintain the site's integrity, but protect sensitive features, such as burials, and eliminate the need for expensive curation.

Curation of archaeological materials excavated from TVA sites has challenged the agency for many years as collections across the valley have been in dire need for improvements in order to meet the standards established through federal regulations (36CFR79). As a result, graduate students' and academic archaeologists' interest in the study of these materials have been limited. In addition to condition, there is also a growing concern for repository space. This space is an issue not only for TVA, but for federal agencies across the United States (Childs and Sullivan, 2004; Sullivan and Childs, 2003). TVA has only recently begun to address these concerns through the establishment of partnerships with the museums and repositories that have maintained these resources since the 1930s. It is also anticipated that improvements to these collections may once again stimulate research interest in the Tennessee Valley region.

Challenges aside, there remains tremendous information potential with the archaeological resources of the Tennessee Valley. TVA will continue to manage archaeological resources in concert with its operation of the Tennessee River. New technology will allow for greater understanding of these resources without permanent loss of data or the expensive long-term cost of curation for the associated archaeological materials. The agency is in the process of establishing through its cultural resource management plan the necessary mechanisms to ensure the long-term, efficient, and integrated management of these resources as it continues to thrive as the one of the few remaining New Deal Agencies in the United States.

On that sunny spring day back in March 1936, President Roosevelt said that Norris Dam was the *"key to the carefully worked out control of a great river and its watershed . . ."* (Morgan, Address, March 4, 1936). The Tennessee River was at the core of TVA's mission in the 1930s, and it remains at the core of TVA's service to the people of the Tennessee Valley today.

References

Boyd, C. Clifford Boyd, Jr. (Editor). 1985. *Archaeological Investigations in the Watauga Reservoir, Carter and Johnson Counties, Tennessee.* Report submitted to the Tennessee Valley Authority, Knoxville, Tennessee.

Childs, S. Terry and Lynne P. Sullivan. 2004. Archaeological Stewardship: It's About Both Collections and Sites. In *Our Collective Responsibility: The Ethics and Practice of Archaeological Collections Stewardship*, ed. S. Terry Childs, 3-21. Washington D.C: Society for American Archaeology.

Clapp, Gordon. 1956. The Meaning of TVA. In *TVA The First Twenty Years.* Ed. Roscoe C. Martin. University, Alabama: The University of Alabama Press and Knoxville Tennessee: The University of Tennessee Press.

Dickson, D. Bruce. 1976. *Final Report on the 1972-1973 Archaeological Site Reconnaissance in the Proposed TVA Columbia Reservoir, Maury and Marshall Counties, Tennessee.* Report submitted to the Tennessee Valley Authority, Knoxville, Tennessee.

Duffus, R. L. 1946. *The Valley and Its People.* New York: Alfred A. Knopf.

Faulkner, Charles H. 2009. The Normandy Project. In TVA Archaeology: Seventy-five Years of Prehistoric Site Research, ed. E. E. Pritchard, 39-61. Knoxville. University of Tennessee Press.

Haag, William G. 1985. Federal Aid to Archaeology in the Southeast, 1933-1942. American Antiquity 50(2):272-280.

Huxley, Julian. 1945. *TVA, Adventures in Planning.* London: The Architectural Press.

Jennings, Jesse. 1994. Accidental Archaeologist. Salt Lake City: University of Utah Press

Kimball, Larry R. and William Baden. 1985. Quantitative Model of Woodland and Mississippian Ceramic Assemblages for the Identification of Surface Collections. In *The 1977 Archaeological Survey: An Overall Assessment of the Archaeological Resources of Tellico Reservoir.* ed. L.R. Kimball, pp. 121-274. Report of Investigations No. 40, Department of Anthropology, University of Tennessee.

Laird, Price K., Emily Kate Tucker, and Jeffrey L. Holland. 2008. *Archaeological Shoreline Survey Adjacent to Bear Creek Reservoir in Franklin County, Alabama.* Report submitted to the Tennessee Valley Authority, Knoxville, Tennessee.

Lewis, Thomas M. N., and Madeline D. Kneberg. 1946. Hiwassee Island: An Archaeological Account of Four Tennessee Indian Peoples. Knoxville: University of Tennessee Press.

Lewis, Thomas M. N. and Madeline Kneberg Lewis. 1961. Eva: An Archaic Site. Knoxville: University of Tennessee Press.

Lewis, Thomas M. N. and Madeline Kneberg Lewis 1995. The Prehistory of the Chickamauga Basin in Tennessee, compiled and edited by L. P. Sullivan. Knoxville: University of Tennessee Press.

Little, Barbara J. 2002. Archaeology as a Shared Vision. In *Public Benefits of Archaeology*, ed. Barbara J. Little, 3-19. Gainesville: University Press of Florida.

Lyon, Edwin A. 1996. *A New Deal for Southeastern Archaeology*. Tuscaloosa: University of Alabama Press.

McKern, William C. 1939. The Midwestern Taxonomic Method as an Aid to Archaeological Culture Study. *American Antiquity* 4(4):301-313.

Morgan, Arthur E. "Address by Arthur E. Morgan at Ceremony of the Closing of Norris Dam Gates, March 4, 1936. Files, TVA Library.

O'Brien, Michael J., and R. Lee Lyman. 2001. The Direct Historical Approach and Analogical Reasoning in Archaeology. *Journal of Archaeological Method and Theory* 8:303–342

Olinger, Danny E. and A. Eric Howard. 2009. In the Beginning.... In *TVA Archaeology: Seventy-five Years of Prehistoric Site Research*, ed. E. E. Pritchard, 17-38. Knoxville. University of Tennessee Press.

Schroedl, Gerald F. 1998. Mississippian Towns in the Eastern Tennessee Valley. In *Mississippian Towns and Sacred Spaces*, edited by B. Lewis and C. Stout, 64-92. Tuscaloosa: University of Alabama Press.

Schroedl, Gerald F. 2009. The Tellico Archaeological Project. In *TVA Archaeology: Seventy-five Years of Prehistoric Site Research*, ed. E. E. Pritchard, 17-38. Knoxville. University of Tennessee Press.

Sullivan, Lynne P. 1995. Foreword to The Prehistory of the Chickamauga Basin in Tennessee, compiled and edited by L. P. Sullivan. xv-xxviii. Knoxville: University of Tennessee Press.

Sullivan, Lynne P. 1999. "Madeline D. Kneberg Lewis: Leading Lady of Tennessee Archaeology." In *Grit-Tempered: Early Women Archaeologists in the Southeastern United States,* edited by N. M. White, L. P. Sullivan, and R. Marrinan, 57-91. Florida Museum of Natural History, Ripley P. Bulletin Series. Gainesville: University Press of Florida.

Sullivan, Lynne P. 2007. "Dating the Southeastern Ceremonial Complex in Eastern Tennessee." In *Southeastern Ceremonial Complex: Chronology, Iconography, and Style*, edited by A. King, 88-106. Tuscaloosa: University of Alabama Press.

Sullivan, Lynne P. and S. Terry Childs. 2003. *Curating Archaeological Collections: From the Field to the Repository*. Walnut Creek, California: AltaMira Press.

Taylor, Nick. 2008. American-Made: The Enduring Legacy of the WPA: When FDR Put the Nation to Work. New York: Bantam Books.

Tennessee Valley Authority. 1983a. *A History of the Tennessee Valley Authority*. Knoxville, TN: TVA Information Office.

Tennessee Valley Authority. 1983b. *The First Fifty Years: Changed Land, Changed Lives.* Knoxville.

Tennessee Valley Authority. 2013. *2013 Factbook*. Knoxville, Tennesseee, internal document.

Tennessee Valley Authority. 2014a. Flood Damage Reduction. http://www.tva.com/river/flood/index.htm. Accessed 26 Nov 2014

Tennessee Valley Authority. 2014b. Integrated Resource Plan. http://www.tva.com/environment/reports/irp. Accessed 26 Nov 2014

Tennessee Valley Authority. 2014c. Natural Resource Plan. http://www.tva.com/environment/reports/nrp. Accessed 26 Nov 2014

Tennessee Valley Authority. 2014d. Reservoir Operations Study. http://www.tva.com/environment/reports/ros_eis. Accessed 26 Nov 2014

Watkins, Joel H. 2014. *A Cultural Resources Shoreline Survey and Erosion Monitoring of Boone Reservoir, Sullivan and Washington Counties, Tennessee.* Report submitted to the Tennessee Valley Authority, Knoxville, Tennessee.

Webb, William S. 1938. *An Archaeological Survey of the Norris Basin in Eastern Tennessee.* Bureau of American Ethnology Bulletin 118. Smithsonian Institution. Washington, DC: Government Printing Office.

Webb, William S.. 1939. *An Archaeological Survey of Wheeler Basin on the Tennessee River in Northern Alabama.* Bureau of American Ethnology Bulletin 122, Smithsonian Institution. Washington, DC: Government Printing Office.

Webb, William S., and David L. DeJarnette. 1942. *An Archeological Survey of Pickwick Basin in the Adjacent Portions of the States of Alabama, Mississippi and Tennessee.* Bureau of American Ethnology Bulletin 129, Smithsonian Institution. Washington, DC: Government Printing Office.

Webb, William S., and Charles G. Wilder. 1951. *An Archaeological Survey of Guntersville Basin on the Tennessee River in Northern Alabama.* Lexington: University of Kentucky Press.

Whitman, Willson. 1939. *God's Valley.* New York: The Viking Press.

Wheeler, William Bruce, and Michael J. McDonald, 1986. *TVA and the Tellico Dam, 1936-1979.* University of Tennessee Press, Knoxville.

Willey, Gordon R., and Philip Phillips, 1958. *Method and Theory in American Archaeology.* University of Chicago Press, Chicago.

Willey, Gordon R., and Jeremy A. Sabloff, 1974. *A History of American Archaeology.* San Francisco: W. H. Freeman.

Development of the WWC world water heritage systems (WHS) program

Avinash Chand Tyagi[a] and Kazumi Yamaoka[b]

a. Secretary General International Commission on Irrigation and Drainage
48, Nyaya Marg, Chanakyapuri, New Delhi 110021, INDIA
tyagi@icid.org

b. Research Coordinator (Governor of World Water Council)
Japan International Research Center for Agricultural Sciences (JIRCAS)
1-1 Ohwashi, Tsukuba-shi, Ibaraki, 305-8686 JAPAN
kyamaoka@affrc.go.jp [Correspondence author]

Abstract

Existing world programs carried out by UNESCO, FAO and ICID are aimed at different concepts of heritage and effectively segmented into suitable niches of products of humanity worth protecting and preserving as heritage. However the existing five programs, namely the World Heritage, the Intangible Cultural Heritage, the Memory of the World, the Globally Important Agricultural Heritage Systems and Heritage Irrigation Structure, still uncover certain areas. People-centred institutions and practices having sustainably carried out sensible and people-inclusive water management for over generations form one of these areas. They also contain in themselves crystals of wisdom that have created coexistent social systems for humanity and a sound environment. We must widely learn from these crystals of wisdom in order to realize a harmonious and sustainable society for the future. It leads to the idea that a innovative program for protecting sites of the people-centred practices, institutions, organizations, regimes and rules serving as soft components of sustainable water management systems across all sectors and geographical areas around the world as intangible water heritages should be established in order to consider their outstanding value. Therefore the World Water Heritage Systems (WHS) Program has been discussed between the World Water Council (WWC), the International Commission on Irrigation and Drainage (ICID) and relevant bodies.

Keywords: *intangible, people-inclusive water management, people-centred institutions, World Water Council, International Commission on Irrigation and Drainage.*

1. Introduction

In order to cater to the growing population and development needs, the food security requires, among others, long-term increased supplies of quality raw materials: water, land and seed. Factors (e.g., unusual weather caused by climate change, growing water scarcity) are causing production and prices to be more volatile in the short term and agriculture production unsustainable in the long term. Irrigation has served since time immemorial as a tool to overcome the temporary water scarcity. Archaeological investigation has identified evidence of irrigation by Mesopotamians, Egyptian, Nubian and many other time-honoured civilizations where the natural rainfall was insufficient to support crops. Study of the history of irrigation, development of irrigation technology, sustainability of the ancient irrigation systems not only provides an insight into the factors that have sustained the outcomes over the generations but have also great potential for exploring the past and past cultures. Cultural movement, settlement and adaptation can be traced and documented by analysing certain cultural markers and features which irrigation systems display. Settlement patterns can also be determined by means of access to exploitable water supplies. A study of the manner in which irrigation systems are constructed can teach us a lot about human ingenuity and traditional knowledge. The ICID has encouraged and supported such studies from the day it was founded.

Within the international frameworks on protecting heritages, the United Nations Educational, Scientific and Cultural Organization (UNESCO) carries out programs concerning the World Heritage (WH), the Intangible Cultural Heritage (ICH) and the Memory of the World (MW), whereas Food and Agriculture Organization of the United Nations (FAO) carries out the Globally Important Agricultural Heritage Systems (GIAHS). They have been aimed at various concepts of heritage and have effectively segmented them into suitable niches consisting of products of humanity worth protecting as well as preserving them as a heritage. The present proposal for World Water Heritage Systems, initiated by the International Commission on Irrigation and Drainage is intended to encourage the study of all people-centred water management systems, including irrigation systems, and their relationship to other objects encountered surrounding them.

2. The World Water Heritage Systems

People-centred institutions and practices in the past had managed water systems for over generations and contain in themselves crystals of wisdom of humanity worth protecting and preserving as a heritage. This wisdom has realized a harmonious and sustainable society through sensible and people-inclusive water management but is not readily available to those engaged in water management at various levels. In order to make available the lessons and good practices learnt over generations in managing various water systems across all sectors and geographical areas through stakeholders' participation, an idea of establishing the World Water Heritage Systems (WHS) Program has been discussed between the World Water Council (WWC), International Commission on Irrigation and Drainage (ICID) and relevant bodies. The proposal was initiated because it is necessary for these people-centred institutions and practices serving as soft components of sustainable water management systems to be protected and the lessons learnt through their successful management over the years to be disseminated widely. None of the current heritage programs or award schemes covers them directly.

The idea originally emerged from a discussion among the authors and the experts participating in the ICID Working Group on History during the 64th International Executive Council (IEC) and the 1st World Irrigation Forum (WIF) held in Mardin, Turkey in October 2013. The meetings are preceded by the International Council on Monuments and Sites (ICOMOS) Conference 'Protecting Deltas: Heritage helps!' held in Amsterdam, the Netherlands in September 2013. It was attended by the present author who found out that such canal drainage systems managed by the Delfland Water Board, one of the earliest drainage associations in Dutch history, have had difficulties even in standing as a national candidate for a World Heritage Site due to a lack of any prominent monument. Sharing this concern with people in the ICOMOS Netherlands that works on the relation between water and heritages: an issue of importance, the author took the idea to Budapest (Hungary) in order to discuss it with key persons during the 50th WWC Board of Governors (BoG) meeting and the Budapest Water Summit held immediately after the meetings in Mardin. After the consultation with the secretariat of the ICID and that of the WWC a proposal note was submitted by the President of the ICID at the 52nd WWC BoG meeting held in Mexico City in June 2014 in order to initiate a collaborative program for the recognition of the WHS as a means for knowledge sharing based on historical expertise as to sustainable water management. In fact the ICID was concurrently involved in establishing a new scheme of the ICID Register of Heritage Irrigation Structures (HIS) which was later launched at the 22nd ICID Congress held in Gwangju (Korea) in September 2014. Moreover, the ICID published the first list of HIS sites. In this manner the idea of WHS crossed the continents to be elaborated step by step.

During the 53rd WWC BoG meeting held in Marseille (France) in October 2014 the governors agreed to establish a Task Force with the terms of reference in order to examine the ICID proposal for setting up of the WHS Program. This Task Force is expected to submit its report to the 54th WWC BoG meeting in April 2015 so that the decision on the program could be taken prior to the 7th World Water Forum (WWF7) to be held in Daegu and Gyeongbuk (Korea) immediately after the 54th WWC BoG meeting with the intention of publicly launching the program during the WWF7. The institutional mechanism such as the Technical Advisory Committee and the International Committee will be setup in order to establish the technical details as to how a 'system' would be included in the Register of WHS enabling the formal launch of the program during the 7th General Assembly of WWC to be held during the final months of 2015.

The WHS program aims at identifying, giving recognition to and preserving the people-centred water management systems, organizations, regimes and rules. The reason for this is that an intangible water heritage is considered to be of outstanding value to humanity creating a coexistent social system for humanity and sound environment. The objectives of the program are to:

1. gain/learn lessons from these heritage systems,
2. disseminate the age-old wisdom gathered through them,
3. extract new ideas from the wisdom aggregated from the past,
4. adapt the knowledge suitably within the present context and
5. disseminate it.

Figure 1. Water itself is worshipped and wisely distributed to terraced paddies on Bali (Indonesia).

The program is expected to create a database i.e., a register of World Water Heritage Systems including (a) data on the system's characteristics with its physical, financial and social context, (b) activities undertaken through the system, (c) its historical development and (d) the nuggets of wisdom they offer. It will also encompass an evaluation of the systems' success.

The WHS is to be a global initiative to provide an appropriate recognition to the water management systems from around the world. The systems would represent the intangible people-centred institutions, practices, regimes, rules and related facilities, which have substantially contributed to the socio-economic development in their respective regions by means of management of water systems for over generations. The WHS targets systems which many stakeholders created together and have developed through collective activities for over generations that have managed water resources by utilizing functions of natural and artificial physical facilities. The *subak* system in Indonesia, for example, is not about the canals that distribute the water alone, but about the social organization of the system that relies on the hierarchy of *subak* temples and on 'hydrological interdependency'. (see Fig. 1) The social organization of Balinese rice farmers is dictated by water temples and is completely separate from the state as they become physical and symbolic sites for determining economic roles for production as well as social roles in an interconnected system. The Balinese study provides excellent information on how irrigation systems can help explain social organization, ritual and religion. As an illustration, certain systems that could qualify as the WHS are presented in the Box on the next page.

The scope encompasses all water management systems as intangible social heritages that serve mankind as well as natural environment systems related to water management regardless of regions and sectors. Institutions (a) managing water for drinking, agriculture, industries, electricity generation, navigation, preserving ecosystems and fisheries, (b) dealing with flood management, (c) measures of defence from storm surge and (d) institutions controlling waste water from drainage and sanitation will be eligible for inclusion in the register of the WHS. The physical facilities and hardware related to the nominated systems might have been renewed, renovated and reformed recently in order to fulfil the necessary functions of water management. This concept is applied from one in the HIS program which is anxious about maintaining the status of sites and not changing their formation forever, as the water users have the right to replace an earlier structure with more efficient ones as to a better and efficient water use.

3. The distinction between the WHS and others as a heritage program

The UNESCO seeks to encourage the identification, protection and preservation of cultural and natural heritage around the world considered to be of outstanding value to humanity. World Heritages are tangible 'properties' (e.g., ruins, historical sites, landscapes, natural settings) registered by UNESCO which targets immovable estates and equivalencies and aims at protection and succession of physical cultural

Potential World Water Heritage Systems

Many people's groups and organizations have developed regimes and rules. The gathered wisdom through the energetic management of Irrigation Systems has continued to serve them for over generations or centuries in many countries. Farmers under these systems have a strong sense of ownership of paddy field irrigation encompassing both software as well as hardware. They are therefore conscious of the fact that they must take the initiative to actively protect and preserve their systems, and thus, they have a firm awareness of their rights. Furthermore, while the above organizations are associated with regulation of water allocation and maintenance/ repair of facilities, there are many cases in which they are closely connected with traditional events, ceremonies, and religious rituals related to water and agriculture.

So and *Igumi* in Japan (the antecedents of the modern Land Improvement Districts), *Funnonge* (the basic unit of farmland improvement districts) in South Korea, *Beichuan* (the basic unit of paddy field water use associations) of Taiwan, *Yutan* of China, *Tsuanferra* in the Philippines, *Subak* in Indonesia, *Mounfai* in Thailand, *Samakumu* and *Colmatage* in Cambodia, *Nawan* in Laos, *Komira* in Bangladesh, *Torisu* in Nepal, *Warabandi* in India and Pakistan, and *Kanna* in Sri Lanka are some of the systems that have heritage value and qualify for the WHS.

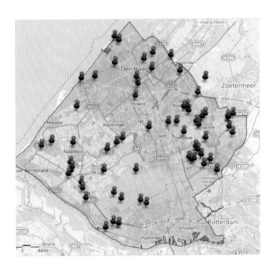

Figure 2. Area and projects, and activities of dredging, water quality check and members meeting of the Hoogheemraadschap van Delfland (Delfland Water Board).

Another candidate is *Waterschappen* or *Hoogheemraadschappen* (Water Boards) in the Netherlands. These regional bodies are in charge of managing water barriers, waterways, water levels, water quality, and sewage treatment in their respective regions. These regional water authorities are among the earliest forms of local governments in the Netherlands, several of which were founded in the 13th century (see Fig. 2).

assets. This is embodied in an international treaty called the Convention concerning the Protection of the World Cultural and Natural Heritage (WH Convention) adopted by the UNESCO in 1972. States parties are encouraged and should submit Tentative Lists to the WH Centre at least one year prior to the submission of any nomination and can submit nomination of at most two sites per year to the WH Committee. A nominated property is independently evaluated by two Advisory Bodies mandated by the WH Convention: the International Council on Monuments and Sites (ICOMOS) and the World Conservation Union (IUCN), which respectively provide the WH Committee with evaluations of the cultural and natural sites nominated.

Cultural heritage does not end at monuments and collections of objects. It also includes the ICH in the form of traditions or living expressions inherited from our ancestors and passed on to our descendants (oral traditions, performing arts, social practices, rituals, festive events, knowledge and practices concerning nature and the universe, knowledge and skills to produce traditional crafts). The UNESCO established Representative List of the ICH of Humanity based on the Convention for the Safeguarding of the ICH adopted at General Assembly of UNESCO in 2003. The Convention entered into force on 20 April 2006. After the proposal or requirement of States Parties to the 2003 Convention the Intergovernmental Committee for the Safeguarding of the ICH decides registration of each ICH with the Convention's Lists as a different heritage from WH sites.

The UNESCO has also started the MW program since 1997 with the vision: the world's documentary heritage belongs to all, should be fully preserved and protected for all and, with due recognition of cultural mores and practicalities, should be permanently accessible to all without hindrance. Its mission is to (a) facilitate preservation, by the most appropriate techniques, of the world's documentary heritage, (b) assist universal access to documentary heritage, and (c) increase awareness worldwide of the existence and significance of documentary heritage. The MW Register lists documentary heritage which has been recommended by the International Advisory Committee (IAC) and endorsed by the Director-General of UNESCO, as corresponding to the selection criteria regarding world significance and outstanding universal value. The IAC is the peak body responsible for advising the UNESCO on the planning and implementation of the program as a whole.

The Earth is dotted with a myriad of home-grown agricultural systems that are humanity's common heritage. These systems provide essential ecosystem goods and services as well as food security for millions of local community members and indigenous peoples, well beyond their borders. In order to safeguard and support the world's ingenious agricultural systems reflecting the evolution of humankind, the diversity of its knowledge, and its profound relationship with nature as agricultural heritage systems, the FAO started an initiative for the dynamic conservation of GIAHS in 2002. The Global Environmental Facility (GEF), the Federal Ministry of Food, Agriculture and Consumer Protection of Germany, the International Fund for Agricultural Development (IFAD), the United Nations University (UNU), the UNESCO and the Islamic Educational, Scientific and Cultural Organization (ISESCO) are designated as resource partners of the GIAHS initiative providing technical cooperation and grants.

As to the UNESCO WH Sites, registration means maintaining status and not changing formation forever. However, it would be incorrect to stipulate the same obligation for irrigation structure, as the water users have the right to replace older structure with more efficient ones for better and efficient water use. The ICID intends to bring historical irrigation structures into the public knowledge and raise people's awareness as to the roles which the structures have played in achieving food security and also provide appropriate technical guidance to the project authority through a team of experts from the ICID for its further sustainability, conservation and safe management as long as possible. Therefore the ICID established the HIS program in 2014 in order to make a historical irrigation structure recognized as a HIS by including it in an 'ICID World List of Heritage Irrigation Structures.' This is an internal system of the ICID in which National Committees of the ICID can nominate their national site or send a proposal as a candidate of the HIS meeting the designated criteria.

Fig. 3 presents us with a conceptual demarcation of these five programs. The entire box is divided into two boxes whereby the left one represents the tangible side and the right one represents the intangible side. Programs in the left box target tangible structures (monuments, ruins, historical sites, landscapes, natural settings, documentaries, irrigation facilities) as registered heritages while those in the left box target intangible performances (oral traditions, performing arts, social practices, rituals, festive events, knowledge and skills regarded as cultural assets, agricultural systems). On the other hand the entire box includes a domain of nature (and non-nature) and culture (and non-culture). Their boundaries are represented as ovals. Within this context the entire box is divided into four territories.

Clearly the programs of the WH and the ICH operated by the UNESCO target domains inside of 'Nature' and 'Culture' boundaries, whereby the former and the latter target the tangible and intangible side respectively. Within the WH program a natural WH site evaluated by the IUCN must be located inside of 'Nature' boundary whereas a cultural WH site evaluated by the ICOMOS and an intangible heritage registered in Representative List of the ICH of Humanity must be located inside of 'Culture' boundary.

The other UNESCO's MW program targets only documents. They are apparently tangible and artificial man-made products so that they must occupy the territory located in the tangible side and outside the 'Nature' boundary at the same time.

The program of the GIAHS operated by the FAO has rather unique characteristics. It targets only the intangible agricultural production systems resembling the ICH program. However a GIAHS site must be located outside of 'Culture' as well as 'Nature' boundaries because agriculture is a kind of production industry. Nevertheless traditional and indigenous agricultural systems may have more flavour of and stronger relations to local culture as well as deeper coexistent relations with nature. The way it will end up is that the program of the GIAHS must occupy an intangible side by and large located outside the 'Nature' and 'Culture' boundaries but partially inside them.

Finally the program of the HIS newly operated by the ICID can be characterized as a mirror image of the GIAHS setting the straight line consisting of a border between the tangible and intangible side as a symmetry axis because the former targets irrigation structures which are artificial and tangible agricultural properties. However, indigenous ones may have more flavour of and stronger relations to local culture as well as deeper coexistent relations with nature.

These five programs cover a considerable part of the whole entire but the GIAHS and the HIS can target only agriculture related sites. Thus many sites worth protecting and preserving as heritages are as yet not covered. People-centred institutions and practices having sustainably carried out sensible and people-inclusive water management for over generations are one these not covered sites. They must be protected as soft components of sustainable water management systems. Their crystals of wisdom of humanity must be studied in order to realize a harmonious and sustainable society for the future. The proposed World Water

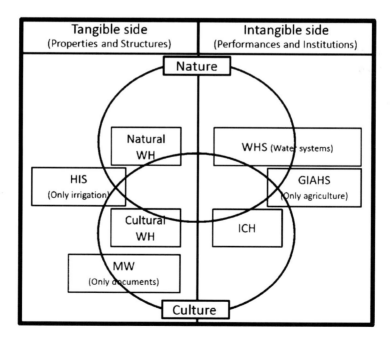

Figure 3. The conceptual picture presenting the location of each program by means of tangibility and a natural-cultural classification.

Heritage Systems has similarities with the ICH and the GIAHS so that they clearly target the intangible side. The nature of the people-centred institutions and practices on water management is not natural but the product of humankind. However the systems to be protected must contain natural resources of water (e.g., river systems, lakes, marshes, ground water aquifers, glaciers, seas, waste water flows, etc.). In addition,. indigenous systems may have more flavour of and stronger relations to local culture. Consequently the program of the WHS must be located in the intangible side and stretch across the boundary of 'Nature' and mostly outside of the 'Culture' boundaries but partially inside them. (see Fig. 3)

4. The proposed criteria for a registration under the WHS program

The World Heritage List includes 1007 properties forming part of the cultural and natural heritage which the World Heritage Committee considers as having outstanding universal value. These include 779 cultural, 197 natural and 31 mixed properties in 161 States Parties and 191 States Parties have ratified the World Heritage Convention. The geographical distribution of properties is that the number of properties per one state party in America and Europe (10.12) looks conspicuous in comparison to that in Africa (2.11), Arab States (4.11), Latin America and the Caribbean (4.18) and Asia and Oceania (5.42) being between 20% and 50% of America and Europe. (see Table 1) In the case of number of sites in the GIAHS program the number is much limited and in more misdistribution by country, for example there are 59 sites worldwide of which 32 are located in Asia of which 11, 10 and 5 in China, India and Japan respectively. A contrast is noted with North America in which only one site is located.

The WHS program aiming at contribution to humanity must learn from these experiences. Based on the elaborative investigation to the institutional frameworks and systems of criteria for registration under five international programs precedent to the WHS, the following procedures, criteria and institutional framework (described in section 5) would be proposed to maximize the number of candidates

Region	Number of sites by country (A)	Proportion (%)	Number of states parties (B)	A/B
Africa	95	8.96	45	2.11
Americas and Europe	516	48.68	51	10.12
Arab States	78	7.36	19	4.11
Asia and Oceania	233	21.98	43	5.42
Latin America and the Caribbean	138	13.02	33	4.18

Table 1. The regional distribution of World Heritage Sites. Source: Data from UNESCO World Heritage Website acquired by the present author. http://whc.unesco.org/pg.cfm?cid=31&mode=table. Note: Certain sites belong to more than one country. Duplicates exist when counting them by country and within a region.

and minimize their misdistribution by countries. National Committee systems which do not yet exist in the WWC are proposed to be newly introduced and the criteria are proposed in a manner simplified as much as possible.

The WWC would encourage national and local governments and WWC members to submit information on the 'candidate systems' to be included in the 'Register of WHS' through the National Committees on the WHS (described in section 5). The proposals are scrutinized by the WHS Technical Advisory Committee for having fulfilled the criteria laid down only after satisfying themselves that all the required information needed for inclusion in the Register is available. On the recommendation of the TAC, the WHS International Committee approves their listing in the Register of the WHS. The people-centred institutions nominated for inscription in the 'Register of the WHS' shall satisfy all of the following primary criteria and one or more of the secondary criteria in the box below.

Proposed criteria for registration of WHS sites

1 Primary criteria

   a.   The nominated institution shall be a people's group/organization managing water systems and has demonstrated sustainable management for over generations, at least 100 years,

   b.   The institution should have realized effective water management by creating a system bringing together people's wisdom, coordinating and developing customs, rules and practices,

   c.   The institution should have contributed to socio-economic development in a given region by means of a sustainable management of water system, and

   d.   The institution should have involved many stakeholders such as citizens and farmers along with experts and authorities.

2 Secondary criteria

   a.   It has an outstanding historical background,

   b.   It has effectively served as an outstanding system that overcame at least one of the adverse natural and social conditions, e.g., droughts, flooding, water quality degradation, waterborne diseases, etc.,

   c.   It has an indispensable element necessary for evolving culture, sustaining bio-diversity and generating socio-economic activities in the region, and

   d.   It has an outstanding universal value common to humanity.

5. The proposed institutional framework for the WHS program

The WHS program is proposed as an activity carried out by means of actions on voluntary initiatives of related international organizations in a manner similar to the 'Memory of the World' by the UNESCO and the 'Globally Important Agricultural Heritage Systems' by the FAO. The World Water Council, in cooperation with the UNESCO, FAO, ICID and other interested global institutions and authorities with expertise in water management, should host the program. The WWC can exploit its strength drawn from its members i.e., national and international organizations, encouraging them to take actions autonomously as to the activation of the WHS program. The program is proposed to have a flexible framework as compared to the World Heritage and/or the Intangible Cultural Heritage of Humanity program carried out by the UNESCO which is based on the Conventions ratified by the States Parties.

6. Conclusion

Existing world programs are aimed at different concepts of heritage and effectively segmented into suitable niches of products of humanity worth protecting and preserving as heritage. However, a dedicated analysis of existing five programs, namely the World Heritage, the Intangible Cultural Heritage, the Memory of the World, the Globally Important Agricultural Heritage Systems and the Heritage Irrigation Structure, clearly revealed the existence of uncovered areas. People-centred institutions and practices having sustainably carried out sensible and people-inclusive water management for over generations comprises one of the areas. They contain in themselves crystals of wisdom of humanity worth protecting and preserving as a heritage because wisdom has realized harmonious and sustainable society by means of sensible and people-inclusive water management. However, it is not readily available to those engaged in water management at various levels. Therefore a new program for protecting sites of the people-centred practices, institutions, organizations, regimes and rules serving as soft components of sustainable water management systems across all sectors and geographical areas around the world as intangible water heritages should be established in order to consider their outstanding value. We must widely learn from the crystals of wisdom to realize a harmonious and sustainable society for the future. It is recommended that the WWC will further elaborate the program and launch it in a timely manner with an effective institutional framework as to an operation-based society as proposed in the present paper.

References

FAO (2014) GIAHS Site, http://www.fao.org/giahs/giahs-sites/en/

UNESCO (2014) World Heritage Site, http://whc.unesco.org/pg.cfm?cid=31&mode=table

UNESCO (2014) Intangible Heritage Site, http://www.unesco.org/culture/ich/

UNESCO (2014) Memory of the World Site, http://www.unesco.org/new/en/communication-and-information/flagship-project-activities/memory-of-the-world/homepage/

Appendix 1

Statement of Amsterdam

Kinderdijk

Woudagemaal

ICOMOS
Netherlands

The Statement of Amsterdam

ICOMOS CONFERENCE * WATER & HERITAGE
PROTECTING DELTAS: HERITAGE HELPS !

Saving the deltas of the world is one of the most critical challenges for a sustainable future. Increasing population density and water related hazards threaten the rich and diverse heritage on the banks of rivers, in low-lying deltas and in vulnerable coastal regions. Climate change affects flood and drought patterns, groundwater and sea levels, pollution and the frequency and intensity of disasters. Societies and professional communities related to water, heritage and spatial planning alike are challenged to change and adapt.

For a world struggling to find sustainable solutions, heritage helps by providing valuable examples of successful and not so successful strategies to deal with uncertainty and risk. It allows us to better understand the dynamic relationship between societies, water management and governance. Human ingenuity and the capacity to share water management experience across cultures shaped iconic cultural landscapes and helped coping with water hazards in the past; they are key to improving wellbeing in the present; and will determine our chance of creating an equitable and sustainable future for all. Similarly, modern water management offers essential technologies to protect world heritage sites acutely threatened by natural disasters and prepare for the impacts of environmental change. UNESCO affirms the connection between heritage, water and sustainable development through its programmes and research bodies, the conventions on World Heritage, Intangible Heritage and Underwater Heritage, and in the declarations on Responsibilities Towards Future Generations and on Culture for Sustainable Development. Climate Change strategy emphasizes the importance cross-sectoral approaches. ICOMOS Netherlands convened the conference "Protecting deltas: heritage !" from 23-28 September 2013 in Amsterdam, to bute towards safe and sustainable communities in gions. More than 100 water, heritage and planning from over 20 countries answered the call to share e strategies on heritage protection and water t, to build and promote linkages within and mmunities, and to identify opportunities to or mutual benefits.

The conference finds that:
• Water, land and societies are constantly evolving. Water heritage is dynamic by nature; its management is 'management of change'. Many historic water structures are still in use, modern waterworks are heritage of the future. They epitomize the need to adapt the function and meaning of sites based on principles of flexibility and resilience. Profound understanding of historical continuity is an essential source of inspiration to improve planning processes. Vice versa, understanding the social function of water infrastructure is crucial to historic research and site protection;

• Attractive, sustainable and resilient cities and regions fully integrate heritage management, water technology, urban and spatial planning. Heritage is a valuable asset as a source of pride and identification, social and economic development, stimulating striving communities. Safety measures preparing societies for the effects of climate change will work best where they are combined with improving cultural landscapes, and implemented with respect for heritage, local institutions and the social context;

• The societal desire for sustainability has found its expression in spatial planning, but the relation of heritage, development and sustainability is still in its infancy. There is an urgent need to create a shared vision, and communicate the links to policy makers, professionals and the public. Spatial planning plays a key role in involving stakeholders in participatory processes, and in connecting decision makers with experts including engineers, archaeologists, historians, geographers, ecologist and landscape architects;

• Education and capacity development are key to facilitate institutional transformations needed to integrate water, heritage and development. Relatively recent advances in water technology created flood protection and water supply technologies too easily taken for granted. Traditional knowledge and heritage plays a crucial role in reminding societies that we have to keep redefining our relationship with water. More research is needed to evaluate the potential of traditional approaches for scaling up to solve today's challenges.